Jesus

Understanding Who Jesus Is and What it Means to be Christ-centred

J. F. Rodrigo

Foreword by Bishop William T. McGrattan

WILLIAM T. MCGRATTAN

BISHOP of CALGARY

RESCRIPT

In accord with Canon 823 of the Code of canon Law, I hereby grant my permission to publish "JESUS THE CHRIST – Understanding Who Jesus Is and What It Means to be Christ-centred" by J.F. Rodrigo.

It is my desire that you will use this work to spread the important message of Who Jesus Is, and the meaning of Christ-centredness that is so desperately needed in our world.

Notice of this rescript is to be printed on the reverse side of the title page of the book.

Given on the third day in the month of May in the year of our Lord two thousand twenty four.

Sincerely in Christ,

+William McGrattan

Most Reverend William T. McGrattan,

Bishop of the Diocese of Calgary

DIOECESIS CURIA EPISCOPALIS CALGARIENSIS

ROMAN CATHOLIC DIOCESE OF CALGARY
Catholic Pastoral Centre | 120 17 Ave SW, Calgary, AB T2S 2T2
Phone: 403-218-5526 | Fax : 403-264-0272

Jesus the Christ

Understanding Who Jesus Is and What it Means to be Christ-centred

2024
Trinity Project Publishing

Nihil Obstat: ✠ Most Reverend William T. McGrattan
Bishop of the Diocese of Calgary

Imprimatur: ✠ Most Reverend William T. McGrattan
Bishop of the Diocese of Calgary
May 3, 2024.

Jesus the Christ
Understanding Who Jesus Is and What it Means to be Christ-centred

ISBN: 978-0-9959644-2-6

Photo Credits:
Front Cover Image: "*Simeon and Jesus*" by Andrey Shishkin, 2012; "*Simeon and Anna in the Temple*" by Rembrandt van Rijn (a.k.a. Rembrandt Harmenszoon van Rijn), *c.* 1626-1628.

Cover and interior design by Blitsprint Inc. and Trinity Project Publishing.

Published in Canada, by Trinity Project Publishing.
Printed and bound in Canada.

To my Ammi (my mother),
may Jesus the Christ be your centre.

Contents

Abbreviations

OLD TESTAMENT							
Genesis	Gen	1 Chronicles	1 Chron	Ecclesiastes	Eccl	Amos	Amos
Exodus	Ex	2 Chronicles	2 Chron	Song of Songs	Song	Obadiah	Obad
Leviticus	Lev	Ezra	Ezra	Wisdom	Wisdom	Jonah	Jonah
Numbers	Num	Nehemiah	Neh	Sirach	Sirach	Micah	Micah
Deuteronomy	Deut	Tobit	Tobit	Isaiah	Isa	Nahum	Nahum
Joshua	Josh	Judith	Jdth	Jeremiah	Jer	Habakkuk	Hab
Judges	Judg	Esther	Esth	Lamentations	Lam	Zephaniah	Zeph
Ruth	Ruth	1 Maccabees	1 Macc	Baruch	Baruch	Haggai	Hag
1 Samuel	1 Sam	2 Maccabees	2 Macc	Ezekiel	Ezek	Zechariah	Zech
2 Samuel	2 Sam	Job	Job	Daniel	Dan	Malachi	Mal
1 Kings	1 Kgs	Psalms	Ps	Hosea	Hosea		
2 Kings	2 Kgs	Proverbs	Prov	Joel	Joel		

NEW TESTAMENT							
Matthew	Mt	2 Corinthians	2 Cor	1 Timothy	1 Tm	2 Peter	2 Pt
Mark	Mk	Galatians	Gal	2 Timothy	2 Tm	1 John	1 Jn
Luke	Lk	Ephesians	Eph	Titus	Ti	2 John	2 Jn
John	Jn	Philippians	Phil	Philemon	Phlm	3 John	3 Jn
Acts	Acts	Colossians	Col	Hebrews	Heb	Jude	Jude
Romans	Rom	1 Thessalonians	1 Thes	James	Jms	Revelation	Rv
1 Corinthians	1 Cor	2 Thessalonians	2 Thes	1 Peter	1 Pt		

OTHER	
New American Bible	NAB
Catechism of the Catholic Church	CCC
Deus Caritas Est	DCE
Misericordiae Vultus	MV

Foreword

The reader of this book will be embarking on a very interesting theological journey, exploring the essential aspects of Jesus' identity. The work covers nine chapters and is founded on a methodology deeply rooted in biblical-based theology and its practical application, aiming to guide readers on a transformative journey toward a connection with Jesus and a Christ-centered life. It not only reflects a profound understanding of our Catholic faith but also presents it in a way that is both accessible and engaging for those with an interest in delving into such content, offering a broader and deeper perspective on the person of the Christ.

As Catholics, we do not only encounter the Christ in Sacred Scripture and the Sacraments, we also experience Him in the Church's liturgy, our personal prayer and meditation, our experience of daily life and of living faithfully our vocation, our relationship with others and our life of service and outreach, and in studying theology. While a personal relationship with the Christ should be constitutive of our life as Christians, the study of the Faith is essential to nurturing and nourishing that personal relationship, guided by the Church's Magisterium, for we belong to the Body of Christ. Otherwise, a faith that has no element of study on the proper interpretation of Scriptures and on the divine truths contained in the Church may be misguided or misled especially in the context of our relativistic society. This book offers elements of the various dimensions and experiences of our life and faith which should provide the reader fresh insights into the person of Jesus the Christ and the communion we are called to live in God, the Father, the Son, and the Holy Spirit.

Aside from the contents of this book which help to ground our ordinary experiences of life to the Sacred Mystery, I am proud of the fact that the author has a local connection and is from the Diocese of Calgary. Rodrigo's passion for writing about the person of the Christ in a relatable manner speaks to the very heart of his apostolate to share God's incarnate love to others. If this book speaks to your heart, may you be compelled to share it with others, especially with those who may need that special encouragement to know the Christ more deeply.

May the Holy Spirit open your mind and heart as you read this book, and may you receive new graces that will inspire you to see the world through the eyes and gaze of the Christ.

✠ William T. McGrattan
Bishop of Calgary

Preface

Always be ready
to give an answer to anyone
who asks you for a reason
for the hope that lies within you;
but do it with gentleness and compassion.

1 Peter 3:15

This biblical passage is unequivocally a firm directive to *all* Christians. Not only am I a huge advocate of this directive, but also these words of Saint Peter have given me the motivation to embark on writing this book.

To give a fuller understanding, let us look at the underlying Greek words. We are to

- *always*, ἀεί (aei/*ah-eye*), not occasionally, but constantly, at all times to
- be *ready*, ἕτοιμος (hetoimos/*het-oy'-mos*), that is to be prepared, equipped
- *to give an answer*, ἀπολογία (apologia/*ap-ol-og-ee'-ah*), an explanation, a logical defence, an articulation, to enlighten
- *anyone who asks you for a reason*, λόγος (logos/*log'-os*), literally a word, or a rational cause, an account, a teaching, a doctrine
- *for the hope*, ἐλπίς (elpis/*el-pece'*), the expectation, the confidence, the trust
- *that lies within you, but do it with gentleness*, πραΰτης (prautēs/*prah-oo'-tace*), mildness, meekness, modesty, humility
- *and compassion*, φόβος (phobos/*fob'-os*) or reverence, fear, and respectfulness (1 Pt 3:15).

This admonition is not optional. I, therefore, hope and pray that this book gives us a clear and logical explanation of Who Jesus the Christ *Is*, so, when required, we are prepared to articulate those specific principles on Who He *is* with humility and respect to all those who ask.

Because we are called to communicate our faith, I present this book as a study, in an explanatory, conversational style, or to be precise, a conversational *preaching* and *teaching* style. Consequently, *Jesus the Christ*: *Understanding Who Jesus Is and What it Means to be Christ-centred* is more of a kitchen table, "Bible on the one side, Catechism on the other side," contemplative, meditative, "let us struggle, grapple, and grow in our faith" type of read rather than a casual "curl up on the couch on a Sunday afternoon" read.

Keep in mind that the fundamentals of what we believe have a direct correlation to how we live. If our beliefs are sound, and we put them into practice, our life will inevitably be sound! If our beliefs are unsound, our life becomes unsound! Moreover, the frequent use of those faulty beliefs will continue to produce a faulty life. Unfortunately, as Christians, we profess a *belief* in Jesus, but too many of us do not really understand *in* Whom (or even what) we believe, nor the *difference* that this belief we profess should make in our lives (*Note*[1]). Some of us are also caught up in private subjective revelations, in private religious practices, or even secular ideologies. These may seem right to us, "but the end of it leads to death" (Prov 14:12).

We Christians are currently led to feel a false sense of security, causing us to be less alert, less aware, or less watchful. It is time for us to *wake up* (Eph 5:14), be alert (1 Thes 5:6), truly understand the beliefs we profess, and live accordingly. With this in mind and with this directive and conviction, I press forward in my *study* of God, so, through His grace, I may do what is asked of me. Interestingly, when writing about Truth (i.e., Jesus) or truths, some readers assume that the writer has *arrived* and is living the written reality. To be clear, that is not so with me. I have *not* arrived! As I preach and teach, a phenomenon happens: I find myself preaching and teaching mainly to myself. "I count myself one of the number of those who write as they learn and learn as they write," to use the words of Saint Augustine (*Note*[2]). You should also know that as the Lord is my witness, I struggle immensely with what I have written. I struggle with the truth that Jesus presents to His Church. As I write, my own words convict me.

Let us pray:
That the God of our Lord Jesus the Christ,
the Father of glory, may give you
a spirit of wisdom and revelation
resulting in knowledge of Him.
May the eyes of your heart be enlightened,
that you may know what is the hope that belongs to His call,
what are the riches of glory in His inheritance
among the holy ones,
and what is the surpassing greatness of His power
for us who believe,
in accord with the exercise of His great might,
which He worked in the Christ,
raising Him from the dead
and seating Him at His right hand in the Heavens,
far above every principality, authority, power, and dominion,
and every name that is named
not only in this age but also in the one to come.
And He put all things beneath His feet
and gave Him as head over all things
to the Church, which is His body,
the fullness of the One who fills all things
in every way.
Amen.

Ephesians 1:17-23

Introduction

Lord, now you let your servant go in peace;
Your word has been fulfilled:
my own eyes have seen the Salvation
which You have prepared in the sight of every people:
a Light to reveal You to the nations
and the glory of Your people Israel.

Canticle of Simeon – Luke 2:29-32

Most Christians know from Scripture of a man named Simeon and a prophetess named Anna who lived in Jerusalem. They were both advanced in years: Anna had been a widow for most of her life; she was constantly at the Temple, worshiping night and day with fasting and praying; Simeon was a righteous and devout man, who was awaiting the consolation of Israel.

The Holy Spirit revealed to Simeon that he would not die before he had seen God's Messiah. One day, prompted by the Holy Spirit, Simeon came into the Temple at the same time that Mary and Joseph brought the little Baby Jesus to fulfill for *Him*[3] what was customary according to the Law.

At which point, Simeon took Baby Jesus into his arms, blessed God, and proclaimed the Evangelical Canticle quoted above.

Anna also came forward at that moment. As a prophetess, she gave thanks to God and spoke of the Messiah to all who were also looking for the redemption of Israel (Lk 2:26-38).

For this book, I would like to propose the *image* of Simeon and the prophetess Anna.[4] The image of Anna, devoting her entire life to fasting and praying; the image of Anna culminating her life by prophesying about the little Baby who was now in the Temple. The image of Simeon, holding little Baby Jesus in his arms, blessing God, and proclaiming this canticle.

These are images of a man and a woman who had wrapped their *entire* lives around the centrality of the Saviour. They had patiently waited for the Messiah—Jesus the Christ—Who has now, to their delight, entered the world and appeared in the Temple (Lk 2:27; also cf. Mal 3:1). Therefore, in true exaltation, they could not help but glorify the Lord.

Anna and Simeon demonstrated the centrality of the Messiah in their lives. Simeon was now ready to die, for his eyes had seen God's Salvation, which He has provided for him and for each of us in this little Baby Boy. All of creation hinges upon this particular Baby, for He *is* the Salvation of God. Simeon and Anna not only recognized this *reality*, they also exalted in the One Who *is* Truth Itself.

The Church, in *Her*[5] wisdom, rightfully places Simeon's Evangelical Canticle on our lips, every day, during Night Prayer.[6] The words of Simeon should be our words. Like Simeon, we too (figuratively speaking) should cradle Baby Jesus every night in our arms—entrusting our *entire* life to Him. Radical love should result in radical service to Truth (3 Jn 1:3-4). Following Simeon's lead, we should also give praise and thanksgiving to God and exalt in this Truth, recognizing, identifying, internalizing, and demonstrating the centrality of Jesus, the Messiah, in our lives.

Seeing the Messiah puts Simeon's and Anna's entire lives into perspective. In Him they experienced a delicate and exquisite peace. We must therefore take on their disposition, for only He can give our life true meaning and peace. As Simeon articulates with deep understanding, we also should articulate with that same conviction and understanding, that not only should our entire life revolve around this little Baby Jesus, Who is our Lord and Messiah now among us, but also so should our death revolve around Him—"For if we live, we live for the Lord, and if we die, we die for the Lord; so then, whether we live or die, we are the Lord's" (Rom 14:8; also cf. Lk 13:23-27).

These words should not be mere lip service. It is not good enough to just know about Jesus the Christ (see Mt 7:21) or simply study Him as a mere academic exercise, we must follow Him with every fibre in our body (Mt 22:37), and, more importantly, allow Him to be the very *centre* of our lives.

Believing in Him in a superficial manner will inevitably create a superficial life. Each and every day, we must wake up and make a conscious decision to follow Him with all that we have. It is not good enough to call ourself a Christian, to say that we love Jesus, or to have high theological knowledge of Him. We must possess Him, and more importantly, allow Him to possess us, just like Simeon and Anna did.

We should not live as if He does not exist, or recognize His existence only when it is convenient, or keep Him on the periphery of our lives. We must allow Him to permeate every action of our lives, and as a result, we must praise Him with our every action. We must have a Christ-centred worldview, and thus live a Christ-centred life.

Christianity depends on the identity of a *Person*,[7] and then on our *covenant-relationship* with that Person. This covenant-relationship is no mere contract, nor is it a pre-negotiated agreement that binds two parties. No, it is a solemn promise made by the Messiah, in love, and thus calls for a complete surrender to Him in response to His love.

For that reason, in Chapter 1 we will study the *basic* fundamentals concerning the Person of Jesus—the *new covenant* Initiator—by looking at the importance of the question: "Who do you say that I AM?" In Chapter 2 through Chapter 6, our primary focus will be on the first part of our subtitle—*Understanding Who Jesus Is*. Chapter 7 is a transitional chapter. Finally, in Chapter 8 and Chapter 9, our primary focus will shift to the second part of our subtitle—*What it Means to be Christ-centred*. That is, how do we now live a Christ-centred life?

In other words, once we understand who Jesus *Is*, we must completely surrender to Him, rest in Him, and *allow* Him to permeate our life. Just like the lives of Simeon and Anna, our lives must ultimately reflect that covenant-relationship with Him.

Fundamentals may be somewhat technical, but not only do they help to keep us from superficiality, they essentially feed us. I think, at some level, most Christians are hungry for these fundamental truths. We know that it is important that we grasp them; if not, we know that we run the risk of living some sort of insipid pseudo–Christianity.

Having said that, by no means is this study an in-depth Christology. Nor is this study about proving that Jesus is the Messiah, or that He is God. This is simply a foundational, biblically based study for a Christian—a *person in the pew*—to build upon. Yet this study will give or remind us of the core truths of Jesus our Christ.

As mentioned, how we live and conduct our life, has a direct correlation with what we believe, our worldview. Our worldview must be aligned with Him and in Him—specifically, it must be Christ-centred.

Consequently, our mission in life must also be aligned with the mission He has given us—our mission is His mission, our purpose is His purpose. In this Baby Boy, the Kingdom of God has now arrived in history. In this Baby Boy the culmination of God the Father's plan for humanity's salvation is now here for all to see.

Our Salvation *is* indeed personified in our Saviour. He is our wellspring of salvation. When we think of salvation, most of us think of the process of *being saved from danger* or calamity, or the *saving act of God from our sins*, or the *deliverance from sin* in an act in the past and present, but mainly in the future (by going to Heaven). Moreover, and "generally speaking, the concept of salvation involves three elements: a condition from which salvation is the release; the means of release; the state to be attained through salvation."[8] That being said and noted, Jesus the Christ is central to all types of salvation, either directly or intermediately. Therefore, my focus will be on the connection of Jesus *as* Salvation. That is to say, making Him central is the aspect of salvation that will be my primary focal point throughout this book, for it is the aspect of salvation demonstrated by both Anna and Simeon, when Jesus was brought into the Temple.

The entire world's Salvation *is personified in Him*! In the Greek, the word for salvation—σωτηρία (sōtēria/*so-tay-ree'-ah*)—is actually a derivative of saviour, σωτήρ (sōtēr/*so-tare'*). Therefore, as we will explore in this book, our *Salvation*, *Sōtēria* (Σωτηρία)—the culmination of God the Fathers plan for humanity's salvation beginning with the incarnation of His Son—is our *Saviour*, *Sōtēr* (Σωτήρ).

At culmination, "all power in Heaven and on earth" (Mt 28:18) has been given to *this* particular Baby Boy who is the Christ. This book is about getting rid of all distractions and solely focusing on Him, for He is Lord and God. He is the Messiah. He is the complete goal of our faith, the *Sōtēria* (Σωτηρία) of our body, mind, and soul—as vividly proclaimed by Simeon and Anna (1 Pt 1:9: also cf. Lk 2:30)—and thus now *in Him*, in our covenant-relationship *with Him*, we have been commissioned to serve Him.

Using the individual talents we have been given and the time allotted to us (cf. 1 Cor 1:17), we are called to go forth and "make disciples of all nations, baptizing them in the Name of the Father, and of the Son, and of the Holy Spirit," thus inaugurating humanity into His Kingdom (Mt 28:19-20).

"Who do you say that I AM?" is *the* fundamental question. Therefore, we must ask and answer this question.

A Note to the Reader

First, I have divided this study into chapters; the chapters, however, should *not* be read in isolation. An integration or synthesis exists within the chapters; I would like, therefore, to present this study as a continuous and unified thought.

Second, because *Jesus the Christ: Understanding Who Jesus Is and What it Means to be Christ-centred* is a *study*, I have started and ended it with a prayer (or Scripture passage). I hope it will guide our thoughts and set the necessary tone.

Third, I am using Endnotes in three different ways: (i) for basic citation, (ii) to define a theological word or term, and (iii) to give additional information. For your ease, when used in this third way, I will state within parentheses the word (*Note*) with the reference number.

Fourth, in Appendix A, you will find my Methodology and Presuppositions. I recommend that you read this section before commencing the study (even though you might find it a little dry). However, if you do not see it as beneficial, feel free to skip it, or skim through it, and pick up whatever benefits you.

Finally, I would like to thank my family and friends who were kind enough to read and critique these studies in their original form. Your questions, concerns, comments, suggestions, objections, discussions, and encouragement have helped bring *Jesus the Christ: Understanding Who Jesus Is and What it Means to be Christ-centred* to this stage. Thank you!

Chapter 1 | Who Do You Say That I AM?

We begin this study with the central question that Jesus asked His disciples, and, by extension, asks all of humanity. This question, found in all three Synoptic Gospels[9] (Mt 16:13-23, Mk 8:27-33, and Lk 9:18-22) is considered the pivotal point of the Gospel message. In Saint Mark's Gospel, especially, it is literally in the middle (Chapter 8). Every aspect of the Gospel message leads to this question and everything proceeds from this question's answer (*Note*[10]).

The importance of this question, "Who do you say that I AM?" lies within the questioner Himself, as many academic theologians[11] and preachers have stated. What other religious leader asks such a question? In fact, academic theologians have noted that there is none. Buddha never asked it—his teaching was never about him. Mohammed never asked it—his teaching was never about him. Similarly, no mainstream prophet, guru, or sage has asked this question.

Therefore, why did Jesus ask such a question? Briefly put, the ontology[12] of Jesus is paramount. Who He *is*, His *Being*, is of utmost importance. Therefore, we also should answer this question!

Who *is* this Jesus?

Let us start with the basics, by looking at the name *Jesus* and the word *christ*. *Jesus,* of course, is the name for God the Son, as a man. Since the word *Christ* (christ capitalized) is often combined with the name *Jesus* some may think that Christ is Jesus' last name. However, *Christ* is a title for Jesus, not His name. In fact, the word *christ* was a word long before it became a title.

However, before we look at the meaning of the word *christ* and how we have come to use it as a title, let us look at the English name *Jesus* first. Jesus comes to us from the Latin *Iesus* (Iēsūs). This is a transliteration of the Greek name, Ἰησοῦς (Iēsous/*ee-ay-sooce'*). In turn, this is a translation from the Hebrew name יְהוֹשֻׁעַ (y^e^hôshûaʿ/*yah-ho-shoo'-ah*)—and its variant spelling, although pronounced the same, יְהוֹשֻׁעַ (yᵉhôshûaʿ/*yah-ho-shoo'-ah*)—which is Joshua in English (*Note*[13]).

Moreover, another variant spelling, or the shortened form יֵשׁוּעַ (yêshûaʿ/*yah-shoo'-ah*), phonetically spelt as *Yahshua*, is how Jesus' name was pronounced (*Note*[14]).

We should know the pronunciation of His name in the original Hebrew. Why? Because His name in Hebrew—*Yahshua* (יֵשׁוּעַ)—is not only the way that Mother Mary[15] would have called her Son, but that name has a profound theological root.

As the Introduction alludes, the name *Yahshua* (יֵשׁוּעַ) literally means "*YHWH* is Salvation" or "*YHWH* saves" (cf. Mt 1:21, Acts 4:12, Heb 3, and 12:2). These four letters are known as the divine Tetragrammaton, meaning the four consonant letters in Hebrew יהוה (*yud-hey-vav-hey*), translated into English in all capital letters—*YHWH*—which is the Name of the God of Israel (*Note*[16]).

Moreover, in our society, a name is mainly used as a label or identity. In contrast, in Hebrew, a name evokes personhood and describes relationship. Scripture takes this a step further by attaching the name to that person's character.

Just as in the Greek, a connection is also made between *Salvation* and *Saviour* in the Hebrew; and is explicitly rooted in the meaning of His name in Hebrew—*Yahshua* (יֵשׁוּעַ). Although the name Jesus in English or any other language has *power* (Phil 2:10) and contains this theological significance—for when we are referring to Him—this significance is unfortunately not as explicit (*Note*[17]).

Therefore, in Hebrew, Jesus' name literally means the power to save—He *is* Salvation. "There is no Salvation [*Sōtēria* (Σωτηρία)] through anyone else, nor is there any other name under Heaven given to the human race by which we are to be saved" (Acts 4:12). A good way to express this is from time to time to use the name *Yahshua* (יֵשׁוּעַ)—*YHWH* is Salvation—God saves!

Now, let us move to the word *christ*, and the title *Christ*. Don't be offended by my writing christ in lower case (although it is inappropriate to do so in English, for in English it is always a title). I am making a point, as we will see when we study this word in Hebrew.

Working backwards, the title *Christ* in English comes from the Latin title *Christus* (ˈKrɪs-tʏs), which is a transliteration of the Greek word and title χριστός (khristós/*khris-tos'*), which in turn is a translation of the Hebrew word and title מָשִׁיחַ (mâshîyach/*maw-shee'-akh*). The Hebrew word and title *mâshîyach* (מָשִׁיחַ) was also transliterated into Greek as a title Μεσσίας (Messias/*mes-see'-as*), from which we get the phonetically spelt title, Messiah, in English (*Note*[18]).

As a result, we have two words (titles) in English that mean the same—Christ, rooted in the Greek, and Messiah, rooted in the Hebrew.

It is also the case in Greek, in Greek we have the translated word and title from *mâshîyach* (מָשִׁיחַ) to the word and title χριστός (khristós/*khris-tos'*), and the transliterated word *mâshîyach* (מָשִׁיחַ) into Greek as a title *Messias* (Μεσσίας).

Further on the original Hebrew word *mâshîyach* (מָשִׁיחַ), we find that it was simply a word, meaning *anointed* or *anointed person*—usually a priest, prophet, or king (*Note*[19]). A person is anointed to accomplish their mission (just as our baptism obligates).

Some examples taken from these three categories help our understanding of the word use.

- Priest: "The *anointed* [*mâshîyach* (מָשִׁיחַ)] priest shall then take some of the bullock's blood and bring it into the meeting tent, where, dipping his finger in the blood, he shall sprinkle it seven times before the LORD, toward the veil of the sanctuary" (Lev 4:5-6).
- Prophet: "Do not touch My *anointed* [*mâshîyach* (מָשִׁיחַ)], to My prophets do no harm" (Ps 105:15).
- King: "Therefore will I proclaim you, O LORD, among the nations, and I will sing praise to your Name, You who gave great victories to your king and showed kindness to your *anointed* [*mâshîyach* (מָשִׁיחַ)], to David and his posterity forever" (2 Sam 22:50-51).

The priests, prophets, or kings were not the Messiah; however, they were messiahs—that is to say, they were *mâshîyach* (מָשִׁיחַ) *anointed*. Seeing *mâshîyach* (מָשִׁיחַ) in this context as a word is important; understanding that it was only over time that the word became a title is just as important. This is also the case within the Greek (*Note*[20]).

When translating *mâshîyach* (מָשִׁיחַ) into the Greek Septuagint (a.k.a., the LXX), the seventy rabbis used the word *khristós* (χριστός). We primarily use *khristós* (χριστός) as a title, thus, it is informative to read the above Scripture passages using *khristós* (χριστός) as a word in place of anointed (*Note*[21]).

As mentioned, the word *mâshîyach* (מָשִׁיחַ) in Hebrew, and its equivalent word *khristós* (χριστός) in Greek, gradually changes into a title. Initially, the title focused on the king—God's anointed, or anointed one, e.g., King David or even a non-Israelite king, Cyrus king of Persia (Isa 45:1-4). Then, as Israel struggled without a king (or without any prophets, for that matter), the word *mâshîyach* (מָשִׁיחַ) takes on an eschatological[22] tone, and now gradually becomes a title for *the* Messiah—*Mâshîyach* (מָשִׁיחַ).

Israel is now waiting, anticipating, and desiring *the* Anointed One—*the Mâshîyach* (מָשִׁיחַ)—to come to deliver them in the Last Days.

Even though not fully recognized by Israel, Jesus, however, is in fact that desired Anointed One! *Iēsous* (Ἰησοῦς) is the awaited for *Khristós* (Χριστός). *Yahshua* (יֵשׁוּעַ) is that anticipated *Mâshîyach* (מָשִׁיחַ).

With Jesus, the word *anointed* has now officially become a title. As we now write:

- Jesus the *Mâshîyach* (מָשִׁיחַ)!
- Jesus the *Khristós* (Χριστός)!
- Jesus the *Christ*!

By the time we come to the Latin and all later translations (including English), Christ is understood only as a title (and thus always capitalized). It is unfortunate that, over time, the definite article, "the" was dropped in English, and Jesus *the Christ—Iēsous* (Ἰησοῦς) *ho Khristós* (Χριστός) as written in the Greek—became just Jesus Christ (confusing some by appearing to be another name for Jesus).

Hence, in this book, I refer to *the* Christ with the definite article (as stated in the book's title), and as written in the original Greek New Testament—*ho Khristós* (Χριστός). This will reinforce the proper usage of the title (for example, Jesus the Christ, Jesus the

Messiah, Jesus the *Mâshîyach* (מָשִׁיחַ), *Yahshua* (יֵשׁוּעַ) the *Mâshîyach* (מָשִׁיחַ), or Jesus the Anointed One).

What we have stated above deals with usage—it does not prove that Jesus is *the* Anointed One (as I am writing to the Christian in the pew, I assume that you already believe that). To a baptized Christian there is no need to prove that Jesus is the Anointed One. Nevertheless, let us briefly see Jesus as the fulfillment of prophecy, as the Anointed One by going back about 400 to 500 years before Jesus' incarnation.

Many Old Testament prophecies are fulfilled in the Person of Jesus; however, I will consider only three. They give us an understanding of Israel's *anticipation* and *expectation.*

Israel's Anticipation of the Messiah: About the time of Jesus' ministry on earth, Israel was clearly looking for the Anointed One.

The first prophecy is from the Prophet Daniel. He refers to the coming of the Anointed One, who will deliver Israel. Daniel sets a 490-year countdown clock—seventy years' time seven (*Note*[23])—until the ultimate Messianic fulfillment (Dan 9:24-27). This clock runs out about the time of Jesus (*Note*[24]).

The second prophecy is also from Daniel. This concerns the Kingdom of God and the Son of Man, which also sees its culmination about the time of Jesus. In Chapter 2, Daniel interprets King Nebuchadnezzar's dream. Daniel outlines five kingdoms (Dan 2:26-45) based upon the portions of the image of the statue in Nebuchadnezzar's dream (Dan 2:31-35).

Academic theologians assign the first kingdom to the Babylonian Empire, the second kingdom to the Medo-Persian Empire, the third kingdom to the Greek Empire and the fourth kingdom (during the time of Jesus) to the Roman Empire. Now, it is during the fourth kingdom, "in the lifetime of those kings" (i.e., the Roman Empire), that "the God of Heaven will set up a Kingdom that shall never be destroyed" (Dan 2:44a); this is the fifth kingdom, the

Kingdom of God. "The great God has revealed to the king what shall be in the future," Daniel concludes (Dan 2:45b).

These academic theologians also line up these five kingdoms with Daniel's dream in which he sees "four immense beasts" (Dan 7:2-7) culminating with a vision of "One like a Son of Man coming, on the clouds of Heaven" (Dan 7:13). These four beasts correspond to the first four kingdoms of Daniel 2 and the Son of Man with the fifth kingdom, the Kingdom of God.

Messianic anticipation, therefore, was at a so-called *fever pitch* at the time of Jesus, for the 490-year countdown clock was coming to an end, and it was the time of the fourth kingdom and the fourth beast, in which God was to set up His Kingship with His own Kingdom (Dan 7:14). Israel was totally attuned to all of this (see Lk 3:15).

Add to this, Israel did not have a king, and Israel had not even seen a prophet for almost 450 years, because there was a drought in God's revelation from the time of the prophet Malachi (the last Old Testament prophet) to the time of Jesus.

This brings me to the third prophecy. The prophet Malachi prophesies: "Lo, I am sending my messenger to prepare the way before Me" (Mal 3:1; also cf. 4:5). As a result, Israel was not only looking for the Anointed One, but also was looking for this messenger.

With all this, we can see why Messianic anticipation was at an all-time high, and thus, messiahs appeared to be popping up everywhere (e.g., Acts 5:36-37). Israel was looking and waiting for the Messiah to deliver them from the Roman Empire, and establish God's Kingdom.

It was in this milieu that Jesus enters the picture. However, He was unlike the other so-called deliverers of that time, for Jesus was from God (Acts 5:38-39). He was the true Anointed One of God. He was the true Redeemer that Israel was anticipating.

The early Church recognized the fact that in *Yahshua* (יֵשׁוּעַ) was the ultimate fulfillment of Messianic prophecy. They went back into the Scriptures (i.e., Tanakh or Old Testament), searched, and understood Jesus to be the fulfilled promise of the Anointed One! He was the anticipated and desired *Mâshîyach* (מָשִׁיחַ)! With this revelation, the New Testament writers proclaimed how in the Person of Jesus all three offices of priest, prophet, and king are fulfilled:

- Priest: Jesus is the "High Priest, who has taken His seat at the right hand of the throne of the Majesty in Heaven" (Heb 8:1).
- Prophet: "When the people saw the sign He had done, they said, 'This is truly the Prophet, the one who is to come into the world'" (Jn 6:14),
- King: "He has a Name written on His cloak and on His thigh, 'King of kings and Lord of lords'" (Rev 19:16; also cf. 1 Tm 6:15).

Yahshua (יֵשׁוּעַ) fulfills all three categories:

> In the Person of Jesus, we have the ultimate "Anointed One," Who unites priestly, prophetic, and monarchical strands of Old Testament expectations about God and the coming of His Kingdom.[25]
>
> | *Catholic Encyclopedia* |

Remember Daniel's prophecy? Four hundred and ninety years later, *Yahshua* (יֵשׁוּעַ) is the ultimate fulfillment of that Messianic prophecy (see Mt 18:22). In addition, He is the Son of Man who establishes the Kingdom of God (see Mk 1:15 and Mt 25:31).

Remember Malachi's prophecy? This was a prophecy about which even Jesus' disciples questioned Him (Mt 17:10; also cf. Mal 3:1 and 4:5). Jesus answered that the messenger (Elijah) had come in the person of John the Baptist (Mt 17:11-13; also cf. Lk 3:3-6, 7:27-28, and Mt 11:13-14); and thus, John the Baptist is the fulfillment of the messenger prophecy, the proclaimer of the coming of the Messiah (*Note*[26]).

Israel's Expectation of the Messiah: If Jesus fulfills all of the categories of the Anointed One, if Daniel's and Malachi's prophecies were fulfilled, why was there an issue?

The answer has two parts, both having to do with Israel's expectation of the *Mâshîyach* (מָשִׁיחַ). The first part concerns Israel's expectation of what the Messiah should *do*; the second part concerns Israel's expectation of who the Messiah *is*, or, more precisely, who the Messiah *is not*.

In the first case, Israel expected the Anointed One to be a new Moses (Deut 18:15; also cf. Acts 3:22 and 7:37). For Moses himself prophesies that "A prophet like me will the LORD, your God, raise up for you from among your own kinsmen" (Deut 18:15). Israel eventually attributed that person to be an end-time prophet (*Note*[27]).

Jesus fulfills this prophecy in its archetypical form. Moses is saved as a baby (Ex 2:3); Jesus is saved as a baby (Mt 2:13-14). Moses goes through the waters of the Red Sea (Ex 13:18); Jesus is baptized in the waters of the Jordan (Mt 3:13). Moses fasts for 40 days (Ex 34:28); Jesus fasts for 40 days (Mt 4:2). Moses chooses 12 princes (Num 1:44); Jesus chooses 12 Apostles[28] (Mt 10:5). Moses appoints seventy elders to assist him (Num 11:16); Jesus appoints seventy disciples to assist Him (Lk 10:1); and so forth.

Israel, in a desire for national self-determination, however, narrowly defined the fulfillment of this prophecy, and thus was expecting a freedom fighter, a liberator, a redeemer from oppression. In particular, this redeemer would liberate Israel from Caesar's oppressive Roman rule, just as Moses liberated Israel from Pharaoh's oppressive Egyptian rule. With this distorted understanding, even King Herod felt troubled by Jesus' birth, for he believed that Jesus would threaten his rule (see Mt 2:3 and 2:16). For it was this understanding which was rooted in Israel's expectation!

Jesus did liberate Israel, however not in the manner that Israel expected. Liberation was at a higher level—a spiritual level—and, sadly, the majority of the Jews[29] missed this liberation. Israel was stuck in limited thinking and understanding.

Consider the two disciples on their way home to Emmaus (Lk 24:13-33). They were emotionally depressed and discouraged, for they hoped that Jesus *was* the *Mâshîyach* (מָשִׁיחַ), the new Moses, the freedom fighter who was going to redeem Israel from Roman occupation (Lk 24:21). However, although He was mighty in deed and word in His ministry, He had now been crucified (Lk 24:19-20), a conundrum indeed (see Lk 24:17). At this point Jesus, Himself, had to correct their understanding of the Messiah's role in His First Coming, by giving them a lesson in Scripture "beginning with Moses and all the prophets" (Lk 24:25-27).

Consider another example. Previously, during Jesus' ministry, even John the Baptist seems to have been confused. The forerunner who boldly proclaimed that Jesus is the Lamb of God (Jn 1:29), and that he is unworthy even to untie His sandal (Jn 1:27), sat in prison wondering if he had made a mistake. Is Jesus the real *Mâshîyach* (מָשִׁיחַ), or should they be looking for another (Mt 11:3 and Lk 7:20), the Baptist questioned?

Interestingly, Jesus' answer gives us some insight. He does not directly answer John's question. He corrects the disciples' thinking, by showing how He fulfills Old Testament prophecy, quoting the prophet Isaiah (Mt 11:4-5 and Lk 7:22; also cf. Isa 29:18-19, 35:5-6, and 61:1). The Messiah's mission at His First Coming was to ensure that the blind regain their sight, the lame walk, lepers cleansed, the deaf hear, the dead raised, and the poor have the good news proclaimed to them (Mt 11:5). This mission functions on both a spiritual and physical level. Moreover, the Messianic mission was not about liberating Israel from Roman occupation. Then Jesus goes on to say: "blessed is the one who takes no offence at me" (Mt 11:6 and Lk 7:23). Don't be offended that I, the Messiah do not fit your plans, and your way of thinking, your ideologies, your criteria, or your expectations of what the Messiah should do.

From this, here are the first of two conclusions. First, Jesus' liberation was not political or earthly as Israel thought (or we might think) it *should* be.

The liberating Messiah being crucified was definitely not part of Israel's desire; being locked in prison was the opposite of freedom, and continual Roman occupation was definitely not liberation. However, God's Messianic mission pointed to something greater, which is what Israel, or for that matter even we, two thousand years later, need to understand.

Here is another way of putting it. Like we, Israel liked Jesus' mighty deeds, like feeding of the 5,000 (Jn 6:14)—remember, they even wanted to make Him king after this miracle (Jn 6:15). Israel liked the "Rise, pick up your mat and walk" part of Jesus' ministry—it met physical needs. However, they did not care much for the "Your sins are forgiven" side of things—for this they grumbled (Mt 9:3-4,

Mk 2:7-8, and Lk 5:21), and considered it blasphemy. In a sense, it was unspectacular. However, forgiveness of sins was the *core* of Jesus' ministry—physical healing points only to that greater reality.

He healed physically to show His authority over spiritual healing (Mt 9:6, Mk 2:10, and Lk 5:24), which is the greater of the two, and which is precisely what He came to do. We might tend to see the list—"the blind regain their sight, the lame walk, lepers are cleansed, the deaf hear, the dead are raised, and the poor have the good news proclaimed to them" (Mt 11:5; also cf. Lk 4:16-21)—merely from a human perspective, but it is not. All of these items point to a greater understanding.

Saint John helps us to make this distinction by referring to Jesus' miracles as signs (Jn 2:11, 4:54, etc.). As we know, signs point to something, in this case, the greater. As a result, by calling the miracles signs Saint John keeps us from making the mistake of seeing Jesus' miracles purely from an earthly perspective.

Unfortunately, like Israel, some of us do not understand that distinction; even today some Christian groups imitate Israel's perspective. These groups tend to limit the meaning of Jesus' miracles to an earthly reality.

They are represented by spectacular faith healers and popular preachers, who convey a very limited message. One example is the *prosperity gospel* preachers (*Note*[30]). This emphasis, regrettably, is more aligned with Israel's misconceptions than with an understanding of the *true* Messiah.

The second conclusion is that, first and foremost, Jesus' liberation is liberation from our slavery to sin—this is the true meaning of Exodus (Lk 9:31). His miracles, therefore, are a sign that points to that reality.

Think about the paralytic that was brought to Jesus (Mk 2:1-12; also cf. Mt 9:1-8 and Lk 5:17-26). After his friends' going through all the trouble of lowering him from the roof, Jesus says to him: "your sins are forgiven" (Mk 2:5). The scribes did not like that comment for theological reasons (Mk 2:7-8); but is it also fair to argue that the paralytic and his friends did not like what Jesus said for very human reasons. They wanted their friend, the paralytic, healed, did they not? "Your sins are forgiven." Really! We went through all this trouble for that; no, we want our buddy to walk. On the other hand, Jesus healed their friend after he saw their faith. We may therefore also argue that they were receptive to spiritual healing as well.

As important as physical healing may be, it was secondary for Jesus. For which is easier: "to say to the paralytic 'Your sins are forgiven,' or to say, 'Rise, pick up your mat and walk'?" (Mk 2:9). It is easier to say that sins are forgiven, since there is no external evidence of that, whereas physical healing is very evident. Jesus contending with the scribes shows the ability to heal physically (the easier) in order to demonstrate the ability for forgive sins (the harder). Do not get me wrong; the human side is important—for Jesus does carry out the miracle—but this is a sign; the glory of God and our reconciliation with Him is way more important.

Theologically speaking, moreover—as we will see in Chapter 7, Why the Death and Resurrection?—saying to the paralytic "pick up your mat and walk" is also the easier of the two to do since in order to legitimately say "Your sins are forgiven" means that Jesus had to die on the *Cross*[31], which points to the fulfillment of the actual healing, the spiritual liberation for not only the paralytic, but for you and me.

Jesus did not come only to do the easier of the two. He did not come *only* to fix our earthly problems, for He mainly came to fix our eternal needs—true and complete spiritual liberation. However, many in Israel did not want the deeper reality. Unfortunately, even today, some Christians focus on earthly issues, not eternal needs. We want miracles, here and now! Don't we?

Consider the rebuke that Saint Peter received from Jesus when Peter tried to deny that Jesus needed to die on the Cross. "Get behind me, Satan!" is Jesus' reprimand to him, "You are an obstacle to me. You are thinking not as God does, but as human beings do" (Mt 16:23 and Mk 8:33). To this day, we are doing the same; we are not thinking like God does; we are looking at things from only a human point of view, and thus, we are also being rebuked by Him.

In summary, Moses, in liberating Israel from slavery, is seen as a type[32] of Jesus. Jesus, as the antitype (the fulfillment of the type), liberates *Israel* (and, all of humanity) from slavery to sin—this is indescribably *more* important.

Moses brings Israel to the Promised Land—he is the type of Christ. Jesus brings *Israel* (and, all of humanity) to the ultimate Promised Land, by reconciling them to God the Father. This, Israel could not comprehend, for the majority continually rejected God (and His reconciliation), wanting an earthly resolution (e.g., 1 Sam 8:1-9), and in that thinking, the Messiah's ministry was not what Israel expected the *Mâshîyach* (מָשִׁיחַ) to *do*.

Let us move to the second part—concerning Israel's expectation of who the *Mâshîyach* (מָשִׁיחַ) *is*. Simply put, Israel also did not fully grasp that the Anointed One could actually be God.

Not realized by most, Scripture (the Tanakh) does make reference to the *Mâshîyach* (מָשִׁיחַ) as being God. For example, subtly stated in Daniel's vision of the Son of Man who establishes His kingship over the Kingdom of God, which will not be destroyed (Dan 7:13-14), indicates that the kingship is not one of human origin.

Another, and not so subtle reference, concerns the ministry of the "voice of one crying out in the desert" (Isa 40:3; also cf. Mt 3:3 and Lk 3:4) who was to "prepare the way of the LORD! Make straight in the wasteland a highway for our God!" (Isa 40:3), and "suddenly there will come to the Temple the LORD whom you seek" (Mal 3:1). Both Scripture passages use the word LORD, the Name of Israel's God in the Hebrew text (we will explore this further within the next chapter).

We can also cite Psalm 110. Amusingly, Jesus questions the Pharisees' lack of understanding of this Psalm—let's listen to this dialogue:

> While the Pharisees were gathered together, Jesus questioned them, saying, "What is your opinion about the Messiah? Whose son is he?" They replied, "David's". He said to them, "How, then, does David, inspired by the Spirit, call him 'Lord,'" saying: "'The LORD said to my Lord, Sit at my right hand until I place your enemies under your feet'? If David calls him 'lord,' how can he be his son?" (Mt 22:41-45)

This is an interesting exchange and telling question, isn't it? Jesus does not deny that the Messiah is a descendent of David; He, however, clarifies who the *Mâshîyach* (מָשִׁיחַ) *Is*—i.e., if He is also the Messiah—according to Psalm 110, He is also David's Lord.

We will return to this in the next chapter but, for now, the point is that even though Old Testament Scripture (the Tanakh) pointed to the *Mâshîyach* (מָשִׁיחַ) as being God (also see, Ps 2:7, Isa 53:2, and 9:6-7), Israel either did not take this Scripture literally, or, they did not think that the God of the universe would actually become a human being, like us (*Note*[33]). In fact, this thought was considered utter blasphemy (cf. Mt 9:3, Mt 26:65, Mk 2:7, Mk 14:64, Jn 10:33, etc.). However, knowing Scripture as they did, they must have wondered at the possibility of the Messiah being God Himself.

To go back to the story of the healed paralytic, the scribes clearly objected to Jesus' deity for their theological reasons. Pun intended, they pick up what Jesus was laying down—they understood precisely what Jesus was implying by what He said—they correctly conclude: "Why does this man speak that way? He is blaspheming. Who but God alone can forgive sins?" (Mk 2:7).

More on this later, but for the moment, as stated in the *Catholic Encyclopedia*: "The historical, religious, and theological horizons of the term 'Christ' are significantly reshaped in the Person of Jesus."[34] *Yahshua* (יֵשׁוּעַ) the *Mâshîyach* (מָשִׁיחַ) not only shatters Israel's expectations of what the Anointed One should *do*, but also of who the Anointed One *is*.

No, He was not a mere rabbi among other rabbis, or a prophet among other prophets, or a preacher among other preachers (in line with Israel's thinking). In the Person of Jesus, the Messianic expectation was totally shattered and the Messiah's understood nature infinitely exceeded; it was not what Israel bargained for—therein lay the issue.

Again, we treat Jesus no differently than Israel did. We say that He is merely a good teacher, a miracle-worker, a holy man, a spiritual or religious founder; a spiritual guru, political revolutionary or insurgent or social disrupter. None of these is adequate.

Shockingly, neither Israel's opinion nor ours matters! Informational or objective truth and Truth Himself are not affected by our personal opinion. Most theologians teach this simple understanding of truth. Truth is equal to "what is" (it reflects reality accurately). Now, there are two kinds of truths: (1) subjective, which is about the subject; and (2) objective, which is about the object. Concerning the latter, our knowing or not knowing, our agreeing or disagreeing, about it does not affect it. To be exact, objective truth is totally independent of us. It does not matter if we like it or not. Our opinion does not determine meaning. Therefore, what we think is irrelevant.

Again, our opinion really does not matter! Informational truth is totally independent of us; it is technically not even our opinion, for it is *common property* (*Note*[35]). For example, if I were to hold this book five feet above the ground, and ask you: What would happen if I let go of it? You would say: It will drop to the ground. Now, that answer is the objective truth—it is not just your opinion. You are actually stating the objective truth concerning the effects of gravity, which is common property—it really does not matter what I think of it; it is objectively true.

In this regard, information truth proclaimed by the Church and Truth Himself is not up for debate. This is not based upon popular opinion. For that reason, the Church is not a democracy.

We see that the Church is not a democracy within Scripture itself. Let us go to the dialogue between Jesus and His disciples concerning the question "Who do you say that I AM?" (Mk 8:27; also cf. Mt 16:13 and Lk 9:18). Note that the original question was: "Who do *people* say that I am?" As academic theologians point out, the question did not concern Jesus' ministry as such, it was about His very Self, His very Being. To this, the disciples answer by giving the consensus of Israel, by stating the popular opinion. They answered: "Some say John the Baptist, but others Elijah, and still others Jeremiah or one of the prophets" (Mt 16:14; also cf. Mk 8:28 and Lk 9:19). As we know, popular opinion got it *all* wrong (*Note*[36]).

It was only after that that Jesus' question gets personal, for now He points directly to His disciples and asks: "Who do *you* say that I AM?" It is to this direct, pointed question that "Simon Peter answered, 'you are the Messiah, the Son of the living God'" (Mt 16:15; also cf. Mk 8:29: and Lk 9:20). Note that that answer was not even *his* answer; it was not *his* opinion. This is key. Jesus clearly states that it was not Simon Peter who made this proclamation—it was a revelation from God (Mt 16:17). Simon Peter declares *Yahshua* (יֵשׁוּעַ) as the *Mâshîyach* (מָשִׁיחַ), but not as his opinion. The proof is that he did not understand the full implication of that confession (Mk 8:31-32; also cf. Mt 16:22). If he had, he would not have been rebuked by Jesus mere seconds later, for saying something contrary to that declaration he just made (Mk 8:33; also cf. Mt 16:23).

So then, who is this *Yahshua* (יֵשׁוּעַ) to you? The general question is now pointed directly to *you:* Who do *you* say that Jesus *IS*? You and I are obligated to answer His question directly. We cannot look around us for an answer from others. The answer comes not from a democratic vote or consensus—it is an infusion of truth from God. How do *you* objectively, theoretically, and theologically understand the Person of Jesus? How do *you* define the term *Messiah*?

Within Saint Peter's answer, we move to the implicit practical second aspect of the answer. Even if our theological response is just as eloquent as Saint Peter's, we must also demonstrate that our answer determines how we live our life. It is a movement from theory to lived reality.

Here is the implicit side of the question: when you, through the revelation of God, proclaim *Yahshua* (יֵשׁוּעַ) as the *Mâshîyach* (מָשִׁיחַ), *what does that proclamation actually mean* in your life? What is the correlation between our answer and our lived reality?

At the time of Saint Peter's answer, he did not know what this implication meant to his life. However, he discovered it over time. Likewise, we must discover its meaning in our own lives. In a nutshell, this movement from theory to reality (or head to heart) is the essence of this book. As we grow in our Christian faith there should be a continuous circular movement from theory (head) to reality (heart)—or even heart to head—and then back again.

Here is a simple thesis: each human being (at a point) needs to answer this fundamental question posed by Jesus directly to him or her, individually: *Who do you say that I AM*? Then, we must live out the true meaning of our answer. I pray that this book helps you and me to achieve that.

As we contemplate the depths of this question and its answers, let us segue into the next chapter by listening to some of the first sermons given concerning Jesus the Messiah.

These following five sermons and conclusion are in their totality, as contained in Scripture, without any commentary. It is sometimes beneficial to read Scripture in context, without regard to chapters and verses, or explanations. Therefore, as you read, I encourage you to place yourself in the crowd, listening to Saint Peter, Saint Stephen, and Saint Paul preaching their Gospel messages *directly to you.*

We will begin with Saint Peter's famous sermon given at Pentecost. This is considered to be the very first homily ever given concerning *Yahshua* (יֵשׁוּעַ) the *Mâshîyach* (מָשִׁיחַ). In the crowd, you are a devout Jew gathered in Jerusalem for the feast. You hear a loud sound and look to see what is happening. At a distance you see this man, Saint Peter, with ten other men surrounding him. He stands and in a loud voice he proclaims:

> You who are Jews, indeed all of you staying in Jerusalem. Let this be known to you, and listen to my words. These people are not drunk, as you suppose, for it is only nine o'clock in the morning. No, this is what was spoken through the prophet Joel: "It will come to pass in the last days," God says, "that I will pour out a portion of my spirit upon all flesh. Your sons and your daughters shall prophesy, your young men shall see visions, your old men shall dream dreams. Indeed, upon my servants and my handmaids I will pour out a portion of my spirit in those days, and they shall prophesy. And I will work wonders in the Heavens above and signs on the earth below: blood, fire, and a cloud of smoke. The sun shall be turned to darkness, and the moon to blood, before the coming of the great and splendid day of the Lord, and it shall be that everyone shall be saved who calls on the Name of the Lord." You who are Israelites, hear these words. Jesus the Nazorean was a man commended to you by God with mighty deeds, wonders, and signs, which God worked through Him in your midst, as you yourselves know. This man, delivered up by the set plan and foreknowledge of

> God, you killed, using lawless men to crucify Him. But God raised Him up, releasing Him from the throes of death, because it was impossible for Him to be held by it. For David says of Him: "I saw the Lord ever before me, with Him at my right hand I shall not be disturbed. Therefore my heart has been glad and my tongue has exulted; my flesh, too, will dwell in hope, because you will not abandon my soul to the netherworld, nor will you suffer your holy one to see corruption. You have made known to me the paths of life; you will fill me with joy in your presence." My brothers, one can confidently say to you about the patriarch David that he died and was buried, and his tomb is in our midst to this day. But since he was a prophet and knew that God had sworn an oath to him that He would set one of his descendants upon his throne, he foresaw and spoke of the resurrection of the Messiah, that neither was He abandoned to the netherworld nor did His flesh see corruption. God raised this Jesus; of this we are all witnesses. Exalted at the right hand of God, He received the promise of the Holy Spirit from the Father and poured it forth, as you (both) see and hear. For David did not go up into Heaven, but he himself said: "The Lord said to my Lord, Sit at my right hand until I make your enemies your footstool." Therefore let the whole house of Israel know for certain that God has made Him both Lord and Messiah, this Jesus whom you crucified. (Acts 2:14-36)

The next public statement on the *Mâshîyach* (מָשִׁיחַ) is also from Saint Peter. This is immediately after he and Saint John cured the crippled beggar at the gate of the Temple. Again, picture yourself within the crowd gathered, witnessing the healed beggar walking, leaping, and praising God. Then you hear Saint Peter proclaim the explanation and implication of this miracle:

You Israelites, why are you amazed at this, and why do you look so intently at us as if we had made him walk by our own power or piety? The God of Abraham, (the God) of Isaac, and (the God) of Jacob, the God of our ancestors, has glorified His servant Jesus whom you handed over and denied in Pilate's presence, when he had decided to release Him. You denied the Holy and Righteous One and asked that a murderer be released to you. The author of life you put to death, but God raised Him from the dead; of this we are witnesses. And by faith in His Name, this man, whom you see and know, His Name has made strong, and the faith that comes through it has given him this perfect health, in the presence of all of you. Now I know, brothers, that you acted out of ignorance, just as your leaders did; but God has thus brought to fulfillment what He had announced beforehand through the mouth of all the prophets, that His Messiah would suffer. Repent, therefore, and be converted, that your sins may be wiped away, and that the Lord may grant you times of refreshment and send you the Messiah already appointed for you, Jesus, whom Heaven must receive until the times of universal restoration of which God spoke through the mouth of His holy prophets from of old. For Moses said: "A prophet like me will the Lord, your God, raise up for you from among your own kinsmen; to Him you shall listen in that He may say to you. Everyone who does not listen to that prophet will be cut off from the people." Moreover, all the prophets who spoke, from Samuel and those afterwards, also announced these days. You are the children of the prophets and of the covenant that God made with your ancestors when he said to Abraham, "In your offspring all the families of the earth shall be blessed." For you first, God raised up His servant and sent Him to bless you by turning each of you from your evil ways. (Acts 3:12-26)

In both of Saint Peter's sermons he not only expresses the importance of the Anointed One, he also demonstrates how the Scriptures point to *Yahshua* (יֵשׁוּעַ) being that Anointed One.

In our next discourse, Saint Stephen takes this a step further. Saint Stephen gave a lengthy historical Scriptural overview to demonstrate how Israel consistently rejected God's chosen ones, ultimately *the* Messiah. These words of Saint Stephen were so obnoxious to the religious leaders that they become the catalyst for his martyrdom at their hands:

> My brothers and fathers, listen. The God of glory appeared to our father Abraham while he was in Mesopotamia, before he had settled in Haran, and said to him, "Go forth from your land and (from) your kinsfolk to the land that I will show you." So he went forth from the land of the Chaldeans and settled in Haran. And from there, after his father died, he made him migrate to this land where you now dwell. Yet He gave him no inheritance in it, not even a foot's length, but He did promise to give it to him and his descendants as a possession, even though he was childless. And God spoke thus, "His descendants shall be aliens in a land not their own, where they shall be enslaved and oppressed for four hundred years; but I will bring judgment on the nation they serve," God said, "and after that they will come out and worship me in this place." Then He gave him the covenant of circumcision, and so he became the father of Isaac, and circumcised him on the eighth day, as Isaac did Jacob, and Jacob the twelve patriarchs. And the patriarchs, jealous of Joseph, sold him into slavery in Egypt; but God was with him and rescued him from all his afflictions. He granted him favour and wisdom before Pharaoh, the king of Egypt, who put him in charge of Egypt and (of) his entire household. Then a famine and great affliction struck all Egypt and Canaan, and our ancestors could find no food; but when Jacob heard that there was

grain in Egypt, he sent our ancestors there a first time. The second time, Joseph made himself known to his brothers, and Joseph's family became known to Pharaoh. Then Joseph sent for his father Jacob, inviting him and his whole clan, seventy-five persons; and Jacob went down to Egypt. And he and our ancestors died and were brought back to Shechem and placed in the tomb that Abraham had purchased for a sum of money from the sons of Hamor at Shechem. When the time drew near for the fulfillment of the promise that God pledged to Abraham, the people had increased and become very numerous in Egypt, until another king who knew nothing of Joseph came to power (in Egypt). He dealt shrewdly with our people and oppressed (our) ancestors by forcing them to expose their infants, that they might not survive. At this time Moses was born, and he was extremely beautiful. For three months he was nursed in his father's house; but when he was exposed, Pharaoh's daughter adopted him and brought him up as her own son. Moses was educated (in) all the wisdom of the Egyptians and was powerful in his words and deeds. When he was forty years old, he decided to visit his kinsfolk, the Israelites. When he saw one of them treated unjustly, he defended and avenged the oppressed man by striking down the Egyptian. He assumed (his) kinsfolk would understand that God was offering them deliverance through him, but they did not understand. The next day he appeared to them as they were fighting and tried to reconcile them peacefully, saying, "Men, you are brothers. Why are you harming one another?" Then the one who was harming his neighbour pushed him aside, saying, "Who appointed you ruler and judge over us? Are you thinking of killing me as you killed the Egyptian yesterday?" Moses fled when he heard this and settled as an alien in the land of Midian, where he became the father of two sons. Forty years later, an angel appeared to him in the desert near Mount Sinai in the flame of a burning bush. When Moses saw it, he was amazed at the sight, and as he drew near to look at it, the voice of the Lord came, "I am the God of your fathers, the God of Abraham, of Isaac, and of Jacob." Then Moses, trembling, did not dare to look at it. But the Lord said to him, "Remove the sandals from your feet, for the place where you stand is holy ground. I have witnessed the affliction of my people in Egypt and have heard their groaning, and I have come down to rescue them. Come now, I will send you to Egypt." This Moses, whom they had rejected with the words, "Who appointed you ruler and judge?" God sent as (both) ruler and deliverer, through the angel who appeared to him in the bush. This man led them out, performing wonders and signs in the land of Egypt, at the Red Sea, and in the desert for forty years. It was this Moses who said to the Israelites, "God will raise up for you, from among your own kinsfolk, a prophet like me." It was he who, in the assembly in the desert, was with the angel who spoke to him on Mount Sinai and with our ancestors, and he received living utterances to hand on to us. Our ancestors were unwilling to obey him; instead, they pushed him aside and in their hearts turned back to Egypt, saying to Aaron, "Make us gods who will be our leaders. As for that Moses who led us out of the land of Egypt, we do not know what has happened to him." So they made a calf in those days, offered sacrifice to the idol, and reveled in the works of their hands. Then God turned and handed them over to worship the host of Heaven, as it is written in the book of the prophets: "Did you bring me sacrifices and offerings for forty years in the desert, O house of Israel? No, you took up the tent of Moloch and the star of (your) god Rephan, the images that you made to worship. So I shall take you

> into exile beyond Babylon." Our ancestors had the tent of testimony in the desert just as the One who spoke to Moses directed him to make it according to the pattern he had seen. Our ancestors who inherited it brought it with Joshua when they dispossessed the nations that God drove out from before our ancestors, up to the time of David, who found favour in the sight of God and asked that he might find a dwelling place for the house of Jacob. But Solomon built a house for him. Yet the Most High does not dwell in houses made by human hands. As the prophet says: "The Heavens are my throne, the earth is my footstool. What kind of house can you build for me? says the Lord, or what is to be my resting place? Did not my hand make all these things?" You stiff-necked people, uncircumcised in heart and ears, you always oppose the Holy Spirit; you are just like your ancestors. Which of the prophets did your ancestors not persecute? They put to death those who foretold the coming of the Righteous One, whose betrayers and murderers you have now become. You received the Law as transmitted by angels, but you did not observe it. (Acts 7:2-53)

Saint Stephen becomes the Church's first martyr. I guess that calling them *stiff-necked, uncircumcised in heart and ears* did not help! In essence, Saint Stephen clearly shows Israel's spiritual leaders' continual rejection of God's chosen ones, culminating in their rejection of the Messiah.

With its rejection of *Yahshua* (יֵשׁוּעַ) as the *Mâshîyach* (מָשִׁיחַ), Israel's leaders now turn to persecution of all those who are making such proclamations. This was the beginning where the lineage eventually (many years later) gets divided. That is, in hindsight, this was the initial start of the separation of what we now refer to as Judaism and Christianity.

This leads me to the next sermon. Saint Peter is invited to the house of Cornelius, a centurion, who is a Gentile, a non-Jew. In a Gentile household, he says the following:

> In truth, I see that God shows no partiality. Rather, in every nation whoever fears Him and acts uprightly is acceptable to Him. You know the word (that) He sent to the Israelites as He proclaimed peace through Jesus Christ, who is Lord of all, what has happened all over Judea, beginning in Galilee after the baptism that John preached, how God anointed Jesus of Nazareth with the Holy Spirit and power. He went about doing good and healing all those oppressed by the devil, for God was with Him. We are witnesses of all that He did both in the country of the Jews and (in) Jerusalem. They put Him to death by hanging Him on a tree. This man God raised (on) the third day and granted that He be visible, not to all the people, but to us, the witnesses chosen by God in advance, who ate and drank with Him after He rose from the dead. He commissioned us to preach to the people and testify that He is the one appointed by God as judge of the living and the dead. To Him all the prophets bear witness, that everyone who believes in Him will receive forgiveness of sins through His Name. (Acts 10:34-43)

As a Gentile, I trust that you pictured yourself in the house of Cornelius listening to Saint Peter inviting you into the fold. This understanding is continued by Saint Paul who demonstrates that the gathering of Jews with the Gentiles is God's ultimate plan.

Saint Paul begins his preaching with Israel's Salvation History[37] and how *Yahshua* (יֵשׁוּע) is *the* fulfillment as the *Mâshîyach* (מָשִׁיחַ). He proclaimed this message at Antioch (as we can see, still within the Jewish fold), in a synagogue, on the Sabbath (Acts 13:14). After he said this, demonstrating that *Yahshua* (יֵשׁוּע) is the Messiah, many Jews and converts to Judaism started to follow (Acts 13:43). They also invited Saint Paul to the synagogue to continue the discussion on the following Sabbath, at which point he finishes his teaching with the invitation of the Gentiles. He begins by proclaiming:

Fellow Israelites and you others who are God-fearing, listen. The God of this people Israel chose our ancestors and exalted the people during their sojourn in the land of Egypt. With uplifted arm He led them out of it and for about forty years He put up with them in the desert. When He had destroyed seven nations in the land of Canaan, He gave them their land as an inheritance at the end of about four hundred and fifty years. After these things He provided judges up to Samuel (the) prophet. Then they asked for a king. God gave them Saul, son of Kish, a man from the tribe of Benjamin, for forty years. Then He removed him and raised up David as their king; of him He testified, "I have found David, son of Jesse, a man after my own heart; he will carry out my every wish." From this man's descendants God, according to His promise, has brought to Israel a Saviour, Jesus. John heralded His coming by proclaiming a baptism of repentance to all the people of Israel; and as John was completing his course, he would say, "What do you suppose that I am? I am not He. Behold, one is coming after me; I am not worthy to unfasten the sandals of His feet." My brothers, children of the family of Abraham, and those others among you who are God-fearing, to us this Word of Salvation has been sent. The inhabitants of Jerusalem and their leaders failed to recognize Him, and by condemning Him they fulfilled the oracles of the prophets that are read Sabbath after Sabbath. For even though they found no grounds for a death sentence, they asked Pilate to have Him put to death, and when they had accomplished all that was written about Him, they took Him down from the tree and placed Him in a tomb. But God raised Him from the dead, and for many days He appeared to those who had come up with Him from Galilee to Jerusalem. These are (now) His witnesses before the people. We ourselves are proclaiming this good news to you that

> what God promised our ancestors He has brought to fulfillment for us, (their) children, by raising up Jesus, as it is written in the second psalm, "You are my Son; this day I have begotten you." And that He raised Him from the dead never to return to corruption He declared in this way, "I shall give you the benefits assured to David." That is why he also says in another psalm, "You will not suffer your holy One to see corruption." Now David, after he had served the will of God in his lifetime, fell asleep, was gathered to his ancestors, and did see corruption. But the One whom God raised up did not see corruption. You must know, my brothers, that through Him forgiveness of sins is being proclaimed to you, (and) in regard to everything from which you could not be justified under the Law of Moses, in Him every believer is justified. (Acts 13:16-39)

As mentioned, Saint Paul concludes his preaching on the following Sabbath; following Saint Peter's lead, he also opens the door to the Gentiles:

> It was necessary that the word of God be spoken to you first, but since you reject it and condemn yourselves as unworthy of eternal life, we now turn to the Gentiles. For so the Lord has commanded us, "I have made you a light to the Gentiles, that you may be an instrument of Salvation to the ends of the earth." (Acts 13:46-47)

Jesus the Christ is Lord and *God*.
Therefore, when we make such a proclamation,
it *must* have a consequence in our life.

Chapter 2 | The Second Person of The Trinity

In the previous chapter we asked the question: Who is this *Yahshua* (יֵשׁוּעַ)? Even if, by God's revelation, we were to answer this question as eloquently as Saint Peter by stating that *Jesus is the Messiah, the Son of the living God*, we now face the question: What are the implications and core meaning of the answer?

As mentioned in the Introduction, by setting the stage with this question—"Who do you say that I AM?"—we now enter the first part of our book's subtitle: *Understanding Who Jesus Is*. While throughout this book we will touch on the second part of the subtitle, *What it Means to be Christ-centred*, our primary focus in Chapters 2 through 6 will be on understanding who *Yahshua* (יֵשׁוּעַ) the *Mâshîyach* (מָשִׁיחַ) is, thus we will continue to answer the question considered in the title of Chapter 1.

At the close of Chapter 1, we looked at some of the first sermons concerning the *Mâshîyach* (מָשִׁיחַ). Sometimes we read Scripture in light of today and forget its context. Therefore, the goal in Chapter 1 was to place us in that particular milieu—smelling, touching, seeing, feeling, and, most of all, listening to what was proclaimed concerning this Man.

As the early Church grew, to codify the Apostles' teachings (the Gospel message), Church leaders orally recited canticles as teaching materials for the believers. These were in use before what we call the New Testament was written. Like the Evangelical Canticles from the Gospel of Saint Luke, these teaching materials were also sacred songs and hymns (easy to remember within an oral tradition). They were also simple professions of faith.

Let us begin this chapter with one such canticle found in Saint Paul's letter to the Philippian believers:

Though He was in the form of God,
Jesus did not deem equality with God
something to be grasped at.

Rather, He emptied Himself
and took the form of a slave,
being born in the likeness of men.

He was known to be of human estate,
and it was thus that He humbled himself,
obediently accepting even death,
death on a Cross!

Because of this,
God highly exalted Him
and bestowed on Him the Name
above every other name,

So that at Jesus' Name
every knee must bend
in the Heavens, on the earth,
and under the earth,
and every tongue proclaim
to the glory of God the Father:
JESUS [THE] CHRIST IS LORD!
| Canticle – Philippians 2:6-11[38] |

In the past few decades, an interesting phenomenon appears. More and more scholars are stating something as follows: The Bible consists of multiple stories tied together to make us good people; or, The Bible is about helping us live a good and upright life; or, The main goal of the Bible is to teach us about caring, kindness, and love.

As a result, some scholars are reducing Christianity to living our life ethically and morally. In trying to appeal broadly to society, they assert that Christianity is just a beautiful philosophy of life that results in treating one another well.

I have also heard some scholars speak of Jesus in terms of only an academic exercise. They blandly speak of Jesus as if He were just another spiritual leader, teacher, preacher, or just another founder of a religious group or sect, or even only a highly enlightened individual. Others have even relapsed into some ancient heresies, which treat Jesus as only a great moralist, philosopher, guru, apocalyptic prophet, or even another buddha. Some, with a highly secular perspective, view Jesus as a political revolutionary, a religious zealot or extremist, or even a feminist.

Granted, some of these statements from these three categories individually or collectively might have merit; nevertheless, without a proper biblical perspective, these statements are totally inadequate, or in cases of those that have no merit, they even could be heretical.

For example, Scripture is not simply a bed-side story book written to keep us on a purported good or right path. The Bible (or Scripture) is the documentation of the God of the Universe's Salvation History, culminating in His Son. It is beyond religion in that it is also the instruction and documentation of the plan for salvation pertaining to all of humanity. Even though the Bible is written by humans—in a time, place, and culture—Scripture is the objective Word of God.

In regard to Christianity, admonitions to exhibit a moral and ethical lifestyle, while important, are actually secondary, and what is more, if a lifestyle merely remains there, it is also theologically inadequate. Living an upright life is important; practical and social issues are important; moral and ethical teachings are important; however, if Christianity is only that, its message is no better than any other religion. In fact, it is no better than any other philosophy or humanistic endeavour.

Finally, in regard to Jesus, such heretical beliefs are only one step removed from syncretism[39] or relativism[40]—as God, He is the One Who places the other two categories of philosophy and humanism in their proper perspective.

A Christian worldview places every other worldview in its proper context and meaning (e.g., ethics and morals), or even makes some worldviews irrelevant (e.g., calling Christianity merely a philosophy of life).

It is only in this full biblical context that we can have proper understanding. For example, being moral, good, and ethical should be understood in the context of love. If we love properly we will act morally. We are not called to love in just any way, but to love with Christian love. As we will study, it is to love as Jesus loves. Jesus is both the example and source of that love, because He is God—and God is love. Love is rooted in God. If Jesus was not God, loving as He loves is meaningless.

Also, morals and ethics are rooted in God. True morality can only be practiced if there is a true God. In other words, we need God in order to have a true framework of morals and ethics. If not, morals and ethics will have no real meaning. Likewise, if Jesus was not God, Christian morality is also meaningless.

To consider *Yahshua* (יֵשׁוּעַ) as just another man is heresy! This heresy makes Christianity irrelevant and impotent to deal with the nature and destiny of humanity and the universe. For that reason, let us start with this fundamental assertion of the deity of the Christ and then build on it—for if He is not God we have nothing!

Of the Three Persons within the Trinity (*Note*[41]), One enters into creation. "The Word was God" Saint John proclaims (Jn 1:1), "and the Word became flesh and made His dwelling among us" (Jn 1:14). The Word, the Son of God, the Second Person of the Trinity, enters the cosmos by becoming Man, with a human body, and lived among us, His creation. The Word of Life Who created the cosmos became physical and visible within His own creation (1 Jn 1:1-2).

> *Homoousios* (Greek for consubstantial) is the term accepted at the Council of Nicaea (A.D. 325) and incorporated into the Nicene Creed to affirm the full divinity of the Son, as He shares the divine substance of His Father (*Note*[42]).
>
> | *Catholic Encyclopedia* |

Jesus, the Son, shares fully in the divinity of God the Father—for He is God (*Note*[43]). Therefore, *Yahshua* (יֵשׁוּעַ) the *Mâshîyach* (מָשִׁיחַ) is true God and true Man—fully God and fully Human—at the same time. He is not part God and part Human, or some mixture of divinity and humanity (*CCC* #464).

The Second Person of the Trinity (*Note*[44]), God the Son—is "God from God, Light from Light, true God from true God, begotten, not made, consubstantial of one Being with the Father" as is stated in the Creed—condescended into the womb of a young girl named Mary, and becomes human (*Note*[45]). He, the all-powerful One, became one of us. Putting aside His essential dignity and superiority, the Creator became human in the womb of Mary. To put it another way, in this act of condescending, He emptied Himself, and limited Himself through human biology (*Note*[46]).

The Council of Chalcedon, nearly 1600 years ago and about 125 years after the Council of Nicaea declared again this truth:

> Therefore, following the holy fathers, we all teach that with one accord we confess one and the same Son, our Lord Jesus Christ, the same perfect in human nature, truly God and the same with a rational soul and a body truly man, consubstantial with the Father according to divinity, and consubstantial with us according to human nature, like unto us in all things except sin, (cf. Heb 4:15); indeed born of the Father before the ages according to divine nature, but in the last days the same born of the Virgin Mary, Mother of God according to human nature; for us and for our deliverance, one and the same Christ only begotten Son, our Lord, acknowledged in two natures, without mingling, without change, indivisibly, undividedly, the distinction of the natures nowhere removed on account of the union but rather the peculiarity of each nature being kept, and uniting in one person and substance, not divided or separated into two persons, but one and the same Son only begotten God Word, Lord Jesus [the] Christ, just as from the beginning the prophets taught about Him and the Lord Jesus Himself taught us, and the creed of our fathers has handed down to us. Therefore,

> since these have been arranged by us with all possible care and diligence, the holy and ecumenical synod has declared that no one is allowed to profess or in any case to write up or to compose or to devise or to teach others a different faith.[47]
>
> | The Council of Chalcedon, 451 A.D. |

This declaration, based on the teaching of Scripture, states that Jesus is both God and Man; however, it is difficult to comprehend its full implications. Even Saint Mary and Saint Joseph could not comprehend it entirely (Lk 2:49-50).

We might be able to apprehend this statement (that is, to grasp mentally the meaning or have an idea of what is being said); however it is impossible to comprehend it (that is, to have a profound knowledge or totally understand what is being said). We use inadequate human language to express best this mystery with our limited vocabulary, all the while acknowledging that finite words always fall short of describing the infinite. That said, however, at some level we need to truly grasp that Jesus is God!

As we continue this study, we will realize that as a Christian this declaration cannot be mere conjecture or optional—this is reality. This is objective truth; this is fact—whether or not we agree with it or like it (*Note*[48]). If Jesus is not God, if He was not physically resurrected, if our hope in Him is only for this life, "we are the most pitiable people of all" (1 Cor 15:19). Note, also, that Jesus cannot be God for just the people who believe Him to be, and not God for those who do not. He is either God or He is not.

By living with and being taught by Jesus directly, the Apostles gained great insight, which enabled them to make earth-shattering declarations. In addition to our discussion of Saint Peter's confession, consider Saint Thomas, who, when confronted with the resurrected *Mâshîyach* (מָשִׁיחַ), boldly declares: "My Lord and my God" (Jn 20:28). As Gentile Christians, we might take this pronouncement for granted; however, for the first-century Jew even to think that a man was God would be blasphemy.

However, although we cannot totally comprehend it, as biblical truth, we can *apprehend* it. I encourage you to read and meditate, on the Athanasian Creed found in Appendix A, 1. For if Jesus is not

God, everything we believe is in vain. We might as well pack up our bags and go home (see 1 Cor 15:12-34).

For Jews, from the first century to today, the essential challenge is believing that the *Mâshîyach* (מָשִׁיחַ) is God Himself. They still await the *Mâshîyach* (מָשִׁיחַ); they cannot accept that *Yahshua* (יֵשׁוּעַ) is He.

The incarnation is important to grasp! So again, God the Father sends His Son—Who is co-eternal with the Father, Who is God Himself (1 Pt 1:18-21)—to assume human form, incarnated in the particular Man named *Yahshua* (יֵשׁוּעַ), born of the particular woman named Mary. This was in accordance with the promise to Israel, in a very Jewish context (*Note*[49]). This *Jewish* Man is not only the Man selected by God to fulfill all the types of the *Anointed One* stated in the Scriptures of old, the *Mâshîyach* (מָשִׁיחַ) that Israel was promised, but He is also God Himself—God incarnate—God's very own Son (*Note*[50]). Academic theologians refer to this as *Divine Condescension.* When seriously contemplated it is truly mind-blowing!

Let us review how the above issue played out in Jesus' time on earth and in the early Church. Some Jews recognized that Jesus was the Messiah, and was also God Himself; others did not. An uncomplicated synopsis would go something like this: Israel, until the time of Jesus, was waiting for the Anointed One of God—the new Moses. Some recognized this awaited *Mâshîyach* (מָשִׁיחַ) in the Person of *Yahshua* (יֵשׁוּעַ). They came to realize that this *Yahshua* (יֵשׁוּעַ) transcended all expectations of what a *Mâshîyach* (מָשִׁיחַ) or a new Moses should be, with an ultimate realization that this Messiah was God Himself! They—from and through the Scriptures (i.e., what we now call the Tanakh or the Old Testament)—apprehended it, moved forward in this Truth, and thus, vigorously proclaimed this Truth (e.g., Acts 18:28). Others, however, questioned this fact. Those who questioned, and their descendants to this day, are still waiting for the coming of an Anointed One.

Furthermore, some from the first group of Jews that accepted Jesus as the Messiah evangelized the Gentiles (the non-Jews). Most of us reading this belong to this last group.

The Christian Church since then is an incorporation of believing Jews and believing Gentiles. Simply put, the lineage is the same for both. We Gentiles are grafted in. "Some of the branches were broken off, and you, a wild olive shoot, were grafted in their place and have come to share in the rich root of the olive tree" (Rom 11:17). Some scholars overly complicate the difference between Israel and the Church; however, all Christians must recognize that all Gentile believers are connected to the olive tree, our Jewish spiritual ancestry.

Consequently, Christianity should *not* be considered a *new religion* per se. A good example of what I mean by this is demonstrated in Saint Paul's conversion. Saint Paul does not convert from one religion to another. He was a devout Jew: as he put it, "a Hebrew of Hebrew parentage, in observance of the law a Pharisee" (Phil 3:5). Thus, as a devout Jew he was waiting for the coming of the Messiah. First, he thought Jesus was not the Messiah; so, he persecuted those Jews who thought Jesus was (1 Cor 15:19). However, later, when he was figuratively kicked off his horse, and he had a revelation of a deeper reality (Acts 26:14-15), he not only realized that Jesus is the long awaited Messiah, but He is also God.

Christians recognize that Jesus is *Israel's* appointed Messiah (Who is also God Himself). Those *Jews* who proclaimed this Revelation were eventually labeled, or called, Christians, Χριστιανός (Christianos/*khris-tee-an-os'), literally, followers of the Khristós* (Χριστός), which first happened in Antioch (Acts 11:26). Likewise, because Jesus is God, Christianity fundamentally became a relationship with that *Mâshîyach* (מָשִׁיחַ). That is, Christians are in a covenant-relationship with this Man named *Yahshua* (יֵשׁוּעַ). His *Being* matters. His ontological makeup matters. Who He *is* matters. He, Himself is the object of our faith. This is precisely what sets Christianity apart from any other religion; while rooted in Judaism, Christianity actually goes beyond all ethnic categories or other religious beliefs. Christianity is *not* merely a religion among a gamut of religions—within a supermarket of religions as some have suggested. In fact, it is more than a religion. It is rooted in the ontology of the Man named *Yahshua* (יֵשׁוּעַ), and He is God Himself—I cannot stress this enough.

Keep in mind that no other leader of a major religion (Krishna, Buddha, Mohammad, etc.) claimed to be God. Jesus' teachings are important because of Who He *is*—not the reverse.

By stating that the Man, Jesus—*Yahshua* (יֵשׁוּעַ) the *Mâshîyach* (מָשִׁיחַ)—is God, we inevitably are faced with an all-or-nothing proposition. Let me explain. We either hate the Man Jesus or love Him with everything we have. We either run away from Him with animus, or bow down and worship Him with all we have. There is no middle ground. Jesus demands an either-or-response. In His own words: "Whoever is not with me is against me, and whoever does not gather with me scatters" (Mt 12:30 and Lk 11:23). Why is this so?

The early Church Fathers adamantly asserted *Aut Deus aut malus homo. Yahshua* (יֵשׁוּעַ) is either God or a bad man with no option in-between. We must make that decision. We cannot state that Jesus was a good moral teacher, a good man, and a wise religious leader who tells us how to live, if He is not God. This would be utter madness. Why? Precisely because He spoke and acted in the Person of God (as we will shortly explore). If Jesus is not God, His teachings are worthless—for He has to be God (to Whom we must bow down and worship), or He has to be a liar (from whom we must run away).

Using the Early Church Fathers, C. S. Lewis formulates the trilemma: "liar, lunatic, or Lord!"[51] Yes, these are our options. *Yahshua* (יֵשׁוּעַ) was a con-man, or a crazy-man, or He was and is precisely whom He claimed to be—God incarnate! We cannot accept what He taught over or without whom He *claimed to be*.

Within the Jewish context of that day, we need either to throw stones at Him, as some Jews wanted to do (Jn 8:59)—which we need to clearly to state is rightful if He was not God—or bow down and worship Him, as Saint Thomas did when he realized He was and is Lord and God (Jn 20:28). These were the only options presented to Israel as a whole at that time; ignoring the trilemma, as some might do today, was not an option (*Note*[52]).

Think about it! If someone walked up to you and claimed to be God, what would you do? What would you say? This was what Israel faced. Do you blame them for rejecting the Messiah? Particularly since such a claim was also utter blasphemy in their eyes—hence the reason they could not simply ignore it (*Note*[53]). On some level, I have a hard time not sympathizing with them. Sometimes I wonder, as twenty-first century Christians, do we really understand the gravity of the situation or the decision Israel needed to make? So, let's do that. Let us walk in Israel's shoes.

Play along. Picture yourself as a first-century Jew following this Man named *Yahshua* (יֵשׁוּעַ).

As we take such a journey, we will see the objection given by some scholars that Jesus nowhere in Scripture claims to be God is flawed.

At face value, within a twenty-first century perspective, we might agree with this objection. We may argue that nowhere in Scripture does *Yahshua* (יֵשׁוּעַ) clearly come out and say: I am God! Upon further investigation, however, we learn that Jesus does make that claim, but His claim is considerably more subtle than twenty-first century way of speaking, and made within a first century Jewish context in a *Jewish way*, so to speak.

Playing along, one day, during the Feast of the Dedication, Jesus was walking about in the Portico of Solomon within the Jerusalem Temple (Jn 10:22-23). You, with others, have gathered around Him and directly asked Him, "How long are you going to keep us in suspense? If you are the Messiah, tell us plainly" (Jn 10:24). Jesus begins by telling you that even if He told you, you would not believe Him; and then He goes on to say that "the works I do in My Father's name testify to Me" (Jn 10:25).

You notice that Jesus is not directly answering the question concerning His Messiahship, however, as a first-century Jew you immediately realize that He is stating something deeper, by calling God His Father, and just in case you missed it, He clearly states: "The Father and I are one" (Jn 10:30; also cf. Jn 14:8-10). Responding to His unambiguous statement, you pick up "rocks to stone Him" (Jn 10:31), and accuse Him of blasphemy. Horrendously, He, a *man*, is saying He is God (Jn 10:33).

Prior to this event, virtually the same thing happened when *Yahshua* (יֵשׁוּעַ) healed the crippled man on the Sabbath (Jn 5:1-17). After this healing, "the Jews tried all the more to kill Him, because He not only broke the Sabbath but He also called God His own Father, making Himself equal to God" (Jn 5:18). Keep in mind, claiming to be the *Mâshîyach* (מָשִׁיחַ) is *not* blasphemy. However, importantly, claiming to be equal to God—which is no different from claiming to be God, from a Jewish perspective—certainly is blasphemy, hence their reaction (*Note*[54]). Here *Yahshua* (יֵשׁוּעַ) did not call Himself a Prophet or even the *Mâshîyach* (מָשִׁיחַ); within a Jewish context He again, in essence, called Himself God, by making Himself equal to God.

On another day, as you are having a heated discussion with Jesus, you ask: "Who do you make yourself out to be?" (Jn 8:53). To this, Jesus answers: "Amen, amen, I say to you, before Abraham came to be, I AM" (Jn 8:58). You see that He is only about 30 years old—or not yet 50 as stated within Scripture (Jn 8:57)—but He is saying that He pre-existed before Abraham (Jn 8:57). More importantly, as a first-century Jew you would have not missed the Great "I AM" that *Yahshua* (יֵשׁוּעַ) just proclaimed Himself to be. Placing the emphasis squarely on Who He *Is*, He is clearly referring to "I AM WHO I AM" (Ex 3:14)—in Hebrew אֶהְיֶה אֲשֶׁר אֶהְיֶה (*Ehyeh Aser Ehyeh*), in Greek ἐγώ εἰμί ὁ εἰμί (*Ego Eimi Ho Eimi*)—the Revelation of God to Moses (*Note*[55]). "I EXIST" not merely a being among beings, but the sheer act of Being Itself, the verb "to be" (thus, it is because of this that I existed before Abraham). It is time to wipe out this blasphemy with stones so you pick them up this time as well (John 8:59)!

Some scholars say that the "I AM" proclamation is only found in Saint John's Gospel. Untrue!

In Saint Matthew's Gospel, Jesus walks on water towards the disciples who were in the boat (Mt 14:22ff). The disciples were terrified, thinking that they saw a ghost (Mt 14:26). Jesus approaches the boat and said to them: "Take courage, it is I; do not be afraid" (Mt 14:27). Unfortunately, some English translation translate this as "it is I" (as noted in the *NAB*), but the Greek words are I AM, *Ego Eimi* (ἐγώ εἰμί), stressing the Great I AM connection. This I AM is clearly acknowledged by the disciples. After Jesus entered the boat, the disciples "did Him homage, saying, 'Truly, you are the Son of God'" (Mt 14:33). If Jesus were not God, He should have stopped the disciples from giving Him homage. The Greek word for the English *homage* is προσκυνέω (proskuneō/*pros-koo-neh'-o),* meaning to prostrate oneself, to do reverence, to adore, to worship.[56]

This incident is also recorded in the Gospel of Saint Mark. Jesus clearly tells His disciples: "take courage, it is I [literally, *Ego Eimi* (ἐγώ εἰμί)], do not be afraid!" (Mk 6:50).

Another explicit I AM incident is found in Saint Mark's Gospel (Mk 14:53-65) and is also recorded in the Gospel of Saint Luke (22:66-71). The theological understanding of this I AM is very precise for it is taken two steps further: first, by the literal Son of God (*YHWH*) question, and second by its connection to the Son of Man title within the answer (*Note*[57]).

Imagine that you are now an elder or scribe (Mk 14:53) at Jesus' trial (as presented in the Gospel of Saint Mark):

> They led Jesus away to the High Priest, and all the chief priests and the elders and the scribes came together . . . The chief priests and the entire Sanhedrin kept trying to obtain testimony against Jesus . . . The High Priest asked Him and said to Him, "Are you the Messiah, the Son of the Blessed One?" Then Jesus answered, "I am" [*Ego Eimi* (ἐγώ εἰμί)]; and "you will see the Son of Man seated at the right hand of the Power and coming with the clouds of Heaven." (Mk 14:53-62; also cf. Mk 13:26)

First, the question from the High Priest is clear-cut. Unfortunately the explicit nature of his question could easily be missed in reading English translations. Here the High Priest plainly asks Jesus: Are you the Messiah, the Son of the *Blessed One*? The underlying Greek word translated as *Blessed One* is εὐλογητό (eulogētos/*yoo-log-ay-tos'*).

"In Jewish circles by this time, since there was reticence to speak the name of God [*YHWH*], God was given the title of 'the Blessed One.'"[58] This word or title therefore refers to the name of God, *YHWH*; hence the reason it is translated into English in capital letters.

As a part of the Sanhedrin you understand that the clarity of the question is unmistakable, the High Priest is literally asking: Are you the Messiah, the Son of the *YHWH*?

Listening to Jesus' answer and testimony, you also do not miss the implications of Jesus' words. Not only does Jesus evoke the Great

I AM, in answering the High Priest's question, He neatly connects identifies Himself with the Son of Man in Daniel's prophecy:

I saw One like a Son of Man coming,
on the clouds of Heaven;
When He reached the Ancient One
and was presented before Him,
He received dominion, glory, and kingship;
nations and peoples of every language serve Him.
His dominion is an everlasting dominion
that shall not be taken away,
His kingship shall not be destroyed. (Dan 7:13-14)

Is it any wonder the High Priest tore his garments (Mk 14:63)? The High Priest's question could not have been any clearer. To this Jesus answers in the affirmative: He is the Messiah, He is the Son of *YHWH*, and He is God Himself—*I AM*!

Moreover, He is the divine Son of Man Who comes on the clouds in judgment. Jesus is stating that He is the One Who has dominion over all nations, and that His enemies will be made His footstool. Jesus is literally saying that He will be the ultimate judge of even this trial. To you, as an elder or scribe standing there, Jesus' meaning is plainly obvious.

Now, further to our discussion concerning Psalm 110, which we started to look at in Chapter 1—"The LORD says to you, my lord: Take your throne at my righthand, while I make your enemies your footstool" (Ps 110:1)—we find an interesting construction. In the Hebrew text, the underlying word for the first LORD is יהוה (*YHWH*) As mentioned in the previous chapter, these four letters are also known as the divine Tetragrammaton, meaning the four consonant letters in Hebrew יהוה (*yud-hey-vav-hey*) which is the Name of the God of Israel; hence translated into English in all capital letters.

The underlying word for the second Lord is אָדוֹן ('âdôn/*aw-done'*), which can mean Lord, or lord, master or sir. In this context (within the Hebrew text) Lord with a capital L is an appropriate translation since this "Lord" is God. Here is the interesting part. When these two words were translated into the Greek Septuagint, the rabbis used the Greek word Κύριος (Kurios/*koo'-ree-os*), in both places, which means God, Lord, or lord, master or sir. They could have used Θεός (Theos/*Theós*), meaning God for the first LORD and *Kurios* (Κύριος) for the second Lord, but they did not; they decided to use the same word twice. Now we move to the New Testament.

Recorded in the New Testament, Jesus quotes this text (which appears in all three Synoptic Gospels: Mt 22:44, Mk 12:36, and Lk 20:42). In this discussion, Jesus questions the ideas concerning the nature of the Messiah, namely, if David's son is the Messiah, as some scribes were claiming. So, how is possible that David could call his "son" "Lord," that is, God? For David said: The Lord said to my Lord, Sit at my right hand until I place your enemies under your feet? (Mt 22:44). In the original Greek (New Testament writings), all three Gospels use the word *Kurios* (Κύριος) in both places, just as the Septuagint does.

I find it interesting that some English translations, translate the first *Kurios* (Κύριος) as LORD (all in capitals—harkening back to the Hebrew), and the second *Kurios* (Κύριος) as lord (as cited in the *NAB* above) or master (sometimes Master in capital). In context, neither of these is accurate. Translating *Kurios* (Κύριος) in two different ways not only goes against the original Greek; it also goes against the point Jesus is trying to make: "If David calls him 'Lord,' how can he be his son?" (Mt 22:45). It is not David's son. The second Lord is a reference to Jesus Himself (capital L). The Apostles got the point that Jesus made. In the first sermons ever given, Saint Peter makes this point loudly and clearly:

> For David did not go up into Heaven, but he himself said: 'The Lord [*Kurios* (Κύριος)] said to my Lord [*Kurios* (Κύριος)], Sit at my right hand until I make your enemies your footstool.' Therefore let the whole house of Israel know for certain that God has made him both Lord and Messiah. (Acts 2:34-36)

Looking at the Hebrew text—"The LORD [*YHWH* (יהוה)] says to you, my Lord ['âdôn (אָדוֹן)]" (Ps 110:1), we can place this text in context and state: "The LORD [The First Person of the Trinity, God the Father] says to you, my Lord [The Second Person of the Trinity, God the Son]: Take your throne at my right hand, while I make your enemies your footstool" (Ps 110:1). This is totally in line with the point Jesus' was making (cf. Phil 2:10 and Rom 14:11).

A further "I AM" and "Son of Man" connection is found in Saint John's Gospel. This happens just before the Abraham discussion that we mentioned above. Jesus said to His audience,

> "You belong to what is below, I belong to what is above. You belong to this world, but I do not belong to this world. That is why I told you that you will die in your sins. For if you do not believe that I AM [*Ego Eimi* (ἐγώ εἰμί)], you will die in your sins." So they said to Him, "Who are you?" Jesus said to them, "What I told you from the beginning. I have much to say about you in condemnation. But the one who sent me is true, and what I heard from Him I tell the world." They did not realize that He was speaking to them of the Father. So Jesus said (to them), "When you lift up the Son of Man, then you will realize that I AM [*Ego Eimi* (ἐγώ εἰμί)], and that I do nothing on my own, but I say only what the Father taught Me. The one who sent Me is with Me. He has not left Me alone, because I always do what is pleasing to Him. (Jn 8:23-29)

As previously mentioned, there were some Jews who believed in the revelation that *Yahshua* (יֵשׁוּעַ) the *Mâshîyach* (מָשִׁיחַ) was presenting and some who did not. In this particular instance, "because He spoke this way, many came to believe in Him" (Jn 8:30).

This is precisely what happened to Saul of Tarsus. Saul was a devoted Jew who was waiting for the coming of the *Mâshîyach* (מָשִׁיחַ). Nevertheless, he just did not believe that *Yahshua* (יֵשׁוּעַ) was that *Mâshîyach* (מָשִׁיחַ). So Saul persecuted the Jews who were calling *Yahshua* (יֵשׁוּעַ), the *Mâshîyach* (מָשִׁיחַ). However, on his way to round up some of these Jews in Damascus, he had an encounter with this Jesus (Acts 9:3-8). During this encounter Saul asks: "Who are you?" (Acts 9:5). To which, the reply came, "I AM [*Ego Eimi* (ἐγώ εἰμί)] Jesus" (Acts 9:5). This encounter with the risen Jesus was the turning point for Saul and his conversion to become (Saint) Paul.

During Jesus' arrest in the Garden of Gethsemane, the Gospel of Saint John records three I AM assertions. When the band of soldiers, guards, chief priests and Pharisees came to arrest Jesus, He asks them:

> Whom are you looking for? They answered Him, Jesus the Nazorean. He said to them, I AM [*Ego Eimi* (ἐγώ εἰμί)]. Judas His betrayer was also with them. When He said to them, I AM [*Ego Eimi* (ἐγώ εἰμί)], they turned away and fell to the ground. So He again asked them, Whom are you looking for? They said, Jesus the Nazorean. Jesus answered, I told you that I AM [*Ego Eimi* (ἐγώ εἰμί)]. (Jn 18:4-8)

Notice the response when Jesus says *Ego Eimi* (ἐγώ εἰμί). There was power in the *I AM*, which made them all fall to the ground. This was not a simple "Yes, I am Jesus" (*Note*[59])—this I AM made them fall to the ground!

Although the next I AM assertions are not as explicit as the ones we have stated above, Saint John records seven other *Ego Eimi* (ἐγώ εἰμί) statements, as follows:

1) I AM [*Ego Eimi* (ἐγώ εἰμί)] the Bread of Life (Jn 6:35 and 6:48; also cf. 6:41 and 6:51).
2) I AM [*Ego Eimi* (ἐγώ εἰμί)] the Light of the World (Jn 8:12).
3) I AM [*Ego Eimi* (ἐγώ εἰμί)] the Door (Jn 10:9).
4) I AM [*Ego Eimi* (ἐγώ εἰμί)] the Good Shepherd (Jn 10:11 and 10:14).
5) I AM [*Ego Eimi* (ἐγώ εἰμί)] the Resurrection and the Life (Jn 11:25).
6) I AM [*Ego Eimi* (ἐγώ εἰμί)] the Way and the Truth and the Life (Jn 14:6).
7) I AM [*Ego Eimi* (ἐγώ εἰμί)] the Vine (Jn 15:1 and 15:5).

Therefore, scholars who claim that Jesus did not refer to Himself as God are plainly mistaken (*Note*[60]). Granted, His claim is not overt—it is done within the Jewish context, and as we have studied, some of which is unfortunately lost in translation.

Moving along, it has been said that the primary reason that the Jews instigated the crucifixion of Jesus was jealousy. Jealousy and envy may have played a part in their decision-making. In fact, Pontius Pilate suspected this on the part of the chief priests (Mk 15:10). We also read of a calculated political power-play among the Pharisees right after Jesus raises Lazarus (Jn 11:45-57). On a human level this argument has validity; nevertheless, jealousy or political calculation must always be secondary, for Scripture shows that the accusation of blasphemy must *always* be primary. There is an overwhelming amount of Scripture telling us precisely that the Jewish leaders wanted to kill Jesus because of His claim to divinity and for nothing else Jesus said or did. The verdict of Jesus' trial was clearly a verdict of blasphemy (Mk 14:64). It is a theological necessity to assert plainly that Jesus was killed *because* of who He *Is*; and that He did not die a martyrs death.

Let me further explain with three simple points: First, if Jesus was killed because of jealousy and envy, or if He was a martyr, He would have been no different than any others who suffered such a fate. However, being God and being killed because of this claim of who He *Is* makes Him unique.

Second, as we will discuss in Chapter 7 (Why the Death and Resurrection?), In God the Father's Providence,[61] Jesus is the *only* Lamb of God; thus He was sacrificed—not martyred—for He is the sacrificial Lamb of the Father.

Third, as we will also discuss further in Chapter 7, out of love for us, it was ultimately God the Father Who delivers up His Son to death (Acts 2:23). His Son came to die for us in order to take upon Himself the sins of the world and thus redeem humanity.

Consequently, we see the Gospels' removing all other reasons and pointing to this particular verdict of blasphemy as the reason needed for Jesus' death.

As we just studied, it was when Jesus answered Caiaphas, the High Priest, in the affirmative and said "From now on you will see 'the Son of Man seated at the right hand of the Power" and "coming on the clouds of Heaven" (Mt 26:64) that Caiaphas tore his robes and said, "He has blasphemed! What further need have we of witnesses? You have now heard the blasphemy; what is your opinion?" To this the Council replied, "He deserves to die!" (Mt 26:65-66; also cf. Mk

14:61-64 and Lk 22:67-71). At this point, all other accusations are irrelevant. This was the *only* charge that mattered. Of course, in the Providence of God, this accomplished God's eternal plan for redemption of humanity.

As another argument, which some scholars claim, is that the primary reason Jesus was killed was His claim to be the *King of the Jews*. This is baseless. This theory is asserted in order to make Jesus into a mere prophet, zealot, revolutionary, or radical activist Under Roman law, if Jesus called Himself the King of the Jews, this would be a capital offence. Scripture, however, is crystal clear that both the Roman governor of Judea, Pontius Pilate, and King Herod, the tetrarch of Galilee, found *no* capital crime committed by Jesus (Lk 23:15 and 23:22).

To briefly elaborate, although segmented, what we essentially have are separate trials with two separate authorities (the Jewish and the Roman). Nowhere in the transcripts of the Jewish trials does the claim—King of the Jews—appear (Mt 26:57-68, Mk 14:55-65, Lk 22:54-71, and Jn 18:13-24).

The Jews had their own law, judicial system (courts), and their own police (soldiers and officers)—and Rome was well aware of this and had made provisions for such governance (Jn 18:31a). Acts such as adultery (see Jn 8:5), or blasphemy (see Mk 14:64) constituted death or stoning in accordance with this law. For that reason, they could have easily convicted and stoned Jesus within their own governance, and Rome would not have bothered them (Jn 18:31a). We see this play out with the stoning of Stephen (Acts 7:58-59). The High Priest and the chief priests had the power to do this (*Note*[62]). If we were to think about it, in more than a few instances they even picked up rocks to stone Jesus (e.g. Jn 8:59; and 10:31), which would have killed Him. Yes, they had the power to put Him to death. Eventually, as time went by, however, stoning Jesus was not good enough for them; they wanted more. They wanted a crucifixion (*Note*[63]), which they had no power to do; so, they now needed Rome (Jn 18:31-32).

With this background, let us move to the Roman trials. Going to Pontius Pilate with an accusation of blasphemy would not have gotten them anywhere—Rome did not care about religious blasphemy—so they had to go to Pilate with a false accusation (Lk 23:2; also cf. Acts

13:28). They accused Jesus of calling Himself a King, and thus rivaling Caesar (a capital offence). They knew that this accusation was treasonous, and called for crucifixion.

Pilate recognized the real underlying cause, and so, even told them to judge Jesus by their own Law (Mk 15:10; also cf. Jn 18:29-31). He also tried to pawn off Jesus on Herod, who was in Jerusalem at the time (Lk 23:7). As we know, they returned to Pilate and pressed on—even pitting Pilate against Caesar (Jn 19:12)—and they eventually got their crucifixion. Interestingly, and to their dismay (Jn 19:21), their lie is the truth. Jesus was ultimately crucified with the inscription: "Jesus the Nazarene, King of the Jews" (Jn 19:19, Mt 27:37, Mk 15:26, and Lk 23:38).

Consider another example. As mentioned in the previous chapter, *Yahshua* (יֵשׁוּעַ) forgave the sins of the paralytic (Mt 9:3-4; Mk 2:7-8, and Lk 5:21). The scribes sitting there asked themselves: "Who but God alone can forgive sins?" (Mk 2:7 and Lk 5:21). Sitting there, would we be wondering the same? (*Note*[64]). *Yahshua* (יֵשׁוּעַ) is clearly speaking in the Person of God when He forgives sins. Almost in unison, the scribes yell out, "Blasphemy" (Mt 9:3, Mk 2:7; and Lk 5:21). Would you have done the same? *Yahshua* (יֵשׁוּעַ), however, ignores that; using His Messianic title, He states: "the Son of Man has authority on earth to forgive sins" (Mt 9:6, Mk 2:10, and Lk 5:21). This is simple logic: *Yahshua* (יֵשׁוּעַ) the *Mâshîyach* (מָשִׁיחַ), i.e., the Son of Man, has the authority to forgive sins, which is the prerogative of God Himself; therefore, He the *Mâshîyach* (מָשִׁיחַ), the Son of Man, must also be God.

This is *not* a delegated authority as some scholars now argue when posed with this text, for the underlying Greek word used here is ἐξουσία (exousia/*ex-oo-see'-ah),* which means physical or mental power or strength of doing as one pleases, the power of authority, the inherent ability to carry out a task.[65] He has the full authority, power, or ability to act and speak in the Person of God, because He is God.

Therefore, in essence, He is telling all of us sitting there: Deal with it! To make sure we get it, He tells the paralytic: "Rise, pick up your mat, and go home" (Mk 2:11; also cf. Mt 9:6 and Lk 5:24). If there were microphones in that day, that was definitely a mic-drop moment. Boom! The veiled power of God in the Person of *Yahshua* (יֵשׁוּעַ) the Messiah was visibly demonstrated "in the sight of everyone" (Mk 2:12); *Yahshua* (יֵשׁוּעַ) spoke and it happened (cf. Gen 1:3). The paralytic "rose, picked up his mat at once, and went [home]" (Mk 2:12; also cf. Mt 9:7 and Lk 5:25).

Unlike the prophets of old, *Yahshua* (יֵשׁוּעַ) does not qualify His pronouncements by stating "Thus says the Lord" (Isa 10:24, Jer 4:27, Ezek 2:4, Amos 1:3; and so forth). Speaking in the Person of God, He simply states with pure authority (cf. Mt 7:29), "You have heard it said . . . but I say to you" (Mt 5:22-48). "But I say to you"! Really? Who is this *Yahshua* (יֵשׁוּעַ) to make such a statement? Could you imagine a Buddhist monk saying, "You have heard Gautama Buddha say, but I say to you"; or an Imam say, "You have heard prophet Mohammed say, but I say to you." No reputable Buddhist monk or an Imam would go beyond simply teaching religious ideas by using the words *but I say to you*. That would be unheard of.

In a Jewish context, Jesus' claim "You have heard it said . . . but, I say to you" is a greater offence. No Jewish rabbi would utter those words. Why? It is a direct reference to the Torah, in particular the 10 Commandments that came down from God Himself (e.g., Mt 5:21 and 5:27). A first-century Jew listening to Jesus' words would have had only one of two opinions. Jesus is crazy, or He actually has the power to speak in the Person of God, i.e., He is the Author of the Torah itself!

Consider also Jesus words, "I say to you, something greater than the Temple is here" (Mt 12:6). As a first-century Jew, how does one reconcile this? The Temple is the dwelling place of God, and this *Yahshua* (יֵשׁוּעַ) is stating that something greater than God's dwelling place is here! Would you believe that statement, or cringe and call it blasphemous?

Again, Jesus is clearly speaking here in the Person of God. Yes, something greater is here. This is precisely why He can also state with all power that, "Heaven and earth will pass away, but [My] words will not pass away" (Mt 24:35, Mk 13:31, and Lk 21:33). He is not only greater than the Temple, His teachings and commands are more permanent than Heaven and earth.

That said, and to use the famous catchphrase popularized by the infomercial guy, Ron Popeil: "But wait, there's more!"

Yahshua (יֵשׁוּעַ) demonstrates the three basic attributes of God: omniscience (all-knowing), omnipotence (all-powerful), and omnipresence (all-present). For instance, He demonstrated His omniscience when He tells Saint Peter, "Before the cock crows this day, you will deny three times that you know me" (Lk 22:34). He demonstrated omnipotence by raising people back to life, thus showing power over death: e.g., the Widow of Nain's son (Lk 7:11-17); Jairus' daughter (Lk 8:49-56); and Lazarus (Jn 11:1-44). Finally, He demonstrates omnipresence by telling His disciples that: "I am with you always, until the end of the age" (Mt 28:20).

As previously mentioned, *Yahshua* (יֵשׁוּעַ) is deliberately polemical, and thus demands a response from His listeners as to His identity and nature, about His very Person, and about choosing Him. "If you love Me, you will keep My commandments" (Jn 14:15). He comes first (see Mt 6:33). It is about *Him* more than His doctrine or teaching. He demands an all-or-nothing response (see Rev 3:16). "Let the dead bury their dead" but you, "follow Me" (Mt 8:22 and Lk 9:60). "If any one comes to Me without hating his father and mother, wife and children, brothers and sisters, and even his own life, he cannot be My disciple" (Lk 14:26). Two thousand years later, we sometimes miss the significance of these statements. Listening to this, as a first-century Jew, how would we respond to these statements?

The Bread of Life Discourse provides another example (and more will be said on this in the next chapter). One day as the disciples were following Him, He says: "Amen, amen, I say to you, unless you eat the flesh of the Son of Man, and drink His blood, you do not have life within you" (Jn 6:53). Wow! How would you handle this statement? Even *Yahshua* (יֵשׁוּעַ) Himself asks: "Does this shock you?" (Jn 6:61). As a first-century Jew would Jesus' proclamation that you need to eat His flesh and drink His blood, shock you? In a way Jesus' question is kind of humorous . . . if I were standing there, I know that it would shock me. Would you follow Him after He says that you need to eat His flesh? Do you see that it is about *Him*, His very Being? It is not hard to wonder why a lot of His followers left Him that very moment (Jn 6:66). Would you be among them?

When we place ourselves in the context of a first-century Jew, it is frightening to think what we would do, or how we would react. My hope is that by placing ourselves within the Jewish context, we can see the gravity of the proposition presented to Israel. In a way, we are quite fortunate compared to the first-century Jew. We have two thousand years of hindsight to help us answer these questions and make a decision.

The purpose here is to giving us some tools to help "give an answer to anyone who asks for a reason for the hope that lies within you" (1 Pt 3:15). This chapter is about reminding and asserting that *Yahshua* (יֵשׁוּעַ) the *Mâshîyach* (מָשִׁיחַ) *is* God, and more importantly, revisiting the consequences of such assertion.

On the flipside, the downfall of having two thousand years of hindsight is that we now take this assertion for granted. It is for that reason that I went through all this. By playing along and placing ourselves in the context of a first-century Jew, we get a glimpse into—or we are reminded of—the implication of this assertion. We are reminded that when we assert that Jesus the Christ is God, we are not only stating that He is *not* just another great teacher—or a prophet, or a highly intellectual philosopher with an enhanced philosophical worldview, or a self-help guru telling us how to improve our quality of life, or a charismatic spiritual leader that started a new religion—we are also adamantly asserting the flipside. No, He is not a bad man! No, He is not a con-man! No, He is not a crazy-man! No, He is not a liar! No, He is not a lunatic! *He is precisely whom He claims Himself to be.*

His Being matters. His ontology matters. His Person matters. For *He is God*!

This assertion would have shaken a first-century Jew—it should also shake us to our core. If not, we still do not get it! Although we know that Jesus is God, we might not realize the full implications of the knowledge that *Yahshua* (יֵשׁוּעַ) the *Mâshîyach* (מָשִׁיחַ) *is* God (i.e., the Second Person of the Trinity).

The point is that believing that Jesus is God is not good enough. Do not even demons confess this fact? "What have you to do with us, Son of God" some demons cried out (Mt 28:29). "I know who you are—the Holy One of God" another proclaimed (Lk 4:34). "What have you to do with me, Jesus, Son of the Most High God" another screamed (Mk 5:7). Even if the Apostles were a little confused about who Jesus is, the demons were certainly not. They believed.

Thus, our asserting that Jesus is God is not good enough, for that does not make us necessarily better than demons. Knowing this truth, they continued being demons—enemies of God. "You believe that God is one. You do well. Even the demons believe that and tremble" (Jms 2:19). Their trembling showed a justifiable fear of God. The sad fact is some of us do not even *tremble* (*Note*[66]).

Going to church on Sundays and engaging in pietistic practices such as saying the novenas, rosaries, and so forth, are extremely important (see 1 Tm 4:7-8); however, they are not an end in themselves. If so, they become mere formalities, or superficial aspects of our faith. Practices without truth-claims are totally inadequate. Christianity is not merely about how we live in this world and how we treat others, important as these are. We as Christians must fundamentally understand that there must be an inner disposition that launches everything we do. We must, through faith, first grasp with all our heart, all our strength, all our being, the assurance that Jesus is God, and let that truth permeate every facet of our lives. This reality goes beyond what we tend to define as a religion. In a sense, we are not a part of a religion per se. Yes, we use the term as a qualification, and note that Christianity has characteristics of religion; however, the reality of Jesus the Christ goes far beyond these characteristics and qualification. Again, He is God! Period! This is *the* starting point from which we launch. Everything is about Him. He is why we believe what we believe, not the other way around. Our lives must be centred in Him.

In closing this chapter, despite what some scholars try to promote, Scripture clearly states that Jesus, the Messiah, is God: "In the beginning was the Word, and the Word was with God, and the Word was God," as Saint John plainly writes (Jn 1:1). This Word was eternal with God; and "was in the form of God"; or to be precise, the Word had the same *nature* as God.

However, here is the astonishing thing, the Word "did not regard equality with God as something to be grasped"; rather this Word condescends to come to earth in human form; Saint Paul tells us that God the Word "emptied Himself, taking the form of a slave" (Phil 2:6-7).

In human form the Person of Jesus "is [at the same time] the image of the invisible God, the firstborn of all creation" (Col 1:15).

Yahshua (יֵשׁוּעַ) is the One who spoke, and everything leapt into being. "For in Him were created all things in Heaven and on earth, the visible and the invisible, whether thrones or dominions or principalities or powers; all things were created through Him and for Him" (Col 1:16). God the Father "in these last days" decides to speak to us "through a Son, whom He made heir of all things and through whom He created the universe" (Heb 1:2). God the Son, "is the refulgence of [God the Father's] glory, the very imprint of His Being, and who sustains all things by His mighty word" (Heb 1:3).

All this Scripture is exactly what the Apostles taught and handed down to us. It is what they had heard, what they had seen with their own eyes, what they looked upon and touched with their own hands, it was what was from the beginning—the Word of life (1 Jn 1:1). This Word of life was made visible, they had seen it and testified to it, and they proclaim it to us (1 Jn 1:2-3). In light of this revelation, their worldview had to be re-thought, in the light of Jesus the Christ. As Christians, two thousand years later, we must do likewise, going back to the basics.

This back to the basics approach may even help us in our evangelization and re-evangelization. We sometimes tend to present to others Christianity as a religion, or a Church, or even Jesus Himself as a *religion* per se, instead of teaching and presenting Jesus as *the* Messiah, and as *God Himself*—exactly the way the Apostles did.

Yahshua (יֵשׁוּעַ) is the Lord of lords (Rev 19:16). He is the King of kings (Rev 19:16). "I AM [*Ego Eimi* (ἐγώ εἰμί)] the *Alpha* and the *Omega*, the first and the last, the beginning and the end" He Himself proclaims (Rev 22:13). Nevertheless, with all that power and dominion, our Creator became a human person such as we are!

If we truly believe this, we should tremble; we should be shaken and rattled to our core. If this is true, everything changes; we must live differently. If this is true, we must give Him our everything; our very life. If this is true, rejecting syncretism or relativism we must boldly take a stand; issue a call to action; and evangelize this truth (*Note*[67]). Like Saint Thomas, confronted with this revelation by the resurrected *Mâshîyach* (מָשִׁיחַ), we must courageously declare "My Lord and my God" (Jn 20:28) and immediately bow down and worship the Christ.

Remember, when we read the words of Jesus the Christ within Sacred Scripture, we are not reading the words of a mere man; we are reading the words of God Himself. It is God Himself speaking to us. Jesus the Christ is Lord and God. Deal with it. Internalize it. React to it. Live it. For like it or not, everyone will eventually come to the conclusion that He is Lord and God:

At Jesus' Name
every knee must bend
in the Heavens, on the earth,
and under the earth,
and every tongue proclaim
to the glory of God the Father:
JESUS [THE] CHRIST IS LORD!
| Canticle – Philippians 2:10-11[68] |

Jesus *is* Supreme.
Therefore, our lives must demonstrate the *supremacy* of Him.

Chapter 3 | The Absolute Primacy of Jesus

Yes, JESUS THE CHRIST IS LORD! As Scripture declares, "For that reason, to the glory of God the Father, at the Name of [*Yahshua* (יְשׁוּעַ)], His Son, every knee will bend, those in Heaven, those on earth, and even those in hell" (Phil 2:10). Why is this so? As other Scripture declares:

[*Yahshua* (יְשׁוּעַ)] is the image of the invisible God,
the first-born of all creatures.
In Him everything in Heaven and on earth
was created,
things visible and invisible.

All were created through Him;
all were created for Him.
He is before all else that is.
In Him everything continues in being.
| Canticle – Colossians 1:15-17[69] |

Everything! From the nucleus of an atom to every other part of the cosmos, everything exists and continues to exist in Jesus the Christ (see Wisdom 11:25 and 12:1). Nothing is excluded! It is the will of God the Father, to make *absolute* fullness reside in His Son (*Note*[70]). Therefore, the primacy *of* Jesus is fundamental. Note:

It is [Jesus] who is head of the body, the Church;
He who is the beginning, the first-born of the dead,
so that primacy may be His in everything.
| Canticle – Colossians 1:18[71] |

Again, everything! This includes God the Father's will to place His Son, *Yahshua* (יְשׁוּעַ), as the head of His Church. Why? Scripture answers:

It pleased God
to make absolute fullness reside in [His Son]
and, by means of Him,
to reconcile everything in [the Person of Jesus],
both on earth and in the Heavens,
making peace through the blood of His Cross.
| Canticle – Colossians 1:19-20[72] |

In His Son,
[God the Father] rescued us
from the power of darkness
and brought us
into the kingdom of His beloved Son.
Through Him we have redemption,
the forgiveness of our sins.
| Canticle – Colossians 1:13-14[73] |

Therefore,

Let us give thanks to the Father
for having made [us] worthy
to share the lot of the saints
in light.
| Canticle – Colossians 1:12[74] |

In Chapter 2, we explored the Philippians canticle; here we consider the Colossians canticle; it is a succinct summary of God the Father's will as professed by the early Church.

In this we see that God the Father declared His pleasure and will that Jesus the *Mâshîyach* (מָשִׁיחַ)—His Son—is supreme.

Therefore, Christianity is not a religion merely showing another way to God—it is not *a* way, or even just *a better* way. It is not simply one religion among others. Why? Christianity is rooted in God the Son, Whom God the Father (the God of the universe) decides to be the *only* way to Him. As a result, all fullness of truth resides *only* in His Son, not in any other religion (*Note*[75]).

This can only be because Jesus the Christ is *the* Way to God, *the* Truth, and *the* Life, as per His self-declaration (Jn 14:6). In our relationship to Jesus, He becomes our very life.

Let me explain. In the above Colossians canticle, the early Church proclaimed that the relation of the Christ to the universe was that "primacy may be His in everything" (Col 1:18). The Greek word translated here into the English word *primacy* is πρωτεύω (prōteuō/*prote-yoo'-o*). This Greek word is used only once in the New Testament.

It means: preeminence, preeminent, supreme, supremacy, supreme in everything, first, to be first, to hold the first place, to have the first place, to rank first, to have the highest dignity, to have the highest place, most excellent, and unsurpassed.[76]

It was God the Father's will and pleasure to have "all the divine fullness (the sum total of divine perfection, powers, and attributes)" dwell in Jesus the Messiah, His Son, permanently, "so that He alone is everything and in every respect might occupy the chief place [stand first and be preeminent]" (Col 1:18-19[77]). This is what is meant by the absolute primacy of Jesus. He is supreme in all things. The crux of this chapter is that *Yahshua* (יֵשׁוּעַ) the Messiah is *first* in everything.

Saint Louis de Montfort offers another summary. He reminds us that Jesus the Christ is the First and the Last, the *Alpha* and the *Omega* of all things (see Rev 1:8, 21:6, and 22:13), and concludes that He is *our* everything:

> Jesus, our Saviour, true God and true Man, must be the ultimate end of all our devotions. Otherwise, they would be false and misleading. He is the *Alpha* and *Omega*, the Beginning and the End of everything. In Him alone dwell the entire fullness of Divinity and the complete fullness of grace, virtue, and perfection. In Him alone we have been blessed with every spiritual blessing. He is the *only* teacher from whom we must learn, the *only* Lord on whom we should depend, the *only* Head to whom we should be united, and the *only* Model we should imitate. He is the *only* Physician who can heal us; the *only* Shepherd who can feed us; the *only* Way that can lead us; the *only*

Truth that we can believe; the *only* Life that can animate us. He alone is everything to us, and He alone can satisfy all our desires. We are given no other Name under Heaven by which we can be saved. God has laid no other foundation than Jesus for our Salvation, perfection, and glory. Every edifice that is not built on a firm rock is founded upon shifting sands and will certainly fall sooner or later. Every one of the faithful who is not united to Him is like a branch broken from the stem of the vine. It falls and withers and is fit only to be burned. If we live in Jesus and Jesus lives in us, we need not fear damnation. Neither angels in Heaven, nor men on earth, nor demons in hell, no creature whatsoever can harm us, for no creature can separate us from the love of God in [Jesus the *Mâshîyach* (מָשִׁיחַ)]. Through Him, with Him and in Him, we can do all things.[78] (*emphasis* added)

| Saint Louis de Montfort |

With these two summations, we have much to unpack. Let us begin by understanding the centrality we place upon Jesus when He declares that He is *the* Way, *the* Truth, and *the* Life (Jn 14:6).

With this initial understanding, I will demonstrate the absolute primacy of Jesus as verified in three key areas: (1) His Holy Name; (2) the Law, including the Sabbath; and (3) the Eucharist (*Note*[79]). As you read this next part, keep in mind that I am speaking as a Christian to those with a Christian understanding.

He is *the* Way, *the* Truth, and *the* Life: In the Gospel of Saint John, *Yahshua* (יֵשׁוּעַ) the *Mâshîyach* (מָשִׁיחַ) clearly states that He is *the Way* and *the Truth* and *the Life* (Jn 14:6). Absolutely *no one* can come to God the Father except through Jesus, His Son (Jn 14:6). Therefore, contrary to some scholars' pronouncements, Jesus is not *a* way, or *one* of the ways to God; He is *the only* way (*Note*[80]). "There is no Salvation through anyone else, nor is there any other name under

Heaven given to the human race by which we are to be saved" (Acts 4:12).

Some Christians have shied away from this truth; on the contrary, we should be bold in declaring it (*Note*[81]). As we have studied, Salvation and Saviour are inseparably connected. *Yahshua* (יֵשׁוּעַ) is God the Father's *instrument of salvation*.

We need to understand clearly that the God of Israel is the God of all nations (e.g., Isa 52:7-10, Ps 22:7, Tobit 13:11, 14:6). The God of the Bible *is* God of the entire universe. He is the God of *all*! Read Genesis! He created everything, thus all creation is His. God's covenant with Noah clearly demonstrates this fact. For not only was God's covenant with all of Noah's descendants (Gen 9:9), but it was with all living creatures (Gen 9:10). Eventually Israel is chosen from all of humanity as God's particular people, as His guiding light to the rest of the world. God pre-selects Israel as a beacon to the other nations: "theirs is the adoption, the glory, the covenants, the giving of the Law, the worship, and the promises; theirs the patriarchs, and from them, according to the flesh, is the Messiah" (Rom 9:4-5).

Therefore, salvation is through Israel, for "Salvation [the One Who is the instrument, the means, the Saviour, the Messiah Himself] is from the Jews" (Jn 4:22). Yes, in the fullness of time, He sent His Son (Gal 4:4), the Messiah. What is more, He establishes all primacy in Him (Rev 15:3-4). As a result, now, in the final days, His Church is that guiding light to the world (Acts 10:9-33).

Therefore, we must conclude that Jesus is also the Lord of all nations, or He is not the lord of any nation (*Note*[82]). In other words, He *has to be* the Lord of every human being or the lord of absolutely none—there is no middle ground. We are, once again, faced with the dichotomy of all-or-nothing. He is the God of the universe or god of nothing. This is non-negotiable. As Christians, we need to make up our minds. We cannot say that He is the Lord of only a particular group. We cannot say He is the Lord of only Christians. That would be illogical and utter nonsense. Christianity is not regional or tribal.

Jesus is either the Lord God of every atom of the entire universe, the entire cosmos, or He is the lord god of absolutely nothing. This is pure logic. He is the Lord God of all Christians, Jews, Hindus, Sikhs, Buddhists, Muslims, agnostic and atheist alike. He must be and has to be, if not He is not even the Lord God of *you*. Without this assertion of primacy over everything, do not call Him your Lord and your God!

This is a fundamental basis of the assertion that He is the *only* Way. It is just simple logic. The word only means exactly that . . . *only*! Therefore, we Christians need to stop the nonsense and stop watering it down, stop apologizing, and simply in His *love* proclaim *this* Truth.

There is another aspect worth exploring. This comes from the uninformed, politically correct backlash that Christians face (*Note*[83]). In our highly secularized, politically correct society, we Christians have become afraid to make an assertion of the Christ's primacy, for fear of repercussions. Within aggressive secularization is a focused anti-Christian sentiment. In this anti-Christian milieu attack, they state: How dare Christians say that Jesus is the *only* way—that is intolerance and exclusion. Others exclaim that Jesus is just one of many ways to God, that Christians' view is narrow-minded bigotry. Therefore, we Christians quickly back away from making this assertion in fear of social-excommunication. Sound familiar?

We might rationalize this backing away from truth by saying to ourselves that we are keeping silent because we do not want to offend anyone. I think the more important question we need to ask is: should we not be more afraid of offending God? Keep in mind that if we deny Him, He will deny us (Mt 10:33); so, empathizing with, or backing away from, or keeping silent about secular statements that threaten social excommunication, is not an option.

"Do not be ashamed of your testimony to our Lord" (1 Tm 1:8), Saint Paul tells Timothy—and, in effect, tells us. "For God did not give us a spirit of cowardice [i.e., fear] but rather of power and love" (1 Tm 1:9). Here, for the word *power*, Saint Paul uses the Greek word δύναμις (dunamis/*doo'-nam-is*), which means miraculous power, ability, strength, and mighty wonderful works.[84] Evoking the directive to us from Saint Peter (see Preface; and 1 Pt 3:15), and Saint Paul's admonitions, we must therefore be prepared with boldness, certitude, and *miraculous power* to explain this truth with gentleness (*calm, well-balanced mind*) and love.

Accordingly, let us address this, Christian to Christian. We begin with articulating the underlying premise, the critic's objection to exclusivity. It begins with a variety of secular humanistic ideas (so-called inclusive thought): there could not possibly be only one way to Heaven; or, there cannot be only one way to live, or only one worldview; or, there must be many ways to God, or equally valid diverse thinking on this subject; or, life is not about a particular faith or religion, it is about an overall abstract spirituality; or, life is about living with an open heart through love. These ideas are pseudo-religious gospels of: acceptance, tolerance, expression, cultural identity, cooperation, harmony, diversity, equity, or inclusiveness (*Note*[85]).

Of the above ideas, living life with a loving heart is what many believe is of utmost importance. Thus, loving kindness and generosity (although again, these terms are all subjective in themselves) supposedly can bring people from diverse perspectives, from the atheist to the spiritually enlightened, to the same point which some might call *Heaven* or some sort of undefined positive final end.

At face value, this might sound amazing. Sad to say, some Christians have bought into this purported inclusive thought argument. It can generate a feel-good *kumbaya* moment. It also reminds us of John Lennon's hit song *Imagine*, which, despite its spurious lyrics, has become a Christian anthem for some.

It is time that we Christians *wake up* and realize that the price we must pay to buy into these purported *gospels* is apostasy. Not only are these thought patterns rooted in ancient heresies such as Pelagianism[86] and Gnosticism,[87] the contemporary versions are just as heretical, to say nothing of being logically contradictory (*Note*[88]).

Again, Christian to Christian, let us stop and ponder this for a moment. The conclusion that *all* we need to do is live a life with an open heart through love, inevitably promotes a subjective faith (hence my calling it a pseudo-religion) which implicitly demands our *right* to Heaven due to our living a so-called love-filled-life.

It also presupposes that we have the ability, the know-how, the talent, the personal will, and the skills to *work* our way to Heaven. This *conclusion* is faulty and reeks of arrogance. As fallen human beings, we *do not* have the self-reliance, the personal entitlement or autonomy, the human will, or the "personal power"—as some self-help gurus' state—to achieve anything and everything we want, including salvation. None of these false gospels can save us!

In humility, we Christians must realize that any good we do is only through the grace of God. Christians need to *wake up* and assert that there is absolutely *nothing* that we can personally or collectively do to get into Heaven—*absolutely nothing*!

Here is a point to ponder: if the good works we perform through our own ability and will (whatever they may be) have the ability to save us (get us into Heaven), did the Christ die for nothing? Besides, the logic of Jesus' having to be *the* Lord of the entire cosmos (as we stated above), is the logic that the entire cosmos is reconciled through Him (Col 1:19-20). Why would God the Father be pleased to reconcile everything in His Son, if there was nothing to be reconciled? In other words, why have a Saviour if we did not need to be saved? Why would God the Son have to go through the ordeal of making peace through the blood of His Cross, if we were able somehow to do this on our own, by our own merit, by our own goodness, by living life with an open-heart through love, or the gospel of inclusiveness?

Although I write this in very strong language, I realize that some Christians reading this—who have bought into this so-called inclusive thought—still might not like this answer; for this thought is highly prevalent in our society. However, as it is written:

> There is no one just, not one, there is no one who understands, there is no one who seeks God, all have gone astray; alike are worthless; there is not one who does good, there is not even one. (Rom 3:11–12; also cf. Ti 3:4–7)

We are *all* tainted. All means *all*, the Christian and non-Christian alike. In humility we must recognize this reality. How can we help a non-Christian when we ourselves have not accepted and eternalized this sound doctrine? We will discuss this further (in Chapter 7, Why the Death and Resurrection?), but for the moment, my point here is this: all of us have sinned and come short of the glory of God (Rom 3:23). All means *all*—we are all sinners (*Note*[89]). It is therefore only through humility, acknowledging the redemptive work of Jesus the Christ and His grace, that we are justified (see Eph 2:1-10). "The righteousness of God has been manifested . . . through faith in Jesus

[the] Christ" (Rom 3:21–22); for, it is *Yahshua* (יֵשׁוּעַ) who reconciles humanity to God (Eph 2:16). It is not our doing; it is His doing. It is He who destroys the "dividing wall of enmity" (which by the way, we created) between us and God the Father (Eph 2:14).

Using the example of gravity, if your daughter decides to put on a super-cape and jump from her third-storey bedroom window, is it intolerance to teach her about gravity? Your daughter might not agree with you, she might not understand gravity, but does that really matter? Gravity is gravity—whether if she believes in it or not, it can kill her. You and your daughter must deal with it.

In a similar manner, teaching others that there is nothing they can do to get into Heaven, is *not* intolerance. It is fact. Teaching others that it is *only* through *Yahshua* (יֵשׁוּעַ), that it is *He* who reconciles humanity to God (Eph 2:16), is not intolerance, nor exclusion (as society currently defines these words). It is just reality.

Pope Benedict XVI put it well when he says, "the Kingdom of God is a gift. And we cannot—to use a classical expression—'merit' Heaven through our works. Heaven is always more than we could merit."[90] In view of that, it does not matter how *good* our works are or how *good* a person we are—for "all our good deeds are like polluted rags" (Isa 64:6). We cannot save ourselves by our own moral efforts or personal merit, collectively or individually. If this was possible, again, we would not need a Saviour, would we? As Christians, we must clearly understand this, internalize this, and clearly state that we do not have the so-called personal power to save ourselves.

Now in stating this, in no way are Pope Benedict XVI or I stating that our behaviour does not matter. For this is not the case, as he goes on to say:

> Heaven is always more that we could merit, just as being loved is never something "merited", but always a gift. However, even when we are fully aware that Heaven far exceeds what we can merit, it will always be true that our behaviour is not indifferent before God. [91]
>
> | Pope Benedict XVI |

On the one hand, we assert that there is nothing we can do to get into Heaven. While simultaneously holding the fullness of this truth, on the other hand—as we will further study in Chapter 7, Why the Death and Resurrection?—we must became a *witness of charity*, and answer our personal *call to holiness*. However, we do this all the while acknowledging that this is only a reciprocation of the unmerited love that we have received from Him—not some means of gaining favour or to work our way into Heaven.

Another problem with the word *inclusive*, is that society *subjectively* defines the word; its meaning keeps changing and becomes *infinitely fluid*.

In comparison, to paraphrase G. K. Chesterton, *it doesn't matter how often we fail to achieve the ideals that we've put before us, but it matters terribly if we keep changing our ideals* (*Note*[92]).

Accordingly, subjective definition means that any words or phrases may differ from one person to the other and may differ over time. Ultimately, these words do not mean anything objectively, they becomes a *word-salad*.

For example, if you claim to have your own informational truth and I have my own truth, could we not also conclude that you have a form of exclusive truth and so do I. See the problem? If each are different, each is subjective. Neither has objective meaning and *float* to whomever accepts it. Moreover, if they contradict each other, they are not objective truth. Our society needs an objective foundation; if not, as we are seeing, things will result in chaos.

This also applies to Church teachings. Some Christians (within all Christian churches) are caught up in this so-called inclusive mentality; they think that truth is up for grabs. Those who align themselves with our confused culture and advocate revisions to Church teaching—which is objectively rooted in Holy Scripture—might not realize the gravity of such an alignment. It is not only heretical, it is confusing. As many academic theologians have pointed out: if the teachings of the previous two thousand years are discarded for a new and improved teaching, it inevitably raises doubts and questions about the legitimacy and veracity of any teaching. How are we to say that the new teaching is correct? If we have been wrong all along for the past two thousand years, who's to say that what is being proposed is now right? Would we not be casting doubt upon the new teaching as well? Moreover, this new teaching could also change at any time in the future, so why abide by it? There is no point.

In alignment with continuous change, Christianity itself will become meaningless and likewise irrelevant. The gravity of this alignment with new teaching is that not only does it undermine credibility, it also treats all doctrine as suspect—it will open a Pandora's Box.

I therefore pray, and we must all pray, that those in leadership roles within the Church do not capitulate to the outside forces who advocate such heretical change; that they hold strong and do not compromise by absorbing secular thought.

To those within the Church, leadership or otherwise, who desire the reimaging of Church teachings (or a reinvented Catholicism) I pray that they take a moment and prayerfully think this through. Jesus our Messiah is *the* Way, *the* Truth, and *the* Life (Jn 14:6). If we persist in this continuous remaking of Christianity it will not only lead to heresy, it will inevitably lead to apostasy.

In addition, it will, without doubt, hinder evangelizing—if it has not already done so (*Note*[93]). In an ever-changing society—filled with cultural fallacies—people inside and outside the Church intrinsically seek clarity and stability in teaching. Jesus the Christ is that stability knowingly or unknowingly craved by humanity—for He is "the same yesterday, today, and forever" (Heb 13:8; also cf. Jms 1:17). In Him the sacred Deposit of Faith (*Depositum Fidei*)—Christian doctrine which is rooted in love—constantly proclaims His unchanging truths with love. Thus, "do not be led away by diverse and strange teachings" (Heb 13:9); do not proclaim another gospel (cf. 2 Cor 11:4 and Gal 1:7); do not be credulous or spread heresy (*CCC* #2089); for He is the stability humanity needs.

If we adamantly go down the path of doctrinal revision, it will undermine credibility—there will be absolutely no reason for anyone to trust the Scriptures, or listen to the teachings, or the hierarchy—of the Church. We will have never ending change, for nothing will be objective, and in its fluid subjectivity, we will end up living in pointless disarray.

Therefore, we should be crystal clear in articulating that, the word *inclusive*, in all its ideological forms, is defined from a subjective perspective; and, in that subjectivity, results in teachings that contradict each other; consequently cannot be objectively true; and thus, the claim to inclusivity is a form of exclusivity and therefore meaningless.

Consider that, and compared to inclusive ideology (and its subjective, floating definitions), Christian theology gives us the true meaning and understanding of *inclusivity* and is very liberating, for the Christian and non-Christian alike. Christian inclusivity welcomes all to an objective understanding of truth. This welcoming is depicted by the structure of the Vatican Basilica—the outstretched arms (the pillars surrounding Saint Peter's Square) invites in all the nations. In fact, the word catholic literally means *universal*.

Christian inclusivity is grounded in objectivity (not subjectivity). It starts by placing all of humanity on the same footing—no matter who we are—without partiality. Then it continues by welcoming all to embrace objective Christian doctrine (rooted in love). We may legitimately argue that Christian inclusivity is *the* true liberating and inclusive message, namely, that we, all of humanity, are in the same boat, and all of us have been liberated in and through the Person of Jesus the Messiah. This is true objective reality, not subjective.

Moving along, Jesus the Christ is the focal point of objective reality. He is *the* Way, *the* Truth, and *the* Life (Jn 14:6), precisely because everything converges in Him. This statement by our Messiah is real objective inclusiveness and a *true inclusive* proposition (*Note*[94]).

It is not about you, it is not about me, as exclusive individuals. It is not about what we can achieve or do, nor is it about how good a person we are, how kind we are to one another, or about the love we show to one another (*Note*[95]). As we will study in Chapter 7, we are all still incapable of doing what the Christ did.

In other words, Jesus the Christ did what we *all* could not do (Phil 2:6-11). That is why it is not about us as exclusive individuals—it is rather about Him, true inclusivity. As we will read in Chapter 8, "Rejoice . . . Always!" we must look away from ourselves and look to Him who unites us. He is preeminent, not us. He brings all of us—all of humanity—together. Unified humanity only happens in Him. God the Father rescues us *in* Him, not based on anything we did or who we are (it is a free gift); therefore, it is *only* through Him that "we have redemption, and forgiveness of our sins" (Col 1:13-14). Again, the enmity that we created was reconciled *only* through Him (Eph 2:16). With this understanding, on Palm Sunday, we pray:

Almighty Father of our Lord Jesus [the] Christ,
You sent your Son
to be born of woman and to die on a Cross,
so that through the obedience of one Man,
estrangement might be dissolved for all men.
Guide our minds by His truth
and strengthen our lives by the example of His death,
that we may live in union with You
in the Kingdom of your promise.[96]

As we pray this, we recognize the sense of humility in this prayer. We recognize that *Yahshua* (יֵשׁוּעַ) the *Mâshîyach* (מָשִׁיחַ) is the *only* Intercessor between us and God the Father (*Note*[97]). He is the Saviour and Redeemer for all of us. How much more inclusive can this get?

Here is the proper stance the Christian and the non-Christian should take. The Christian should—in humility—unequivocally assert that Jesus the Christ is the *only* Way. As we can see, anything else is illogical.

As for the non-Christian, they are free to state that there are multiple ways to God (or Heaven); however, they should not state that Jesus the Christ is included in any one of those multiple ways. He must be excluded from the list. Jesus is the only way or He is absolutely not any one of the ways. There is no negotiating here—it is all or nothing. Those who persist in saying that Jesus can be one of the ways does not understand the claim the Christ is making (wait for Chapter 7, Why the Death and Resurrection? where we will more deeply reflect on this).

All this said, some of you might have already determined the ultimate meaning of this Scripture passage. The reason I deliberately wrote, *Yahshua* (יֵשׁוּעַ) the *Mâshîyach* (מָשִׁיחַ) is *the* Way, *the* Truth, and *the* Life (Jn 14:6) in capital letters, is because these words ultimately refer to a Person. The *Way* is the avenue of access in the form of a Person, the Christ. The *Way* does not reference a course of action, a way of life, a path that we take, or a way of living in this world (e.g., being a good, kind, and loving person), in and of itself. No! The *Way* is the Person of Jesus the Messiah. The Way *is* He. With this understanding, the claim of multiple ways really does not make any sense, does it?

In view of that, we Christians who are getting this wrong need to fix our thinking. Next time someone (biblically based or not) tells us that there are multiple ways, we need courageously to declare that *the Way* referred in Scripture is actually a Person—and that Person is Jesus the Christ.

In fact, *Yahshua* (יֵשׁוּעַ) the *Mâshîyach* (מָשִׁיחַ) is also *the Life*. The Greek word used here is not βίος (bios/*bee'-os)*, expressing the following meanings: the course of life, livelihood, or the present state of existence.[98] No, it is ζωή (zōē/*dzo-ay')*, which means the following: the absolute fullness of life, real and genuine life, or even life eternal.[99] *Zōē* (ζωή) indicates a deeper state of reality or life than *bios* (βίος). In this context, it is true *Life*, Jesus Himself. True *Life* is He; it is Jesus the Messiah.

Finally, *the Truth* is also a Person. The objective *Truth* is manifested in the Person of Jesus the Christ—the Son of God, who is both divine and human. The *Truth* is not an idea, thought, moral concept, or a state of mind. An idea cannot set you free, but the *Truth*—the Son of God—can (Jn 8:32). He is Truth incarnate. Consider the conversation between Jesus and Pontius Pilate (Jn 18:37-38). Pilate vehemently exclaims, "What is *Veritas*?" That is, what is *Truth*? Jesus is that *Veritas*, He is *the Truth* standing in front of Pontius Pilate.

In this we have a paradox: on the one hand, we humans do not find the Truth, the Truth finds us; on the other hand, we must go in search of the Truth ourselves, as demonstrated by the Magi, we must put aside worldly comforts and burdens, look up, take a risk, get up, set out, and be open to discovering the Truth. Question: if we think about our own busyness—does our busyness take us closer to the Messiah? Are we spending most of our lives with diversions and distractions? Are we deliberately avoiding getting closer to our Messiah?

In addition to this paradox, we have an inner contradiction. We are inherently designed with a *restless heart* to search for truth. Unfortunately, however, most of us do not like the Truth (see Jn

8:45). We prefer darkness as opposed to Light (Jn 3:19). Therefore, we do not allow Truth to find us, nor do we search for Truth.

Like it or not, Jesus is the Truth. He is *the* Way and *the* Truth and *the* Life. Those of us who place the Sign of the Cross upon ourselves are announcing to the world that we belong to the triune God. This is an imitation of the Magi: the longing, the searching, the eventual finding, the giving of gifts, and the final culmination of worshiping. Saint Augustine spoke about this when he eloquently states: "Thou hast formed us for Thyself, and our hearts are restless till they find rest in Thee."[100]

With this, we understand that life is not about us, it is about Him. This is the opposite of modern secular thought that promotes self-determination and self-sufficiency. Money, fame, achievements, worldly pleasures, honours, and success become the guiding stars. This attitude, found even in Christians, is a form of relativism. Relativism is the notion that there is no universal, absolute truth. All criteria or judgments are relative to the individual (*Note*[101]). As we stated earlier, the popular mantra is: I have my truth; you have your truth (*Note*[102]). In this, Jesus (the Truth) is now an inconvenience.

A close relative of relativism is syncretism, defined as: "the attempted reconciliation or union of different or opposing principles, practices, or parties, as in philosophy or religion."[103] I think the key word in this definition is *attempted*. Syncretism is an exercise in futility since principles that are the opposite of each other are logically irreconcilable.

We live in a world that is becoming increasingly relativistic and syncretistic (*Note*[104]). Although denounced by popes, bishops, and multitude of other Christian leaders, its influences have worked their way into Christian thinking, for their warnings have not been heeded. I believe that the main reason we are influenced by these nonsensical thought patterns is lack of Christian theology. Saint Paul explains,

> if only you would put up with a little foolishness from me! Please put up with me . . . I am afraid that, as the serpent deceived Eve by his cunning, your thoughts may be corrupted from a sincere (and pure) commitment to [the] Christ. For if someone comes and preaches another Jesus than the one we preached,

> or if you receive a different spirit from the one you received or a different gospel from the one you accepted, you put up with it well enough. (2 Cor 11:1; and 11:3-4)

It is now time we stop putting up with these nonsensical worldviews. We need to stop preaching *another Jesus* or a *different gospel*. We need to stop the corruption of our thoughts.

As previously mentioned, although for the sake of classification we call Christianity a religion—in the sense of the following definition: "a specific fundamental set of beliefs and practices; a set of beliefs concerning the cause, nature, and purpose of the universe; devotional and ritual observances, and often containing a moral code governing the conduct of human affairs"[105]—in its strictest sense, Christianity is *not merely* a religion. It is definitely *not* a religion among a supermarket of religions. Consider Islam and Buddhism. Although Christianity presents a body of doctrine, and a belief structure that guides individual living, as does Islam, unlike Islam, Christianity is *not* solely a conveyance of revelation, a body of doctrine. Although Christianity uses philosophical terms, methodology, and terminology to convey theological truths, unlike Buddhism, Christianity is *not* just a philosophy or a path to follow. Christianity goes beyond simple classifications of religion or philosophy.

> We must remember the way in which Jesus is Saviour. He did not limit Himself to showing us the way to encounter God, a path we can walk on our own by being obedient to His words and by imitating His example. Rather, [the] Christ opens for us the door of freedom, and becomes, Himself, the way: "I am the Way" (Jn 14:6). Furthermore, this path is not merely an interior journey at the margins of our relationships with others and with the created world. Rather, Jesus gave us a "new and living way that He inaugurated for us through His flesh" (Heb 10:20).[106]
>
> | Congregation for the Doctrine of the Faith |

Christianity is fundamentally a covenant-relationship with a Person, God Himself, who has created everything that exists. He is *the Way*. We can't classify that! Although we *may* use these terms (such as religion) for the sake of classification, we must recognize that this goes beyond all classifications (*Note*[107]).

Relativism and syncretism must not be entertained by any genuine Christian (*Note*[108]). We must keep our eyes fixed on Jesus. He is our inspiration and the perfecter of our faith (Heb 12:2). The priority for *every* human being is to know God, in the *Mâshîyach* (מָשִׁיחַ) He sent, and grow in that faith.

Regrettably, many have moved from the centrality of Jesus the Christ. We speak of being open-minded to other religions (*Note*[109]), which is necessary from a free will point of view, but not as if somehow these other religions are a part of God's final plan. Simply put, they are not! Jesus the Messiah is God's final plan. God *does not* promulgate multiple truths (as in multiple religions), for that will only bring about confusion. Although God allows humanity to choose any other religion, this is not His plan—His *plan* is His Son. Confusion is the sign and work of the devil, "because he is a liar and the father of lies" (Jn 8:44), the enemy of God. Other religions are created by humans. However, God, in His sovereignty has carried out His own plan of salvation in the fullness of time, in and through His Son (Gal 4:4). He wants *all* to come to His Son and not to any other substitute. True love is calling others to accept God's ultimate plan (Acts 17:22-30). Therefore, the fundamental act of true Christian love is to share Jesus the Christ with others. To bring *all* to Him, for this *is* His ultimate plan.

Apprehension of the Truth in any aspect does not make us inherently superior to others. This is the mistake Christians have made over the centuries. If you are inclined this way, remember:

> You were dead in your transgressions and sins in which you once lived following the age of this world, following the ruler of the power of the air, the spirit that is now at work in the disobedient. All of us once lived among them in the desires of our flesh, following the wishes of the flesh and the impulses, and we were by nature children of wrath, like the

> rest. But God, who is rich in mercy, because of the great love He had for us, even when we were dead in our transgressions, brought us to life with Christ (by grace you have been saved), raised us up with Him, and seated us with Him in the Heavens in Jesus, that in the ages to come He might show the immeasurable riches of His grace in His kindness to us in Jesus. For by grace you have been saved through faith, and this is not from you; it is the gift of God; it is not from works, so no one may boast. (Eph 2:1-9)

Therefore, accept God's gift of salvation and do not boast. The harsh tone of these last few pages should *never* be used with non-Christians. Avoid triumphalism. It is *only* through His grace and mercy that we are grafted into God's family, and in a like manner we can be pruned out (Rom 11:11-24). We cannot sit on our high-horse. There is no place for superiority within a Christian. Our *modus vivendi*—that is, our manner of living—is Christian love (*Note*[110]).

Recognizing that God calls every human being in and through His Son, we therefore, do not disqualify others, nor do we put them into a separate box—i.e., as in *we* versus *they* mentality. Even in the Old Testament, we see that Salvation is for all. The culmination of God the Father's plan for humanity's salvation; Jesus His Son is for all. In the Book of Jonah (3:1ff), God tells Jonah to go and preach repentance to Nineveh, a pagan city. The sinful Ninevites heeded Jonah's preaching, believed in the God of Israel, and repented. As a result, God spares them. That said, we must also acknowledge that some people do not like the Truth, that some "people prefer darkness to Light" (Jn 3:19). God gives each one of us free will.

Saint Peter came to understand that "God shows no partiality" (Acts 10:34). In every nation whoever fears Him (not anyone or anything else, but only Him), and then acts uprightly *in* Him, is acceptable *to* Him (Acts 10:35; also cf. Jonah 3:1ff).

Let us repeat the words of Saint Peter, as he—filled with the Holy Spirit—boldly proclaimed in front of the Sanhedrin: "Leaders of the people and elders . . . There is no Salvation through anyone else, nor is there any other Name under Heaven given to the human race by which we are to be saved" (Acts 4:8, 12). Again, Salvation and

Saviour are connected. He is Salvation—His Name, *Yahshua* (יֵשׁוּעַ), literally means *YHWH* is Salvation!—salvation is not as much something we acquire, but it is *Someone*.

As Christians, we should not only internalize that there is no other name and there is no other person from whom that salvation comes, we should also, like Saint Peter, filled with the Holy Spirit, boldly declare this truth from the rooftops.

Some of us, to somehow rationalize our un-Christian thinking, use a popular quote attributed to Saint Francis, which goes something like this: "Preach the Gospel always, and only when necessary use words." I know I have personally used this line. However, looking back, I also know that at some level I used this as a copout. Moreover, more and more Franciscan theologians are concluding that Saint Francis never said those words. We could even conclude that the quotation is unbiblical—following the footsteps of *Yahshua* (יֵשׁוּעַ), we need to preach the Gospel in *both* word and deed.

In addition, we Christians may build a straw-man by saying something like: What about people on a remote island or some undiscovered jungle or some hidden corner of the earth, who have never heard of Jesus . . . would God smite them and send them to hell? Now, if we were to think about this for a moment . . . doesn't this straw-man objection take us away from the real issue? For, I personally do not know *any* adult who has *not* heard of Jesus. Do you? Just try and name one adult person you personally know who has not heard of Jesus? Even if you have traveled the world, have you ever met anyone who has *not* heard or at least know of Christianity or Jesus? By saying this, I am not suggesting that every single human being on the earth has heard of Jesus; the point I am trying to make is that to this day I have not met even one.

What I do have are friends and family who are not Christian, but they *all* have *heard* of Jesus (obviously so, for they know I am a Christian). Accordingly, is this not the root of the better question we should be asking? That is to say, the real issue or question is: What about our friends and family, who have heard of Jesus, but do not believe that He is the Messiah, that He is Salvation, that He is Lord and God? That's the root of the matter, isn't it? That is the real issue most of us face, not the ridiculous straw-man argument and its fabricated objection.

The straw-man argument is mostly made to take the onus off of us. Maybe that is why we erect it. All that said, keep in mind that: "Ever since the creation of the world" God has made it possible to know Him, as the Creator God; for "His invisible attributes of eternal power and divinity have been able to be understood and perceived in what He has made" (Rom 1:20; also cf. Ps 19:1-2). He has also written His *law* (e.g., natural law, morals, ethics) within our hearts (Rom 2:14-15). Therefore, there is "no excuse" (but only our own doing) in not knowing a Creator God (Rom 1:18-24). However, although this has been evident to all humanity for all of history, and moreover, the possibility of knowing a Creator God can also be established using scientific logic (see Appendix B), as we are now in the second part of history, knowing Jesus the Christ takes faith and proclamation. The "times of ignorance" is no more (Acts 17:30). The *onus* is on us to make this proclamation. For, God the Father "wills *everyone* to be saved and to come to knowledge of the *Truth*" (1 Tm 2:4; *emphasis* added).

Intriguingly, we are worried about people that we have not seen or might not even exist, but we are not worried about the family member, the friend, or our neighbour standing right next to us. Now, there are many other insights that may be given on this issue, but my focus here is on our responsibility as Christians.

Let us therefore not flutter with the winds of society. Let us state publicly *the* Truth in and out of season and "be persistent whether it is convenient or inconvenient" (2 Tm 4:2). Recall, we are given a spirit of courage and *miraculous power*, not a spirit of cowardice and fear (2 Tm 1:7; also cf. Rom 8:15), and always bearing in mind, "if we deny Him He will deny us" (2 Tm 2:12). However, if we acknowledge Him before others, He "will acknowledge [us] before the angels of God" (Lk 12:8). "So do not be ashamed of your testimony to our Lord" (Tm 1:8).

God proclaims only one Truth, His Son Jesus our Lord. In no other way is there any salvation. This is the true understanding of Christianity (*Note*[111]). What is more, He destines us to be adopted sons and daughters in and through His Son, Jesus the Christ (Eph 5:1; also cf. Gal 4:4-5 and Rom 8:14-17). In Him we become a *child of God*. This is *who we are*. This is the great exchange, He became human and we become the children of the Most High. Yes, we become children of God, but only by His grace, through His Son—for *Yahshua* (יֵשׁוּעַ) the *Mâshîyach* (מָשִׁיחַ) is unequivocally the *only* Way and the *ultimate objective* Truth and the *absolute fullness* of Life!

Having now studied the centrality of Jesus the Christ as *the* Way, *the* Truth, and *the* Life (Jn 14:6), we will continue this study by demonstrating the absolute primacy of Jesus in the first of three key areas; namely, the primacy of Jesus verified in His Holy Name.

The Absolute Primacy of Jesus as Verified in Three Key Areas

Key Area Number 1, His Holy Name: Inspired by Saint Paul, the fourteenth century Franciscan friar, Saint Bernadine of Siena, spent his life fervently preaching on the primacy and power of the Holy Name of Jesus. "The Name of Jesus that makes us children of God is a firm foundation of faith" he professed; and he continues:

> Nothing can stop you from being carried away in anger, nothing can keep you from puffing up with pride, nothing can heal the wound of envy, resist the surge of sensuality, extinguish the flame of passion, temper the thirst of greed, consume the rust of every dishonour, like the Name of Jesus! . . . The Name of Jesus is the glory of those who believe . . . The Name of Jesus is the remedy for all our infirmities.[112]
>
> | Saint Bernadine of Siena |

Our faith,

> is based upon the knowledge and recognition of Jesus, who is the light of the soul, the gateway to life, the foundation of eternal Salvation. Whoever lacks this knowledge and recognition, or has abandoned it, is like a man who walks through the darkness of night without a light and like a person who rushes headlong through dangers with his eyes shut.[113]
>
> | Saint Bernadine of Siena |

Saint Bernadine's assessment is as follows:

> [it does not matter how] brilliant such a person's mind may be, [for] he follows a blind leader when he follows his own understanding to grasp the secrets of Heaven. He attempts to build a house without laying a foundation, he wants to enter through the roof because he left out a door. Jesus, then, is the foundation, light and door . . . This foundation supports the Church built on the Name of Jesus.[114]
>
> | Saint Bernadine of Siena |

Saint Bernadine of Siena recognizes that true wisdom knows who God *Is*, and the revelation of His Truth. Scripture makes a distinction between worldly wisdom and godly wisdom (see Appendix A, 8). Wisdom that is from God "is the refulgence of eternal light, the spotless mirror of the power of God, the image of His goodness" (Wisdom 7:26). The Greek word for refulgence is ἀπαύγασμα (apaugasma/*ap-ow'-gas-mah*), which means reflected brightness, or perfectly reflect; thus we may conclude that true wisdom perfectly reflects the brightness of God. Saint Augustine, about a millennia earlier, teaches us that true wisdom knows objective Truth, as follows:

> For whereas the wise man is so joined to God in mind, as that there is nothing set between to separate; for God is Truth; and no one is by any means wise, unless his mind come into contact with the Truth.[115]
>
> | Saint Augustine |

As mentioned, this understanding is all built upon Jesus the Messiah—*the* objective Truth (see 1 Cor 2:6-7). Understanding all of this is *true* wisdom. In this, we must take a vital step of recognizing primacy of the Name of Jesus. Within Scripture, there is a transfer of emphasis from the Name of God to the Name of Jesus (from God the Father to God the Son). Let me explain.

Old Testament Scripture clearly states that at the Name of *YHWH* (יהוה), every knee will bend, and every tongue will confess that He is LORD and God (Isa 45:23). Remember, when the word LORD is translated or written in all capitals, it is the actual Name of God, *YHWH* (יהוה). With that, we will describe the movement from the Name of *YHWH* (יהוה) to the Name of *Yahshua* (יֵשׁוּעַ).

First, at this point in history the pronunciation of the Name *YHWH* (יהוה) is unknown—all that we definitively know are the four consonants. The Holy Name of God in Hebrew (יהוה) was written only with the Hebrew consonants *yud-hey-vav-hey*. In English it would look something like this: G-D or to be exact GD. We do not know the vowels; therefore, we do not know how to pronounce the Name (*Note*[116]). Many books have discussed this point.

Additionally, *YHWH* (יהוה), God the Father's Name as proclaimed to Moses on Mount Sinai, was not even translated or transliterated into any other language. Even the rabbis while translating the Scriptures into Greek Septuagint did not translate His Name; they used the Greek word *Kurios* (Κύριος) instead, which in this case, means Lord. Saint Jerome, while translating the Holy Scriptures into Latin used the word *Domins*, which again simply mean Lord; and as mentioned, the Name of the God of Israel is translated into English as LORD, but in all capital letters.

The effect is that, with our ignorance of the pronunciation of God the Father's Name, the primacy of the Name of God the Son, Who is Lord and God become emphasized (and by the way, the Son's Name has been translated into many languages). Primacy is *now* in the Son, the Name of Jesus not in God the Father's Name. Scripture states that this is the *intentional* will of God the Father.

Therefore, we now proclaim it is no longer at the Name of *YHWH* (יהוה), but it is *now* at the Name of *Yahshua* (יֵשׁוּעַ), that

every knee must bend
in the Heavens, on the earth,
and under the earth,
and every tongue proclaim
to the glory of God the Father:
JESUS [THE] CHRIST IS LORD!
| Canticle – Philippians 2:6-11[117] |

For,

It pleased God [the Father]
to make absolute fullness reside in [His Son]
and, by means of [His Son],
to reconcile everything in [His Person],
both on earth and in the Heavens,
making peace through the blood of His Cross.
| Canticle – Colossians 1:19-20[118] |

God the Son will and must reign—this is a continuous action in the time period in-between (to speak in temporal terms)—until in the end, when God the Father has put all His Son's enemies under His feet (1 Cor 15:25).

The Reign of God the Son has already begun. God the Father's "commandment is this: we should believe in the Name of His Son" (1 Jn 3:23), and we must *listen* to His Son; for Jesus is God the Father's *beloved* and *chosen* (Mt 17:5, Mk 9:7, and Lk 9:35)—the *full* fulfillment of God's plan for humanity's salvation.

All of salvific history is rooted in His Son (as mentioned throughout this book); however, temporally speaking, there are two periods in history—we can call them B.C. and A.D.[119] Although forgiveness of sins was physically accomplished in the second period through the death of the Christ, it was effective throughout both periods. The first period was the *type* which pointed forward to Jesus the Messiah. He is the fulfillment of the first period. Therefore, forgiveness of sin really did not come from rams, bullocks, goats, or lambs, these were merely the types fulfilled in Him. Only from Him is true forgiveness of sin. It is only through His Name (Acts 10:43) and by calling on His Name (Acts 2:21) that anyone is saved: There is "no salvation through anyone else, nor is there any other Name under Heaven given to the human race by which we are to be saved" (Acts 4:12). A universal Lordship is in effect until the last enemy, death itself (1 Cor 15:26), is placed by God the Father under His Son's feet—which will be at the climax of history as we know it (*Note*[120]). It is only through the Son that we have access to the Father (Jn 14:9-10), or for that matter to know Him clearly (Eph 1:17).

In the first letter to the Corinthians, Saint Paul further develops this emphasis from God the Father to God the Son, by stating that although God the Father was subjecting *everything* under the feet of His Son, it does not include Him, for Saint Paul writes:

> when it says that everything has been subjected, it is clear that it excludes the One who subjected everything to Him. (1 Cor 15:27)

Moreover (*Note*[121]),

> when everything is subjected to Him, then the Son Himself will (also) be subjected to the One who subjected everything to Him, so that God may be all in all. (1 Cor 15:28)

Therefore, at this point in history, the emphasis on the primacy of God the Son and His Name (cf. 1 Jn 5:12, Heb 7:25, and Eph 1:15-23) is important.

This is illustrated in the eye-opening moment when Saint Paul encountered the Messiah on his way to Damascus. Saint Paul realized the primacy of Jesus as Lord and in that he develops a Christ-centred worldview (Acts 9:1-18).

We fully know God the Father through His Son. This applies to all nations. All nations will now come to know (and obey) God the Father—Who up to this point intentionally remained the God of Israel—now through His Son. Israel, His chosen beacon, has now become the opening in His movement in His Son (now for all nations). The Name of Jesus is for all nations. The Name of *Yahshua* (יֵשׁוּעַ) is universal.

In Jesus' Name, times have changed. The time we Gentiles went our own way is now over (Acts 14:16). The time of ignorance for us Gentiles is no longer (Acts 17:30). This is a decisive movement on the part of God the Father. His Son is now the centre of worship. Everything converges on His Son, Who now is revealed to all of humanity as the centre of His saving work.

In this, Saint Paul understood the "mystery of the Christ" (Eph 3:4). With this understanding, Saint Paul wants to be a slave of

Yahshua (יֵשׁוּעַ) the Anointed One (Rom 1:1). Thus, he counts absolutely everything as loss, as rubbish, literally as *dung,* for the surpassing worth and gain of knowing Jesus the *Mâshîyach* (מָשִׁיחַ) his Lord (Phil 3:8; also cf. Eccl 12:13). This is the realization and disposition every Christian (Jew and Gentile) should have. Thus, this is now our worldview and our lived reality.

It is strange that Christians (and sometimes non-Christians) say that they want to be immortal; they say that they want to go to Heaven and spend eternity there, yet they refuse to give their life completely to the *only* One who makes that possible. Jesus the Christ has triumphed over death. He has destroyed the power of death so that, in Him, we may be victorious in this life and with Him in eternity. That is only possible if we live in Him and *only* for Him, for this is the will of God the Father.

His Name—*Yahshua* (יֵשׁוּעַ)—should always be on our lips. We must seek Him with an undivided heart. We must ask ourselves: Do we love Jesus for His sake, or for what we can get from Him? Do we love Jesus, just so we can avoid hell, or, do we love Jesus simply for His sake, no strings attached?

Some preachers and teachers (even popular songs) tell us that all we need is love. Sorry to The Beatles, but love is not all we need when defined in a worldly sense; all we need is *Yahshua* (יֵשׁוּעַ) the *Mâshîyach* (מָשִׁיחַ), for He is God the Father's love for us, and He is *Love*! Only in Him do we find true love, and the truth of love. In other words, it is only in Him that we love, and moreover, find the true meaning of Christian love. So yes, all we need is *Love*—but with a capital "L"—which means all we need is *Jesus*!

For that reason, in His love, "whatever you do, do from the heart, as for the Lord and not for others, knowing that you will receive from the Lord the due payment of the inheritance; be slaves of the Lord" (Col 3:23-24)—Jesus the Messiah—Whose Holy Name surpasses every other name!

Key Area Number 2, The Law, including the Sabbath: Understanding the power and primacy of the His Holy Name, we now move to the second key area, the primacy of Jesus verified in the Law, including the Sabbath.

To do this, first it would be helpful to understand the way the word *law* is used in the New Testament:

> There are four important references intended by the word "*law*" when used in the New Testament: (i) all commandments and stipulations which God gave to Moses (also known as the Mosaic law); (ii) the historical as well as juridical material in the Pentateuch [the first five books of the Bible]; (iii) all of the Old Testament, which can collectively be regarded as "law" [which also includes moral and liturgical law]; and, (iv) the oral traditions embodying the teachings of great rabbinical figures.
>
> Jesus fulfills these definitions of *law*, and thus surpasses it (Mt 5:17–20), because Jesus is the way to God. The "*law*"—as a reference to Old Testament as a whole—is comprehensive, revelatory, permanently valuable and consists of an intrinsic and indissoluble amalgam of moral, liturgical and juridical guidelines . . . [However] the Gospel announces the Christ-centred fulfillment of law, pointing out that contact with God is not by means of physical circumcision (Rom 2:28, 3:1, Gal 2:3, 7, and 5:6) or observance of traditional applications of the Mosaic law (Gal 2:16, 3:2, 5:10, Rom 2:15, 3:20 and 28). So, while the law is holy and good (Rom 7:12 and 16), an expression of God's will (Rom 2:27), and it does teach, it does not have the power to make holy, to transform, to renew.[122]
>
> | *Catholic Encyclopedia* |

That power to transform us and make us anew is found *only* in Jesus (*Note*[123]). This renewal also includes the Sabbath (which is part of the Law, in the sense of being part of the Old Testament).

The New Testament clearly establishes that *Yahshua* (יֵשׁוּעַ) the *Mâshîyach* (מָשִׁיחַ) is Lord of the Sabbath (Mt 12:8, Mk 2:28, and Lk 6:5).

Unfortunately, some confusion concerning the Sabbath exists among Christians. Some Christian groups claim that the Catholic Church forcefully changed the Sabbath from Saturday to Sunday. Some Catholics claim that Sunday is the Sabbath or the new Sabbath. Technically speaking, they are both wrong.

Using the *Catechism of the Catholic Church* let me explain. The Sabbath, now and always refers to the last day of the week:

> The third commandment of the Decalogue recalls the holiness of the Sabbath: "The seventh day is a Sabbath of solemn rest, holy to the LORD." (*CCC* #2168)

To be precise, for Israel, the Sabbath was from Friday sunset to Saturday sunset. The meaning of the Sabbath, however, is declared from the beginning of revelation:

> in speaking of the Sabbath Scripture recalls creation: "For in six days the LORD made Heaven and earth, the sea, and all that is in them, and rested the seventh day; therefore the LORD blessed the Sabbath day and hallowed it." (*CCC* #2169)

Scripture provides other aspects of the Sabbath:

> Scripture also reveals in the Sabbath day a memorial of Israel's liberation from bondage in Egypt: "You shall remember that you were a servant in the land of Egypt, and the LORD your God brought you out thence with mighty hand and outstretched arm; therefore the LORD your God commanded you to keep the Sabbath day." (*CCC* #2170)

With that,

> God entrusted the Sabbath to Israel to keep as a sign of the irrevocable covenant. The Sabbath is for the Lord, holy and set apart for the praise of God, His work of creation, and His saving actions on behalf of Israel. (*CCC* #2171)

As you have just read, right from the *Catechism*, the Catholic Church has not changed the Scriptural meaning of the Sabbath.

Sunday, the first day of the week, is not the Sabbath, it is the day of the Lord, or the Lord's Day. However, it is the fulfillment of the Sabbath. For the Lord's Day, is the day of Resurrection, it is the day of the New Creation:

> Jesus rose from the dead "on the first day of the week." Because it is the "first day," the day of [the] Christ's resurrection recalls the first creation. Because it is the "eighth day" following the Sabbath, it symbolizes the new creation ushered in by [the Messiah's] resurrection. For Christians it has become the first of all days, the first of all feasts, the Lord's Day (*he kuriake hemera, dies dominica*). (*CCC* #2174)

This first day, recalling the first creation, harkens back to Genesis. Early Church Father, Saint Justin Martyr, spoke about this:

> We all gather on the day of the sun, for it is the first day (after the Jewish Sabbath), but also the first day when God, separating matter from darkness, made the world; and on this same day Jesus Christ our Saviour rose from the dead.[124]
>
> | Saint Justin Martyr |

This connection, the separation of light from darkness, is intriguing, requiring further exploration.

Most of us are familiar with the creation story found in Genesis Chapter 1: "In the beginning, when God created the Heavens and the earth, the earth was a formless wasteland, and darkness covered the abyss, while a mighty wind swept over the waters. Then God said, 'Let there be light,' and there was light" (Gen 1:1-3).

When we hear the words *let there be light* we might instinctively think of the creation of the sun and moon. We confuse the *light* created on the first day with those lights. However, the sun was created on the fourth day: "Then God said, 'Let there be lights in the dome of the sky, to separate day from night. Let them mark the fixed times, the days and the years, and serve as luminaries in the dome of the sky, to shed light upon the earth.' And so it happened . . ." (Gen 1:14-15).

The Hebrew word in Genesis 1:3 אוֹר ('ôr/*ore*), for light, and 1:14 מְאֹרֹת ($m^{e'}$ôrâh/*meh-o-raw'*) are actually different words. Most English translations miss that. Thus, they also miss the nuance between Genesis 1:3 and 1:14.

Genesis 1:3 (Hebrew is read right to left):

אוֹר	וַיְהִי־	אוֹר	יְהִי	אֱלֹהִים	וַיֹּאמֶר 1:3
light	and-there-was	light	let-there-be	God	and-He-said

Compared with Genesis 1:14 (read right to left):

מְאֹרֹת	יְהִי	אֱלֹהִים	וַיֹּאמֶר 1:14
light	let-there-be	God	and-He-said

We do not need to know Hebrew to see that the underlying words for *light* in Genesis 1:3 and 1:14 are two different words; and thus these two words have two different meanings. The primary definition of $m^{e'}$ôrâh (מְאֹרֹת) in Genesis 1:14, is as a luminous body or luminary, i.e., the sun and the moon reflecting its light; on the other hand, the primary definition for 'ôr (אוֹר) in Genesis 1:3 is an illumination.[125] So then, what is this *illumination* which laminated the earth in the beginning?

Before we answer this question, note that Sacred Scripture ends as it begins. At the end of the last book of Scripture—The Book of Revelation—it states: "Night will be no more, nor will they need light from lamp or sun, for the Lord God shall give them light" (Rev 22:5). Although the original language used here is Greek, Greek also distinguishes different words translated into the one English word *light*: "Night will be no more, nor will they need [φῶς (phōs/*foce*)] from lamp or sun, for the Lord God shall give them [φωτίζω (phōtizō/*fo-tid'-zo*)]" (Rev 22:5). With a similar definition as the Hebrew word m^e'ôrâh (מְאֹרת), the Greek word phōs (φῶς) describes the light from lamps or the sun; and correspondingly the Hebrew word 'ôr (אוֹר) and the Greek word phōtizō (φωτίζω) share that illumination aspect.[126]

Therefore again, what is this *illumination*? Speaking of Genesis in particular, in his 2012 Easter Vigil homily, Pope Benedict XVI touched on the two different lights found in the creation account. Referring to Genesis 1:14, he states that "the creation account calls them lights, set by God in the firmament of Heaven," which is a deliberate act that "takes away the divine character that the great religions had assigned to them."[127] For the sun and the moon "are not gods"—"they are shining bodies created by the one God."[128] Pope Benedict XVI goes on to say that the sun and the moon are nevertheless "preceded by the light through which God's glory is reflected in the essence of the created being"—referring to the "light" that was created in Genesis 1:3.[129] This light was created to make the world "a space for knowledge and truth"—the *knowledge and truth* of the true Eternal Light of Jesus Christ:

> At Easter, on the morning of the first day of the week, God said once again: "Let there be *Light*". The night on the Mount of Olives, the solar eclipse of Jesus' passion and death, the night of the grave had all passed. Now it is the first day once again—creation is beginning anew. "Let there be *Light*", says God, "and there was *Light*": Jesus rises from the grave. Life is stronger than death. Good is stronger than evil. Love is stronger than hate. Truth is stronger than lies. The darkness of the previous days is driven away the moment Jesus rises from the grave and Himself becomes God's pure *Light*. But this applies not only to Him, not only to the darkness of those days. With the resurrection of Jesus, light itself is created anew. He draws all of us after Him into the new *Light* of the resurrection and He conquers all

> darkness. He is God's new day, new for all of us.[130] (*emphasis* added)
>
> | Pope Benedict XVI |

Yahshua (יֵשׁוּעַ) the *Mâshîyach* (מָשִׁיחַ) *is God's new day*. He is God's new Light. We may easily connect what Pope Benedict XVI teaches us to the text we looked at from the Book of Revelation: Night or darkness will be no more, nor will we need phōs (φῶς) from lamps or the sun, for the Lord God shall give us *pure* phōtizō (φωτίζω) (Rev 22:5)—Jesus *is pure Light*, pure illumination, He is God's new first day. This is clearly stated: "The city had no need of sun or moon to shine on it, for the glory of God gave it Light, and its lamp was the Lamb" (Rev 21:23).

This new day shows the primacy of Jesus. It is fitting, therefore, that this new day, the first day, the Lord's Day, fulfills the Sabbath in all aspects. As the Early Church Father Saint Ignatius of Antioch states:

> Those who lived according to the old order of things have come to a new hope, no longer keeping the Sabbath, but the Lord's Day, in which our life is blessed by Him and by His death.[131]
>
> | Saint Ignatius of Antioch |

So, what of Sunday?

> Sunday is expressly distinguished from the Sabbath which it follows chronologically every week; for Christians its ceremonial observance replaces that of the Sabbath. In Christ's Passover, Sunday fulfills the spiritual truth of the Jewish Sabbath and announces man's eternal rest in God. For worship under the Law prepared for the mystery of [the] Christ. (*CCC* #2175)

Without taking away from the covenantal, ceremonial, and perceptual components in the observance of Sunday, the Lord's Day as a fulfillment of the Sabbath, we as Christians must also emphatically articulate the understanding that it is more than just a day of rest, for it represents an eternal rest in Jesus the Christ: "Come to me, all you who labour and are burdened, and I will give you rest" (Mt 11:28). It is a full and complete *rest* in Him—the pure illumination. Sunday is broader than just one day—it is not merely a one-day rest; some sort of escapism from work, as a day to do what is pleasurable—it is a complete Sabbath rest in *Yahshua* (יֵשׁוּע), every day here and now and for all eternity!

To gain additional insight, consider Ezekiel Chapter 20. It relates a conversation concerning Israel's rebellion and infidelity after they came out of Egypt under Moses. *YHWH* (יהוה) clearly states why He gave Israel His statutes and ordinances (i.e., the Law), and why He gave the Sabbath. *YHWH* (יהוה) states:

> I gave them my statutes and made known to them my ordinances, which everyone must keep, to have life through them. I also gave them my Sabbaths to be a sign between me and them, to show that it was I, the LORD, who made them holy. (Ezek 20:11-12)

Statutes and ordinances are *not* given as a killjoy, to dampen the party, or to make our lives miserable. On the contrary, in His infinite wisdom, God knows precisely what we need to give us true life and fullness of life. In the words of a popular preacher: The Law was given not to kill our joy, but to make our joy complete (*Note*[132]). As we know, however, Israel rebelled. They did not keep God's statutes and ordinances, and they desecrated the Sabbath (Ezek 20:13). Moreover, they did not want *YHWH* (יהוה) to make them holy; which is life itself, the true sign of the Sabbath. Instead, they wanted to be self-determined, self-emancipated, and thus, opting for nonlife. So, they were left to follow their own heart desires, worshipping pagan idols, which did not bring life (see Rom 1:18-32). This theme of rebellion and the Sabbath are picked up in the letter to the Hebrews:

> We have become partners of [the Messiah] if only we hold the beginning of the reality firm until the end, for it is said: Oh, that today you would hear His voice: "Harden not your hearts as at the rebellion."

> Who were those who rebelled when they heard? Was it not all those who came out of Egypt under Moses? With whom was He provoked for forty years? Was it not those who had sinned, whose corpses fell in the desert? And to whom did He swear that they should not enter into His rest, if not to those who were disobedient? And we see that they could not enter for lack of faith (Heb 3:15-19) . . . Therefore, let us be on our guard while the promise of entering into His rest remains, that none of you seem to have failed. For in fact we have received the good news just as they did. But the word that they heard did not profit them, for they were not united in faith with those who listened. For we who believed enter into (that) rest, just as He has said: As I swore in my wrath, "They shall not enter into my rest," and yet His works were accomplished at the foundation of the world. For He has spoken somewhere about the seventh day in this manner, "And God rested on the seventh day from all His works"; and again, in the previously mentioned place, "They shall not enter into my rest." Therefore, since it remains that some will enter into it, and those who formerly received the good news did not enter because of disobedience, He once more set a day, today, when long afterwards He spoke through David, as already quoted: Oh, that today you would hear his voice: "Harden not your hearts." Now if Joshua had given them rest, He would not have spoken afterwards of another day. Therefore, a Sabbath rest still remains for the people of God. And whoever enters into God's rest, rests from his own works as God did from His. Therefore, let us strive to enter into that rest, so that no one may fall after the same example of disobedience. (Heb 4:1-11)

A Sabbath rest still remains for the people of God. The Sabbath is a sign. The promise of rest still remains. This sign is fulfilled and thus now *only* found in *Yahshua* (יֵשׁוּע) the *Mâshîyach* (מָשִׁיחַ). What is more, it is a complete rest. Not so much a rest from external activity, but more an inner disposition. A deeper reality of *rest* than cessation from work is conveyed by the Sabbath. Keep in mind, Jesus cures on the Sabbath (Mt 12:9-14, Mk 3:1-6, and Lk 6:6-11; also cf. Lk 14:1-6), and clearly states that He and the Father are still at work (Jn 5:17).

Rest has another aspect deeper than the physical. "Come to me, all who labour and are heavy laden, and I will give you rest" Jesus tells us (Mt 11:28). Does He mean only one day? If this is so, why would He say: "Do not worry about your life" (Mt 6:25). Do not worry and say, "What are we to eat?" or "What are we to drink?" or "What are we to wear?" (Mt 6:31).

The rest that *Yahshua* (יֵשׁוּעַ) is conveying is a complete release and rest *in* Him. We should not be anxious about earthly things. Let us not be disobedient as the Israelites.

Let us not provoke Jesus our Saviour, but let us try to enter into *His* rest. Let us seek Him with every fibre of our being (Mt 6:33 and Lk 12:31), and trust in His Divine Providence, for He will take care of us (Mt 6:30 and Lk 12:30). Commit to memory this truth: unless Jesus builds our house, in vain do we labour and build (Ps 127:1). Unless Jesus guards over us, in vain do we keep guard (Ps 127:1). In vain is our earlier rising, and going late to bed, working hard for the bread we eat, for Jesus pours His gift on His beloved while they sleep (Ps 127:2).

As He Himself says: "Look at the birds in the sky; they do not sow or reap, they gather nothing into barns, yet your Heavenly Father feeds them. Are not you more important than they?" (Mt 6:26). "Notice how the flowers grow. They do not toil or spin" (Lk 12:27). "If God so clothes the grass in the field that grows today and is thrown into the oven tomorrow, will He not much more provide for you, O you of little faith?" (Lk 12:28).

All the Saints understood the power of Divine Providence. In our own time, Saint Teresa of Calcutta comes to mind. She knew that Jesus the Messiah would provide even if it was at the last minute.

All things has been handed over to *Yahshua* (יֵשׁוּעַ) the *Mâshîyach* (מָשִׁיחַ) by God the Father (Mt 11:27). "No one knows the Son except the Father, and no one knows the Father except the Son" (Mt 11:27). In this, Jesus tells us to come to Him for rest (Mt 11:28). He calls us to come to Him with all our anxieties, our labours, and our burdens (Mt 11:28). He tells us to take up His yoke, for His yoke is easy and His burden is light (Mt 11:30). He has revealed Himself to us (Mt 11:27), and in this revelation He asks us to learn from Him, to be meek and humble and we will find true rest (Mt 11:29).

It takes humility and meekness to rest in *Yahshua* (יֵשׁוּעַ). We live in a world of doing, striving, accomplishing, and being our own masters with self-determination and self-sufficiency. Our mantra is that life is about *me* and my accomplishments, isn't it? This in some ways is juxtaposed to what Jesus is calling us to do. More will be said on this in Chapter 8, "Rejoice . . . Always!". For the moment, however, we will leave the admonition to strive for humility and focus on resting in Jesus the Anointed One, right here, right now, in this life, and then for all eternity. This is the true Sabbath rest.

Key Area Number 3, The Eucharist: Now that we understand that primacy of Jesus related to the Law and the Sabbath, and that the Sabbath is more than just one day of rest, we should also look at the covenantal, ceremonial, and prescriptive aspects of Christian living fulfilled in the observance of taking Sunday rest as the Lord's Day. In this, we now move to the third key area, the Eucharist. It is difficult to speak of the primacy of Jesus without speaking of the Eucharist.

First we must acknowledge that the Eucharist is "the source and summit of the Christian life" as Vatican Council II emphatically asserted.[133] The Church is a church with a *Eucharistic faith*. Second, we also acknowledge that we cannot speak of the Eucharist without speaking of the Church that God established (i.e., the Mystical Body of the Christ or the Bride of the Christ).

Beginning with the latter and then moving to the former, I think it is crucial that in today's climate—where virtual reality in some ways have become reality or proclaimed as such—Christians clearly articulate the irrevocable nature of community, the physical gathering as Church (which is absolutely essential). Christianity is not only a personal relationship or merely a spirituality in isolation. All of us, in distinction within our personal relationship and encounter with the Christ, are incorporated into one body—the Body of the Christ—in which He is the Head. If we are in an isolation mentality regarding our faith—e.g., stating that: I believe in Jesus and my relationship is with Him, but I don't believe in the Church—it is as if we are dismembering the Head from the body.

Corporately, we are also *His* bride. We are created by Him, and for Him. This creation comes from and through *Yahshua* (יֵשׁוּעַ) the *Mâshîyach* (מָשִׁיחַ).

Concerning the Body of the Christ, I will now focus on two pertinent points, namely: the underlying word used in Scripture for *church*, and the connection between Adam and his bride, Eve, and Jesus and His bride, the Church.

The Greek word for church is ἐκκλησία (ekklēsia/*ek-klay-see'-ah*). Although, this word is a compound derived from ἐκ (ek), and καλέω (kaleō), which literally means to call out, it is primarily defined as a gathering, meeting, community, or congregation.[134] In its secular Greco-Roman roots, *ekklēsia* (ἐκκλησία) was mainly used as a reference to the gathering of law-makers. In the New Testament, however, *ekklēsia* (ἐκκλησία)—used 114 times, mainly in the First letter to the Corinthians and the Book of Revelation—has a more *particular* meaning.

To understand that meaning, we should note that even though there is a connection, there is really no equivalent word for *ekklēsia* (ἐκκλησία) in Hebrew. Let me explain. There are three main Hebrew words that come close: (1) עֵדָה (ʿêdâh/*ay-daw'*), translated mainly as congregation, community, or assembly; (2) עַם (`am/*am*), translated mainly as people and nation, and even as a proper name; and (3) קָהָל (qâhâl/*kaw-hawl*), translated mainly as assembly, congregation, or community. However, none of these words has been translated from Hebrew into the English word church (or synagogue). That is, we do not see the words church or synagogue appear anywhere in the English translations of the Old Testament (only in the English translations of the New Testament).

That said, the exception is the Septuagint, in which a connection is made, for we find these three words interchangeably translated as *ekklēsia* (ἐκκλησία) or συναγωγή (sunagōgē/*soon-ag-o-gay'*), that is, synagogue. However, we may argue that both *synagogue* (συναγωγή) and *ekklēsia* (ἐκκλησία), particularly *ekklēsia* (ἐκκλησία), do not seem to have the same connotation as it has in New Testament Greek. Conversely, we may argue that *ekklēsia* (ἐκκλησία), as used in the New Testament, finds its roots in *sunagōgē* (συναγωγή), which in turn finds its roots in the three words *'êdâh* (עֵדָה), *`am* (עַם), and *qâhâl* (קָהָל).

In a New Testament text, referring to Moses, Saint Stephen states that Moses "in the assembly [*ekklēsia* (ἐκκλησία)] in the desert, was with the angel who spoke to him on Mount Sinai" (Acts 7:37). This is the connection; *ekklēsia* (ἐκκλησία) is God's people who have been *called out*. In that connection, therefore, *ekklēsia* (ἐκκλησία) becomes an important new term for the New Testament writers.

The early Christian community not only used this word to signify the gathering or *calling out* of God's people right from the time of Moses, but more importantly, they now emphatically rooted *ekklēsia* (ἐκκλησία) *in* Jesus the Christ: "He is the Head of the body, the *Ekklēsia* (ἐκκλησία)" (Col 1:18; also cf. Col 1:24, 1 Cor 12:12-27, and Rom 12:4-5). He is the Head and we are His body. The *Ekklēsia* (ἐκκλησία) is now clearly rooted in Him.

Unfortunately, over the centuries, some Christians have lost this interconnection of the Church (the body) with Jesus (the Head). We usually think of Church as in hierarchy or a building, which it also is, but, more importantly it—*Ekklēsia* (ἐκκλησία)—is profoundly connected to Jesus Himself (*Note*[135]).

Moving on to the image of *Ekklēsia* (ἐκκλησία) as bride, a commonly held view is that the *Ekklēsia* (ἐκκλησία) was officially created on the Cross—to be precise, through the pierced side of the Christ—this image gives us a profound visual insight into this union (*Note*[136]). This view has a graphic connection with that of the creation of Eve from the side of Adam as the typology with that of the creation of the Church—the *Ekklēsia* (ἐκκλησία)—from the side of the Messiah, as the fulfillment of that type.

If we were briefly to explore this, it would go something like this: a deep sleep was cast upon the first Adam (Gen 2:21), and the Christ being the new Adam, or the second Adam (1 Cor 15:22 and 15:45) has an even deeper *sleep* cast upon Him (Jn 19:33); while the first Adam was asleep, his side was opened, a rib was taken from his side, and it was used to create Eve (Gen 2:21-22); as the second Adam slept while being dead upon the Cross, His side was pierced and water and blood poured out (*Note*[137]), this is the creation of the second Eve (Jn 19:34), the *Ekklēsia* (ἐκκλησία), the Church which is

His bride. Just as Eve, created from the side of the first Adam, is closely united to Adam (Gen 2:23), the *Ekklēsia* (ἐκκλησία), is closely united to the second Adam (Acts 9:4). This unity is that of bridegroom and bride. Both creations—Eve and the *Ekklēsia* (ἐκκλησία)—become the bride of the one from whom they were created (see Gen 2:24 and Jn 3:29 respectively).

The Mystical Bride of the Christ is the new Eve, the *Ekklēsia* (ἐκκλησία), the sacramental-church, the New Jerusalem that comes down from Heaven, adorned for Her Bridegroom (Rev 3:12 and 21:2). So, do the words of the first Adam become the words of the second Adam? Does He also look at His bride and say: "This one, at last, is bone of my bones and flesh of my flesh" (Gen 2:23)? Unequivocally, yes! We, the *Ekklēsia* (ἐκκλησία) as His bride, are unquestionably the bone of His bones, and the flesh of His flesh. Now "this is a great mystery" (Eph 5:31-32).

Keeping this image in mind, it will help to understand the Eucharist, which, as mentioned, is the source and summit of the Christian life![138]

Lex Orandi, Lex Credendi, the Early Church Fathers asserted. That is to say, the law of worship (or rule of prayer) reflects, or is, the law of belief (or rule of faith). How we worship and pray fundamentally demonstrates our underlying belief structure—our foundational beliefs.

"The Eucharist is the sum and summary of our faith: 'Our way of thinking is attuned to the Eucharist, and the Eucharist in turn confirms our way of thinking,'" Saint Irenaeus goes on to say (*CCC* #1327).

To understand the implications of the reason for the Eucharist, we should study Salvation History and consider various typologies that eventually come to fulfillment in the Eucharist. Keeping in mind that this topic is far beyond the scope of this book, a brief overview is nevertheless necessary.

Before this overview, I would like to mention three things. First, my focus is mainly on the foundational understanding of the Real Presence of Jesus the Christ in the Eucharist (*CCC* #1373-1377 and 1407-1413) conveying the primacy of the Christ, and the implications of this understanding for Christians to gather as community.

Second, with this focus, we will provide a brief glimpse of Salvation History, particularly its sacrificial aspect.

Third, I am writing this in particular to a growing number of Catholics who are questioning or no longer believing in the Real Presence of the Christ in the Eucharist (*Note*[139]).

Now with these three things, let us begin.

Due to the fall of humanity (resulting in everyone's having a sinful nature), God set up a system of sacrifice, a payment for sin. Although this sacrificial system was formally established with the covenant of Moses, we find a sacrifice in Genesis 3:21 that is a veiled reference to the Christ's sacrifice. Shortly after our first parents sinned, the LORD God replaced the fig leaves, which the two of them sewed to clothe themselves, with "leather garments" (Gen 3:7 and Gen 3:21). An animal was sacrificed to produce the garments.

We see a parallel between this incident and Genesis Chapter 4. Cain brings an offering of fruits to the LORD God, and Abel, for his part, offers the LORD God, one of his sheep (Gen 4:3-4). The latter was acceptable to God and the former was not (Gen 4:5). Unfortunately, when we read this in English it makes God sound capricious. We might ask: Why did God reject Cain's offering (Gen 4:4-5)? Did he not give what he had produced from his agricultural effort? Was that not appropriate or good enough?

However, the Israelites, most likely, would not have asked these questions. In the Hebrew language, the answer is apparent. In Scripture, the sacred writers sometimes used a play on words. This technique, may get lost in English translation. The Hebrew name, Cain קַיִן (qayin/*kah'-yin*) has an affinity with the Hebrew term קָנָה (qânâh/*kaw-naw'*), which literally means *I produce*. This understanding is demonstrated in Cain's offering itself. For example, Cain's offering was the produce that he produced (I guess we can have a play on words also in English). Consequently, the underlying meaning is that he, Cain, brought it forth, it was *his* doing. He produced his offering by his own efforts.

Abel's offering, the sheep he had raised, which was given to God in faith (Heb 11:4), is rooted in the realization that even though he raised the sheep, he did not bring it forth, it was not of his doing. In this, it looked forward to the sacrificial system that God established for Israel that was the type which was fulfilled in the Christ's death on the Cross. Within the sacrificial offering there is a declaration that what happened to this animal should have happened to the one offering it. As we know, eventually, this does happen to Abel at the hands of his brother (Gen 4:8). Thus, Abel is a type or figure of the Christ (see Heb 12:24).

We should note that both Cain and Abel exercised priestly roles, as they both preformed sacrifices. This is also true for Abraham and Isaac. They had an equal priesthood, i.e., the two of them "walked on together" (Gen 22:7). Isaac is also a figure of the Christ, i.e., he carries "the wood for the offering" (Gen 22:6). Just like the Christ, Isaac is both victim and priest, who willingly obeys his father's command (Gen 22:9).

Moriah (Gen 22:2), where Abraham and Isaac go to make the offering is eventually where Jerusalem was built (2 Chron 3:1). Today, archaeologists also state that there is good evidence that Golgotha (Calvary in Latin), where Jesus was crucified, is the exact place where Abraham built the altar to offer his son Isaac. "God Himself will provide the sheep" (*Note*[140]), Abraham answers his son (Gen 22:8). How prophetic! The sheep (or ram) as a substitute for Isaac was at that time, provided by God (Gen 22:13). In like manner, God the Father provides God the Son as the ultimate Sacrifice for sin.

As we move to Exodus, sacrifice is taken a step further in relation to the Passover, and there are a vast amount of typologies within Exodus that eventually come to fulfillment in the Eucharist. Here, I will touch on some of the major ones.

When we speak of the theology (i.e., the understanding of God) of the Passover, in Exodus, we note that there were three stages: first, the procurement and slaughtering of the lamb (Ex 12:3-5); second, the shed blood was to be marked on the door posts (Ex 12:6-7); but, this still was *not* enough, for third, the sacrifice *must* be eaten (Ex 12:8-11). Israelites were told literally to devour אָכַל ('âkal/*aw-kal'*), the flesh בָּשָׂר (bâśâr/*baw-sawr'*) of the lamb (Ex 12:8). This is important as we will shortly see (we will also return to the graphic nature of these two words, *devour* and *flesh*).

Right after the saving effect of the blood of the lamb is pronounced in Verse 13, Israel is told to keep this day as a memorial feast day (Ex 12:13-14). This is highly significant. It is more than just a commemoration; to this day Jews speak of this in the present tense, identifying themselves as if they walked out of Egypt, by the hand of Moses, through the power of Almighty God. This is "what the LORD did for *me* when *I* came out of Egypt" (Ex 13:8; *emphasis* added), is stated even today. Therefore, this memorial is not just something of the past; it is here and now.

In Exodus, the typologies continue. Hearing Israel murmuring concerning the lack of food, the LORD God conveys to the Israelites through Moses: "In the evening twilight you shall eat flesh, and in the morning you shall have your fill of bread" (Ex 16:12). There are two key points that need to be made here.

First, the order starts with the evening, and goes to the morning. This order is not incidental—consider: "At evening you will know that it was the LORD who brought you out of the land of Egypt; and in the morning you will see the glory of the LORD" (Ex 16:6-7)—the order of evening then morning is actually significant. The sacrifice comes first, in the evening (Ex 16:6); i.e., the quail comes first: "In the evening quail came up and covered the camp" (Ex 16:13). Important to note, it is in reference to *quail* that the word *flesh*, *bâśâr* (בָּשָׂר) was used in the previous verse (Ex 16:12; also cf. Ex 12:8). Only then the glory of God comes or is seen in the morning (Ex 16:7); i.e., in the morning when the dew evaporated there were: "fine flakes like hoarfrost on the ground" (Ex 16:14; also cf. Ex 16:31).

Second key point is that the *fine flakes*, the bread, the manna that came down from Heaven, takes preference over the quail, the flesh. For right in Exodus, the emphasis is placed on the manna; i.e., the glory of the LORD. For example, it is the gathering of the manna that is mostly discussed (Ex 16:14-36). It is *only* the manna that was—gathered the day before and—eaten on the Sabbath (Ex 16:22). More significantly, it is the manna that was placed in a jar for safekeeping (Ex 16:33). This vessel was placed in front of the Ten Commandments (Ex 16:34), and eventually was placed inside the Ark of the Covenant (Heb 9:4).

The importance of the manna does not stop there. After the Ark of the Covenant was designed and built (Ex 25:10-22), a special table was made to display the manna (Ex 25:23-30). A new term was given to the manna: "Showbread" (Ex 25:30). As in English this is a compound word in Hebrew. Show, פָּנִים (pânîym/*paw-neem'*), which expresses the meaning *face* or the presence of a person; and bread,

לֶחֶם (lechem/*lekh'-em*), which means food made out of grain—bread.[141] Put together this compound word literally means the "bread of the Presence" (see Mt 12:4). In addition, when the Hebrew Scriptures were translated into Greek (LXX), the seventy rabbis upgraded the Hebrew word צִנְצֶנֶת (tsintseneth/*tsin-tseh'-neth*), found in Exodus 16:33—which simply means, vase, pot, jar, or vessel, most likely made out of clay—into a jar made of gold, χρύσεος (chruseos/*khroo'-seh-os*). It is this LXX term and not the Hebrew word that is used in the letter to the Hebrews: "a gold [chruseos (χρύσεος)] jar containing the manna" (Heb 9:4).

So, why upgrade from a simple pot to a golden vessel? Why the overt emphasis on the manna? May we argue that it is because the manna is a type; it is the prefigurement that finds its ultimate fulfillment in Jesus the Messiah, the true and everlasting bread from Heaven—the true *Bread of the Presence* and the *Face of the Presence* (Jn 6:31 and 6:41).

The LORD declares a *new covenant* to be made with the house of Israel (Jer 31:31). This new covenant is established by *Yahshua* (יֵשׁוּעַ), the Anointed One (Lk 22:20). The old covenant is now transformed in the new covenant, and the centrality of the Exodus Passover is now fulfilled in the new Passover with the centrality on *Yahshua* (יֵשׁוּעַ) the *Mâshîyach* (מָשִׁיחַ).

With this in mind, we discuss the implications of the purpose of the Eucharist.

When we took this quick glimpse into Salvation History we saw various typologies. These types are important and still relevant, because of their fulfillment. Pertaining to the Eucharist, this includes the slaughtering and the eating of the lamb.

For the most part, we tend to understand the *sacrificial aspect* of the slaughtering of the lamb, which is fulfilled by Jesus on the Cross. As Abraham prophetically exclaims, "God will provide the lamb" (Gen 22:8) for the sacrifice, and about twenty-two centuries later He provides the *Ultimate Lamb*. God the Father provides His Son, as depicted in all four Gospels.

To explain the second part, the eating of the lamb as alluded in graphic terms, let us turn to the Bread of Life discourse found in the Gospel of Saint John, which gives us the most articulate explanation and demonstration of the fulfillment of eating.

This teaching happens the day after Jesus feeds the 5,000 (Jn 6:1-15 and 6:22). Not only did the crowds want to make Jesus king after He fed them (Jn 6:15), they came looking for Him the next day (the day in question) wanting more food for their stomachs (Jn 6:26 and 6:34). Jesus, realizing the crowd's motives—wanting free manna from Heaven just like their ancestors; it was all about eating their fill—hence, He tells the crowds that, "it was not Moses who gave the bread from Heaven, my Father gives you the true bread from Heaven" (Jn 6:32). Then He goes on to teach them the fulfillment, namely that He is "the bread of life" (Jn 6:35). To this statement the crowds murmur (Jn 6:41) so, Jesus repeats His statement: "I am the bread of life" (6:48). More emphatically, Jesus asserts, "I am the living bread that came down from Heaven; whoever eats this bread will live forever; and the bread that I will give is my flesh for the life of the world" (Jn 6:51).

The underlying Greek word translated in this verse as eat is φάγω (phagō/*fag'-o*), expressing the meaning: to consume, to take food, to eat a meal in the usual manner, basically to *eat*.[142] The underlying Greek word translated into the English word *flesh* is σάρξ (sarx/*sarx*), which means a strip of skin or meat, again properly translated as *flesh* (*Note*[143]). There is another word *body*, σῶμα (sōma/*so'-mah*) in the Greek language (see 1 Cor 10:16), which could have been used (and is the world Saint Paul uses, which in turn is also the word we use in our Liturgy); but giving heed to Exodus, the word *flesh* is vividly used here (Ex 12:8 and 16:12; also cf. Gen 2:23).

To this the crowd's murmuring now turns into quarreling, "How could this man give us His flesh to eat?" they protest (Jn 6:52). Does Jesus quickly reduce His message to symbolism? No! He restates it and adds a new element: "Amen, amen, I say to you, unless you eat the flesh of the Son of Man and drink His blood, you do not have life within you" (Jn 6:53). Then, He goes on to say that you need to do this to have eternal life (Jn 6:54). When we are questioning *why* the Eucharist, it is important we understand this part, i.e., "For my flesh is true food, and my blood is true drink; whoever eats my flesh and drinks my blood remains in me and I in him" is Jesus' teaching (Jn 6:55-56).

Not only does Jesus tell the crowds that they need to eat His flesh and drink His blood, to have eternal life, He changes the word

He uses (unfortunately, not reflected in the English translation). Remember, the word eat, *phagō* (φάγω)? Well, here Jesus changes the word from *phagō* (φάγω), again basically to eat a meal, to τρώγω (trōgō/*tro'-go*), which expresses the meaning to gnaw, or crunch, or take apart. This is a graphic word which again harkens back to Exodus, remember Israel was asked literally to devour and consume, *'âkal* (אָכַל), the flesh, *bâśâr* (בָּשָׂר), of the lamb (Ex 12:8). This is exactly what He is telling the crowds, they must do—devour and consume.

As the crowds increasingly murmur, grumble, and quarrel, Jesus' words become vivid, graphic, and explicit. He does not water down His message. On the contrary, He gives the crowds absolutely no wiggle room; He continually doubles down on His teaching, for He is *not* conveying some metaphorical message.

Now let us place ourselves in the crowds as a first-century Jew. How would we react? We know that many around us said, "This is a hard saying" and, went on to question "who can accept it?" (Jn 6:60). Would we have said the same? Here is a question: Why would this be the crowds' reaction if it were symbolic, or a metaphor, or merely spiritual?

As mentioned, a growing number of Catholics claim that Jesus' statement is only a metaphor—we cannot take it literally. Jesus is speaking in symbolic language. Really? If so, then why would He ask the crowds, and by extension you and me, "Does this shock you?" (Jn 6:61). Why would it shock us if it was just a metaphor? Likewise, "as a result of this, many of His disciples returned to their former way of life, and no longer accompanied Him" (Jn 6:66). In this crowd were some of His true disciples (Jn 6:60). Why didn't He then call them back? Telling them: Come back—I wasn't speaking literally, for this was just a metaphor! Again, why didn't He call them back to clear up the misunderstanding? There is only one logical answer. It was not symbolic language. It was not a metaphor. It was *not* a misunderstanding. The crowds got it right. Jesus' words were crystal clear. He did not ease up. He continually doubled down, harkening back to Exodus.

We miss this in English translations, but the word change from *phagō* (φάγω) to *trōgō* (τρώγω) is highly significant. This is real. Today Catholics (and we can also say all Christians) just like the first-century Jews need to grapple with this question from Jesus. "Does this shock you?" (Jn 6:61). It should! Placing this discourse in proper context, we need to decide: are we going to be among those who walk away and "no longer accompanied Him" (Jn 6:66).

As we study this analysis, looking at the vocabulary and typologies, I think that most of us realize that there are no two ways about it. Yes, *Yahshua* (יֵשׁוּעַ) the *Mâshîyach* (מָשִׁיחַ) is asking His disciples to eat His flesh and drink His blood, if we want eternal life, and life in Him (Jn 65:3-54).

As an objection to this understanding, some quote the following: "It is the spirit that gives life, while the flesh is of no avail. The words I have spoken to you are spirit and life" (Jn 6:63). However, this text has to do with *cannibalism*, not to justify figurative speech. If it had to do with understanding what He said metaphorically, why did "many of His disciples returned to their former way of life and no longer accompanied Him" (Jn 6:66) even after He said that? So, what is being said here is that His disciple must eat His flesh and drink His blood but this is not cannibalism (*Note*[144]). This is the only clarification Jesus makes concerning what He said (as we will study shortly).

For the moment, cannibalism or not, the more pressing question is that none of this makes any sense if Jesus does not give us a way to do this. Remember the question, "How could this man give us His flesh to eat?" (Jn 6:52). Well, to answer this question we come to the Last Supper.

This event not only takes place on the feast of the Passover, it becomes the new Passover, the true fulfillment of the Exodus Passover. In Exodus, Israel is released from their slavery to Egypt. At the hand of Moses, through the power and might of the LORD, Israel is taken out of bondage and cleansed through the Red Sea. In the fulfillment of this type, the new Exodus, we, humanity are released from bondage, at the hand of the new Moses, *Yahshua* (יֵשׁוּעַ) the *Mâshîyach* (מָשִׁיחַ), through the power and might of God the Father, removes us from the bondage and slavery to sin by cleansing us through the waters of baptism in Him. This is the fulfillment.

Just as Israel was asked to keep the Passover as a memorial (Ex 12:13-14), we are asked to keep the new Passover in memorial of Him (Lk 22:19). Just as keeping the Passover was not a mere commemoration, keeping the new Passover is not a mere recollection or reenactment of past events (*CCC* #1363-1364). I intentionally wrote all this in the present tense, for it is important that we understand that this memorial—mainly the sacrificial aspect—transcends time.

The Eucharist is a sacrifice, because it is the memorial of Jesus the Christ's Passover (*CCC* #1365). We are proclaiming the death of Jesus—Lord and Messiah—our Paschal sacrifice (1 Cor 5:7). However, we are not re-crucifying the Messiah. This is a grave misconception. "The sacrifice [*Yahshua* (יֵשׁוּעַ) the *Mâshîyach* (מָשִׁיחַ)] offered once for all on the Cross remains ever present" (*CCC* # 1364). The Eucharist, therefore, is not a reenactment, "it *re-presents* (makes present) the sacrifice of the Cross" (*CCC* #1366). Just like Israel spoke of the Passover in present terms, so do we.

"The sacrificial character of the Eucharist is manifested in the very words of institution" (*CCC* #1365). In the species of bread and wine, Jesus gives us the means of participating and consuming His flesh and blood: "While they were eating, Jesus took bread, said the blessing, broke it, and giving it to His disciples said, 'Take and eat; this is my body.' Then He took a cup, gave thanks, and gave it to them, saying, 'Drink from it, all of you, for this is my blood of the covenant, which will be shed on behalf of many for the forgiveness of sins'" (Mt 26:26-28; also cf. Mk 14:22-24 and Lk 22:17-20; also cf. Jn 6:27-56 and Gen 14:18). The bread and wine *become* His Body and Blood, His Soul and Divinity (*CCC* #1376 and #1413).

At the Last Supper, He gives us the means to carry out what He asks of us in the Bread of Life discourse. This is the mode of eating His body and drinking His blood. He gives us the answer to the question posed by the crowds (Jn 6:52). This is how we partake in the Lamb. Also keep in mind that if Israel had to eat the lamb, what makes us think we do not have to, for He is the true "Lamb of God, who takes away the sins of the world" (Jn 1:29).

Once more, like Israel, we must also eat the lamb; it is therefore not metaphorical. If it were, we must also acknowledge that there was *no lamb* to be found at this Passover meal (*Note*[115]). Exactly, where was the lamb at the Last Supper, which was a Passover meal? Well He, the Paschal Lamb—*Our Paschal Lamb*, Jesus the Christ, Who "has been sacrificed" (1 Cor 5:7)—*the* sacrificial Lamb, the fulfillment of Exodus was right there at the table. In the species of bread and wine, those at the table—the Passover meal—ate the Lamb. Although Jesus was there, present in the body, at the Last Supper, the efficacious action of the Cross transcends time; therefore, the sacrifice offered on the Cross was present at the Last Supper. When Jesus says—"This *is* my body" . . . "This *is* my blood" (Mt 26:26-28, Mk 14:22-24, and Lk 22:17-20)—the word *is*, means *is*, not *isn't*; even in Greek *is* means *is*. Therefore, in and through the words He spoke, the Paschal Lamb was consumed by the Apostle.

The Real Presence of the Christ *is* found in the Eucharist (*Note*[146]). This understanding of the Eucharist did not change; it was there right from the beginning, articulated in the early Church.

Saint Paul tells us, "Whoever, therefore, eats the bread or drinks the cup of the Lord in an unworthy manner will be guilty of profaning the Body and Blood of the Lord" (1 Cor 11:27). Why would Saint Paul tell us to watch out when we eat the bread or drink the cup of the Lord? Why would this be an issue if it was a mere metaphor? Why do we need to examine ourselves: "Let a man examine himself, and so eat of the bread and drink of the cup. For anyone who eats and drinks without discerning the body eats and drinks judgment upon himself" (1 Cor 11:28-29).

Again, if this is just symbolic language, and it is only bread and wine, not the Real Presence of the Christ, why would eating and drinking this cause judgment upon us? This is clearly not something merely figurative. We definitely know Saint Paul is being literal as he refers to this judgment, because he clearly states the actual consequences: "many of you are weak and ill, and some of you have died" as a result of this judgment (1 Cor 11:30). Getting ill and dying from eating symbolic bread and drinking symbolic wine (*Note*[147])—really? How is this even possible if it is not the Real Presence?

Even historians of the early Church, including historians of first and second century secular Rome (in an odd way) attest to the understanding of the Real Presence. They state that charges of cannibalism were brought against the early Church (*Note*[148]), and that this charge of having cannibalistic feasts was a misunderstanding of the Eucharist. This is highly significant, for if the early Church did not believe in the Real Presence, where and how would Roman authorities get this misunderstanding? Why would they conclude and accuse Christians of cannibalism? The only logical explanation, as stated, is that they misunderstood the Real Presence aspect of the Eucharist.

Returning to the concern of cannibalism, the Early Church Fathers, as mentioned, used Jesus' words found in the Gospel of Saint John—"It is the spirit that gives life, while the flesh is of no avail. The words I have spoken to you are spirit and life" (Jn 6:63)—to reject any notion of cannibalism and thus removing any form of difficulties arising from the Bread of Life discourse. However, at the same time they asserted that the Real Presence of the Christ is found in the Eucharist (*Note*[149]). On the one hand He—Body and Blood, soul and divinity— is really and truly found in the Eucharist (*Note*[150]); on the other hand consuming the Eucharist is not cannibalism; and if we had a third hand, we humbly capitulate that all of this is a mystery.

Yes, similar to the Trinity, the Eucharist is also an ineffable mystery. These mysteries go beyond human capacity. We use terms and human concepts in order to apprehend this mystery; however, we will never be able to comprehend this mystery totally.

> I speak as to sensible men; judge for yourselves what I say. The cup of blessing which we bless, is it not a participation in the blood of [the Messiah]? The bread which we break, is it not a participation in the body of [the] Christ? Because there is one bread, we who are many are one body, for we all partake of the one bread. (1 Cor 10-15-17)

There is something happening here that is beyond us. The mystery continues. We also become His body (*Note*[151]). We become the flesh of His flesh, the bone of His bones (cf. Gen 2:23). We go through a transformation; the people of God collectively becomes the temple of God, God's very own dwelling place (see 1 Cor 3:16). We go through a transfiguration; we become God's tabernacle, now reflecting God's glory. All of this is a mystery. Again, we may apprehend it, but we will not be able to comprehend it.

In summary, the new covenant is established (Lk 22:20). Jesus the Messiah is the mediator of that covenant (Heb 8:6-13). When Jesus "speaks of a new covenant, He declares the first one obsolete.

And what has become obsolete and has grown old is close to disappearing" (Heb 8:13). Sacrificial offerings at the Temple are no longer required. In fact, they have not taken place since the destruction of the Temple. Once the fulfillment has arrived, we do not go back to the type (as we will see in the next chapter). The type has now become obsolete. These types are important; nevertheless we do not go back to carrying them out, or participating in them. They are still relevant in the sense of understanding, and their need to be fulfilled.

Therefore, as Israel had to eat the lamb (*Note*[152]), we must also eat the lamb. Israel was asked literally to devour and consume, *'âkal* (אָכַל), the flesh, *bâśâr* (בָּשָׂר), of the lamb (Ex 12:8); we are also asked to gnaw or crunch, *trōgō* (τρώγω), the flesh, *sarx* (σάρξ), of the Lamb of God (Jn 6:54-55).

Just like Israel was told to keep the Passover as a memorial feast day (Ex 12:13-14); we are told to keep the new Passover as a memorial of Him (Lk 22:19; also cf. 1 Cor 11:24-25). This was more than a commemoration on the part of Israel, and thus it is more than a commemoration on our part. They spoke of it in the present tense, as if they, themselves, walked out of Egypt, at the hand of Moses, through the power of Almighty God. We also speak of it in the present tense. We are not re-crucifying the Messiah. We are not reenacting the Last Supper. This is not something of the past; it is here and now. This transcends time. It is a mystery.

Just like the *fine flakes*, the bread, the manna that came down from Heaven, takes preference over the quail, the flesh; the flesh of Jesus the Christ, in a manner of speaking, is veiled in the species of the bread. The significance of the manna increases and thus is placed in a gold container, given its own table and placed in the Ark of the Covenant, given a new term, Showbread, which is the bread of the Presence. The Eucharist is also placed in a gold container (ciborium and chalice), given its own altar (e.g., Eucharist Adoration), placed in the tabernacle (the new Ark), and given a new term, the Eucharist—which is the Real Presence of the Christ (*CCC* #1378).

"At evening you will know that it was the LORD who brought you out of the land of Egypt; and in the morning you will see the glory of the LORD" (Ex 16:6-7). Freedom or redemption comes first, in the evening (Ex 16:6). The Last Supper, and the sacrifice on the

Cross comes first, in the evening (Mt 26:20, Mk 14:17; also cf. Mt 27:45, Mk 15:33, and Lk 23:44). Then the glory of God comes second; it is seen in the morning (Ex 16:7); the Resurrection, the glory of God comes in the morning (Mt 28:1, Mk 16:1, Lk 24:1, and Jn 20:1).

The early Church gathered in the morning to break bread on the Lord's Day (Acts 2:42; 2:46, 1 Cor 10:16; 11:17, Heb 10:25). The new day, a new creation (Gen 1:3-5) was the first day of the week (Mt 28:1 and Mk 16:2). This signifies the *new creation*; it is a new beginning (*Note*[153]). It is "man's eternal rest in God" (*CCC* #2175). The old—including the Passover, the Law, and the Sabbath—is now obsolete, in the sense that now these are renewed and fulfilled in *Yahshua* (יֵשׁוּעַ) the *Mâshîyach* (מָשִׁיחַ).

Recall the assertion of the Early Church Fathers: *Lex Orandi, Lex Credendi* (the law of worship reflects, or is, the law of belief). Christianity is not some mere spiritual practice that simply teaches us how to live in this world, and how to treat others. It is not a spiritual practice without truth claims. How we worship must reflect *the* Truth. Without worship, without liturgy, without the Eucharist, we are without the fullness of the Messiah. So yes, because the Eucharist reflects the Truth—reflects His very Self—as Christians we are in a sense *obligated* to participate and thus demonstrate its truth claims (see *CCC* #2042). Having said that, may I suggest five reasons we should go beyond mere obligation and *want* to participate in the Eucharist (*Note*[154]).

First, we go because of *love*! He, the One who loves us, asked us to eat this bread and drink this cup in remembrance of Him (*CCC* #1341-1344). In our obedience to this request is a reciprocation of our love to the God who loves us. Although the celebration of community is important, it is always secondary; for the primary focus of the Eucharist is to receive, worship, and adore the One we love. This is not a motivation of calculation or obligation. No! We want to be with the One we love. We want to spend time with our beloved. We want to encounter Him. We want to listen to Him and completely follow Him. We desire to receive Him and worship Him. Again, Christianity without the Eucharist is a Christianity without the fullness of Jesus the Christ.

Second, we go to say, *Thank You*! The God who spoke and all things were created out of nothing (*ex nihilo*), humbled Himself in the form of bread and wine. To this, we, in humility, say Thank You! In fact, the word Eucharist comes from the Greek word εὐχαριστία (eucharistia/*yoo-khar-is-tee'-ah*), which means thanksgiving, giving thanks, thankfulness, and gratitude—especially to God as an act of worship.

Third, we go to exercise our *priestly role*, our royal universal Priesthood in our Messiah! Just like Abraham and Isaac who exercised their priestly roles, we are also called to exercise our Messiah's priestly office, through spiritual worship and sacrifices through Him. In our baptism we are baptized as priest, prophet, and king (as we will further study in Chapter 5, An Ontological Event). All three must manifest themselves in our life; for in our baptism we are bound to the mystery of the Messiah. When we participate in the Eucharist, although the primary role is the priestly one, we exercise all three.

Fourth, we go to be *nourished*, we go to be healed! In faith, with humility, we acknowledge our sinfulness, our brokenness, our imperfections, our flaws, our deficiencies. In that acknowledgement we realize that it is only in Him that we can be purified. We do not participate in the Eucharist (i.e., go to church or Mass) because we think we are *holier than thou*—No! we go because we know, without Him, we are not. Just as we eat food to nourish our bodies, we consume the Eucharist, His body, blood, soul and divinity, to nourish ourselves, body and soul (*Note*[155]).

Fifth, we go, for in that nourishment, we grow to be more and more like Him, *Christ-like*! We recognize that we gather in community as the Body of the Messiah. We are His mystical Body. We are flesh of His flesh. We are bone of His bones. We are His Bride. We are His *Ekklēsia* (ἐκκλησία), and we must gather and exemplify that reality. As we gather we are signifying our communion, union, and oneness with each other.

In the Eucharist there is not only this presence of Jesus the Christ within our community, but also the mysterious presence of Jesus the Christ within those who commune. Christianity is not in isolation, nor is the Eucharist (i.e., Communion) some sort of membership in the club. As mentioned, placing His blood on our doorpost is not enough; we need to eat the Lamb (Ex 12:8-10). There is no such thing as an individual Christian spirituality, for Christianity is in community. Nor is there Communion without its implications, for as we (with intentionality) continually participate and consume the Eucharist, we are changed. It is the continual process of slowly but surely moving away from self-centredness, self-pity, self-admiration, self-absorption, self-will and so forth, that is, in essence, the movement from our natural-self to our spiritual-self, in Him.

We have all heard the saying: You are what you eat. This is preeminently true in its application to the Eucharist. To paraphrase Saint Augustine: *we become what we eat* (*Note*[156]). In faith, as we consume the Body and Blood of Jesus the Christ we become more and more Christ-like—an image of the Messiah. This is not us just representing the Christ; it is us actually becoming Him—which is our true-self. For that reason, we encounter Jesus not only in the Eucharist, not only in the Word of God being proclaimed, but also in each other, the body of the Christ.

Over the centuries, there has been much division. This division is caused by humans, not by God. The God who loves us sent His only Son to destroy enmity, estrangement, and alienation, not only between us and God, but also between each other. There is no more race or colour (Jew or Greek)—we are all one in Jesus the Anointed One (Gal 3:28; also cf. Col 3:11).

You are my brother. You are my sister. We must unequivocally, as His *Ekklēsia* (ἐκκλησία), make this declaration. This is not just a metaphorical or a symbolic sentiment. This is literal fact.

In this, we must therefore stand up and say that Jesus the Messiah is the answer. He is the only *Way* and the ultimate objective *Truth* and the absolute fullness of *Life* (Jn 14:6). He is the answer to everything. He is unity. For through the Holy Spirit *diversity finds unity only in Him* (see Acts 2:7-8)

Although people do not like the truth (Jn 3:19), we are inherently designed to search out the truth. We have a mind to discern and to know; the very object of that discernment is always truth—for none of us inherently wants to live a lie. Therefore, we grasp and acquire with an innate desire to know truth.

As Christians, we must stir up these natural desires—in ourselves and those around us—in the search of truth (see Acts 17:22) and thus more and more lead ourselves and others towards ultimate objective Truth (see Acts 17:23). We must not shy away from proclaiming that everything converges on Him, for He is supreme. He is Truth in and of Himself. The moral and ethical decay, and divisive crisis that we are plainly seeing ever more in our current society (and for that matter also in our Church), is due to our abandoning of God and adapting ourselves to the spirit-of-the-world without objective Truth.

He is the Bread of Life, and happy are those Who are called to His Heavenly banquet; He is the true Manna from Heaven, Who nourishes His bride with His Body and Blood; He is the Priest of the new and eternal covenant, Who offers the perfect sacrifice to the Father on the altar of the Cross; He is the King of true justice and peace, Who in His sacrificial offering unites us.[157]

We are one in Him!

As we have studied (and further study) there can be only one Unifier, one Answer, one *Way*, one *Truth*, and one *Life*. We state this to be Jesus Himself.

Only in Him are we one. We become a *unified new creation* only in Him. Yes, He is first; He is above all; He is supreme, therefore there is an absolute primacy of Jesus.

Let us end this chapter by praying the Colossians canticle:

Let us give thanks to the Father
for having made you worthy
to share the lot of the saints
in light.

He rescued us from the
power of darkness and brought us
into the kingdom of His beloved Son.
Through Him we have redemption,
the forgiveness of our sins.

He is the image of the invisible God,
the first-born of all creatures.
In Him everything in Heaven and on earth
was created,
things visible and invisible.

All were created through Him;
all were created for Him.
He is before all else that is.
In Him everything continues in being.

It is He who is head of the body, the Church;
He who is the beginning, the first-born of the dead,
so that primacy may be His in everything.

It pleased God
to make absolute fullness reside in Him
and, by means of Him,
to reconcile everything in His person,
both on earth and in the Heavens,
making peace through the blood of His Cross.

| Canticle – Colossians 1:12-20[158] |

Fullness of Revelation, the complete Deposit of Faith, is found *only* in Jesus. Therefore, why are we looking for anything more?

Chapter 4 | No New Revelation Needed

In all wisdom and insight, God the Father has made known to us the mystery of His divine will. This is expressed by His acting (deeds) and His speaking (words) throughout history; and which culminates—in accord with His favour that He has set forth—in His most definitive Act and very Word, His Son Jesus, our Christ (Eph 1:9).

This chapter is an extension of Chapter 3. For as we studied in the preceding chapter, when we say that all primacy is in Jesus the Christ, this includes the fact that the fullness of Divine Revelation dwells *only* in *Yahshua* (יֵשׁוּעַ) the *Mâshîyach* (מָשִׁיחַ). God the Father's definitive act of Divine Revelation is the ultimate and complete revealing of Himself in His Son (Eph 1:9). Stated in reverse, in all primacy, Jesus is the ultimate and complete Divine Revelation of His Father. This is what is meant by saying that the fullness of Divine Revelation only dwells in Him.

That being said, while we are in the temporal (that is, while we are on this earth, within time), the source of God's Divine Revelation is Holy Scripture handed down through the Tradition of the Apostles (*Note*[159]).

Therefore, Revelation with a capital "R" is not only *the* Person of Jesus—Who is the *fullness* and *complete* Revelation, for He is the *complete utterance* from God the Father—it is also *the* source of revealing (i.e., Holy Scripture).

These two are somewhat interchangeable but keep in mind that this is only while we are in the temporal. For the source of revealing does not supersede the complete Revelation found *only* in His Son; for "paramount among these is Jesus [the] Christ—the very Word of God—Who communicates, definitively and unsurpassably, all that the Triune God wants humankind to know about Himself and His saving purposes."[160]

Accordingly—and as controversial as this may sound—Saint Augustine states that at one point we will *not* even need Holy Scripture.[161] This is important to note, so let me explain. In temporal times, before the end of this age, Scripture is the Revelation of *the*

Revelation; Scripture is the living document or the continual means for revealing the Person of Jesus. In this, we rightfully say that Holy Scripture is *enduring*, this is so, however, this is *only* so concerning the truths contained within, and in the context of temporal times; for, in the world to come, when the truths are completely fulfilled, Scripture itself will no longer be needed. Why would it be needed? Thus, the word *enduring* should be understood only in temporal terms and concerning the truths therein. Consider for example, we need faith and hope in the sense in which they are used today *only* while on this earth. For when we see Him—the fullness of Revelation—*face to Face* (1 Cor 13:12-13), none of this will be needed.

As Saint Paul tells us, everything will cease (1 Cor 13:8), everything will pass away (1 Cor 13:9-10)—*everything* also includes Scripture—again excluding the truths therein (Mt 24:35). Just like faith and hope will pass away, for faith will eventually yield to sight, and hope will eventually yield to possession (1 Cor 13:13a), Holy Scripture will eventually yield to *Truth* Himself—Jesus the Christ

Therefore, Scripture will pass away, for Holy Scripture—the Revelation of *the* Revelation—will eventually yield to the fullness of Revelation, the fullness of perfection, when we see Him *face to Face*. "If there are prophecies, they will be done away with; if tongues, they will fall silent; and if knowledge, it will be done away with. For we know only imperfectly" but here is the key, when we see Him *face to Face*, which is to say once Perfection comes "the partial will pass away" all things which is in part will be done away with (1 Cor 13:8-10).

The main point I am trying to make here is that He is *Revelation* with a capital "R"—the fullness and total perfection of all revelation (e.g., even creation itself)—therefore, we need nothing more! Currently and ultimately our possession is He, Jesus the Christ, and in Him *is* the Revelation of God Himself, in all perfection.

"God has revealed Himself fully by sending His own Son, in whom He has established His covenant forever; the Son is His Father's definitive Word;" what is more, is that because of this "there will be no further Revelation after Him" (*CCC* #73; also cf. #65-67). *All* of Sacred Scripture points *to Him*. God the Father says all He needs to say in His Son. Period! He is the ultimate Deposit of Faith.

> It pleased God, in His goodness and wisdom, to reveal Himself and to make known the mystery of His will (cf. Eph 1:9). His will was that men should have access to the Father, through [the] Christ, the Word made flesh, in the Holy Spirit, and thus become sharers in the divine nature (cf. Eph 2:18; 2 Pt 1:4) . . . After God has spoken in many times and in various ways through the prophets, "in these last days He has spoken to us by His Son" (Heb 1:1-2). For He sent His Son, the eternal Word who enlightened all men, and dwelt among men and to tell them about the inner life of God . . . The Christian economy, therefore, since it is the new and definitive covenant, will never pass away; and no new Public Revelation is to be expected before the glorious manifestation of our Lord, Jesus (cf. 1 Tm 6:14 and Ti 2:13).[162]
>
> | *Dei Verbum* |

We are enlightened *only* by Him. True enlightenment comes *only* through Him. Therefore, there is *no new Public Revelation to be expected*, for it is *rooted* in Jesus the Messiah.

While we are on this earth (in time) Holy Scripture (which we have designated the Old Testament and the New Testament), is God's authoritative communication to us handed down by the Apostles. It is the Revelation of *the* Revelation, which is also called Public Revelation. As Saint John put it, Holy Scripture is the proclamation of the Revelation of God the Father in and through His Son, which they the Apostles have handed down to us (see 1 Jn 1:1-4).Therefore, in the temporal, this is all we need—we do not need to search for additional Divine Revelation, as we eagerly wait to see Him *face to Face.* For that reason, Christians should not look for any other prophet or any new Divine Revelation. As the *Catechism* clearly teaches: "There will be no further Revelation" (*CCC* #73).

In addition, it would not make any sense to accept any so-called new Divine Revelation, for by that we would be saying that the Divine Revelation of the Father was inadequate.

More and more Christians (mainly Catholics) are searching for *new divine revelation* in various ways—this unfortunately, is a grave error. Sadly, for some Christians, the ultimate complete Divine Revelation of God the Father in His Son, *Yahshua* (יֵשׁוּעַ) the *Mâshîyach* (מָשִׁיחַ), as expressed in Scripture Revelation and the Apostolic Tradition, is somehow not good enough.

To help us clarify the issue, the Church has always made a clear distinction between Divine Revelation that is *public* (hereafter "Public Revelation") and revelation that is *private* (hereafter "Private Revelation"). This distinction, while it may be confusing is grounded in the theological understanding of its comparative validity.

Therefore, let us first begin with the distinction, look secondly at the theological understanding, and finally at its consequences if the distinction is not adhered to.

What is the difference between Public Revelation and Private Revelation? First, the words *Public* and *Private* do not refer to the extent to which the revelation is distributed or known.

For example, if someone thinks that he has had a physical vision of Jesus and decides to share it with others by describing the vision on the internet or in a book, that does not now make it Public Revelation. So then, what exactly is Public Revelation and Private Revelation?

Public Revelation: This revelation is expressed through Holy Scripture and the Tradition that was handed down to us from the Apostles (which we referred to as the source of Revelation or Divine Revelation, or to be more precisely, the complete Deposit of Faith—*Depositum Fidei*).

Revelation does not change or need anything added or developed over time. That being said, however—that is, for the ease of understanding we might want to make a sub-category—we over time understand Public Revelation more and more. Although Public Revelation "is already complete, it is not always completely explicit to the Christian; it remains for Christians to gradually to grasp its full significance over the course of the centuries" (*CCC* #66). This applies not only to the Church (at the macro level), but also to you and me as we grow in our Christian faith (at the micro level). We, collectively and singularly are the limitation, not Revelation. Revelation is complete in Him. "For no other foundation can any one lay than that which is laid, which is Jesus [the] Christ" (1 Cor 3:11). Revelation does not need to be developed in the sense of something new; Revelation only needs to be grasped and understood.

This understanding of Public Revelation *is not,* however, considered Private Revelation—this is critical to remember. We should avoid confusing this *gradual grasping* (or unveiling) of Public Revelation with that of Private Revelation (*Note*[163]). Only a gradual unveiling of the initial Deposit of Faith over time has been given, so we may grasp its totality (*CCC* #66). Therefore, we should not confuse this gradual grasping with *so- called* development of doctrine (*Note*[164]).

In that regard (and just in case you are wondering), you will have noted that the contents of this book falls under this sub-category, the *gradual grasping* of Public Revelation, explicit for our time.

Here is an analogy that might help. It is like having a full jug of water placed on our kitchen counter. This represents the fullness of Revelation. The jug is totally full, so nothing more can be added. Now it would be impossible to drink the entire 20-Liter jug of water, so using the spout we pour and drink one glass at a time. This represents the *gradual grasping* of the fullness of Revelation. For every glass we pour is the same water—it is not *new* water—we are only consuming it gradually.

In this, it is also essential that we understand the sacred objective status of Holy Scripture as the codified Revelation of *the* Revelation (*Note*[165]) and thus, not supersede it with any subjective understandings. This includes (but is not limited to) even if it comes from our own personal readings and interpretation of Holy Scripture or from others.

Private Revelation: Now in contrast to what has been stated, all other revelation—e.g., our personal understanding of God, apparitions, visions, Saints (excluding the Apostles within Public Revelation; and some writings of the Saints' which we may classify within the above stated sub-category within Public Revelation, as in the gradual unfold aspect of Divine Revelation), meditation, private prayer, and so forth—is thus considered private revelation.

Private Revelation is revelation that is ostensibly revealed privately to an individual, revelation that only that person knows.

In case you are wondering, incidents in Scripture that appear to be what is called Private Revelation are not so. Because these incidents describing revelation to an individual (e.g., the Holy Spirit's direction to Simeon and Anna or Saint Joseph's dreams), are actually part of Public Revelation; for they are included in Holy Scripture and do not originate from the idea of an individual that is not contained within.

That being said, to avoid confusion, we should note that Private Revelation has two groups within it: (1) Church approved private revelations, e.g., visions that the Saints experience or approved Marin apparitions, etc.; and (2) all non-approved private revelations, e.g., our understanding of God via personal prayer, meditations, or reading of the Scriptures, or even from seers or visionaries who are not Church approved, etc.

Now this is important, if *anything* in Private Revelation contradicts Public Revelation in any shape or form, it should be *immediately* rejected by all Christians. "Christian faith cannot accept 'revelations' that claim to surpass or correct the Revelation of which [the] Christ is the fulfillment" (*CCC* #67)—even if this comes from a world renowned seer, sage, or visionary or from our own thinking or personal experience. Although, personal experience may be profound; however it does not and cannot override objective Public Revelation.

Some of us reading this might not like this; nevertheless, this need be said: our personal thinking, experiences, and private revelations must be highly vetted. Period!

Two good measuring sticks help us to discern. First, we should subject our thinking or experience, and Private Revelation with that of Public Revelation. If it corresponds, great, but if it does not—even in the very slightest manner—discard it immediately. Second, always keep in mind what the Catechism teaches us—"There will be no further Revelation" (*CCC* #73)—so, if this non-approved revelation is new revelation it must also be discarded immediately.

Having said that, we should acknowledge the benefit of non-approved Private Revelation during our own personal prayer or discernment—for the will of the Holy Spirit for our lives as individuals is conveyed through these means. As we will study (in Chapters 7 and 8) the will of the Holy Spirit for us, as in our particular mission for Him, is subjective to us, and thus is individually revealed to each of us within this particular sub-category of Private Revelation. This type of Private Revelation is of utmost importance to us as individuals within the collective (the body of the Christ); however, for that reason, we must diligently make sure our mission is congruent with Public Revelation—we must use the measuring sticks prudently in discerning our mission in life (in Him).

Again, God speaks to us individually in our own personal prayer, meditations, or reading of the Scriptures. Nevertheless, we still must vigorously test this revelation to discern if it is the Spirit of God speaking or another spirit (see 1 Jn 4:1). The time and effort we spend doing this is time well spent.

Every other type of non-approved Private Revelation, which comes from others, may be beneficial, but it is not really important. We do not need it. It may lead us astray and consume time and energy that should be better spent discerning and carrying out our personal mission, in our Messiah.

Consider this admonition for what it's worth: if you do decide, or before you embark in the pursuit of every other type of non-approved Private Revelation, first read your Bible cover to cover, then read the *Catechism* (*CCC*) cover to cover. At that point, you will be somewhat equipped to apply the first measuring stick noted above. Also diligently apply the second measuring stick—if it is new revelation, discard it immediately.

As for Church approved Private Revelation, by definition, we need not worry about contradictions with that of Public Revelation, for the Church in Her wisdom has already vetted this for us. At this point we also know that it does not contain any new revelation. In addition, at this point it also may be included in the sub-category of Public Revelation—in the gradual unfold aspect of Divine Revelation.

Having said all that, interestingly Church approved Private Revelation nevertheless is still not mandatory.

> Throughout the ages, there have been so-called "private" revelations, some of which have been recognized by the authority of the Church. They do not belong, however, to the Deposit of Faith. It is not their role to improve or complete [the] Christ's definitive Revelation. (*CCC* #67)

This might sound contradictory, but, approved Private Revelation *does not* belong to the Deposit of Faith. For example, the Marian apparition at Lourdes and the consequent understanding of God revealed by this apparition can be edifying to the faithful. Knowing this, the Church in Her wisdom has given us the green-light; for these Private Revelations may help us get closer to God, may expound further understandings of Public Revelation, may be beneficial to our lives, e.g., sanctification. Nevertheless, this understanding of God (or even the apparition itself), is not binding upon any Christian or the Church as a whole (that is we do not have to believe in it). Knowing this fine nuanced distinction is of utmost importance.

On that note, we may say that even the non-doctrinal gradual unveiling of Public Revelation is not mandatory. For example, as stated, although this book falls under the sub-category of the gradual grasping of Public Revelation made explicit for our time, and is approved by the magisterium of the Church (i.e., the Diocesan Bishop's *Imprimatur*), and it contains nothing contrary to our Catholic faith (i.e., the Diocesan Bishop's *Nihil Obstat*), it is nevertheless not binding, and you do not have to believe in what is written throughout this book (except for the doctrinal and scriptural statements within). My hope is that this book is edifying, helps with our personal process of sanctification, and brings us closer to our Messiah; however, you may all the same discard it and use this as a paperweight if you so wish.

By the way, some scholars say that Public Revelation is necessary for our *salvation,* but, we *need* Private Revelation for our *sanctification*. Chapter 7 will show that this is not entirely accurate. I also think the distinctions made above helps us consider a nuanced approach to this argument made by scholars.

To further help us, here is a quick summary of Public Revelation opposed to Private Revelation in point form:

- Public Revelation: It is the full and complete Deposit of Faith codified and manifested in Jesus the Christ, revealed in Sacred Scripture and Apostolic Tradition; in Public Revelation there is no so-called development, but an acknowledgement that there is a harmonic unveiling of truth, not only for the individual, but also for the Church as a whole; Public Revelation is objective and thus supersedes any Private Revelation.

- Private Revelation: It is subject to Public Revelation; it must not contradict Public Revelation; it does not add to Public Revelation; it does not complete or improve Public Revelation; it is not binding or mandatory to believe. It has two sub-categories:

  (1) Church approved Private Revelation, in which there is no error or contradiction to the faith; this would include the writings of Saints, approved Marin apparitions, which may be beneficial but are not essential and therefore optional for belief.

  (2a) Non-approved Private Revelation, this does not necessarily mean that it is in error; this would stem from personal prayer, meditation, or reading of the Scriptures; as such, it is absolutely needed for personal understanding of one's particular mission or vocation; it is therefore necessary for growth in sanctity, however, it must be vigorously vetted by Public Revelation (sometimes with the help of a good spiritual director), for it must be hand-in-hand with Public Revelation.

  (2b) Non-approved Private Revelation, the *everything else* part; again, this does not necessarily mean that it is in error; but, it is something we really do not need; it is not really necessary to believe; and although it may help in personal growth in sanctity, we should be careful in its participation, and thus must highly vet it with Public Revelation (again, it must be hand-in-hand with Public Revelation).

All said, there is *no new* Divine Revelation; only the expounding of its content. For that reason, the only absolute necessity is our understanding of God revealed to us in the Person of Jesus, through Sacred Scripture and Apostolic Tradition, and our carrying out that understanding in and through Him.

What has been stated concerning Private Revelation is not intended to diminish it—Private Revelation has a role to play, especially in discerning our particular mission in Him—on the contrary, these assertions are there to inform us of the nuance and thus keep us from error that could move us away from our Christ. To help us further understand this let us now look at the theological understanding behind this assertion.

In his treatise on *The Ascent of Mount Carmel*, the sixteenth century Doctor of the Church, Saint John of the Cross asserts that in the "Christ, God has spoken to us." He writes:

> Under the ancient law prophets and priests sought from God revelations and visions which indeed they needed, for faith had as yet no firm foundation and the gospel law had not yet been established. Their seeking and God's responses were necessary. He spoke to them at one time through words and visions and revelations, at another in signs and symbols. But however He responded and what He said and revealed were mysteries of our holy faith, either partial glimpses of the whole or sure movements toward it. But now that faith is rooted in [the] Christ, and the law of the Gospel has been proclaimed in this time of grace, there is no need to seek Him in the former manner, nor for Him so to respond. By giving us, as He did, His Son, His only Word, He has in that one Word said everything. There is no need for any further revelation. This is the true meaning [in the letter] to the Hebrews when [the writer] urged them to abandon their earlier ways of conversing with God, as laid down in the Law of Moses, and to set their eyes on [the] Christ alone: *In the past God spoke to our fathers through the prophets in various ways and manners; but now in our times, the last days, He has spoken to us in His Son.* In effect, [the writer] is saying that God has spoken so completely through His own Word that He chooses to add nothing. Although He had spoken but partially through the prophets He has now said everything in [the] Christ. He has given us everything, His own Son. Therefore, anyone who wished to question God or to seek some new vision or revelation from Him would commit an

> offence, for instead of focusing his eyes entirely on [the] Christ he would be desiring something other than [the] Christ, or beyond Him. God could then answer: *This is My beloved Son in whom I am well pleased; hear Him.* In my Word I have already said everything. Fix your eyes on Him alone for in Him I have revealed all and in Him you will find more than you could ever ask for or desire. I, with my Holy Spirit, came down upon Him on Mount Tabor and declared: *This is my beloved Son in whom I am well pleased; hear Him.* You do not need new teachings or ways of learning from me, for when I spoke before it was of [the] Christ who was to come, and when they sought anything of me they were but seeking and hoping for [the] Christ in whom is every good, as the whole teaching of the evangelists and Apostles clearly testifies.[166]
>
> | Saint John of the Cross |

History has been divided into two periods. The first period, before the Christ, we call the Old Testament period (or B.C.). In this period, God the Father spoke to His sons and daughters in different ways, including prophets, prophesies, visions, typologies, signs and symbols, and the like. All ways of communication in the past have their centre in Jesus the Christ. Everything points to Him.

Now that the Christ has revealed Himself—the fulfillment of typologies and communications referring to Him—we no longer need to learn of Him in those former ways (Heb 1:1). This second period, we call the New Testament (it is the time in which we are living in right now, or A.D.). In this period—"when the fullness of time had come" (Gal 4:4)—God the Father clearly spoke to His sons and daughters ultimately *through* His Son, Jesus the Christ. We need to fully grasp this truth (cf. Heb 1:2).

God has given us His ultimate and complete Revelation in Jesus His Son, therefore, we no longer *need* to seek any other revelation in any other manner as times of old.

As we can see, this has been the Church's teaching right from the beginning, right within Holy Scripture. To quote Cardinal Gerhard Müller:

> For 2,000 years, the Catholic Church has infallibly taught that Holy Scripture and Apostolic Tradition are the only sources of Revelation and that no further Revelation can be added in the course of history.[167]
>
> | Cardinal Gerhard Müller |

Adding to this, in his second letter to the Corinthians, Saint Paul (quoting the Septuagint version of the Isaiah 49:8 text), states "In an acceptable time I heard you, and on the day of Salvation I helped you; behold, now is the acceptable time; behold, now is the day of Salvation" (2 Cor 6:2).

This *now* is this present time period, in which God bestows His Salvation upon all of humanity in Jesus the *Mâshîyach* (מָשִׁיחַ), the wellspring of salvation. Very important to note, this *now* is "when the fullness of time had come" (Gal 4:4). That is, God sent His Son and He gives us His ultimate and full Revelation in *Yahshua* (יֵשׁוּעַ), His Son, at the *fullness of time*. The word *now* not only means the very moment Saint Paul is writing, but also means the current time that you and I live in—this is the *fullness of time*.

Again: "In times past, God spoke to our fathers through the prophets in various ways and manners; but *now* in our times, the *last days*, He has spoken to us in His Son" (Heb 1:1-2; *emphasis* added). The prophets of old had an individual particular message—it was piecemeal. However, the ultimate, complete, and full utterance of God is given to us in these last days in and through His Son, and thus nothing more is needed. Jesus the Messiah is the clearest and concise voice of God!

Interestingly, the Greek word used here for *last* is not τελέω (teleō/tel-eh'-o), which means conclusion, end, end-goal, or last; and it is not *Parousia*, the Christ's Second Coming, at the end of history as we know it. It is the word ἔσχατος (eschatos/es'-khat-os), which means the end times (it is the source of the word eschatology). The end times—the *eschatos* (ἔσχατος)—are the times in which we are currently living. It is important we grasp this fact so we do not fall into error.

For the past two thousand years we have been living in the end times, the *now*, the *eschatos* (ἔσχατος). Therefore during this entire period—of approximately the past fifty generations, no other Divine Revelation is needed.

Think about the Apostles and disciples of the early church. If we were to scour the New Testament and early church writings we would find that there is no indication any of them were looking for further revelation. What they were looking for was the Second Coming, the *Parousia*. Their wait is our wait!

Not understanding the real meaning of *eschatos* (ἔσχατος), some scholars try to tell us that we are now in the so-called *actual* end times, and thus we need new prophesies for the times we are in. Well, knowing this—that Scripture tells us that we are currently living in the *eschatos* (ἔσχατος), the end times, and have been so for the past two thousand years—in effect answers and dismisses this claim made by these scholars.

For we live in A.D., *Anno Domini*—the year of our Lord—thus all the two thousand years and any in the future until the Second Coming are the end times, the singular year of the Lord.

Another claim that scholars make is that we are now living in the time of the *Parousia.* This is also invalid on its face, for Public Revelation clearly states that no one really knows this (cf. Mt 24:36). Also interestingly, almost every generation of the past fifty generations also thought as such.

The Old Testament was the first period (B.C.), the time of promise. This was the time of the Law (Torah) and the Prophets (Nevi'im), which lasted until John the Baptist (Lk 16:16 and Mt 11:13). In the second period (A.D.), God speaks to us *only* in His Son (as fully revealed in the New Testament). The transition from fragmentary to full has been made. That movement includes how God *now* speaks to us. Clearly stated there is a change in how He speaks to us—for He no longer speaks to us via prophets of old. Why would He? For now that He has made His complete utterance through His Son (as stated, Holy Scripture is the Revelation of *the* Revelation).

John the Baptist was the transitional prophet, and thus made room for and ushered in *Yahshua* (יֵשׁוּעַ) the *Mâshîyach* (מָשִׁיחַ) the fulfillment and total Revelation of God (the second period). Those who argue for a current need of prophets of old, in the likeness of Isaiah, Jeremiah, Elijah, and so forth are mistaken. This is clearly not scriptural. This desire effectively bypasses our Messiah. We no longer need prophets of old for we now have the fullness of Revelation.

Adding to this understanding is the fact that in Jesus the Messiah the Law and the Prophets are now fulfilled—in its totality—in *His* Person: "Do not think that I have come to abolish the Law or the prophets, I have come not to abolish but to fulfill" our Messiah directly tells us (Mt 5:17). In this Scripture passage, Saint Matthew uses the Greek word πληρόω (plēroō/play-ro'-o), which is translated into English as *fulfill* (*Note*[168]).

This Greek word has two dominant meanings. The first definition of *plēroō* (πληρόω) has an eschatological sense (in line with what we just mentioned), and the second definition means to complete, carry out through to the end, render perfect, bring to pass, ratify, or accomplish.

In the New Testament writings, we find a *key,* which is that Jesus the *Mâshîyach* (מָשִׁיחַ) is the lens through Whom the entire Old Testament Scriptures are to be interpreted. This key was taught by Jesus Himself. Recall the personal Bible study with the two disciples on the road to Emmaus (Lk 24:25-27). Starting with Moses and all the prophets, *Yahshua* (יֵשׁוּעַ) the risen Christ, interprets and teaches *all* things concerning Himself, in *all* the Scriptures (Lk 24:27). He clearly teaches that *all* of Holy Scripture points to Him—this teaching, He gives us as *the key* to the entire Bible!

As mentioned by Saint John of the Cross, on Mount Tabor God the Father boldly declares: "This is my beloved Son, with whom I am well pleased; listen to Him" (Mt 17:5, Mk 9:7, and Lk 9:35). We do not need to listen to anything or anyone else (*Note*[169]), if we do we are bypassing Him. In contrast, we must focus on Him, keep our eyes fixed on Him, and listen *only* to Him—a total centrality in Him. Grippingly, here at the Transfiguration on Mount Tabor, we are literally given a visual of the fulfillment of the Law and the Prophets. Saint Peter wanted to make three tabernacles (booths or tents) one each for Jesus, Moses, and Elijah (Mt 17:4 and Lk 9:33). However, Saint Peter "did not know what he was saying" (Lk 9:33)—three tabernacles are not needed. Moses represented the Law and Elijah represented the prophets; they are witnesses to the fulfillment; they now *disappear*; and Jesus is found alone: "when the disciples raised their eyes, they saw no one else but Jesus alone" (Mt 17:8). Notice the dual emphasis—*no one else* and *alone*—this significance should not be minimized. The fulfillment of the Law and the Prophets is done, and thus from this point forward both the Law and the Prophets must always be viewed thought the prism of the Messiah. That is to say, we now *only need one tabernacle*, for the transition is made!

Why is all of this important? What are the consequences of not understanding this? As mentioned, we sadly see more and more Christians desiring *new* revelation. The consequences of this desire are detrimental, for this search not only moves us away from Jesus our Messiah, it actually eradicates the primacy of the Messiah.

Concerning the former: "Anyone who runs on ahead and does not remain in the doctrine of the Christ [*that is, one who is not content with what He taught*], does not have God" (2 Jn 1:9[170]). In our search for new and exciting revelation, we no longer search and rest in Him. We might think we are in this search but in fact we are not. In this pursuit it is easy to forget that Christianity is a relationship with a Person. The pursuit easily becomes a distraction. When this so-called new Private Revelation is discovered, it tends to eclipse Public Revelation, and sometimes even acts as a substitute. As we get caught up in this new revelation, it inevitably takes us away from the Truth—from Him—and as mentioned it distorts Who He actually *Is*; for we now have shifted primacy away from Him.

When an event, a person, or thing acts as a prerequisite for God's Revelation in our Messiah, the prerequisite *automatically* becomes greater than God the Father's complete Divine Revelation in His Son. To elaborate, *whatever* that prerequisite may be (e.g., as in language, nationality, historicity; or consecrations, apparitions, visions; or to receive graces, the distribution of graces, to receive salvation, a particular or special knowledge or insight to know God, or a knowledge that we need for our time; or any particular seer, individual, prophet, or sage for our time; or event or thing) once we place that *whatever* as the prerequisite, that prerequisite automatically takes precedence over the Messiah—for now the primacy power is in that *whatever*—as mentioned we end up bypassing and thus overriding the primacy power of our Messiah. Unavoidably, even if it is not our intention, Jesus the Messiah, becomes secondary.

Here is an example with which we are all too familiar. Let's say you buy an airline ticket to go to your friend's wedding happening six months from now. You do all the necessary due diligence for the purchase. Two days before your flight you receive a notification that you need a particular vaccine to permit you to board your flight. Although you hold a first-class ticket, it is now secondary. The required vaccine, while it has nothing to do with your flight—takes primacy. It now has the power over and above your ticket. Doesn't it?

Here is another example using Public Revelation. When God the Father places God the Son as the only conduit to Him (as we studied in the previous chapter), even though this does not diminish the primacy of the Father, He in actuality is relinquishing His power to His Son (cf. Mt 28:18 and Dan 7:13-14). That is to say, now all the primacy power resides in His Son. For absolutely no one can go to the Father except through His Son (Jn 14:6). The primacy is therefore now in His Son—not in God the Father. The prerequisite automatically takes precedence. Again, this is unavoidable.

For this reason, there is in fact an absolute *theological necessity* to state that "there will be no further Revelation after Him" (*CCC* #73); and thus, also state that there is no seer, prophet of sage as the times of old. For if we say that there is a new revelation given by a so-called prophet of our time, Jesus the Messiah can no longer be fulfillment or the fullness of Revelation.

To help us further understand this, here are a few subtle examples.

Example Number 1: Some Christians are caught up in purported end-time prophecies. In one such prophecy, they are waiting for the rebuilding of the Jerusalem Temple (i.e., the third temple), and with that the recommencement of temple sacrifice (i.e., the red heifer). This is ludicrous! Desiring either is akin to trampling on the blood of the Messiah.

The Temple, was a copy, a shadow of things to come. Now that the fulfillment is here, the copy is no longer needed (Heb 8:5). Why go back to the type when you have the fulfillment? Temple sacrifices are no longer needed. Christians should therefore assert that the third temple will not be sanctioned by God.

Once we place this alleged prophesy as a prerequisite for the Second Coming, it eclipses Jesus. Once we say that we need a perfect red heifer to be sacrificed, we are saying that the blood of Jesus the Christ was not enough. The Temple was destroyed for a reason (Mt 24:1ff; and Mk 13:1ff). Public Revelation clearly states that there is no need for Temple sacrifice or the Levitical priesthood. The blood of a red heifer will not sanctify anyone (see Heb 10:4).

Further, a third temple will not be sanctioned by God, for there is a new High Priest (Heb 4:14). There is a new "minister of the sanctuary and of the true tabernacle of the Lord" (Heb 8:2). There is a new High Priest declared by God not in the line of the Levitical priesthood, but in the order of Melchizedek (Heb 5:10). Because of Jesus, the holiness of God is open to us, the sanctuary veil was torn into two, so we may enter the Holy of Holies through Him (Mt 27:51 and Mk 15:38).

The Temple was the type or the shadow of things to come; the fulfillment is Jesus in His body, and by extension it is you and I—for we, the Church, as bride, become the temple of God. "Do you not know that you [yourselves] are the temple of God, and that the Spirit of God dwells in you [as a bride]? If anyone destroys God's temple, God will destroy that person: for the temple of God, which you [as bride] are, is holy" (1 Cor 3:16-17).

We worship in Spirit and Truth (Jn 4:24), not in any geographic location (Jn 4:21). There is no Temple now. In fact, there is no Temple even within the New Jerusalem (Rev 21:22). Jerusalem will be transformed and made anew (Rev 3:12 and 21:2) with *Yahshua* (יֵשׁוּעַ) the *Mâshîyach* (מָשִׁיחַ) as our centre! The glory of God will not rest upon a Temple made of stone. Animal sacrifice is no longer needed. The fulfillment in Jesus the Christ is here!

It is one thing for our Jewish brothers and sisters to desire this end-time temple, but we should not be teaching Christians to desire the fulfillment of such so-called prophesies.

Example Number 2: Another example is Christians running after visionaries, who are predicting things about the Church and the signs of the times in various capacities (i.e., non-approved Private Revelation). With easy access to the internet we are seeing this more and more—some of it is quite shocking. This falls under that *everything else* within non-approved Private Revelation which we referred to above.

I can see the appeal for such visionaries; however, I wonder why the Divine Revelation in Jesus our Messiah is not good enough? I also find it fascinating that some of us we are willing to read the manifestos of non-approved visionaries, 300, 400 or even 800 pages long, but not Divine Revelation—i.e., the Bible.

That being said, and adding to the previous discussion, we know that the Holy Spirit works among us and He should not be stifled (1 Thes 5:19). However, we must *test everything*, and *only retain* what is in line with Public Revelation. "Do not despise prophetic utterances" (1 Thes 5:20), conversely, be skeptical and vigorously test these utterances (1 Thes 5:21) so you would not be led astray (cf. Rev 19:20 and 2 Pt 2:1).

"Do not trust every spirit but test the spirits to see whether they belong to God, because many false prophets have gone out into the world" (1 Jn 4:1). We must guard and keep safe the Deposit of Faith entrusted to us (1 Tm 6:20). Godless ramblings of self-professed knowledge have led some into error, and thus away from the faith (1 Tm 6:21).

For that reason, ask ourselves, how do we know that these visionaries are actually speaking with Jesus, or Mother Mary, or Saint Michael the Archangel (or whomever)? How do we know that what they are saying is true? How do we know that they are not very slightly tainting the truth (cf. Gen 3:1)?

As mentioned, to answer these questions we should prepare ourselves with the proper tools. For that reason, read your Bible and *Catechism* (*CCC*) cover to cover so you may have the necessary tools to detect what the counterfeit is. Keep in mind that Satan's deceptions are very subtle. They are not overt. If they were, they would easily be recognized. The counterfeit note that is close to the original may pass from hand to hand virtually undetected. Nonetheless, it is still worthless. In the same manner as banks use tools to recognize counterfeit currency, we also must use proper tools to know which *prophetic utterances* are counterfeit (*Note*[171]).

Be solid in your faith. Be well grounded in Scripture Revelation. "Be sober and vigilant. Your opponent the devil is prowling around like a roaring lion looking for someone to devour" (1 Pt 5:8), so resist him, lest you end up getting swept away in deceptions.

If we do not know Scripture Revelation, the Devil will twist it and use it against us. Recall the first measuring stick: hold all thinking, experiences, and Private Revelations from visionaries and the like up against Public Revelation to see if they pass.

Also, recall the second measuring stick: "There will be no further Revelation" (*CCC* #73). So, be on guard. Remember, God the Father is done with speaking to us in this former manner (Heb 1:1-2).

Intriguingly, even our Messiah Himself does not look to Private Revelation. His technique in discerning the signs of the times is not rooted in Private Revelation. If we were to scour the Scriptures we notice that He points the way by quoting the Old Testament section of Public Revelation in His disputes with others (e.g., Jn 2:14-22), His teachings (e.g., Mt 19:3-9), His parables (e.g., Mk 12:1-10), and His prophecies (e.g., Lk 4:16-21).

A vivid example is during Jesus' temptations from Satan in the desert. *Yahshua* (יֵשׁוּעַ) the Christ rebukes Satan by strictly using Public Revelation (*Note*[172]). In all three temptations (representing the temptations of the world) He does not turn to other sources, He simply says, "It is written . . ." referring to Scripture Revelation (Mt 4:1-10).

With all this in mind, *in Him*, the gift of prophecy remains among the faithful. We are all prophets, but not in the limited sense of Old Testament prophecy (see Num 11:29). We are all prophets and prophetesses in the broad sense of the word via our baptism, in Him. For the word prophecy means:

> The expression and deliverance of a message from God which constitutes a true judgment of the present, in the light of the future, arrived at in obedience to the will and under the authority of God. In common parlance, "prophecy" is often synonymous with "prediction of the future." But in the Christian and

> scriptural sense, prophecy refers to any message from God . . . more often prophecy is a divinely inspired word about the present, in the light of God's purposes for the whole of history.[173]
>
> | *Catholic Encyclopedia* |

Also, keep in mind that this use of the word prophecy, within the New Testament, does not mean new revelation. It is the unveiling of Public Revelation. As academic theologians have stated, prophecy is more about telling forth God's truth in Scripture Revelation, not foretelling the future.

When we present Jesus the Messiah to others we are prophesying. As we will study in Chapter 9, The Good News, every Christian takes on the role of John the Baptist in a sense. Just like he, we become the prophet or prophetess of the Most High—you and I also go before the Lord to prepare His way, to give His people knowledge of Salvation by the forgiveness of their sins (see Lk 1:76-77). Accordingly, in the sense of pointing to salvation through Jesus the Christ, Zechariah is not only talking about his son John, but also talking about *you* and me!

Example Number 3: Keeping with this thought pattern, our individual experience or anyone else's is not at the same level as objective Divine Revelation. We therefore cannot use current worldly philosophies to make Public Revelation (or Church teaching, i.e., doctrine) congruent and acceptable to current culture.

No so-called new revelations, within any of the arts or sciences, culture, new practices, new anthropology, or new sociological viewpoints equal Public Revelation. Who are we to adjust Church teaching to fit our time? Who do we think we are to manipulate and reinterpret of Holy Scripture to make God's Word fit with our new societal worldviews? We do not have the authority or ability to change Church teachings. Worldly ideologies are all human creations. The *Church is not a political structure, dictated by public sentiment.*

On that note, as Christians, we must also assert that, based on Public Revelation, things that once were bad (for the past two thousand years), cannot suddenly be good. Likewise, things that were once good cannot now be bad, harmful, or forbidden. *We* are not the ones reformulating what is true and what is not, what is right and what is wrong, or what is ethical and moral and what is unethical and immoral. Public Revelation does not change with the tides of society, or some sort of reimagined new enlightenment. Absolutely nothing is more enlightened or enlightening than God's Revelation in His Son. In this, Public Revelation should reject and replace the cultural fallacies of society, not vice-versa.

Example Number 4: Unfortunately, some Christians are buying into doomsayers who are predicting the immediate end of the world. This, again, is nonsense! As mentioned, almost every generation thought their generation was going to be the last.

On the one hand, we must live life as if the *Parousia*—the Second Coming—will happen in our lifetime. In fact we should live as such, and hope that our generation is the end of history as we know it (*Note*[174]). In this, we call for the *Parousia* and pray every Advent: *Maranatha—Come Lord Jesus*!

On the other hand, in Public Revelation, Jesus clearly states that no one on this earth knows the day or the hour of the Second Coming (Mt 24:36)—we must stop this craziness of following *Parousia* prophesies. This new revelation is eclipsing true Revelation found only in Jesus the Messiah (cf. Gal 3:16).

Example Number 5: Some Christians, including some Catholics, have bought into the idea of the *Remnant*. The general underlying thought is that there is (and always has been) a special group of God's people who are faithful to Him at any given time whereas the majority of people go astray. For example, starting from Genesis, Noah, Abraham, and Joseph all are seen as God's chosen Remnant. As the nation of Israel forms, and then goes astray by forsaking God's covenant, God still had a dedicated Remnant within. For example when Elijah complains that he is the only one left who serves God, God corrects Elijah by telling him that He has "seven thousand men in Israel, all those who have not knelt to Baal or kissed him" (1 Kgs 19:14-18). This is an example of God's Remnant. Basically, God will not allow His people to be wiped out or die out; He will intervene and aid His people to continue.

Unfortunately, some Christians are transferring this Old Testament situation to the Church, saying that God has His Remnant, a special group of dedicated servants who diligently serve Him even now. By transferring this Remnant idea onto the Church, one might even say that they are creating a church within the Church. This is problematic. Additionally, this idea (in some cases) is taken a step further by attaching the Remnant to the *Parousia*; saying that their supposed Remnant will usher in the Kingdom of God since they are the faithful ones.

I can see the attraction to this thought pattern. You might even say that I am a little sympathetic to the desire of this Remnant idea (although it is misguided). The impetus for this Remnant theology stems from church leadership that has apparently faltered or has gone astray in some way.

For instance, as a growing number of those in various church hierarchies and leadership roles capitulate more and more to godless secular thought—in the form of inclusivity and a distorted understanding of pastoral accompaniment of inclusivity and love (*Note*[175]); and as some are creating new revelations (as noted above) by distorting or confusing Church teachings of the past two thousand years, and thus, are leading the sheep entrusted to them to live a sinful life—the faithful Christians in the pews are searching for meaning and existence in face of some of these heretical propositions.

For these Christians, the desire to leave the Church is a nonstarter, therefore, why not say that there is a church within the Church? This is the misguided aspect of Remnant theology. Remember, confusion automatically creates division, for it is from the evil one (see 1 Cor 14:33).

As I write this example I realize that there are a lot of facets which cannot be explained here, including the two primary and three secondary Greek words used for the word *remnant* in the New Testament and the context in which they were used. Therefore I will simply state that the main theological problem with the Remnant idea (within the Church) is that it is actually new revelation. Although we may argue a Remnant theological understanding within the Old Testament (B.C.) times, this understanding cannot be applied to the Church (A.D.) times; for if so, we are now dividing the body of the Christ. Nowhere in New Testament Scripture is such a notion of a

Remnant idea found. This would not make any sense; for we are all called to diligently serve Him. In addition, in some cases Remnant theology also assumes that the *Parousia* will need to happen in our lifetime (which is also non-scriptural).

When Saint Peter (our first Pope) was faltering and being a hypocrite (Gal 2:13), Saint Paul did not consider himself as the Remnant. Remaining in Saint Peter's authority, Saint Paul "opposed him to his face because he [Saint Peter] clearly was wrong" (Gal 2:11-14). This is our methodology. We reform from within. We are a loyal opposition to each other. We, the Church, are one Church; we are the body of the Messiah. Therefore, we are called to admonish one another (Rom 15:14, 1 Cor 4:14, Col 3:16, 1 Thes 5:14, 2 Thes 3:15, and so forth). In this, within our particular ministries, we are called to build the body of the Christ (Eph 4:12), not create a Remnant.

Let us not desire a partial Remnant church, but desire a complete Church of all "those who keep God's commandments and bear witness to Jesus" our Messiah (Rev 12:17).

Example Number 6: There are some Christians (mainly Catholics) who place a high emphasis on a particular Saint (*Note*[176]). We must not forget that Saints, including Mother Mary (and approved Marian apparitions), point us to the Messiah. They *are* Saints because they point us to Him not to themselves. They reveal no Private Revelation. On the contrary, over the centuries, they gradually help us to grasp and deepen our understanding of the full significance of Public Revelation (see *CCC* #66).

The lifestyle and teachings of Saints may be highly beneficial to us; however, the primacy must always be in *Yahshua* (יֵשׁוּעַ) the *Mâshîyach* (מָשִׁיחַ). The Saints and Mother Mary point us to Him, not the reverse. Do not mistakenly place them or her above Him. If we need to know about any particular Saint or event (e.g., Marian apparition) for our salvation—or as we will study in Chapter 7, even our sanctification—that Saint or event becomes greater than the Christ.

Example Number 7: Reliance on political causes, even those that might be considered worthwhile are theologically problematic.

For example, end of the world inferences made from claims of global warming or climate change or climate catastrophes are fraught. To be clear, it is not the change in climate, itself, but the inferences made from the data about those changes that are the issue (e.g., the new revelation of environmentalism).

Christians need to be careful about some politically-driven conclusions, ideologies, rhetoric, and pontifications. Moreover, Christians must shun politically charged words such as: "existential threat," "catastrophe," "crisis," in reference to changing climate. Unfortunately, because of these extreme positions, we are missing out on needed sensible environmental action.

Theologically speaking, when we state that humanity can bring about the end of the world—a societal behavioural-inflicted apocalypse so to speak—an inherent arrogance exists within such an assertion. We are in essence stating that we, *humanity*, have the power to bring about the end of the world (i.e., Second Coming). In this we are bypassing Public Revelation. Are we not?

We are stating that we are in control of the earth's existence or extinction of its inhabitant, not God. This ideology is consciously or subconsciously rooted in the thought that humans are *all-knowing*, we are the ones in control, and thus that we are our own master.

Therefore, similarly to the doomsayers' endless prediction of the end of history (e.g., the year 2000, 2012, 2017), predictions of total environmental ruin should also be shunned (*Note*[177]). Amusingly, these predictions are far more egotistical and conceited than the predictions of the fanatical doomsayer; for here, we are arrogantly asserting to God that not only are we predicting the end of the world—a day and hour that no one knows (Mt 24:36 and Mk 13:32)—we are also the ones in total control of it. In essence, we are not only stipulating that we have the capability and ability to usher in the end, but we are also saying that we are God, for we are in control of the earth's existence and non-existence.

By no means am I saying that it is all right to destroy the environment, or that we are *not* currently destroying the environment, or we need not worry about the environment.

Our appetites are insatiable. We live in a consuming, throw-away-culture, especially here in the West, which we are regrettably exporting to the rest of the world. Major companies are making an endless array of throw-away product that they themselves forcibly make obsolete within short periods of time. In this we are exploiting our environment. We are sucking it dry! So, quite the reverse, we Christians should take care of our environment. We are *called* to conserve, protect, and take care of this beautiful world and all its creatures that have been created for us by a loving God (Gen 1:28; also cf. Mt 5:5), with prudent and sensible environmental action; however, all the while knowing that the earth was made for humanity, not the other way around.

With this, two things must be stressed. First, we cannot claim to love the environment if we do not love the One Who created all of it. Using the example of Saint Francis, the love of God and the love of creation go hand in hand. It is a misconception that Saint Francis was some sort of a tree-hugger. He was neither an environmentalist nor into environmentalism. His love of nature, his love for the environment directly stems from his total and absolute love for the One Who created it.

Second, the conceit underlying climate change claims—the assertions, new revelations, and conclusions—and the egotism of humanity thinking that we are God, inevitably show a total lack of understanding of Who God *Is*. Humanity needs a dose of *humility*! How dare we think that we can force God's hand? Shame on us if we do!

Christians should not be fooled into thinking that the single most existential threat that we are facing is climate change or the environment or anything else. It is not! This is a diversion. There is primacy in Jesus the Messiah. There is no new so-called revelation needed. For that reason, the *single most existential threat* that humanity is currently facing is our floundering or lack of belief in and respect for our Creator; it is a godless society, it is a society without Jesus the Christ at the centre!

**The Christ Event changes our very being itself.
Therefore, we must understand this change.**

Chapter 5 | An Ontological Event

In Chapter 1, we looked at the most important question ever to be asked with respect to Jesus: Who do you say that I AM? This question is important for both Christians and non-Christians alike.

In Chapter 2, we stated that Jesus is God. In Chapter 3, we studied the absolute primacy of Jesus. In Chapter 4 we looked at the particular aspect of the Revelation as it applies to *Yahshuu* (יֵשׁוּעַ) the Messiah Whom God sent (it is an extension of Chapter 3).

Chapter 5 is a culmination of Chapters 2, 3 and 4. We circle back to the original inquiry of Chapter 1: Who do you say that I AM?

If you recall, we stated that this is a strange question, at face value. However, the question points to the fact that Jesus the Christ's essential Being, His ontological makeup is paramount. So then, what is ontology? It is a branch of metaphysics, which is:

> that portion of philosophy concerned with the most fundamental aspects of *being* and *existence*. It reaches from consideration of the lowest forms of matter up to the reality of God.[178]
>
> | *Catholic Encyclopedia* |

This chapter is not an in-depth study of philosophical metaphysics (so you need not worry). However, it is about the change to *our* being, the *ontological effects* that the incarnation, death, and resurrection of the Christ have on all of humanity.

Remember, in Chapter 2 we explored the Philippians canticle; this canticle is mainly a reference to Jesus being God. In Chapter 3 we explored the Colossians canticle, which is mainly a summation of the primacy of Jesus as per God the Father's will. Now, we consider the Ephesians canticle. To the understanding of the incarnation of Jesus (celebrated at Christmas) and the death and resurrection of Jesus (celebrated at Easter or Paschal Triduum), this canticle gives us the ontological effects, the change in our being, that emerge from these three events (hereafter we will call these three events collectively as the *Christ Event*).

Therefore, before we continue with this study, let us prayerfully reflect on this early Church profession of faith, in the Ephesians canticle:

Praised be the God and Father
of our Lord Jesus [the] Christ,
who has bestowed on us in [the] Christ
every spiritual blessing in the Heavens.
God chose us in Him
before the world began
to be holy
and blameless in His sight.

He predestined us
to be His adopted sons through Jesus [the] Christ,
such was His will and pleasure,
that all might praise the glorious favour
He has bestowed on us in His beloved.

In Him and through His blood, we have been redeemed,
and our sins forgiven,
so immeasurably generous
is God's favour to us.

God has given us the wisdom
to understand fully the mystery,
the plan He was pleased
to decree in [the] Christ.

A plan to be carried out
in [the] Christ, in the fullness of time,
to bring all things into one in Him,
in the Heavens and on earth.

| Canticle – Ephesians 1:3-10[179] |

Now that we have read all three canticles, you have probably noticed that each one in its own nuanced way speaks of our salvation in the Christ. Each canticle was designed as a profession of faith. We are therefore witnessing to the fact that we cannot speak of Jesus the Christ without speaking of the mystery of His incarnation, death on the Cross and resurrection—*plus* the consequences of each event. In fact, these three events are so intertwined that theologically, the term, *Christ Event*, as one event, is appropriate (*Note*[180]).

This mystery of the Christ Event changes everything, including our very being. For ease of explanation, we will look at this ontological change individually via Jesus' incarnation, death and resurrection.

Yahshua (יֵשׁוּעַ) is the One who spoke, and everything leapt into being. Beyond any human comprehension this Creator becomes a created being, Emmanuel, God with us in the Person of Jesus the Messiah (Mt 1:23; also cf. Isa 7:14). Just the thought of this is truly mind blowing. "But wait, there's more!" Because of Who He *is*, because He *is* God as well as Man, in the event of the incarnation—in God becoming human—humanity changes. Our being changes. As we will study, all of humanity—the Christian and non-Christian alike—past, present and future (that is, speaking in temporal terms) goes through an ontological change. This is a fundamental change in our nature, which is a profound mystery that goes beyond comprehension, for now humanity will be eternal like He is.

With this event, we may even argue that we are better off than Adam and Eve were in the Garden of Eden. For not only will humanity live forever more (for eternity) because of the incarnation, but there is also now a physiological bond between God and humans, for our mortal bodies are now incorporated into His resurrection. Adam and Eve were in an earthy paradise; we, however, will be enthroned in a heavenly paradise. "Marvelous is the mystery proclaimed [by the incarnation]: man's nature is made new as God becomes Man."[181]

God becomes Man—God takes on our human nature—in Jesus the Christ. This may seem ludicrous but it is the most amazing and loving action ever. The statement, "In the beginning was the Word, and the Word was with God, and the Word was God" (Jn 1:1), "and the Word became flesh and made His dwelling among us" (Jn 1:14), is spectacularly profound. Do not take this event for granted. This event is *not* just another historic event. All things—Heaven and earth—are now being restored in Jesus the Christ (Eph 1:10). This restoration through the Messiah is an ontological event that changes the very *being* of all of humanity. A response to this change is now up to us!

Although this ontological change applies to all of humanity, as we are baptized into Him, it is taken a further step. Baptism is not simply a ritual or formality; nor is it some sort of initiation that makes us a part of a religious group, or institution, or club; and it is not some sort of pledge of loyalty. In our baptism, the ontological change is deepened; an ontological bond exists that changes the depths of who we now are.

So, who are we after the change? Well, we become a new creation. "Whoever is in [the] Christ is a new creation" (2 Cor 5:17; also cf. Gal 6:15), for we become a part of His corporal body, and He becomes our Head (Col 1:18). We are directly connected to Him. Therefore we are taken into Heaven in Him and that—ontologically—happens right now at the time of our baptism (we will discuss this further in Chapter 8, "Rejoice . . . Always!").

Another way of putting this is that in this connection, through Jesus the Christ, we become adopted sons and daughters of God (Eph 1:5). We become a *child of God*—this is *who we are.* As we become children of God, by adoption—in and through Jesus the Messiah—we are placed in a beneficial standing. For in Him we are now immersed into the Divine Trinity. In Him, we become the "salt of the earth" and the "light of the world" (Mt 5:13-14). God as Creator loves His creation; however, He has a very special love for His Son. Through the Messiah, this relationship is bestowed upon us, because we are His Son's body, thus, we *de facto* become His sons and daughters.

Therefore, God the Father's proclamation at His Son's baptism also applies to us. At our baptism, the heavens open and God the Father proclaims: . . . you are my beloved son . . . you are my beloved daughter . . . with you I am well pleased (cf. Mk 1:11, Mt 3:17, and Lk 3:22). In other words, His special love for His Son is imputed to us, those who are baptized into Him, for we are now a part of Him, and thus a part of the Blessed Trinity. In a *lectio divina* mentioning the Great Commission (Mt 28:19), Pope Benedict XVI gave this reflection, which describes this reality:

> We have already heard that the Lord's last words to His disciples on this earth were: "Go therefore and make disciples of all nations, baptizing them in the Name of the Father and of the Son and of the Holy Spirit" (cf. Mt 28:19). Make disciples and baptize them. Why is it not enough for disciples to know Jesus' teaching, to know the Christian values? Why is it necessary to be baptized? This is the topic of our reflection, in order to understand the reality and depth of the Sacrament of Baptism. A first door opens if we read these words of the Lord carefully. The choice of the word "in the Name of the Father" in the Greek text is very important: the Lord says "eis" and not "en", that is, not "in the name" of the Trinity—as when we say that a vice-prefect speaks "on behalf" of the prefect, an ambassador speaks "on behalf" of the government: no. It says: "eis to onoma", that is, an immersion in the Name of the Trinity, a being inserted in the Name of the Trinity, an interpenetration of being in God and of our being, a being immersed in God the Trinity, Father, Son and Holy Spirit; just as it is in marriage, for example. Two people become one flesh, they become a new and unique reality with a new and unique name . . . Consequently, being baptized means being united to God; in a unique, new existence we belong to God [in and through His Son], we are immersed in God Himself.[182]
>
> | Pope Benedict XVI |

In His Son, we become a *new creation* (2 Cor 5:17), a *chosen race*, and a *holy nation* (1 Pt 2:9-10)—we become God the Father's *very own* (1 Pt 2:10).

As a result of the special love which is now bestowed upon us through our baptism—and in our becoming adopted children—we also become "royal priesthood" (1 Pt 2:9). As we are baptized, we are pronounced to be priest, prophet, and king.

We partake in the priesthood of the Messiah, as we offer spiritual worship and sacrifices through Him.

We participate in the prophetic ministry of the Messiah, as we are a witness of Him.

We share in that kingly ministry of the Messiah, as we spread His Kingdom, "namely, a Kingdom of truth and life, a Kingdom of holiness and grace, a Kingdom of justice, love and peace. In this Kingdom creation itself will be delivered from its slavery to corruption into the freedom of the glory of the sons of God" (Rom 8:21).[183]

In our baptism, we share in this triple-office of the Messiah. In humility, we Christians must take hold of the honour He has bestowed upon us—that we "may know what is the hope that belongs to His call, what are the riches of glory in His inheritance" (Eph 1:18). We should not diminish the hope, wealth, and dignity of this honour—"for we are the temple of the living God" (2 Cor 6:16). Scripture clearly tells us that in Him, God the Father bestows on us "every spiritual blessing in the Heavens" (Eph 1:3; also cf. Isa 61:10), this includes the triple-office of the Messiah (*Note*[184]).

Again, all this happens because in our baptism we have been baptized into His death and resurrection. This is a profound mystery, which is illustrated in the discussion Jesus had with Nicodemus (Jn 3:1-8). Jesus tells Nicodemus, "I say to you, no one can see the kingdom of God without being born from above" (Jn 3:3). "How can a person once grown old be born again? Surely he cannot reenter his mother's womb and be born again, can he?" (Jn 3:4), Nicodemus confusingly asks. Yet, in our baptism we are born again; we are born from above (see Jn 3:6-7).

In his letter to the Romans, Saint Paul asks: "Are you unaware that we who were baptized into [*Yahshua* (יֵשׁוּעַ) the *Mâshîyach* (מָשִׁיחַ)] were baptized into His death?" (Rom 6:3).

As we are plunged into the primordial waters of baptism "we were indeed buried with Him through baptism into death" (Rom 6:4a; also cf. Col 2:12). As we are raised "just as [the] Christ was raised from the dead by the glory of the Father" we are also raised so that "we might live in newness of life" (Rom 6:4b; also cf. Eph 2:5-6). We are now re-born through our baptism in Jesus the Messiah. We are made *anew*. We are *a new creation*.

In that plunge into the water, we also die to sinful flesh (cf. Jn 3:6 and Rom 6:1-4). Sin need not have any power over us (Rom 6:14). Jesus bore our sins on the Cross; therefore, it is upon the Cross in His *death* that we are made righteous (1 Pt 2:24 and Rom 8:10).

Through *Yahshua* (יֵשׁוּעַ) the *Mâshîyach* (מָשִׁיחַ), we received a new life. Our baptism is a life-changing ontological event. In this ontological change—through our baptism into His death and resurrection—His very life becomes ours. This is a mysterious and profound transformation. There is *absolutely* nothing we can do to bestow upon ourselves a greater dignity than this.

In addition, as we will also discuss in Chapter 7, pietistic practices (rosaries, novena prayers, and the like) done for all the right reasons are highly beneficial as we submit to the process of our sanctification journey (cf. 1 Tm 4:7-8). Private consecrations may also help us in our sanctification response. Nevertheless, praying one thousand rosaries or multiple consecrations will not and cannot bestow upon us a greater dignity than which was bestowed upon us in our baptism.

The key is that we must live out this baptismal change. That is to say, our calling now is to live out this dignity that He has bestowed upon us (*Note*[185]). Yes, we must "live in a manner worthy of the call [we] have received" (Eph 4:1). "Let us cleanse ourselves from every defilement of flesh and spirit, making holiness perfect in the fear of God" (2 Cor 7:1).

We are re-born of the Spirit (see Jn 3:6). Just like branches receive their life, nutrition, and sustenance from a tree, we are grafted into the very life of the Messiah, whose very life and Spirit pass through to us, the branches (Jn 15:5 and Rom 11:17).

He is our Source, His Light becomes our light, we are not autonomous—we become His *Ekklēsia* (ἐκκλησία). We are completely dependent on Him (1 Pt 1:3). This is a profound union that goes beyond any human comprehension. This is a transforming ontological change. Commit to memory the day of your baptism (your most important date of birth), for it is this day that we are *born again in Him*, and made a *new creation in Him* (2 Cor 5:17; also cf. Gal 3:26).

Some of you reading this might think, my life does not feel like it is a *new creation*. May I suggest that we answer this dilemma in three different ways?

First, note Saint Paul's proclamation: "I am crucified with Christ, it is no longer I who live, but [the] Christ who lives in me" (Gal 2:20). In our baptism there is the old "I" who no longer lives (i.e., dies), and a new "I" that now lives (i.e., been raised from the dead). There is still an "I" but a new "I"—a new self (Eph 4:24 and Col 3:10)—has been imparted.

Using the words we studied earlier, *zōē* (ζωή) this new life is a spiritual life, a fullness of life, genuine life. We may say it is the new self, the new "I"; *bios* (βίος) is the old "I" the fleshly-self that now has died, but lives as *zōē* (ζωή). "If anyone is in [the] Christ, he is a new creation; the old has passed away, behold, the new has come" (2 Cor 5:17). Therefore, we must now live in the "I" of *zōē* (ζωή).

Second, without getting too philosophical, dare we liken this change to what happens in the Eucharist? On the one hand, we still physically see bread and wine. We may argue that there is no difference in the bread or wine before or after consecration. On the other hand, the bread and wine goes through an ontological change, and thus becomes the real Body and Blood of the Messiah.

Third, the above emphasis has been on the objective aspect of our baptism. However, we cannot ignore the subjective aspect, how it affects you and me personally (as alluded to in the first way). Both aspects are important, we should not ignore or minimalize either one.

Subjectively, we may choose to remain in the "I" of *bios* (βίος). Note the admonition from Saint Paul to the church in Corinth (which would have consisted of mainly baptized individuals):

> Brothers and sisters, I could not talk to you as spiritual people [e.g., in the realm of *zōē* (ζωή)], but as fleshly people [e.g., in the realm of *bios* (βίος)], as infants in [the] Christ. I fed you milk, not solid food, because you were unable to take it. Indeed, you are still not able, even now, for you are still of the flesh [e.g., even after baptism they remained in the realm

of *bios* (βίος)]. While there is jealousy and rivalry among you, are you not of the flesh [e.g., the trait or indication that they are still in the realm of *bios* (βίος)], and behaving in an ordinary human way? (1 Cor 3:1-3).

In Chapter 8, "Rejoice . . . Always!" we will give this some further attention; for now, however, we should note that we *will* experience the fullness of this change at the *Parousia*, when "the trumpet will sound, the dead will be raised incorruptible," for "in an instant, in the blink of an eye" those who are remaining on earth shall also be changed (1 Cor 15:52). We will now fully experience the physical reality of being a *new creation* in Him. "He will change our lowly body to conform with His glorified body" (Phil 3:21). We will now participate in the fullness of His resurrection (*Note*[186]).

This event is not resuscitation or reincarnation. For example, the raising of Lazarus was a resuscitation (*Note*[187]). Eventually, Lazarus died an ordinary, earthly death. The concept of reincarnation, taught by Eastern religions and New Age philosophies, is not congruent with Christian theology, anthropology, or science (*Note*[188]).

In contrast, Jesus' body was physically resurrected from the dead. The bodily resurrection of the Messiah is a foundational belief with historical evidence. It is one of a kind. This is not reincarnation, in which the soul is living in a totally different body, nor resuscitation, in which, the body is brought back to life but will eventually experience an earthly death.

The Christ was raised from the dead, and so will we be bodily raised (1 Cor 15:13). If the Christ was not raised from the dead (*Note*[189]) our faith is futile (1 Cor 15:17). If the Christ was not raised from the dead, we are living a fraud. "We are the most pitiable people of all" (1 Cor 15:19).

The resurrected body of Jesus is the *same* body, but different in attributes (Phil 3:21). For example, when the resurrected Jesus encounters Mary Magdalene, she confuses Him for the gardener (Jn 20:15). He was different. Then she recognized Him when He called her by name (Jn 20:16). He was somehow the same.

On the road to Emmaus the two disciples were chatting with the resurrected Jesus for quite some time but they did not recognize Him

(Lk 24:15-28). He was different. Then the two of them recognized Him, in the breaking of the bread (Lk 24:30-31). He was somehow the same.

At the Sea of Tiberius, the resurrected Jesus appeared to seven of His disciples (Jn 21-2). Well into their encounter with the resurrected Jesus, it is stated that: "Now none of the disciples dared ask Him, 'Who are you?'" (Jn 21:12). Interesting. Why would that be an issue? At this point they all knew it was the risen Lord (Jn 21:7 and 21:12), so He was the same, but something was clearly different, hence the questioning in silence (Lk 24:37-38).

In His bodily resurrection, the risen Jesus was the same, e.g., He ate and drank with His disciples (Acts 10:41; also cf. Lk 24:41-42), and He showed them the wounds He received on the Cross (Lk 24:39-40 and Jn 20:27). It was the *same* body. However, He was different, e.g., He walked through walls (Jn 20:19 and 24:26; also cf. *CCC* #999), and He could just vanish from sight (Lk 24:31).

Some scholars say that Jesus' resurrected body was restored at a particular age (e.g., age 18), hence the non-recognition. Others state that the disciples were kept from recognizing Him (see Lk 24:16), that is, the resurrected Jesus could change His appearance. Both are interesting speculations, but it still does not fully account for the confusion at the Sea of Tiberius, which clearly happens after they knew that it was He. At that point, why did He continue to veil Himself?

I think that the most vivid analogy I have heard is the metamorphosis of the butterfly. In this analogy, our physical bodies are now in the state of a caterpillar. In our death, we enter the tomb, or the cocoon. In our resurrection, we break out of the tomb, leaving the cocoon behind; we are now this beautiful butterfly, in our resurrected body—the *glorified body*. Our DNA is the same. On the one hand, it is the *same* body, for the caterpillar is no longer in the cocoon. On the other hand, it is different. The resurrected body is no longer crawling around—it is soaring to the heights. Unless we are aware, we will not recognize one (the caterpillar) from the other (the butterfly), but both are the same individual (cf. Phil 3:21).

This is what Scripture tells us about the resurrected body:

> [So,] someone may say, How are the dead raised?

> With what kind of body will they come back? You fool! What you sow is not brought to life unless it dies. And what you sow is not the body that is to be but a bare kernel of wheat, perhaps, or of some other kind; but God gives it a body as he chooses, and to each of the seeds its own body. Not all flesh is the same, but there is one kind for human beings, another kind of flesh for animals, another kind of flesh for birds, and another for fish. There are both Heavenly bodies and earthly bodies, but the brightness of the Heavenly is one kind and that of the earthly another. The brightness of the sun is one kind, the brightness of the moon another, and the brightness of the stars another. For star differs from star in brightness. So also is the resurrection of the dead. It is sown corruptible; it is raised incorruptible. It is sown dishonorable; it is raised glorious. It is sown weak; it is raised powerful. It is sown a natural body; it is raised a spiritual body. If there is a natural body, there is also a spiritual one. So, too, it is written, The first man, Adam, became a living being, the last Adam a life-giving spirit. But the spiritual was not first; rather the natural and then the spiritual. The first man was from the earth, earthly; the second man, from Heaven. As was the earthly one, so also are the earthly, and as is the Heavenly one, so also are the Heavenly. Just as we have borne the image of the earthly one, we shall also bear the image of the Heavenly one. (1 Cor 15:35-49)

Now we see dimly, but then we will see with total clarity (1 Cor 13:12). We do not fully know what we will be, "but we know that when He appears we shall be like Him, for we shall see Him as He is" (1 Jn 3:2). Baptized into His death and resurrection, we are born again to a living hope:

> Blessed be the God and Father of our Lord Jesus [the] Christ, who in His great mercy gave us a new

> birth to a living hope through the resurrection of Jesus [the] Christ from the dead, to an inheritance that is imperishable, undefiled, and unfading, kept in Heaven for you who by the power of God are safeguarded through faith, to a Salvation that is ready to be revealed in the final time. In this you rejoice, although now for a little while you may have to suffer through various trials, so that the genuineness of your faith, more precious than gold that is perishable although tested by fire, may prove to be for praise, glory, and honour at the revelation of Jesus [the] Christ. (1 Pt 1:3-7)

We usually place our emphasis on the resurrection. In fact, this is rightly so. Consider Saint Paul's statement: "if [the Messiah] has not been raised, then empty too is our preaching; empty, too, your faith" (1 Cor 15:14).

Yes, if Jesus the Messiah had not been bodily resurrected, our faith is in vain (1 Cor 15:17). If that is the case we might as well just party: "let us eat and drink, for tomorrow we die" (1 Cor 15:32). If the resurrection did not happen, we are the most pitiable of people, Saint Paul also tells the Corinthian church, and by extension tells us (1 Cor 15:19).

However, we cannot hold the theology of the Cross and the Resurrection without holding the theology of the Incarnation. The sacrifice, the Messiah's death and resurrection, is not possible if He did not take on a body (Heb 2:14). Bethlehem, Golgotha, and the empty tomb cannot be separated. All three are one event—the Christ Event. All three ontologically change who we are, collectively as one body, the Church and individually as part of that body.

This interwoven connection between Christmas and Easter was vividly demonstrated by the life of Saint Francis. Like most of us, Saint Francis went through many conversion experiences. As his conversion journey unfolded, Saint Francis saw a connection between the events of Christmas and Easter. His devotion to the Cross brought about a profound vision of the incarnation. He identified a unique humility in the incarnation of Jesus the Christ. Both Christmas and Easter intersect. Understanding this, he created a re-enactment of the Nativity in Greccio:

> Finally, the day of joy has drawn near;
> the time of exultation has come.
> From many different places
> the brethren have been called.
> As they could,
> the men and women of that land with exultant hearts
> prepare candles and torches to light up that night
> whose shining star has enlightened every day and year.
> Finally, the holy man of God comes
> and, finding all things prepared,
> he saw them and was glad.
> Indeed, the manger is prepared,
> the hay is carried in,
> and the ox and the ass are led to the spot.
> There simplicity is given a place of honour,
> poverty is exalted,
> humility is commended,
> and out of Greccio is made a new Bethlehem.[190]
>
> | *The Life of Saint Francis* |

When we look at paintings depicting this scene of Christmas in Greccio you will notice that at a far distance, or sometimes even in the hand of Saint Francis, you see a crucifix or a cross.

I have personally made this a part of my Nativity scene. Every year in setting up the scene, I place a small, olive-wood cross, which I got from Bethlehem, at a distance, thus reminding myself of the magnificent interwoven tapestry of God the Father's plan in His Son, which ontologically changed me.

The God of the universe becomes human.
Therefore, should we not ask *Why*?

Chapter 6 | Why the Incarnation?

We ended the last chapter stating that the incarnation, the death, and resurrection of His Son, was God the Father's plan. With that, now we turn to the question: Why was this His plan?

- Why the incarnation of the Christ?
- Why the death of the Christ?
- Why the resurrection of the Christ?

Since we are defining the Christ Event as the unified accomplishment of Jesus the Christ while on earth seen in three aspects, His incarnation (Christmas), His death, and His resurrection (Easter/Paschal Triduum), we may ask:

- Why the Christ Event?

Important to note, that concerning this question, we are not arrogantly questioning God's judgment with reference to the nature of His plan; we are simply seeking to understand His purpose behind it. What can we learn about God and His purposes in examining these three events? In this, we ask *Him*: Why did *You*, God's Son, the God of the universe, go through all that You did?

We are approaching this question regarding His purpose in *humility*, knowing that our brains are finite, and thus, we will never be able to totally comprehend this ineffable mystery.

We will study this question in the two main parts, considering the second and third events together. Using Scripture as our guide, the answer to the first part— Why the Incarnation?—is found in the first part of John 3:16: "For God so loved the world that He gave His only Son" (Jn 3:16a; also cf. 1 Jn 4:9a), which is the question of this chapter. In the next chapter, to answer the second part—Why the death and resurrection?—we will look at the second part of this verse:

"so that everyone who believes in Him might not perish but might have eternal life" (Jn 3:16b; also cf. 1 Jn 4:9b).

Why the incarnation? The most succinct answer is: *love*. The Creator of the universe loved us, His creation, so much that He becomes one of us (Jn 3:16a). This is the greatest love the world has ever known. This is *the greatest love of all* (not what Whitney Houston sang)! The incarnation gives life true meaning; this is what we celebrate at Christmas (Lk 2:12). As we said in the Introduction, the absolute fullness of God's Being is revealed in that little Baby Boy, wrapped in swaddling clothes, lying in a manger. This is truly mind blowing.

Some of us might remember the lyrics from the children's song, *Jesus loves me*. Here is a condensed version:

Jesus loves me!
This I know,
for the Bible tells me so.
Yes, Jesus loves me!
Yes, Jesus loves me!
Yes, Jesus loves me!
The Bible tells me so.

In the simplicity of this song there is much truth. However, as adults we must go deeper and understand what His *love* for us means. That is, when Saint John writes, "God so loved the world that He gave His only Son" (Jn 3:16a), what does this really mean (*Note*[191])?

First, the Greek word that is translated into the English word *love*, is ἀγάπη (agape/*agápā*), meaning sacrificial, self-sacrificing, unselfish, selfless love. This *love* is unconditional, unlimited, and an uncalculated love. It is also the love used to define covenant love or the downward movement from God to us.[192]

Society does not define love in this way. To society, love is mainly associated with emotion, feeling, impulse, affection, inclination, or sentiment. Although *agape* (ἀγάπη) does not exclude affectivity, the secular understanding of *love* is not *agape* (ἀγάπη). This love, *agape* (ἀγάπη), is not fleeting affection; it is not subjective;

and it is an objective, unblemished love. Such love goes beyond emotions and feelings to a rational act of the will. The incarnation is about God the Father's infinite *agape* (ἀγάπη) for us. Jesus, in obedience to the Father, takes on a body (celebrated at Christmas) to carry out God the Father's will in His death and resurrection (celebrated at Easter).

This *agape* (ἀγάπη) in the temporal life is revealed as *mercy*: i.e., He gave His only Son (Jn 3:16a). As written in the encyclical *Dives in Misericordia* (*On the Mercy of God*):

> In the eschatological fulfillment mercy will be revealed as love, while in the temporal phase, in human history, which is at the same time the history of sin and death, love must be revealed above all as mercy and must also be actualized as mercy.[193]
>
> | Saint Pope John Paul II |

Through His mercy we received the fullness of grace (i.e., divine assistance) needed to mend our enmity and estrangement from God.

Consequently, what do these two words—mercy and grace—mean? In Hebrew, there are two predominant words used for mercy. The first word is חֶסֶד (chêsêd/*kheh'-sed*), transliterated into English as *hesed*. The second Hebrew word is רָחַם (râcham/*raw-kham'*); transliterated into English as *rahamim* (*Note*[194]). It is unfortunate that we translate these two different Hebrew words and their meanings into only one English word: *mercy*.

Moreover, according to *Mounce's Dictionary*, *hesed* (חֶסֶד) "is one of the richest, most theologically insightful terms in the Old Testament"; for that reason, *hesed* (חֶסֶד) "cannot be adequately translated into many languages, including English."[195] Gordon Clark would concur, adding that *hesed* (חֶסֶד) "is not merely an attitude or an emotion; it is an emotion that leads to an activity beneficial to the recipient."[196] For it not only denotes kindness, loving-kindness, love, loyal-love, loyalty, and mercy, but also it most poignantly denotes covenant-love, "employed in the context of relationship between God and humans"[197]—in which the recipient is the beneficiary. In addition, in this Hebrew word, we not only have the meaning for *grace* and mercy as a gift but the meaning of legal quality or the *justice* of mercy.

However, when translating *hesed* (חֶסֶד) into Greek (the Septuagint), the translators used the Greek word ἔλεος (eleos/*el'-eh-os*). In turn, Saint Jerome translates it into the Latin word *misericordia*. Both *eleos* (ἔλεος) and *misericordia* predominantly mean *mercy* in English. We should note that *eleos* (ἔλεος) is linked to the Greek word *agape* (ἀγάπη) and *misericordia* is linked to its Latin equivalent, *cāritās* (charity). With this, we can see how the English word *mercy* (which is rooted in the Latin word *misericordia*) is also linked to love.

The second Hebrew word is *rahamim* (רָחַם). According to *Mounce's Dictionary*, this word means to have compassion on, show mercy, take pity on; to find compassion, be loved; feelings of compassion are usually accompanied by acts of compassion.[198] This act of compassion is a love from the *womb,* so to speak, because *rahamim* (רָחַם) is rooted in motherly love. It is therefore a mercy that is unmerited and undeserved. We see a combination of both *hesed* (חֶסֶד) and *rahamim* (רָחַם) in our English word, *mercy*.

"In the Old Testament, mercy is predicated of God (Deut 7:9), and His attitude toward the repentant sinner is mercy rather than punishment."[199] Divine mercy is real (Ex 34:6, Ps 86:15, and 103:8), and *Yahshua* (יֵשׁוּעַ) *is* the face of this reality. Despite our human parents' disobedience (Gen 3:6), a promise of mercy is given (Gen 3:15), and in the fullness of time, this promise is carried out *in* and *through* Jesus the Anointed (Gal 4:4). This is the reality of divine mercy; it is *the* act of a God who saves us. We would *not* exist, the cosmos would not exist without God's *agape* (ἀγάπη), without God's mercy, without God's grace, without God's forgiveness, without God's saving act (Gen 6:5–7, Isa 48:9, and Ex 32:9–14). God keeps us physically alive despite our deserving death because of our sinful nature. In God's mercy, we see the *gift* of mercy from the word *hesed* (חֶסֶד), and we see the mercy that is *unmerited* and *undeserved* from the word *rahamim* (רָחַם). This is divine mercy. This is how God demonstrates His *agape* (ἀγάπη).

Although *hesed* (חֶסֶד) connotes grace, the word חֵן (chên/*khane*) is the actual Hebrew word for grace. This word appears almost 70 times in the Old Testament, however, most English Bibles translate this word as *favour*, it is translated as *grace* only about 10% of the time (*Note*[200]). We might argue that the reason for this is that in the Old Testament *chên* (חֵן) is more in tune with favour, and that it is only in the fullness of revelation that this meaning is taken a step further.

Thus, in the New Testament, the word χάρις (charis/*khar'-ece*), which is the Greek word for grace, is translated as *grace* about 80% of the time. Moreover, *charis* (χάρις) is directly tied to the incarnation (Jn 1:14). It was through Moses that the Law was given, and, the total realization of the Law was given through *Yahshua* (יֵשׁוּעַ) the Christ. His mission is a mission of "[*charis* (χάρις)] and truth" (Jn 1:17). In fact, "from His fullness we have all received, [*charis* (χάρις)] in place of [*charis* (χάρις)]" (Jn 1:16), or grace upon grace. The first *grace* is the grace of the Law, and upon that grace, more *grace* is given, which is the Messiah Himself. He is the fullness of *grace*, thus, the fulfillment of the Law. Here is how the *Catholic Encyclopedia* defines "grace":

> The term "grace" refers generally to any Divine assistance given to persons (human or angelic), in order to advance them toward their supernatural destiny of fellowship with God. In its most proper sense, grace transforms a person's nature so that it can function at an entirely new interpersonal level, where the object of knowledge and love is none other than God Himself and where other persons are known and loved in God. This new level of existence and activity is properly supernatural: It involves the transformation and elevation of the natural states and capacities of the creaturely person. Grace in this sense is traditionally termed habitual or sanctifying grace. This grace involves both the transformation of the whole nature and the infusion of dispositions (the theological virtues and the gifts of the Holy Spirit) that permit real engagement with the indwelling Triune God. As a quality transforming the soul in this way, grace is something created. But because the term "grace" refers also to the very indwelling of

> God, there is an important sense in which grace is uncreated, identical with God Himself.
>
> | *Catholic Encyclopedia* |

When we read this definition does it not harken back to what we studied in Chapter 5, An Ontological Event? Grace is God the Father's will *fully established* in His Son. God the Father's ultimate fulfillment of love is revealed through the action of sending His Son. *Yahshua* (יֵשׁוּעַ) is the incarnation of God's *agape* (ἀγάπη). He wants us to focus on His Son, and on the love He shows us in and through His Son. Jesus is the full actualization of the Father's *agape* (ἀγάπη) for us—which in temporal life is revealed by God's *mercy* and *grace*. In His mercy, we receive the fullness of *grace* (i.e., divine assistance) through His Son, thus removing our enmity to God (Eph 2:1-10). In Jesus His Son, our relationship with God the Father is reinitiated (Rev 21:5).

Let us state clearly: the *fullness* of God's love, mercy, and grace, is *only* in Jesus, His Son. Therefore *all* love, mercy, and grace comes *only* through His Son. God the Father's ultimate fulfillment of *agape* (ἀγάπη) is revealed in and through the action of sending His Son (Jn 3:16). "Once you were no people but now you are God's people; you had not received mercy but now you have received mercy" (1 Pt 2:10). This wonderful change from before (we were people without mercy) to after (we are now His people because of mercy) happens *only* because of Jesus the Christ. For that reason, it is only whoever believes in the Son who will have eternal life, "but whoever does not believe in the Son will not see life, but the wrath of God remains upon him" (Jn 3:36). In God's mercy we received the fullness of grace (i.e., divine assistance) in and through His Son—"through Whom we have gained access by faith to this grace in which we stand" (Rom 5:2)—which in faith is the *absolute only thing* needed to reverse enmity with God.

Now I say *thing*, but without offence, for as stated in the *Catholic Encyclopedia* "the term 'grace' refers also to the very indwelling of God; there is an important sense in which grace is uncreated, identical with God Himself"—i.e., His Son (*Note*[201]).

God the Father is not against us. He does not have a scale in which He is weighing our good deeds versus bad deeds. On the contrary, "God shows His love for us in that while we were yet sinners" He sent His Son (Rom 5:8) to show us His love, mercy, and grace (*Note*[202]). In this He shows us His Holiness. His love for us is not based upon how good we are (our good deeds) or on how bad we are (our bad deeds). For He does not give us what we justly deserve. In fact, in His grace He gives us—sinful disobedient creatures—His favour or grace which we do not deserve. He gives us an undeserved gift.

Here is a simple way of understanding the difference between grace and mercy that I once heard. God's *grace* is our receiving all the good things (favour) that we do not deserve—that is, we receive what we don't justly deserved (unmerited Divine favour). Moreover, through Jesus, we receive all the good things (favour) that only He deserves.

Mercy, on the other hand, is our not receiving all the bad things (or punishment) that we deserve—that is, we do not receive what we justly deserve. Moreover, Jesus took on our punishment that we justly deserve.

"In this is love, not that we loved God but that He loved us and sent His Son" (1 Jn 4:10). Although we made a mess of our lives, God loves us. He is on our side. In His love, He shows us His mercy and gives us His grace—with the ultimate fulfillment inherent in these three words—in His Son (*Note*[203]).

God did *not* need to create us. God created us because He *wanted* to, out of His *agape* (ἀγάπη) for us (*Note*[204]). In addition, the angels and the cosmos were all created, not to fulfill any *need* that God had, but purely out of *agape* (ἀγάπη). He created all of this because of His overabundant love. In that love, He is present with us *without* disturbing our autonomy.

We may thus argue that even hell[205] was created because of His total love for us. There are some scholars who are now arguing that: If there is a *hell* there is no one in it. If that conclusion is correct, God is *not* love. *Love* gives the other the freedom to decide without overpowering, overwhelming, duping, coercing, or twisting the other's arm. God would no longer be *agape* (ἀγάπη) if He somehow coerced us or *forced us* to be with Him in Heaven against our will. This is not *agape* (ἀγάπη). Scholars making this argument mainly base it upon a distorted notion of forgiveness and grace, by taking it to an extreme. Be that as it may, the argument totally ignores *love*, thus its conclusion becomes nonsensical.

God loves us so much that He gives us the free will to accept or decline His love. That is to say, God is with us in *agape* (ἀγάπη), but, does not force His *agape* (ἀγάπη) upon us. As a result, we have the God-given right to say "No" to Him, decline His offer of salvation, and thus choose not to be with Him in eternity—and He will honour that decision because He is *agape* (ἀγάπη). In that sense, God does not send us to hell—we decide to be sent there of our free will (cf. Jn 12-44-50). This is to say, hell is to be without God, which indeed is the torment; this is purely the result of our decision, not His. For *His will* is for us to be with Him (*CCC* #51 and #74).

God wants *all* of humanity to be with Him, to belong to Him, and have life purpose in Him (1 Tm 2:4), but He does so without taking away our free will. Because of the vastness of His love for us, He not only sent His Son to become a human being like we are, He also allowed His Son to die on the Cross for us, so we, the creature, may have eternal life with Him, the Creator. He does this without forcing any of this on us.

We tend to see the *love* of God *within the act* of sending His Son for us, and allowing Him to die on the Cross for us; but, I hope we also see the *humility* on the part of God *within this very act* of His *agape* (ἀγάπη). He "wills everyone to be saved and to come to knowledge of the Truth" (1 Tm 2:4); nevertheless, *He sets aside His own will in favour of ours*!

Let us now take a moment to revisit sections relevant to the incarnation from the three canticles that we studied. Each of them, in its own way, speaks of God's love for us. Remember, these canticles were formed as early Christian creeds, for there was no complete New Testament at that time in the early Church. The canticles speak to a very early understanding of the incarnation and God's love for us shown through His Son:

> Praised be the God and Father
> of our Lord Jesus [the] Christ,

who has bestowed on us in [the] Christ
every spiritual blessing in the Heavens.
God chose us in Him
before the world began
to be holy
and blameless in His sight.

He predestined us
to be His adopted sons through Jesus [the] Christ,
such was His will and pleasure,
that all might praise the glorious favour [grace, *charis* (χάρις)]
He has bestowed on us in His beloved.

In Him and through His blood, we have been redeemed,
and our sins forgiven,
so immeasurably generous
is God's favour [grace, *charis* (χάρις)] to us.

| Canticle – Ephesians 1:3-7[206] |

Though He was in the form of God,
Jesus did not deem equality with God
something to be grasped at.

Rather, [God the Son] emptied Himself
and took the form of a slave,
being born in the likeness of men.

| Canticle – Philippians 2:6-7[207] |

[*Yahshua* (יֵשׁוּעַ) the Christ] is the image of the invisible God,
the first-born of all creatures.
In [Jesus] everything in Heaven and on earth was created,
things visible and invisible.

All were created through Him;
all were created for Him.
He is before all else that is.
In Him everything continues in being.

It pleased God
to make absolute fullness reside in Him
and, by means of Him,
to reconcile everything in His Person,
both on earth and in the Heavens,
making peace through the blood of His Cross.
| Canticle – Colossians 1:15-17; 19-20[208] |

God the Father blesses us with every spiritual blessing (Eph 1:3). The ultimate blessing is the incarnation of His very Son, in whom we are selected to be sons and daughters by adoption (Eph 1:4-5). In His Son, enmity has been removed according to the riches of His favour—His *charis* (χάρις) for us (Eph 1:7).

Yahshua (יֵשׁוּעַ), Who is God Himself, does not cling or exploit His Godliness for personal gain, but releases His rightful dignity, strips Himself of all privileges, and becomes like us. In fact, the actual word used here is: He becomes a *slave*—δοῦλος (doulos/*doo'-los*)—for us (Phil 2:6-7). Thus, in this Christ Event—in Jesus the *Mâshîyach* (מָשִׁיחַ)—we have been rescued and reconciled in His very Person (Col 1:12-20). This is God the Father's plan. This is God's love *agape* (ἀγάπη), mercy *hesed* (חֶסֶד) and *rahamim* (רַחַם), and grace *charis* (χάρις) for us!

> "O blessed light, O Trinity and first Unity!" God is eternal blessedness, undying life, unfading light. God is love: Father, Son, and Holy Spirit. God freely wills to communicate the glory of His blessed life. Such is the "plan of His loving kindness," conceived by the Father before the foundation of the world, in His beloved Son: "He destined us in love to be His sons" and "to be conformed to the image of His Son," through the "spirit of sonship" [Eph 1:4-5 and Rom 8:15]. This plan is a "grace [which] was given to us in [Jesus the Christ] before the ages began," stemming immediately from Trinitarian love [2 Tm 1:9-10]. It unfolds in the work of creation, the whole history of salvation after the fall, and the missions of

> the Son and the Spirit, which are continued in the mission of the Church. (*CCC* #257)

As mentioned in the Introduction, Christianity depends on the identity of a Person and then on our *covenant-relationship* with that Person. It all begins and hinges upon His identity, and on our response to His identity.

Here is how Pope Benedict XVI put it, "Being a Christian is not the result of an ethical choice or a lofty idea, but the encounter with an event, a Person, which gives life a new horizon and a decisive direction."[209]

Jesus is not merely a religious leader among leaders. He is not simply someone we should mimic or follow, or some sort of ideal we should try to attain. Again, "Being a Christian is not the result of an ethical choice or a lofty idea"[210] such as, being a good person or keeping the Law. Being a Christian is an encounter with the Christ Event. It is an encounter with God, revealed in the Person of *Yahshua* (יֵשׁוּעַ) the *Mâshîyach* (מָשִׁיחַ), His Son. Once we have experienced this encounter we must respond to it. Not as if it is just another historical event, but *the* Event, which gives history all its meaning. Not as if He is just another being, but *the* Being, Who gives life all its meaning. He is the true meaning of life; accordingly, it is only He Who gives our lives meaning.

All told, our lives must respond and ultimately reflect this covenant-relationship with Him. This is the time we live in: a time of His favour, a time of His grace *charis* (χάρις). Use it! Take full advantage of it.

Following is an image based on Scripture that has been used throughout the centuries to help us further understand God's *agape* (ἀγάπη) and this covenant-relationship with Him. It is the image of a man's love for a woman, specifically, a husband's love for his wife (Isa 62:5).

Jesus is the Bridegroom, we, the Church, are His bride. We are "called to the wedding feast of the Lamb" (Rev 19:9). He wants and, desires to marry us. He wants a *covenant-relationship* with us. However, a man cannot force a woman to marry him; likewise, Jesus will not force His *agape* (ἀγάπη) on us. As a woman may reject a man, even when he is on bended-knee asking her to marry him, we may also reject Him.

Moreover, we were not created to love God mindlessly. With free will, we have the power to enter into that *covenant-relationship* with our Creator, or say *no*. The choice is ours. However, if we say *yes*, like a marriage, this relationship is permanent. This requires a continual daily choosing on our part to remain in fellowship by accepting His *agape* (ἀγάπη).

Jesus loves us! Despite our faults and failings, He loves us. Even if we are unfaithful, He is faithful (2 Tm 2:13). He loves us unconditionally, even if His *agape* (ἀγάπη) for us is not reciprocated.

The incarnation, which we celebrate every Christmas, gives our lives its true meaning. The fullness of God's Being is revealed to you and me in Jesus the Christ. This is the first part of John 3:16: "God so loved the world that He gave His only Son" (Jn 3:16a; also cf. 1 Jn 4:9a).

Let us now prayerfully reflect on the following Scripture passages as we move to the next chapter, the second part of this verse: "that whoever believes in Him [i.e., our choice and response to Him] should not perish but have eternal life" (Jn 3:16b; also cf. 1 Jn 4:9b), which is the necessary faith response to His love, mercy, and grace (*Note*[211]).

> God, who is rich in mercy, because of the great love He had for us, even when we were dead in our transgressions, brought us to life with [the] Christ (by grace you have been saved), raised us up with Him, and seated us with Him in the Heavens in [*Yahshua* (יֵשׁוּעַ) the *Mâshîyach* (מָשִׁיחַ)], that in the ages to come He might show the immeasurable riches of His grace in His kindness to us in [*Yahshua* (יֵשׁוּעַ) the *Mâshîyach* (מָשִׁיחַ)]. For by grace you have been saved through faith, and this is not from you; it is the gift of God; it is not from works, so no one may boast. (Eph 2:4-9)

> Whoever is without [*agape* (ἀγάπη)] does not know

God, for God is [*agape* (ἀγάπη)]. In this way the love of God was revealed to us: God sent His only Son into the world so that we might have life through Him. In this is [*agape* (ἀγάπη)]: not that we have loved God, but that He loved us and sent His Son as expiation for our sins. (1 Jn 4:8-10)

Moreover, we have seen and testify that the Father sent His Son as Saviour of the world. Whoever acknowledges that Jesus is the Son of God, God remains in him and he in God. We have come to know and to believe in the [*agape* (ἀγάπη)] God has for us. God is [*agape* (ἀγάπη)], and whoever remains in love remains in God and God in him. In this is love brought to perfection among us, that we have confidence on the day of judgment because as He is, so are we in this world. There is no fear in [*agape* (ἀγάπη)], but perfect love drives out fear because fear has to do with punishment, and so one who fears is not yet perfect in love. (1 Jn 4:14-18)

The God of the universe goes through His Passion.
Therefore, should we not ask *Why*?

Chapter 7 | Why the Death and Resurrection?

Before we begin this chapter, let us briefly remind ourselves of the three things we discussed at the beginning of the preceding chapter. First, the Christ Event is one event; nevertheless, for study purposes we are looking at it through Jesus' incarnation, and death and resurrection.

Second, the question we ask in the chapter title is faith-filled, not a skeptical one. We acknowledge that there was no plan "B" for the Christ Event!

Third, this is a mystery, so we sit at His feet and ask this question in humility.

Having looked at the incarnation, ("God so loved the world that He gave His only Son"—Jn 3:16a), and in that context studied the words, *love*, *mercy*, and *grace*; we now move in this chapter to Jesus' death and resurrection ("that whoever believes in Him should not perish but have eternal life"—Jn 3:16b), and in this context, we will study the words, *atonement*, *righteousness*, *justification*, and *sanctification*.

To do this, let us revisit the sections pertaining to Jesus' death and resurrection from the three canticles we studied, and then, we will take a brief Scriptural overview of the Christ Event, and then work our way through this question.

Each canticle in its own way speaks of the death and resurrection of God's Son—our Messiah:

> [The Son of God] was known to be of human estate,
> and it was thus that
> [Second Person of the Trinity] humbled Himself,
> obediently accepting even death,
> death on a Cross
> | Canticle – Philippians 2:7-8[212] |

In [*Yahshua* (יֵשׁוּעַ)] and through His blood, we have been redeemed,
and our sins forgiven,
so immeasurably generous
is God's favour [grace, *charis* (χάρις)] to us
| Canticle – Ephesians 1:7[213] |

It pleased God to make absolute fullness
reside in [His Son, *Yahshua* (יֵשׁוּעַ) the Messiah]
and, by means of Him, to reconcile everything in His Person,
both on earth and in the Heavens,
making peace through the blood of His Cross.
| Canticle – Colossians 1:13-14; 19-20[214] |

Recall that these canticles were formed as early Christian creeds, and thus they speak to a very early understanding of the Messiah's death and resurrection.

The following is a brief Scriptural overview of the Christ Event.

God *is agape* (ἀγάπη), as Saint John boldly proclaims; He is the ultimate source of love; and, He loves all humanity (1 Jn 4:16). In His love for us He shows us mercy and gives us grace, through the ultimate fulfillment of His *agape* (ἀγάπη), by sending His Son as a human. What is more, God visibly *proves* His *agape* (ἀγάπη) for us (although He does not have to), by the fact that "while we were still sinners" He allows—in fact, He wills (Lk 22:42)—His very own Son to die for us on the Cross for all of humanity (Rom 5:8). In this act of love, through His Son, God ensures that our sins may be forgiven; those who through faith believe in the Christ, God declares them righteous before Him (Rom 5:1). God the Father allows His Son to ransom, redeem, purchase us—human beings—for Him from every, tribe, language, people, and nation (Rev 5:9).

Through faith in the *Mâshîyach* (מָשִׁיחַ), we have peace with God the Father in and through God the Son, *Yahshua* (יֵשׁוּעַ) the Messiah (Rom 5:1). Through Jesus the Christ, we, by faith, have access to this amazing state of grace, in which we may stand firm (Rom 5:2). When we acknowledge this fact—that Jesus is the Messiah, He is our

Saviour, He is our God, and He is the *only* One Who reconciles us to God—God abides in us and we abide in Him (1 Jn 4:14-15), that is, the enmity between God and us is no longer. That is why. although it's illogical from an unbeliever's perspective, we proclaim the Christ crucified (1 Cor 1:22-25) and we only boast in the Cross of the Messiah (Gal 6:14). As we pray on the Feast of The Exaltation of the Holy Cross (the Feast day I selected to publish this book):

How radiant is that precious Cross which brought us our salvation.
In the Cross we are victorious,
through the Cross we shall reign,
by the Cross all evil is destroyed.
Death itself died when life was slain on the tree.[215]

Now, in this *covenant-relationship* with Jesus the *Mâshîyach* (מָשִׁיחַ), "love is completed *and* perfected with us, so that we may have confidence in the Day of Judgment," that is, confidence to face God the Father because as Jesus the Christ is, and was, in this world, "so are we [now] in this world" (1 Jn 4:18[216]). Therefore, in *Yahshua* (יֵשׁוּעַ) the *Mâshîyach* (מָשִׁיחַ) there should be absolutely no *fear* for the Christian on this earth, and no fear of final judgment, for

> we have peace with God [the Father] through our Lord Jesus [the] Christ, through whom we have gained access (by faith) to this grace in which we stand. (Rom 5:1-2)
>
> [T]here is no fear in love [*dread does not exist*]. But perfect (complete, full-grown) love drives out fear, because fear involves [*the expectation of divine*] punishment, so the one who is afraid [*of God's judgment*] is not perfected in love [*has not grown into a sufficient understanding of God's love*]. (1 Jn 4:18[217])

We Christians need to firmly and resolutely grasp this fact! Here is succinct summation is from the letter to the Hebrews:

> Since [*these His*] children share in flesh and blood [*the physical nature of mankind*], He Himself in a similar manner also shared in the same [*physical nature, but without sin*], so that through [*experiencing*] death He might make powerless (ineffective, impotent) him who had the power of death—that is, the devil—and [*that He*] might free all those who through [*the haunting*] fear of death were held in slavery throughout their lives. For, as we all know, He (the Christ) does not take hold of [*the fallen*] angels [*to give them a helping hand*], but He does take hold of [*the fallen*] descendants of Abraham [*extending to them His hand of deliverance*] [Isa 41:8-0]. Therefore, *it was essential that* He had to be made like His brothers (mankind) in every respect, so that He might [*by experience*] become a merciful and faithful High Priest in things related to God, to make atonement for the people's sins [*thereby wiping away the sin, and providing a way of reconciliation between God and mankind*]. Because He Himself [*in His humanity*] has suffered in being tempted, He is able to help *and* provide immediate assistance to those who are being tempted *and* exposed to suffering. (Heb 2:14-18[218])

With this brief Scriptural overview of the Christ Event, we will now turn our attention to the question of this chapter: Why the Death and Resurrection?

Using the same method from the previous chapter (as we looked separately at the words *love, mercy,* and *grace* in connection with the incarnation), in this chapter we will also treat the four aspects of the Messiah's death and resurrection separately; by first looking at the words *atonement* and *righteousness* in connection with the Christ's death, and then, the words *justification* and *sanctification* in connection with His resurrection. Although we are separating this for the ease of study, keep in mind that the four aspects are integrated—we must hold all four aspects as a continuous and unified thought.

Just a reminder as we study this question, the Christ Event as a whole is far more multifaceted than our finite minds may handle. Therefore, our proper disposition as we study this should be a disposition of mystery, adoration, and awe.

Aspect Number 1, Atonement: The first aspect in relation to the Christ's death is *atonement.* Traditionally atonement has been thought of as appeasement, but the more accurate or primarily definition would be: reconciliation. To appease, or other words used, such as, to cover up, or propitiate, or reparation, or to wipe clean, or to blot out, or to purge, have more to do with how that reconciliation is brought about. Many theories of atonement have been put forward throughout the centuries dating back to the Early Church Fathers (*Note*[219]).

> Theories that emphasize the love and obedience of [the] Christ in suffering for our sake are preferable to those theories (either penal or substitutional) that center on the appeasement of divine wrath or the ransom paid to Satan.[220]
>
> | *Catholic Encyclopedia* |

It is also important to note that,

> the New Testament witness does not put forth any theory of atonement but makes clear that [the] Christ is the Source of "at-one-ment" (Middle English for "atonement") with God (Mk 10:45, Rom 5:10, Eph 2:13,1 Pt 2:24, Heb 9:28, and 2 Cor 5:19).[221]
>
> | *Catholic Encyclopedia* |

The etymology of the English word, *at-one-ment,* signifies unity. That unity is brought about *only through* Jesus the Messiah. He is the *only* One Who can repair the rift between humanity and God. He is the only One Who brings about *at-one-ment*. We can explicitly say this without stating *how* that was accomplished.

As stated, the Christ Event is complex. If the New Testament writers did not present a clear theory of atonement, may we conclude that this is meant to be a mystery? We can use finite words to somewhat apprehend such mystery, yet all the while acknowledging that no singular theory can suffice in giving us total comprehension.

The usual understanding of atonement is that *we* have to do the work (or some of the work) in order to obtain reconciliation; however, atonement completely is God's act, and thus, various sacrifices foreshadowed the Messiah's ultimate and only effective sacrifice. Goats and bulls were merely placeholders, pointing forward to the fulfillment in the Messiah (Heb 10:1-6). As the letter to the Hebrews states, "it is impossible that the blood of bulls and goats should take away sins" (Heb 10:4).

As we just read in the Scriptural overview above, it was necessary for the Son of God (the second Person of the Trinity) to become human (Jesus the Messiah), not only so He could relate to us humans, but also, so He could be that perfect High Priest in the presence of God, and thus, make that perfect *atonement* for our sins once and for all (Heb 2:17).

In this, we unequivocally state that God is the Actor in the transaction. God the Father, in His Son, Jesus the Christ does the atoning. As a result, every single human being—past, present, and future—has been *atoned* for, even if they do not realize this reality.

Perfection did not come through the Levitical priesthood, based on the Law (Heb 7:11), or animal sacrifice. *Yahshua* (יֵשׁוּעַ) is from the Tribe of Judah, wherein there is no mention of priests (Heb 7:14). Therefore, Jesus' Priesthood is not based on legal requirements or ancestry, that is to say, His being a physical descendant of the Tribe of Levi (Ex 28:1-3).

Moreover, the High Priest needed to "offer sacrifice day after day, first for his own sins and then for those of the people" (Heb 7:27); but Jesus' Priesthood is "by the power of a life that cannot be destroyed" (Heb 7:16).

Jesus' Priesthood is a priesthood in the order of Melchizedek (Heb 7:1). "Melchizedek, king of Salem"—that is, king of peace, also an early name of Jerusalem—"brought out bread and wine" and was "a priest of God Most High" (Gen 14:18).

Some academic theologians refer to Melchizedek as an Old Testament *Christophany* (which is to say, an appearance of the Christ within the Old Testament). For, "without father, mother, or ancestry, without beginning of days or end of life, thus made to resemble the Son of God, he [Melchizedek] remains a priest forever" (Heb 7:3), the letter to the Hebrews states. A connection is made as God the Father attributes this to His Son in Psalm 110: "You [His Son] are a priest forever according to the order of Melchizedek" (Heb 7:17 and Ps 110:4).

Now, "it was fitting that we should have such a High Priest: holy, innocent, undefiled, separated from sinners, higher than the Heavens" (Heb 7:26). This High Priest does not need to offer sacrifices *day after day* to atone for sins, "He did that once for all when He offered Himself" (Heb 7:27). As we can see, God is the Actor, for not only is He the one doing the offering, He Himself is also the Offering. He is *the* perfect High Priest, Who offers *the* perfect Sacrifice—Himself, the sinless Lamb—as *the* perfect atonement for sins.

The words *atone* and *atonement*, in the Greek ἱλάσκομαι (hilaskomai/*hil-as'-kom-ahee*), and ἱλασμός (hilasmos/*hil-as-mos'*), occur only two times each in all of the New Testament. What is more, unfortunately, these four words are rarely translated as atone or atonement into English (*Note*[222]). Let us briefly look at all four occurrences.

The first occurrence of the word atone is in the Parable of the Pharisee and the Tax Collector, found in the Gospel of Saint Luke (Lk 18:9-14): "But the tax collector stood off at a distance and would not even raise his eyes to Heaven but beat his breast and prayed, 'O God, be merciful [*hilaskomai* (ἱλάσκομαι)] to me a sinner'" (Lk 18:13).

It is unfortunate that this word *hilaskomai* (ἱλάσκομαι)—atone—is translated as *merciful*, for the word *atone* gives us a deeper insight into the disposition of the Pharisee versus the tax collector. The Pharisee thinks that righteousness comes from himself (Lk 18:9), atonement is from his own works (Lk 18:11-12), he is the actor, so he does not need God to *atone* for him. He is self-righteous because he is doing the work (see Lk 18:12). The common understanding, even among Christians, that *we* have to do the work to be reconciled to God is flawed.

In this, we could also refer to Judas Iscariot, for he had that same inner disposition as the Pharisee—as in, he is the actor of his own atonement. This was not demonstrated by his words as much as it was demonstrated by his actions. To get that full picture let us then go through his actions after he betrayed the Messiah.

First, he "deeply regretted what he had done" (Mt 27:3). Second, "He returned the thirty pieces of silver" (Mt 27:3). Third, he recognized that he "sinned in betraying innocent blood" (Mt 27:4).

When we think of Judas (after his betrayal) we sometimes forget that he whet through this process. Seeing this, at first we might be inclined to say that this is a good thing. Judas seems to be repentant and disgusted by what he had done, and even wanted to make amends. Interestingly, Saint Peter does not go through a similar process after his denial.

However, the underlying Greek word translated as *deeply regretted* in referring to Judas is μεταμέλλομαι (metamellomai/*met-am-el'-lom-ahee*). Some translations translate this as "he repented" (*NRSV*), or he was "filled with remorse" (*NJB*), or as stated "deeply regretted" (*NAB*). In a way this is correct, but the Greek word also indicates an *action on to one's self*—to repent one's self.[223] Therefore, it is more of "he *self*-repented"; or he was "filled with *self*-remorse"; or "deeply *self*-regretted." Judas' first, second, and third actions are based on this flawed inner disposition, which is fascinatingly highlighted by the chief priests and elders, for after this they say: "What is that to us? Look to it yourself" (Mt 27:4). This is precisely what Judas ends up doing—*he looks to himself.*

Judas' answer to the chief priest should have been that he does not need to look to himself—that is, he does not and cannot atone for himself—but what he needs to do is look to his Messiah. Moreover, if he hung around (pun intended) he would have seen that very fulfillment from his Messiah. As we know however, Judas does not turn to God. As a result, in his final act "he departed and went off and hanged himself" (Mt 27:5). Judas had a flawed understanding that he needed to *look to himself*—that he is the one atoning for His sins. Judas does not ask God to atone for him. This was his disposition (*Note*[224]).

In contrast, going back to the tax collector, in his disposition he realizes that there is nothing he can do except to ask God to be more than merciful—so he asks God to atone for his sins. The tax collector wants God to *blot out* or *wipe clean* his sins, something that he knows he cannot (under any circumstances) do for himself, only God can reconcile him to God. This is the proper disposition.

Unlike the Pharisee, the tax collector does not exalt himself, saying: Hey, look at me and all the great works I'm doing. On the contrary, he humbled himself. The tax collector realized that *God* has to be the Actor here; and thus, placing his trust on the grace of God he goes home *justified* (Lk 18:14). The word *justified* is important, so keep it in mind, we will return to it in the third aspect.

The second occurrence of the word *atone* is in the letter to the Hebrews, which we just quoted: "Therefore, He [Jesus] had to become like His brothers in every way, that He might be a merciful and faithful High Priest before God to expiate [*hilaskomai* (ἱλάσκομαι)] the sins of the people" (Heb 2:17).

Here, the word *atone*, *hilaskomai* (ἱλάσκομαι) in Greek, is translated into English in most translations as *expiate*, which holds the exact same meaning as atone—the only difference is that the English word *expiate* comes from the Latin *expiare*.

Now let us consider the word *atonement*, *hilasmos* (ἱλασμός), of which we find both occurrences in the First Letter of Saint John: "He is expiation [*hilasmos* (ἱλασμός)] for our sins, and not for our sins only but for those of the whole world" (1 Jn 2:2); and "In this is love: not that we have loved God, but that He loved us and sent His Son as expiation [*hilasmos* (ἱλασμός)] for our sins" (1 Jn 4:10).

Here, the English translations are a little mixed. Some translate the word *hilasmos* (ἱλασμός) as "atoning sacrifice" (*NRSV* and *NIV*), others as "propitiation" (*Douay Rheims* and *KJV*), and others as "expiation" (*NAB*).

As we can see it seems like most translators do not like using the work atone or atonement. This is somewhat unfortunate. Although we may argue that the words they use virtually mean the same, these words do not overtly reflect the reality nor the wording of the Old Testament (cf. Lev 16:30 and 2 Chron 29:24).

I think the reason for these varying translations is that the interpretations of the word *atone* or *atonement* are misunderstood.

Some Christians, incorrectly, view the concept of atonement as some sort of appeasement that satisfies an angry, vengeful God, as if God somehow desires a bloody sacrifice or the smell of burning flesh (Old Testament), or the excruciating slaughtering of His Son (New Testament).

However, this is a grave misunderstanding of atonement. The concept of atonement is not in isolation, and need not relate to physical sacrifice. God has wrath toward sin (Rom 1:18)—atonement is needed for *justice* to be just, as we will shortly study—however "God did not destine us for wrath," but to gain salvation through His Son (1 Thes 5:9). Therefore, Christians must understand and simultaneously hold atonement in the light of the preceding chapter: "God so loved the world that He gave His only Son" (Jn 3:16a); and thus, "In this is love: not that we have loved God, but that He loved us and sent His Son as [*hilasmos* (ἱλασμός)] for our sins" (1 Jn 4:10).

In case we forget, *Yahshua* (יֵשׁוּעַ) *is* God. He could have called upon twelve legions of angels to assist Him from being put to death (Mt 26:53). He could have easily come down from the Cross and smitten all those involved in crucifying Him. In a millisecond He could have done exactly what the crowds jeered and taunted Him to do: "If you are the Son of God, come down from the Cross" (Mt 27:40: also cf. Mk 15:29-30 and Lk 23:35-37). Yet He did not! Why? Because in obedience to His Father, He atoned for our sins, out of love.

Also, we must keep in mind that "God did not make death, nor does He rejoice in the destruction of the living" (Wisdom 1:13). "He fashioned all things that they might have being" (Wisdom 1:14a). "For God formed man to be imperishable; the image of His own nature He made him. But by the envy of the devil, death entered the world" (Wisdom 2:23-24).

Therefore, atonement is not an appeasement of a cruel and vicious God; on the contrary, in atonement for sin, God sends His Son to do what we are incapable of doing, and thus, releases us from the grip of sin and death (which Adam's sin brought about). It is about reconciliation of the estrangement and enmity between God and humans that was brought about by Adam's sin.

Also, take into account, God the Father does not *sanitize* our sins by making excuses for them. He gets involved by sending His

Son to atone for them, thus doing what we cannot do. This is the ultimate helping hand from a God who loves us. As a result, everyone who believes in the Son He sent, through His atoning sacrifice will have eternal life with Him (Jn 3:16b).

Yahshua (יֵשׁוּעַ) is *the* atonement for *all* our sins. "Jesus atoned for our faults and made satisfaction for our sins to the Father" (*CCC* #615). On the Cross He takes our place, He replaces *all* of us. "No man, not even the holiest, was ever able to take on himself the sins of all men and offer himself as a sacrifice for all" (*CCC* #616). Only through Jesus, and in Him—through the blood of *Yahshua* (יֵשׁוּעַ) on the Cross—reparation is made, that is to say, two parties (God and we) are brought together in reconciliation. Through divine love—mercy and grace of God we are reconciled with God (cf. 2 Cor 5:18-19 and Rom 3:23-25), in and through His Son. God is the Actor of atonement, and the final and complete sacrifice is His Son.

> The Christian doctrine is that through [the] Christ's passion, death and resurrection, infinite satisfaction is made to God for the sins of humankind. Through this satisfaction, we are reconciled to God.[225]
>
> | *Catholic Encyclopedia* |

"But wait, there's more!" The Christ's

> atonement consists, not primarily in the intensity of the suffering He endured, but in the perfectly obedient and loving acceptance of the Will of the Father which He displayed in embracing this suffering for our sake. Christ's perfect obedience atones for the disobedience of Adam and wins for us the grace of obedient discipleship and divinizing sanctification.[226]
>
> | *Catholic Encyclopedia* |

In summary, this is atonement: *Yahshua* (יֵשׁוּעַ) the *Mâshîyach* (מָשִׁיחַ) is the "Lamb of God who takes away the sin of the world" (Jn 1:29). Through obedience, His atonement is universal and atones for all, dissolving the wrath and enmity between God the Father and all humanity—from the first human being to the last. Through God's love, He is the perfect, innocent, sinless Sacrifice, Who takes our place, suffers in our place, and dies in our place; and in consequence, *blots out* or *wipes clean* our sins, and thus *appeases* and *reconciles* us to God.

Aspect Number 2, Righteousness: With this in mind, let us move to the second aspect in relation to His death, *righteousness*. Upon the Cross, Jesus pays our debt so that we may be just, right, innocent, pure and holy before God—i.e., *righteous* (*Note*[227]).

So then, to whom was this debt paid? How does the Cross constitute reparation? As mentioned, Scripture *does not* give us these answers. We may look to different theories of atonement for some answers. (*Note*[228]); nevertheless, the focus here, with an emphasis on love and obedience, is the *Source* of atonement, not the *how*.

That is to say, although the *how* part of atonement is not stated in Scripture, Scripture clearly states the *Source* of atonement, therefore, this Source should be our primary focus: "He Himself bore our sins in His body upon the Cross, so that, free from sin, we might live for righteousness. By His wounds you have been healed" (1 Pt 2:24; also cf. Rom 8:10).

Furthermore, Scripture tells us that *Yahshua* (יֵשׁוּעַ) the Christ knew no sin, but became sin; not by any sinful action on His part, but because God the Father "made Him to be sin" for our sake, so that we may be righteous in Him (2 Cor 5:21). God the Father could have just forgiven us our sins, but He was not content with a mere forgiveness of sins (not to mention that that would go against His justice, as we will shortly study), so, in His love He took it a step further by sending His very own Son to take those sins upon Himself (in which His justice is retained). Jesus the *Mâshîyach* (מָשִׁיחַ) was obedient to this will of His Father. As a result, His obedience atones for our sins, which in turn makes us righteous in Him.

The words righteous and righteousness are interesting words. In fact, in both the Hebrew and Greek there are actually four different words each that are rendered as *righteousness* or *righteous* in English.

Each language has two different words that are nouns, one word that is an adjective, and one word that is a verb.

According to *Mounce's Dictionary*, "righteousness is first and foremost a quality ascribed to God."[229] It connotes right action and right relations. Speaking generally, the Hebrew nouns convey the understanding that because we are created in the image and likeness of God, we in some sense have the capability to live righteous lives.

This quality, ascribed to God, is a quality we need to accomplish. However, it also conveys the understanding that we are unable to become righteous before God. This understanding is virtually the same in the Greek nouns, but with a stronger emphasis on the fact that we cannot achieve righteousness on our own, for righteousness comes from God (Rom 10:3, Rom 3:21-22, and Phil 3:9). It is God's righteousness that we receive through grace which comes from faith (cf. Rom 4:13 and 10:6). Thus, in the Greek, righteousness is no longer tied into the keeping of the Law (Gal 3:21, Rom 3:21, and Phil 3:9).

The adjectives in both languages connote the same meaning—describing those who act or behave righteously, are innocent or just; and it describes God's righteousness and those who are God-fearing. Again, the Greek adjective, like the Greek nouns, once more takes it a slight step further. It conveys the understanding that no one is really righteous (Rom 3:10) in and of ourselves.

Finally, the verb in both languages conveys the declaration of righteousness, i.e., *to be* righteous. Again, however, in the Greek this meaning is elevated by conveying the understanding that good deeds, or behaviour, or keeping the Law does not declare us righteous (*Note*[230]), for something more is needed.

The theological understanding of the means of *righteousness* is clarified as we move from the Old to the New Testament (also within the Hebrew to the Greek language itself). Israel's understanding of righteousness is clarified, and the fullness of meaning is found and demonstrated through the finished work of *Yahshua* (יֵשׁוּעַ) the *Mâshîyach* (מָשִׁיחַ).

On the Cross, "when Jesus had taken the wine, He said, 'It is finished'" (Jn 19:30). The Greek word used here for *finished* is τελέω (teleō/*tel-eh'-o*), which not only means to end, to complete, to conclude, but also has an inherent meaning that the debt has been discharged, that the debt has been paid, in full (*Note*[231]).

God in His righteousness—in and through His Son—declares us righteous because He has paid off our debt in full; thus, completely dealing with the problem of sin. Jesus the Christ consumes all of God's judgments against us, on the Cross. Therefore, it is only in Him that we are declared righteous. He, the true Righteous One, the One who is without sin (*Note*[232]), takes on our sin and becomes a sin offering so that we may become sinless before God (1 Pt 3:18; also cf. Gal 3:13).

We are now declared righteous to God the Father, because of *Yahshua* (יֵשׁוּעַ) the Christ. Why? Because a quality inherent to Him—righteousness—is imputed to us. "For our sake God made Him to be sin who did not know sin, so that we might become the righteousness of God in Him" (2 Cor 5:21). Most conclusively, righteousness is not accomplished by our doing. This is "expressed paradoxically in terms of sharing and exchange of attributes."[233] In short, we are made righteous because of Him and only in Him!

> When you were dead in your sins and in the uncircumcision of your flesh (worldliness, manner of life), God made you alive together with [the] Christ, having [*freely*] forgiven us all our sins, having canceled out the certificate of debt [literally, the debtor's handwritten note acknowledging the debt] consisting of legal demands [*which were in force*] against us and which were hostile to us. And this certificate He has set aside *and* completely removed by nailing it to the Cross. (Col 2:13-14[234])

We were in debt, now our debt has been completely paid (Col 2:14); this is not from our own doing, but from His pure grace.

Yahshua (יֵשׁוּעַ) the Messiah is really the only One Who can be described as righteous, for He perfectly fulfilled all righteousness through obedience (Rom 5:19; also cf. 6:16)—and then by His grace because of our faith, imputes that righteousness to us. That is to say, His righteousness is credited to us. As a result, God the Father does not look at us, and our sinfulness, but rather, looks at His Son's perfect righteousness, and thus, declares you and me righteous *in Him*.

We should also clearly note that while payment of our sin debt has a quality like paying off a mortgage in full, it also has a judicial quality. It is like the paying of a bail bond, or even more precisely, it is like the completion of a prison sentence. The guilty sentence, which is rightfully ours the Christ takes on; He suffers for us; He takes on our punishment, and He pays our punishment-debt in full. This is the meaning behind Jesus' words: "I did not come to condemn the world but to save the world" (Jn 12:47). His incarnation is tied into His *death*, which pays our debt, i.e., He saves us from condemnation, e.g., like going to prison.

The Law is perfect in identifying sin. However, when it does not find perfection within its object (you and me), it can only confer judgment and punishment—this is the *nature* of the Law. However, the Messiah, unlike the Law, makes the payment in full for us. The suffering, the penalty, the punishment, which we rightly and truly deserve, He takes upon the Cross. In this we "have been purchased at a price" (1 Cor 6:20), as a result, we are not our own (1 Cor 6:19)—we no longer belong to ourselves.

What the Law could not do—i.e., remove the penalty of sin and thus make us righteous—God does for us by and through His Son (Rom 8:3-4). Our righteousness is *not* a righteousness of our own; it is not accomplished by or derived from any obedience to the Law—any good works we perform, any rituals, or pietistic practices, or religious formalities, or devotions we partake in—it strictly comes from the grace of God through faith in *Yahshua* (יֵשׁוּעַ) the *Mâshîyach* (מָשִׁיחַ). He removes the penalty of sin, therefore, it is a righteousness that comes from Him; it is His righteousness that is imputed or credited on us, as a result we are counted, declared, and described righteous only because of Him (Phil 3:9).

We also see this in the categories of *righteous* and *sinners* in some of Jesus' statements, for example: "I did not come to call the righteous but sinners" (Mt 9:13 and Mk 2:17; also cf. Lk 5:32). When reading the passage most of us tend to see this as two different groups—those who are righteous and those who are sinners. May I suggest however, that *all* we have is one group—*sinners*. All of humanity, all of us are sinners!

The difference in the two qualifications demonstrates the difference in disposition: some of us acknowledge this reality that we are sinners (e.g., the tax collector), and some of us do not (e.g., the Pharisee), in which, there is a self-proclamation of righteousness (i.e., self-righteousness). Also, as mentioned within the latter category are those who acknowledge that they are sinners, but in self-righteousness want to atone or pay for their own sins, as we saw in the case of Judas.

To put it another way, *Yahshua* (יֵשׁוּעַ) came to call all of us, however, He cannot call those who have self-proclaimed righteousness in one form or another. It is not as if He is incapable of calling them, or His mission does not include them, it is the attitude and disposition of the one called.

When we call ourselves righteous, Jesus will not impose Himself on us. Why? Because He loves us, all of us, including those who are self-righteous, and thus, He gives all of us freedom—a freedom to reject Him. In that sense, He has not come to call the righteous, in other words, those sinners who proclaim themselves righteous, but, He came to call sinners, in other words, those sinners who know that they are sinners (Mt 9:13).

When we understand this, we also gradually come to understand the paradox between the two statements that He did not come "to condemn the world but to save the world" (Jn 12:47), in which He was referring to His mission during His First Coming, and that He also "is the judge of the living and the dead" (Acts 10:42), which will be most clearly seen at His Second Coming. If He is the judge, does not a judge have to pronounce judgment? Furthermore, knowing that we are guilty—which we all are—would not that judgment result in condemnation?

Aspect Number 3, Justification: Keeping the first two aspects in mind, let us now move to the third aspect—now in relation to the Christ's resurrection—*justification.* "Because of our sins the Father gave the Lord Jesus up to death, and for our justification, He raised Him up again."[235]

The word *justification* is closely related to the word *righteousness*, and they both transform our inner nature. Intriguingly however, there is no equivalent Hebrew word (in the Old Testament) for justification—this is only a Greek word (found in the New Testament). The word *justice* is in Hebrew, but not *justification*. The only instance of *justify* in the Old Testament is in connection with the Messiah (e.g., Isa 53:11—*NAB* translation) or in connection to justice or righteousness (used in other translations). The reason for this is that *justification only* comes with the Resurrection, moreover, faith in the *Christ* and *His* resurrection (Gal 2:16)—for "You could not be justified under the Law of Moses" (Acts 13:38; also cf. Gal 3:24). We are justified *only* in His resurrection and made righteous in the eyes of God, in Jesus the Christ (Acts 13:39; also cf. Gal 3:24b).

In case you are wondering, Abraham was not justified by the Law, for the Law came after he was justified by faith (Rom 4:2-3), and participated in the efficacy of Jesus' resurrection, for Scripture points out that Abraham saw the day of the Messiah (Jn 8:56). Faith equals trust, which equals confidence that we are justified in Him.

There is an important second part to this, which we will discuss shortly, but for the moment, we should mention that justification is the action of God, whereby we the sinners are made righteous and just, declared free of guilt and sin, and its penalty in the eyes of God, and it is He Himself Who does this by raising the Christ from the dead (1 Cor 15:17).

That said, justification is about justice; for in the action of God's justifying us, He practices His justice as presented in the Old Testament. We should note that there is a difference between amnesty or being forgiven, versus being justified by God. Amnesty or forgiveness, in its meaning implies that we did something wrong, that we are actually guilty, but in the mind of the one wronged, we are pardoned or the wrong is no longer considered. Justification, on the other hand, is a legal declaration, which *declares* us *not* guilty, because we are righteous in Him. We are not guilty of the crime. We are declared just.

This action frees us from objective guilt, feelings of guilt, and the need of paying the penalty of the sin. Our sin is not held against us; it is as if we never done it—that we did not sin at all (cf. Isa 43:25 and Ps 103:12). This is not because of anything we have done; it only happens *in* Jesus the Christ, or to be exact, by faith in His death and resurrection we are now seen through the prism of the Messiah.

As mentioned, being made and declared righteous does not usurp justice itself. God is just, therefore He can be both just and the justifier of those who believe because the penalty has been paid by Him. We all are undeservedly justified, declared free of guilt, free of sin, righteous and just before God, by God's freely given gift of grace through His redemptive work, the actual payment for sin, provided by *Yahshua* (יֵשׁוּעַ) the *Mâshîyach* (מָשִׁיחַ) (Rom 3:24)—this is how God decided to manifest His justice (Rom 3:25–26). Sin no longer defines us, for "there is now no condemnation [*no guilty verdict, no punishment*] for those who are in Jesus the Christ" (Rom 8:1[236]; also cf. Jn 3:18).

To help us further understand this, we can describe two parts of justice: (1) justice-righteousness; and (2) justice-judicial. Therefore, when we speak of God's justice, are we speaking of God's justice (righteousness) or God's justice (judicial)? With either the former or latter, we can proclaim without hesitation that God is just, because truth, reason, and fairness are inherent in His nature.

We can further state that God's justice (righteousness) is demonstrated through His mercy, in His Son. When speaking of God's justice (judicial), we might place His justice (judicial) in opposition to His mercy. Nevertheless, His justice (judicial) is still rooted in His *agape* (ἀγάπη), His love, for He cannot act in injustice, for this is in violation of His justice (righteousness). God may not choose to demonstrate His justice (judicial), rather demonstrating His justice (righteousness) and His mercy. However, we should not confuse this as injustice. Moreover by His demonstrating His justice (judicial), we should not say that this is unloving or unmerciful, for He cannot go against Himself—He cannot go against His justice (righteousness).

The former would make God merciful for no reason and the latter would make Him a vindictive, vengeful God. Neither position is correct, for we must keep in mind that *both* His justice (judicial) and His justice (righteousness) are *rooted* in His love. It is not a zero-sum situation. God is *all* justice and *all* mercy, *all* at the same time. For we cannot have true justice without mercy, and we cannot have mercy without justice.

In brief, the Scriptural understanding is that one person sinned (Adam) by breaking a particular law God gave him. Through that "one person sin entered the world, and through sin, death, and thus death came to all" (Rom 5:12). Now, from the time of Adam until the time of Moses, before the Law was given, humanity continued to sin, but the sins humanity committed were not held against them by an external, codified *Law* (Rom 5:13). Yet the penalty of "death [still] reigned from Adam to Moses" (Rom 5:14). Examples include the Flood, God's judgment on Sodom and Gomorrah, and the very fact that everyone dies.

Through Moses, God gave us the Law (i.e., the Ten Commandments and their accompanying regulations) to specify what sin *is* (Rom 5:13). In black and white, it listed the gamut of sinful behaviour (Rom 3:20). This was the precise purpose of the Law.

As many preachers have preached, the Law is just, but, it cannot justify us; the Law is holy, but, it cannot make us holy; the Law is perfect, but, cannot make us perfect. What is more, in the Law's perfection it results in a deadly consequence, the punishment for sin demonstrated via His justice (judicial).

We see this consequence of the Law, 50 days after the Passover, on the day of the first Pentecost (*Shavu'ot*). On that Pentecost 50 days after the Law was given on Mount Sinai, 3,000 people died on the foot of the mountain (Ex 32:15-28). In its perfection, the Law perfectly identified sin, and thus, when it did not find this perfection on the foot of Mount Sinai—due to the *nature* of the Law—it can only confer judgment and punishment. This is God's justice (judicial).

However, God revealed His justice (righteousness) totally independently and apart from the Law (Rom 3:21), in His Son. It is the will of God the Father, "that everyone who sees [His] Son and believes in Him may have eternal life, and [He] shall raise him on the last day" (Jn 6:40). We get to choose which one we want—God's justice (judicial) or His justice (righteousness). On this basis, if we acknowledge our sinfulness (and also recognize that we cannot stop sin by our own effort), and ask God for His justice (righteousness) in His Son, He will pour out that justice (righteousness) upon us, which is His mercy (1 Jn 1:8–9). Unlike the effects of the Law, this is life-giving. As a result, in the New Testament *fulfillment*, 50 days after Jesus' Passover, on the day of the Pentecost, when repentance and baptism were preached on Mount Zion, 3,000 people were saved (Acts 2:38-41). The Law given to Moses on Mount Sinai finds the perfection it seeks in Jesus the Christ on Mount Zion. This is God's justice (righteousness).

When we recognize our need for His mercy (in faith), and ask for His mercy (e.g., the tax collector in the parable), we will be justified in Him (Rom 5:1–11). However, if we claim self-righteousness (e.g., the Pharisee), we will be choosing God's justice (judicial). Therefore, we will be judged according to the Law (Rom 2:12). We are either choosing *Jesus the Messiah* or *the Law*—these are our *only* two choices.

Before we choose, however, keep in mind two things: (1) *none of us keeps the Law* entirely (Jn 7:19), "for whoever keeps the whole Law, but falls short in one particular, has become guilty in respect to all of it" (Jms 2:10)—a good analogy I have heard is that it is like a *necklace of pearls*, when it breaks every pearl falls; (2) even if we somehow did keep the Law, *justification does not come from the Law*, for the word itself is not found within the Law (or is it even related to the Law).

Therefore, do not fool yourself: "Do not nullify the grace [or mercy] of God, for if justification comes through the Law, then Christ died for nothing" (Gal 2:21). If you *nullify* God's grace and mercy through His Son by choosing to justify ourselves by keeping the Law rather than through Him, but do not keep the entire Law, "you will die in your sin" (Jn 8:21).

"Mercy does not override justice [judicial], but rather transcends it and converts the sinner into a just person by bringing about repentance and openness to the Holy Spirit."[237]

When we understand this, we have further insight into the paradox between the two statements that He did not come "to condemn the world but to save the world" (Jn 12:47), and that He "is the judge of the living and the dead" (Acts 10:42). Remember the questions we posed earlier: If He is the judge, does not a judge have to pronounce judgment? Knowing that we are guilty would not that judgment be condemnation?

Both are His justice. It is simply exercised in two different times and manners, so to speak. In His First Coming , the Son of God came to "save the world" (Jn 12:47; also cf. Jn 6:40), by dealing with sin

(Heb 9:28). This is His justice (righteousness). This is the time we are living in right now—this is the *end times*—the *eschatos* (ἔσχατος). Yes, we are in the time of His justice (righteousness).

In the Second Coming, the Son of Man "is the One ordained by God to be judge of the living and the dead" (Acts 10:42). He [God the Father] has given Him [God the Son] authority to execute judgment, because He is [also] a Son of Man [*sinless humanity, qualifying Him to sit in judgment over mankind*] (Jn 5:26-27[238]; also cf. Dan 7:13-14).

This will be His justice (judicial), which will happen ultimately at His Second Coming (the *Parousia*), or intermediately through judgment upon our physical death (consider 1 Cor 11:30).

At the Second Coming the *Mâshîyach* (מָשִׁיחַ) will no longer be dealing with sin; He will be coming in power, bringing the completion of Salvation to those who await Him (Heb 9:28; also cf. Mt 24:30 and Jn 11:25-26), and justice (judicial) to those who are not. In other words, now we are in the time of His mercy and grace; in essence He is giving us a chance or a way out from perishing (2 Pt 3:9)—which is He Himself—for afterward we will be in the time of His judicial judgment.

These concepts keeps us from the unfounded notion that God is a vengeful God waiting to smite us if we slightly step out of place; that could not be further from the truth. We are the ones who are greatly distorted by the effects of sin and the Christ is the One who invites us back and restores us. Yes, after all we have done, Jesus the Christ still *invites* us back. He does not force us back. This is paramount. What is more, that is even after all we have done, He makes it *our choice* to accept or decline His invitation.

God loved us so much that "while we were still sinners" He gave His only Son to die for us (Rom 5:8). Then He raised His Son, *Yahshua* (יֵשׁוּעַ), so we who are now justified by His blood, will be saved through Him (Rom 5:9; also cf. Rom 4:25). Justification detaches us from sin (*CCC* #1990). It includes the remission of sins (*CCC* #2019), which infuses us with the necessary grace—unmerited Divine favour—for renewal. "Our justification comes from the grace of God. Grace is *favour*, the *free and undeserved help* that God gives us to respond to His call to become children of God, adoptive sons, partakers of the divine nature and of eternal life" (*CCC* #1996).

We may respond to this positively, that is receive His gift, or we have the option to say "No" to it. The choice is ours to make. This is our free will. The God of the universe, although He does not have to save us (for He could have smitten us), bends over backwards for us (Phil 2:6-7)—this is the act of His love!

Another way of putting it (which some of us do not realize) is that we will technically *not* be judged! Yes, we will need to appear before the *judgment seat* (2 Cor 5:10), however, it is with the realization that our Messiah has already been judged in our place. If we would be judged according to our deeds that are considered sufficient for salvation, then the Christ died for nothing. He was cursed; He was punished; He was executed on a Cross, in our place, for our sins. That is to say, He was *judged in our place*. He paid the penalty that the Law demands for our sins. He became sin for us (2 Cor 5:21). He is the *Source* of our atonement, our righteousness, and our justification. When we have *died in Him*—that is, our baptism and the continual living of our baptismal promise—our life is *hidden with Him* in God (Col 3:3). It is as if we are hidden behind His mantle or cloak as we appear before the judgment seat (*Note*[239]); in which the Judge is looking at Him, not at us; and then sees that He has paid the penalty that the Law demands for sin; as He Himself became sin for us and bestowed upon us His righteousness (2 Cor 5:21); and in turn justifies us.

Accordingly, as a result of His action, we will *not* be judged. "God did not send His Son into the world to condemn [judge] the world, but that the world might be saved through Him" (Jn 3:17).

Now, all that said, here is the first caveat: it is whoever that believes *in Him* who will not be condemned or judged by Him (Jn 3:18). With that, here is the second caveat: even if anyone hears His voice, does not accept His word, and rejects Him, He will still not condemn or judge them, because, it is essentially the word that He spoke (in His First Coming) that will eventually condemn and judge them on the last day (Jn 12:47-48).

Moreover, this leads us to the second part to this *justification*, which is our response to or cooperation with it (this is the third caveat). It is the process by which, we the sinners, are transformed and thus made righteous:

> Justification in the Catholic Tradition comes about by means of faith in [the] Christ, and [the second part] in a life of good works lived in response to God's invitation to believe. Against classical Lutheran doctrine, the Catholic Faith holds that faith without good works is not sufficient to merit justification, for good works show one's willingness to cooperate with the initiatives of grace. Catholic doctrine rejects any notion that justification comes about through an "inwardness" or merely a disposition, but it also objects to the mere performance of a physical act (*actus externus*) without an inward disposition of faith, hope and charity. What is necessary for Salvation is a faith that represents itself both externally through acts and internally through faith. Given the fact that the person exists concretely in the universe, it is necessary for the Salvation which occurred objectively and historically, that the person respond historically and objectively to that gift of Salvation. As the human person is an embodied spirit, there is a dialogical relationship between the person and the world. Works are necessary for faith simply because they posit an act, accepting the gift of Salvation that is necessary to be redeemed. That works are clearly required in the New Testament for union with [the] Christ is seen in the many parables such as the Good Samaritan, Lazarus and Dives, and others. The true disciple of Jesus is one who labours in the vineyard, who tills the soil, who proclaims the Good News.[240]
>
> | *Catholic Encyclopedia* |

Therefore, the paradox here is that, on the one hand, we must realize it is only by God's mercy, grace, and through faith in *Yahshua* (יֵשׁוּעַ) the Messiah that we are justified. However, on the other hand, we also must recognize that the faith we profess is not a mere internal reckoning, but it must concretely manifest itself in works, which in turn give credence to our justification and the faith we profess.

A simple example is Saint Peter's mother-in-law, through faith (and mercy and grace of the Messiah) her fever was rebuked and healed, and then what did she do? (Lk 4:38). "She got up immediately and waited on them" a reciprocation of love as a concrete manifestation of her faith (Lk 4:39). Our works are the loving reaction to the love we have received. We need to hold both at the same time, for it is a compulsory harmonic movement from one to the other. If not, as Saint James argues, our faith is nothing; it is useless; it is dead (Jms 2:14ff.).

Unfortunately, this paradox has been muddied by Martin Luther's *faith alone* (*Note*[241]) argument for the past five centuries. The back-and-forth of this argument has created many misunderstandings and misconceptions of the actual Christian teaching on the subject (*Note*[242]).

Summation of Aspects 1, 2, and 3: To help us bring together what we have studied, thus far, and move us to the final aspect, let us go through a vivid example from Scripture on these first three aspects—*atonement, righteousness,* and *justification*—by briefly looking at the story line of the Woman Caught in Adultery (Jn 8:3–11).

Studying the incident strictly from Jesus' point of view and not that of the accusers (i.e., the scribes and the Pharisees), this story will help us further understand the first three aspects and move us to the fourth and final aspect, *sanctification*.

Looking at the end of this narrative in Saint John's Gospel, we see that *Yahshua* (יֵשׁוּעַ) is the only One remaining with the woman (Jn 8:10) because He is the only One without sin (Jn 8:7). At this point, based on His own criteria (Jn 8:7), He may justly stone her. Nevertheless, *Yahshua* (יֵשׁוּעַ) does not justly condemn her (Lk 23:41) or put her to death as prescribed by the Law (Lev 20:10 and Deut 22:22), but He releases her. Among many questions, at first, we might ask: Did the Christ think that her sin should go unpunished, or did He somehow think that the Law is no longer in effect?

What we see in Jesus' action does not usurp the Law. Why? He is the actual writer of the Law, which in essence was demonstrated by His writing on the ground. Throughout the centuries scholars have tried to guess what the Messiah actually wrote on the ground. This is irrelevant.

What we do know, though, is that this incident takes place in the Temple area (Jn 8:2); therefore, Jesus' writing "with his finger" (Jn 8:6) would have been, in all probability, on stone, not on sand or dirt. If so, is that not an image of the Law, the stone tablets inscribed with God's own finger (Ex 31:18)? Jesus was visually demonstrating His authority as being the Writer of the Law. What is more, He is also the actual fulfillment of the Law (Mt 5:17). Therefore, the *Mâshîyach* (מָשִׁיחַ) well knows that sins do not go unpunished, thus, justice (the Law) must be fulfilled, which means that justice demands payment (i.e., Aspect 1—atonement).

Yahshua (יֵשׁוּעַ), within Himself, *fulfills* (completes, carries out through to the end, renders perfect, brings to pass, ratifies, and accomplishes) the Law's requirements (i.e., Aspect 2—righteousness), which is imputed to the adulterous woman (*Note*[243]). The sin she had committed is not imputed to her, but His righteousness is imputed to her. God the Father made His Messiah—"Who did not know sin"—to be sin for our behalf, so that in Him, "we would become the righteousness of God" (1 Cor 5:21).

God, in His Son, *fulfills* the Law's literal requirements in Himself. He makes the *payment* that justice (the Law) demands, and it is only because of His loving action (purely the grace of God), that He allows the adulterous woman to go free (i.e., Aspect 3—*justification*).

If you are tempted to question how this could be since that event clearly takes place before Jesus' death, it is that the efficacy of the Christ's death is not dependent on its time in our history The Christ's death was sufficient for the forgiveness of sins (and payment for sins) for all time (even though it happened in history before the Christ died).. Also keep in mind, that in Saint John's Gospel, *Yahshua* (יֵשׁוּעַ) is well aware of His imminent crucifixion (cf. Jn 2:19–22, 11:25, 12:24, 12:33, and 18:32). What is more, the Gospel of Saint John takes it a step further by framing this particular event with the crucifixion in sight, by referring to the Mount of Olives (Jn 8:1). That reference is not made anywhere else in this Gospel, or outside of the Passion week in any of the other three Gospels.

Justice (judicial) demands payment—Jesus knows that. Jesus does not usurp the Law—the Gospel writers know that (*Note*[244]). Therefore *yes*, Jesus *pays* her penalty of being put to death. He takes it on and makes payment for it by atoning for it on the Cross, and thus fulfilling the Law's requirements, making her righteous, and for her justification, God raised Him up (Rom 4:25).

Before I forget, this same principle applies to the tax collector who asked for atonement, for in light of the Resurrection he goes home receiving much more than he bargains for—he goes away being justified (Lk 18:14). This can only happen through the efficacy of the death and resurrection if the Messiah.

To recap: God, in *Yahshua* (יֵשׁוּעַ), demonstrates His justice (judicial), precisely through justice (righteousness), through His mercy. Mercy has not nullified justice (judicial). Also, keep in mind, that both justice (judicial) and justice (righteousness) are rooted in *agape* (ἀγάπη). Nevertheless, justice (righteousness) surpasses and fulfills justice (judicial). It transcends it and converts it.

In this narrative—and, by extension, as it affects you and me—*Yahshua* (יֵשׁוּעַ), in His mercy, has taken on our penalty; He has taken on *our* judgment; He has taken on *our* prison time; He has paid *our* debt in full; thus fulfilling the demands of the Law (*Note*[245]). We are now dead to sin (Rom 6:11), its guilt and shame, condemnation, and punishment (Rom 8:1). The Messiah is not unjust in dispensing His justice (righteousness) for He has fulfilled the legal requirements the Law demands on the Cross. It is for that reason that Saint Paul says, "Do not nullify the grace of God, for if justification comes through the Law, then Christ died for nothing" (Gal 2:21; also cf. Rom 5:21).

Aspect Number 4, Sanctification: Understanding the details of the first three aspects, we now move to the fourth aspect in relation to His resurrection—*sanctification.* For that reason, the story of the adulterous woman does not end there; it ends with *Yahshua* (יֵשׁוּעַ) telling her: "Go, and from now on do not sin any more" (Jn 8:11; also cf. 5:14).

> Sanctification is thus nothing other than the perfection of the life of charity. The chief means of sanctification is the infusion of habitual grace which enables us to turn to God in faith, hope and love. The life of grace is continually enhanced in us through our membership in the Mystical Body of [the] Christ and through our sharing in the sacramental grace that is at the very heart of the Church's life . . . We become holy as God is holy so that we can be fit company for Him for all eternity.[246]
>
> | *Catholic Encyclopedia* |

This directive from Jesus to the adulterous woman—"Go, and from now on do not sin any more" (Jn 8:11); and also note what Jesus said to the man healed at the pool called Bethesda, "Do not sin any more, so that nothing worse may happen to you" (Jn 5:14)—is also directed to you and me. Yes, "sin must not reign over our mortal bodies" (Rom 6:12).

Like justification, sanctification also has two parts: (1) it is developed through God's grace, for He is the Actor; and (2) our response and submission in a continual action of answering Him (*Note*[247]). Now here is a quick summation chart to help us:

Atonement	**God is the Actor**
Righteousness	**God is the Actor**
Justification	**God is the Actor** + **We respond and cooperate (the process)**
Sanctification	**God is the Actor** + **We respond and submit (the process)**

So then, although *sanctification* and *justification* are connected, the difference is that justification is a declaration, an act on the part of God; and then, on our part, it is our response and a process of our cooperation to that act, in faith in God's act—through works. Stated in reverse, we show the fact that we have been justified by God, by our works in faith (see Jms 2:20-24). Therefore, we may conclude that our response to the declaration of justification has to do with our personal *witness of charity*—which is our responds and collaborative cooperation to the declaration of justification through works, to become a witness of Him.

Sanctification, in a sense, takes justification a step further by perfecting it, and thus is synonymous with holiness, or to be holy. In view of that, we may conclude that sanctification has to do with our *call to holiness*. God sanctifies us, He is the Actor, we must now respond by submitting to the process of virtue in becoming holy. It is the "process of the personal supernatural transformation by which we become intimates of the indwelling Trinity."[248]

To sum up, sanctification is the infusion of grace, and then our response to that grace, through submission—an obedient personal transformation—and then our demonstration of that transformation through exhibiting virtue in being Christ-like. It is the process . . . "Go, and from now on" . . . a continual action on our part, to make us holy . . . "sin no more" (Jn 8:11).

Why is this distinction important? It demonstrates our personal responsibility. It shows that God loves us, and thus, will not push anything on us. Also, having a clear understanding of the distinction between justification and sanctification keeps us from error.

For example, some Christians (mainly non-Catholics) have a form of the thought *once saved, always saved*. This is rooted in the rationale that we are justified by faith alone (e.g., Rom 3:28). Some (mainly Catholics) say that we Christians must *do works* for our justification comes from our own good works (e.g., Jms 2:17).

Both groups use Scripture to advance their particular point of view (as examples cited). By understanding this distinction, we are able clearly to see the paradox, and thus hold both views as stated simultaneously without compromise.

Although the idea of the former group is too simplistic (as we will see in the next chapter), the core mistake is that they tend to forget our continual personal response—our cooperation in justification, and thus, become a *witness of Him*; and our submission in sanctification, and thus, allow the personal *supernatural transformation in Him*—to God's act.

The mistake the latter group makes is thinking it is their own doing through their own works that justifies them, not God's act of grace.

We can avoid both errors by clearly seeing both, and thus concluding that we need to hold both equally and in harmony (cf. 2 Cor 5:6-10). Sanctification and justification are not only connected, but they both require a particular response from us (*Note*[249]).

There is more to be said regarding our response to each: *justification* and *sanctification*, for this response is extremely important; therefore, we will revisit this response within the next chapter.

However, for this part of the study it is important to note here that both our *justification* and *sanctification* come from the grace of God and require a response on our part. God gives us the grace needed, through the sacraments—primarily through baptism, which you recall changes our being—to live the faith we profess.

In other words, we may say that we are justified and sanctified only by our faith in the resurrected Messiah. The order is important for, by definition, *atonement*, *righteousness*, and *justification* (in that order), must occur before *sanctification*.

Justification not only precedes but is also needed to secure sanctification. Justification is an instant declaration (to which we freely respond and cooperate—if we desire) whereas sanctification is the infusion of the grace of God (to which we freely submit—if we desire), which results in our progressive transformation of life. It consists of continual submission to the resurrected Messiah (in order to be like Him—*Christ-like*).

Keep in mind: although the choice is ours to make, as a Christian we are obligated to submit. In other words, if we *do not* desire this continual submission—in obedience—to the resurrected Messiah, we need to stop calling ourselves Christian! For, in this infusion we are accepting our consecration—we are in the realm of the sacred, the supernatural; if we reject this infusion, we are simply not.

Therefore: "Go, and from now on do not sin any more" (Jn 8:11). "We have been justified [*that is, acquitted of sin, declared blameless before God*] by faith, [*let us grasp the fact that*] we have peace with God [*and the joy of reconciliation with Him*] through our Lord Jesus [the] Christ (the Messiah, the Anointed)" (Rom 5:1[250]). In "this is the will of God, your holiness" (1 Thes 4:3), your sanctification. "For God did not call us to impurity but to holiness" (1 Thes 4:7). The Messiah loved the Church and handed Himself over for Her to sanctify Her (Eph 5:25b). In the same manner we must hand ourselves over to Him and allow His sanctification. "So submit yourselves to God [give in to the *authority* of God]. Resist the devil [*stand firm against him*], and he will flee from you. Draw near to God, and He will draw near to you" (Jms 4:7-8). For, "the nearer you go to God, the nearer God will come to you" (Jms 4:8[251])

A Deeper Refection on Why the Christ Event?

I once heard the criticism that Christians may have all the right theological understandings in their head without internalizing them in their heart. For example, laypeople in the pew, reading their Bible, may be more in tune in their hearts with the life changing Christ Event than the academic theologian or scholar (*Note*[252]).

However, the opposite holds true. Christians may have fervor in their hearts but without any theological roots—at the slightest challenge they do not have the theological wisdom to back up that fervor. Something similar is taught to us in the Parable of the Sower (Lk 8:4-15).

Great Saints are, first and foremost, great theologians. Likewise, although sadly not always the case, great theologians should be great Saints. We should transform our lives based on Truth—a continual movement from *head to heart* and *heart to head.*

Scripture tells us that we *must* love the Lord our God with all our mind and all our heart, with all our strength and soul; that is to say, with the *totality* of our being (Mk 12:30, Lk 10:27, and Deut 6:5). As we have quoted Saint Augustine, "God is Truth" and our mind needs to "come in contact with the Truth."[253] Then we must allow the Truth to transform us. We must enter into that *covenant-relationship* with the Truth.

This chapter, thus far, has been very heady. However, we need these truths, so that we may have a solid foundation with which to move from head to heart (*Note*[254]). As mentioned in the Introduction, this chapter is the transitional chapter. Hence, let us start that gradual movement.

To do that, let us return to our original inquiry in this chapter and the previous one: Why does the Creator of the universe go through this ordeal of an incarnation, death, and a resurrection? Our theological-Scriptural answer is that it is because of His *love* for us. He shows *mercy* towards us, and He desires to infuse us with His *grace*. He also takes the infusion a step further by doing what we are unable to do. On the Cross He takes our place and *atones* for our sins. In that act He imputes His own *righteousness* to us. As if this were not enough, through His resurrection He *justifies* and *sanctifies* us.

God is the only one who is able to do this.

All that said, at some level the Christ Event *still* does not completely make sense. Even with what we have studied, in some ways it still seems somewhat illogical, does it not?

Scripture also attests to this irrationality. To some extent, knowing what we have just studied, Saint Paul warns that, based on worldly philosophies and wisdom, the Christ Event is utter nonsense and foolishness (1 Cor 1:23), and he continues by saying that based on the Messiah's lineage, the Christ Event is an obstacle and the stumbling block (1 Cor 1:23; also cf. Rom 9:33).

The God of the universe becomes Man. Really?

How does that make any sense?

To die on a cross! Again, really?

If we truly sit and contemplate the Christ Event, it is extremely perplexing, to say the least. However, this is reality. This so-called absurdity is precisely what the Apostles proclaimed—and this is what we proclaim to this day.

What the world calls absurdity is the Wisdom of God (1 Cor 1:23-24). This is the *mystery of God* (1 Cor 2:1).

So then, what *is* this Wisdom of God? In this mystery, we get a glimpse of who God *Is*. Especially, in Jesus on the Cross we come to see the true identity of God. He is not a power-hungry megalomaniac

Who, as mentioned, could have easily come down from the Cross to smite everyone who put Him there; on the contrary, He is a God of *agape* (ἀγάπη)—self-sacrificing, unselfish, selfless love—Who in obedience and humility lays down His life for us. We need to take a moment and let that sink in.

As we let that sink in, let us turn to Saint Thomas Aquinas, who grappled with this very issue. In this, he gives us some helpful insights:

> [the Christ Event] can be considered in a twofold way: in the first place, as a remedy for sin, and secondly, as an example of how to act. [First place] it is a remedy, for, in the face of all the evils which we incur on account of our sins, we have found relief through the [Christ Event, which we just studied]. [Second place, which we will now discuss] it is no less an example, for the [Christ Event] completely suffices to fashion our lives. Whoever wishes to live perfectly should do nothing but disdain what [the] Christ disdained on the Cross and desire what He desired, for the Cross exemplifies every virtue.[255]
>
> | Saint Thomas Aquinas |

The above quotation gives us a secondary understanding of the Wisdom of God that will help us with a deeper reality of the Christ Event. That is, Saint Thomas Aquinas gives us *two* major reasons for the *why* of Jesus' incarnation, death, and resurrection.

The first reason is essentially what we have already discussed in this chapter (and the previous). The Christ Event ultimately is a remedy for sin—it exemplifies *love* and in that accomplishes our *atonement*, *righteousness*, *justification*, and *sanctification*. Only God is able to carry out what we required; and thus He chose to become one of us in order to do that.

This is "God's wisdom, mysterious, hidden, which God predetermined before the ages for our glory, and which none of the rulers of this age knew; for if they had known it, they would not have crucified the Lord of glory" (1 Cor 2:7-8). No one could even imagine what God had in mind (1 Cor 2:9). If the powers of darkness had an inkling of God's plan, and had known that *Yahshua* (יֵשׁוּעַ) the *Mâshîyach* (מָשִׁיחַ) was the ultimate *atonement* for sin they would not have killed Him, thus initiating the chain reaction (i.e., *righteousness*, *justification*, and *sanctification*).

The second reason adds to our understanding. I hope that it will move us from head to heart. God also chose to become human to give us an example of particular *virtues*; thus, He *exemplified to us* what it really means to be human.

This second reason is truly fascinating. Recall that when we discussed *justification* and *sanctification* we acknowledged that we have our own role to play. God, Himself, teaches us what our role is in *justification* and *sanctification.* In His actions, He shows us precisely what our cooperation and submission should look like.

As we go through this, note that the *virtues* outlined by Saint Thomas Aquinas are not only beyond the scope of this book, they require an entire book. Therefore, here, we will consider only the Wisdom of God demonstrated in the seemingly irrationality of the Christ Event.

Starting with *love*—for the true meaning of Christian love is always the starting point for virtues—Saint Thomas Aquinas outlines *five* exemplifying virtues that *only* God Himself could demonstrate fully to humanity. They are as follows: *love*, *patience*, *humility*, *obedience*, and *despising earthly things*.

To paraphrase Saint Thomas Aquinas: We must disdain what He disdained on the Cross and desire what He desired.

The First Virtue, Love:

> If you seek the example of love: Greater love than this no man has, than to lay down his life for his friends. Such a man was [the] Christ on the Cross. And if He gave His life for us, then it should not be difficult to bear whatever hardships arise for His sake.[256]
>
> | Saint Thomas Aquinas |

When we look to the Cross we see the *greatest* example of *love*, of which we are called to be a *witness of.*

Adding to the definition of Christian love, which we started to develop in the prior chapter: love—*agape* (ἀγάπη)—according to Saint Thomas Aquinas, goes beyond a sentiment or feeling "to will the good [*bonum*] of another" or "willing the good [*bonum*] of the other as other."[257] We, as Christians, should will the good of the other, not for our sake but for the sake of the other and the sake of Truth (Phil 2:4).

As a result, we do not seek our rights, our advantage, or our way. The good (*bonum*) of the other is not determined by what we can gain. The only consideration is the good of the other, not our interest, no matter what our feelings might be towards the other.

Christian love, although it does not exclude emotions and feelings, it is action based on a *rational decision.* It properly aligns our emotions and feelings, if necessary, to our actions. We must *decide* to *agape* (ἀγάπη) the other "from a pure heart, a good conscience, and a sincere faith" (1 Tm 1:5b).

Individuals do not act rationally easily. We are constantly moved by our emotions and feelings. They tend to be subjective and fleeting. Often, we calculate our own gain. I know that I'm guilty of this. This is why the Second Person of the Trinity had to become human: to exemplify the true virtue of Christian love—in which its subjectivity is corrected by objectivity.

Taking this a step further, we Christians must unequivocally state that the greatest act of love for a Christian goes beyond merely feeding, clothing, caring for the other, or even worrying about their soul, or helping them get into Heaven. The greatest act of Christian love—the good (bonum) of the other—is to give the other the gift of Jesus the Christ, Who exemplifies and demonstrates the greatest example of agape (ἀγάπη). He is the ultimate gift we can give to another, including our enemy.

Two quick points, first concern souls: I think as Christians we sometimes tend to create a false dichotomy between the body and the soul, and thus concern ourselves with saving souls or stating that God desires souls. This separation can be problematic if taken too far. God is concerned with the totality of our being—our body and soul are truly one (*CCC* #362-368). If not, He would not have bodily resurrected His Son. Thus, God desires more than just our souls, He desires us in our totality. The second point, concerns Heaven: I also think as Christians we sometimes tend to make Heaven our ultimate goal (e.g., being with or seeing our loved ones). It isn't! Heaven is a byproduct. Our ultimate goal is to be in union with Him, our Creator—our Lord our God. He is our total focus. Heaven is only the result of being with Him. We should not be in love with Heaven; we should be in love with Him. Thus, the good of the other is not just to help them get into Heaven; it is to bring them into relationship with our Lord and God. All that said, maybe we should stop concerning ourselves with saving souls or helping people get into Heaven, and start leading others to fall in love with Him.

As we read this, we might object by saying: I thought that the greatest act of love, as just mentioned and according to Jesus, is "to lay down one's life for one's friends" (Jn 15:13). Well, this statement needs to be understood in context. It is a circular argument connected with love in a new commandment: "love one another as I love you" (Jn 15: 13:12; also cf. 13:34). Once again building on our definition of love: Christian love is fundamentally different from all other types of love, for we must love as He loves. Christian love, therefore, is rooted in Him.

It is with this that Jesus goes on to say: "No one has greater love than this, to lay down one's life for one's friends" (Jn 15:13). Then He qualifies what He means by *friend*, by stating that—*you*—we are His friends (Jn 15:14a). Then, leading by example, He shows us the greatest act of love by laying down His life *for us*. In His act of love was Him being *lifted up* (cf. Jn 3:14 and 12:32a), by this, He *will draw everyone* to Himself (Jn 12:32b). To complete the circle—if He is our friend, we must conclude that we are His friend—in turn, we must first lay down our lives for Him, and *in Him*, lay down our lives for the other, for this is stated in His *new commandment*. That is, we are His friends *only* if we do what He has commanded us to do (Jn 15:14b); which is rooted in *agape* (ἀγάπη): "If you love Me, you will keep My commandments" (Jn 14:15), which by the way, is not in reference to the Law.

Therefore, Christian love—*agape* (ἀγάπη)—is rooted in our Messiah, and is connected with the laying down one's life for Him, and in Him, for the other, which is to draw others to Him as a continual circle. Therefore, giving Jesus the Messiah to the other is *the greatest act of love*!

Adding to this understanding of love, let us now juxtapose the mission of Moses with that of the Messiah to give us some further insight.

The book of Exodus could be considered a typology. Egyptian enslavement of the Israelites is a type of our greater enslavement to sin. Egyptian slavery would pass; slavery to sin has eternal consequences. Just as the Israelites in bondage in Egypt needed a saviour, i.e. Moses, each of us needs a Saviour, One who saves beyond the earthly realm.

We need to understand this biblical type, Moses, expressed in terms of earthly *reality* so we can understand the deeper *spiritual reality* of its fulfillment in the Messiah.

To understand the deeper spiritual reality, we must recognize the purpose, ministry, or mission of each saviour. Moses' core mission was the giving of the *Law.* The core Mission of Jesus is a mission of *love*, *mercy*, and *grace* (*Note*[258]). Let us look at the covenantal aspect of each. To do this, we need to consider Abraham.

In his letter to the Galatians, Saint Paul reminds the Galatians that God's promise made to Abraham was a covenantal decree to Abraham and his *seed* (Gal 3:16). Unfortunately, some English translations translate the word *seed*, זֶרַע (zeraʿ/*zeh'-rah*) in the plural as descendant*s* (which academic theologians refer to as the *collective singular*).

However, Saint Paul uses the literal singular rendering of the word—*seed*—to reference only one Person, the Christ (Gal 3:16)—which is also in concert with the singular in Hebrew: "and to his seed" (Gen 12:7, 13:15, 15:18, 17:8, and 22:17-18). He continues to say that the promise granted to Abraham is a gift; it is not dependent on keeping or observing the Law (as some false teachers were teaching), for if it was, it is no longer a gift (Gal 3:18).

So then, what is the purpose of the Law? (Gal 3:19). Saint Paul states (as we have studied), that it was given to show Israel what sin is and to make them conscious of their sinfulness and guilt (Gal 3:19). The Law does not abrogate the promise given to Abraham, nor does it supersede it, for as stated the Law came well after the promise (Gal 3:17 and 3:19).

Now, unlike a promise—which is a pure gift, given by only one party, the giver—the Law needs the consent of both parties, i.e., God and Israel (Gal 3:20). Therefore, Saint Paul continues, the Law needed a go-between, a mediator, or an administrator, which was Moses (Gal 3:19-20).

We may argue that, for Saint Paul, the Law seems to be more of a contract-covenant—for there was an agreement by both parties (Ex 19:5-8)—in contrast, the promise is clearly a gift-covenant. Additionally, the Law itself was a mediator or guardian, until the time of the *promise*, until the *revelation* of the *Seed*, and consequent *faith* in the *Seed* (Gal 4:1-2).

To speak in *human terms*, as Saint Paul put it, a mediator or guardian is needed for children, for they are spiritually immature. Upon adulthood (i.e., spiritual maturity), however, the guardian is no longer needed (Gal 4:1-2). Accordingly, Israel was kept under the disciplinary custody of the Law until the proper time at which the Seed was revealed (Gal 3:23-24, 4:4). Once the Seed was revealed, there was no longer a need for the disciplinarian, no longer need of the Law (Gal 3:25).

The mission of Moses was to administer a temporary earthly reality (the Law) and the Mission of Jesus was to inaugurate an eternal, ultimate spiritual reality arising from the Law: *love*, *mercy*, and *grace*. The Law, given while we are spiritually immature, is based on an *earthly reality*; alternatively, the promise, the gift of salvation is based on a *spiritual reality*.

"When we were children (spiritually immature), we were kept like slaves under the elementary [*man-made religious or philosophical*] teachings of the world" (Gal 4:3[259])—i.e., *earthly reality*. "But when [*in God's plan*] the proper time had fully come, God sent His Son, born of a woman, born under the [*regulations of the*] Law, so that He might redeem *and* liberate those who were under the Law, that we [*who believe*] might be adopted as sons [*as God's children with all rights as fully grown members of a family*]" (Gal 4:4-5[260]; also cf. Rom 11:17-24)—i.e., *spiritual reality*.

This is why the *Seed* must be the *collective singular*, i.e., descendant. For as we studied in Chapter 5, An Ontological Event, when we are baptized into the Christ we are in spiritual union with the one Person, the Anointed One (Gal 3:27). In other words, we are baptized into that singular *Seed*, into the promise, into the gift. For Saint Paul clearly tells us: "you [*who are born-again have been reborn from above—spiritually transformed, renewed, sanctified and*] are all children of God [*set apart for His purpose with full rights and privileges*] through faith in Jesus the Christ" (Gal 3:26[261]).

With this, Saint Paul concludes: "if you belong to Christ [*if you are in Him*], then you are Abraham's descendants, and [*spiritual*] heirs according to [*God's*] promise" (Gal 3:29[262]); "and because you [*really*] are [*His*] sons, God has sent the Spirit of His Son into our hearts, crying out, 'Abba! Father!'" (Gal 4:6[263]).

Wow! This is truly amazing! Through *Yahshua* (יֵשׁוּעַ) the *Mâshîyach* (מָשִׁיחַ), we not only become a part of the promise made to Abraham, we become the spiritual descendents of Abraham (*Note*[264]).

Here are some quick points before we continue.

First, if we were able to be saved by the Law (i.e., the mission of Moses), God would not have become human (in the Mission of the Messiah).

Second, meticulously following the Law to receive divine approval is futile, because the Law cannot save us.

Third, when Jesus says , "the truth will set you free" (Jn 8:32), this is literal, for Jesus the Messiah is the Truth, and only He will set us free, not the Law.

Fourth, in our baptism we now (on this earth) have new life in the Spirit.

Fifth, just as Jesus was "put to death in the flesh" (the *earthly reality*) and "was brought to life in the Spirit" (the *spiritual reality*), so are we right now in that *spiritual reality* (1 Pt 3:18; also cf. Gal 3:26): "So, too, it is written, The first man, Adam, became a living being [*earthly reality*], the last Adam a life-giving spirit [*spiritual reality*], but the spiritual was not first, rather the natural and then the spiritual" (1 Cor 15:45-46).

With these five points let us now continue, for why is it important that we understand the distinction between earthly and spiritual reality? When we look at the Christ on the Cross purely from an earthly reality, we *do not* see an act of love; we see an execution. This is exactly what the bystanders saw that Friday. Israel was caught up in the Law and therefore was caught up in this earthly reality and could not see the spiritual reality the promise unveiled. As we discussed earlier, in this lens of an earthly reality, all they saw and thus wanted was the *Mâshîyach* (מָשִׁיחַ) to liberate them from Roman rule, their current earthly struggle, just like Moses liberated Israel from their earthly struggle, the enslavement to Pharaoh. They could not see the spiritual reality, the act of love—the more important one of the two—which contributes to their missing the Mission of the Messiah.

Like Israel, today some Christians are also caught up in our own earthly reality. Even being baptized in Him (which Israel did not have), some still wear the wrong lenses. Do we not qualify successes and failures strictly within earthly or worldly terms? In this, even living within the time of the fulfillment, we may miss the Mission of the Messiah. It is to our detriment, as it was to Israel's. It is time to change our lenses.

For those who are murmuring while you read this (I agree that this is hard to digest), let us return to Saint Paul for some clarity. Saint Paul acknowledges that he (and us) live in the flesh, yet he adamantly and clearly asserts that it is no longer he who lives, but it is the Messiah, who lives in him (Gal 2:20). This is the paradox in which we currently live: we are on this earth, but we do not belong to this earth. After our baptism, we belong to *Yahshua* (יֵשׁוּעַ) the Christ (to His Kingdom). We live our earthly reality; however, at the same time it is no longer we that live, for we live as the promise, in the Seed. We simultaneously live in an earthly reality and a spiritual reality of the Messiah who lives in us, and we in Him (and this eventually will come to full maturity).

In saying this, we are not denigrating earthly reality, which would be a heresy. God created the universe and "looked at everything He had made, and He found it very good" (Gen 1:31). God loved all things He created, if not, He would not have fashioned it (Wisdom 11:24). Earth is the created environment in which humanity is to live. The Fall of humanity (Gen 3:1-24) has not eliminated that, it only distorted it.

We will discuss this further in the next two chapters, but for now, we need to recognize that, through the Mission of the Messiah (a mission of *love*, *mercy*, and *grace*), we are living in something greater, something beyond the natural; something beyond what we see. We do this while at the same time knowing that the something greater is yet to come.

Consider the *Our Father* (the Lord's Prayer) that the Christ teaches us. We ask for God's Kingdom to come, and His will to be done on earth as it is in Heaven (*Note*[265]).

Some scholars are now saying that this is in reference to a Kingdom of God (a reign of peace) on this earth during a period of time in between the final trial and His Second Coming. This is not the case (see *CCC* #675-676). This is a deception. The Church has rejected every instance in which "the claim is made to realize within history that messianic hope which can only be realized beyond history through the eschatological judgment" even if presented in a modified form (*CCC* #676).

As we live in this world, do His will, and to allow Him to reign over us, we realize that we are actually living that spiritual reality in *Yahshua* (יֵשׁוּעַ) the Messiah, for His Kingdom has come, in Him. Yes! His Kingdom is here right now—*we live as He lives right now*—for the Kingdom of God is in our midst as we speak (Lk 17:21). However, with this understanding we acknowledge that His Kingdom also refers to the eschatological—the *Parousia*—event which is to happen at the end of history as we know it. This is the full and complete fulfillment of the Christ's Kingdom, the part which is yet to come.

Simply put, on the one hand, the Kingdom of God is within history (i.e., in time and space) right now as we speak, and on the other hand, the phrase refers to a dominion and reign outside of history after the Second Coming.

God's "Kingdom does not belong to this world" (Jn 18:36), but has now, in a spiritual sense, come into the world *in Him* and remains *in us*, His bride. "The coming of the Kingdom of God cannot be observed, and no one will announce, 'Look, here it is,' or, 'There it is.' For behold, the Kingdom of God is among you" (Lk 17:20-21) right now, in the Christ. However, eventually at the *Parousia* the present kingdom of this world will be no longer, because at that point: "The kingdom of the world now belongs to our Lord and to His Anointed, and He will reign forever and ever" (Rev 11:15).

According to worldly wisdom, the Cross was disaster. However, from God's Wisdom the Cross makes total sense. In His First Coming, the Christ fulfilled God the Father's plan for introducing the Kingdom and securing eternal salvation for those who would believe in Him. In His Second Coming, God the Father's plan for uniting the Christ's earthly and Heavenly Kingdoms will be fulfilled.

A crucified *Mâshîyach* (מָשִׁיחַ) is the Wisdom of God. It demonstrates a wisdom far beyond our understanding. It demonstrates a spiritual reality. Only in this spiritual reality do we move beyond the lens of merely viewing the crucifixion as an execution—if on that Friday we were a bystander by the Cross—to an ultimate act of love!

Yahshua (יֵשׁוּעַ), in total love for His Father, obediently does the total will of His Father by going to the Cross, thus demonstrating His *agape* (ἀγάπη) for us. Thus, the Cross is the true exemplification of this virtue.

With this, between the two (First and Second Coming), we are called to do exactly the same. We are called to be a *witness of* this virtue: a *witness of* charity; a *witness of* love; a *witness of* mercy; a *witness of* grace; and a *witness of* Him—Jesus the Christ. Radical love is to walk in the Truth, to love in the Truth, and to service to the Truth (3 Jn 1:1-4). This must be our desire.

To do this, first and foremost, just like Saint Paul, we must also "consider everything as a loss, because of the supreme good of knowing [Jesus the Christ our] Lord" (Phil 3:8). We must, for His sake, accept "the loss of all things and consider them so much rubbish [literally dung], that [we] may gain Jesus [the] Christ" (Phil 3:8; also cf. Eccl 1:2).

We must, in *Yahshua* (יֵשׁוּעַ) the *Mâshîyach* (מָשִׁיחַ), make a *rational decision* to lay down our life for our brothers and sisters in love. We must *agape* (ἀγάπη) them just as Jesus the Christ loved us. This is the sacrificial, self-giving Christian *love*, which we are all called to be a witness: "Love one another; as I have loved you" is His New Commandment to us (Jn 13:34).

This is why the Second Person of the Trinity had to become human: to demonstrate and exemplify the true *virtue* of *Christian agape* (ἀγάπη) so we may be a *witness of* His love. Left on our own, we would definitely not understand the Wisdom of God as it pertains to the true meaning of Christian love (*Note*[266]).

Yahshua (יֵשׁוּעַ) the Messiah did not come to us with a rod of discipline and correction—i.e., the Law—He came with love, mercy, and grace (1 Cor 4:21). This was the foundation of His Mission.

To paraphrase Saint Thomas Aquinas: We must disdain what He disdained on the Cross and desire what He desired.

The Second Virtue, Patience:

> If you seek *patience,* you will find no better example than the Cross. Great patience occurs in two ways: either when one patiently suffers much, or when one suffers things which one is able to avoid and yet does not avoid. [The] Christ endured much on the Cross, and did so patiently, because when He suffered He did not threaten; He was led like a sheep to the slaughter and He did not open His mouth. Therefore [the] Christ's patience on the Cross was great. In patience let us run for the prize set before us, looking upon Jesus, the author and perfecter of our faith.[267]
>
> | Saint Thomas Aquinas |

When we look to the Cross we see the *greatest* example of *patience.*[268] The Cross is the true exemplification of this virtue, which we in turn are called to *cultivate.*

Going back to Exodus, we see that the mission of Moses was a mission of power. Although this was part of God's plan (fulfilled within its particular context), and it was God's power (for it was His mighty arm that removed Israel from the hand of Pharaoh) we would not be mistaken if we were to use the word *power* even within a earthly sense; and thus, juxtaposing it against a demonic worldly-power. For example, Pharaoh's minions turn a staff into a snake, while Moses, through the power of God, turns Aaron's staff into a snake that devoured the Egyptians' snakes (Ex 7:9-12). Each time that Pharaoh resisted God, God showed His might and power in very earthly terms. Pharaoh with all his riches, armies, horses, and chariots was met and crushed by the strong arm of God (Ex 15:4). God shows His might and power through the mission of Moses.

In contrast, in the Providence of God, the Mission of *Yahshua* (יֵשׁוּעַ) was not a mission of earthly power. Jesus the Christ did not confront Caesar, to the chagrin of Israel, nor was His mission to overthrow Roman rule. Unlike Moses, He did not *fight the political power* (e.g., Rome). In fact, He avoided confrontation. Before Pontius Pilate (Caesar's political governor of Judah), Jesus declared that His Kingdom was not political in nature; it was not of this world, *nor did it have its origin in this world*. Pilate understood this, thus he found no guilt in Him (see Jn 18:33-38). Jesus the Christ came to "testify to the truth" (Jn 18:3)—His Kingdom is not of this world; therefore neither is ours (*Note*[269]). This is the Wisdom of God.

As stated, even on the Cross, Jesus could have easily come down, foregoing all the suffering and humiliation, but He did not. He patiently endured the long suffering to glorify His Father. Without the incarnation, we would not understand long suffering (i.e., the virtue of patience). We need His physical example to demonstrate this virtue to us. This is the Wisdom of God.

Don't get me wrong, I am not calling this some sort of pacifism. I am merely presenting the biblical text for our reflection. Recall John the Baptist sitting in prison wondering what is happening. Adding to that discussion, we should acknowledge that Jesus starts His ministry by saying that He has come to "let the oppressed go free" (Lk 5:18; also cf. Ps 146:7). Well, when John the Baptist, His forerunner, was unjustly sitting in prison, but, Jesus does not go out to help him. Jesus does not even try to set him free (cf. Mt 4:12 and Mk 1:14). Actually, Jesus ignores his plight and just leaves him to be eventually beheaded (Lk 7:18-35). What does this mean? As the saying goes: Actions speak louder than words. So then, what is Jesus' action teaching us? There is something deeper happening here. There is something beyond this earthly reality happening here. This is the Wisdom of God, with which you and I need to deeply ponder and grapple.

As we struggle with His examples, we must also acknowledge that all power and political rule comes from God—"there is no authority except from God" (Rom 13:1). He *allows* earthy political authority, and their just or unjust rulings (*Note*[270]). We must live in the tension of living in two worlds, the earthly realm and that of the spiritual Kingdom of God. On one hand, we are social beings with the right to be involved in public political life. However, we must keep in mind that, in another sense, we are mere pilgrims and sojourners on this earth. Our Messiah endured evil. He did not fight against earthly rulers—He did not *fight the power*, so to speak. Therefore, we may want to ask ourselves: Should we?

Again, as I am presenting this, I hope we do not see this merely as pacifism. I think that conclusion is too simplistic. On the contrary, I hope we see this for what it is—the *Wisdom of God*!

Saint Paul urges us to aspire to live tranquil, quiet, and peaceable lives, to mind our own affairs, and to work with our own hands (1 Thes 4:11), to live in harmony with others (Rom 12:16), and "to conduct ourselves properly toward others" (1 Thes 4:12). "Your kindness should be known to all" (Phil 4:5) says Saint Paul. He also urged us to "put away ambitious thoughts and associate with those who are lowly" (Rom 12:16[271]). "Let every person be subordinate to the higher authorities" (Rom 13:1), and "obedient to the officials in authority; to be ready to do good at every opportunity; not to go slandering other people but to be peaceable and gentle, and always polite to [all] people" (Ti 3:1-2). We must also pray for our leaders and those in authority "that we may lead a quiet and tranquil life in all devotion and dignity" (1 Tm 2:2). We must not argue or fight; "do everything without grumbling or questioning, that you may be blameless and innocent, children of God without blemish in the midst of a crooked and perverse generation, among whom you shine like lights in the world" (Phil 2:14-15). To sum up, we must patiently endure, that is endure longsuffering (1 Tm 4:5).

Do not worry; God is in charge. He has made you "the light of the world. A city set on a mountain that cannot be hidden" (Mt 5:14). At the same time, however, live "as aliens and sojourners" Saint Peter tells us, and "keep away from worldly desires" (1 Pt 2:11)—don't get entangled in it (2 Pt 2:20). We are ultimately not of this world (Jn 8:23), so be careful to "not run in vain or labour in vain" (Phil 2:16). Always remember that "the wisdom from above is first of all pure, then peaceable, gentle, compliant, full of mercy and good fruits, without inconstancy or insincerity" (Jms 3:17).

Cultivating the example set forth by Jesus our Messiah, we must be patient and stay focused, placing our eyes on the prize (which is not of this world), and run the race to win (1 Cor 9:24), for our long suffering "produces endurance, and endurance produces character, and character produces hope" (Rom 5:3-4).

All the while we are to keep in mind that "our struggle is not against flesh and blood [*contending only with physical opponents*], but against the rulers, against the powers, against the world forces of this [*present*] darkness, against the spiritual *forces* of wickedness in the Heavenly (supernatural) *places*" (Eph 6:12[272]). Therefore, we are not fighting against earthly rulers, as such. Our battle is a spiritual warfare. "Although we are in the flesh, we do not battle according to the flesh, for the weapons of our battle are not of flesh but are enormously powerful, capable of destroying fortresses" (1 Cor 10:3-4).

This is why the Second Person of the Trinity had to become human: to exemplify the *virtue* of *patience*, so we may *cultivate* it; left on our own, we would not understand the Wisdom of God as it pertains to the meaning of Christian patience, nor that we must unwearyingly endure long suffering, for our warfare is not an earthly one, but a spiritual one.

Therefore, cultivating the example of *Yahshua* (יֵשׁוּעַ) the *Mâshîyach* (מָשִׁיחַ), let us patiently endure whatever comes our way. "For to this you have been called, because [the] Christ also suffered for you, leaving you an example that you should follow in His footsteps" (1 Pt 2:21). Bear in mind that "the sufferings of this present time are as nothing compared with the glory to be revealed for us" (Rom 8:18).

To paraphrase Saint Thomas Aquinas: We must disdain what He disdained on the Cross and desire what He desired.

The Third Virtue, Humility:

> If you seek an example of *humility*, look upon the crucified one, for God wished to be judged by Pontius Pilate and to die.[273]
>
> | Saint Thomas Aquinas |

When we look at the Cross we see the *greatest* example of *humility*.[274] The Cross is the true exemplification of this virtue, which we should *understand*.

Acknowledging that all good ultimately comes from the grace of God; I would like to emphasize the Wisdom of God in the virtue of humility from a slightly different perspective.

Continuing to juxtapose the mission of Moses with that of the mission of *Yahshua* (יֵשׁוּעַ), we see an interesting dichotomy between what we typically label as, *something practical* or *good in theory*. In our human nature, most of us like things to be practical. Thus, we might more easily relate to Moses' mission than that of Jesus'. Moses' mission was clearly practical from an earthly point of view, whereas we may argue that the mission of *Yahshua* (יֵשׁוּעַ) was not. From an earthly, practical point of view, a crucified Messiah makes very little sense.

Going through Scripture, we have many more examples of this impracticality, or impossibility. Just to name a few: it is not possible for someone in their old age to have a child; Sarah knows this, she laughs at the thought; giving expedient advice in very practical terms, she gives Abraham, her husband, their slave girl to have a child with him (Gen 18:13 and 16:3) for in theory having a child at Sarah's age was an impossibility.

An untrained boy is not normally successful against a giant seasoned enemy warrior; in practical terms, Saul knows this, so he tries to stop David from fighting Goliath (1 Sam 17:33 and 17:4).

In practice, it is impossible to feed five thousand men plus women and children with five barley loaves and two fish; the disciples know this, so they put their hands in the air and ask: "Where do we get this money?" (Mk 6:44).

It is not practical for the *Mâshîyach* (מָשִׁיחַ), the Son of the living God, to be judged by an earthly ruler and be put to death, Saint Peter knows this, so he rebukes this very thought (Mt 16:16 and 16:22).

So then, what's my point? To *understand* humility in this context, we need only to look at Jesus' return rebuke to Saint Peter (when Peter rebuked Jesus, denying that He should be killed): Jesus ". . . turned and said to Peter, Get behind me, Satan! You are an obstacle to me. You are thinking not as God does, but as human beings do" (Mt 16:23).

This is very harsh. The implication is that God's thinking and ungodly human thinking are polar opposites. In our practicality, looking at possibilities, we are not thinking as God does. This is an understanding about God which we need to grasp. However, like Saint Peter we tend to think in practical human terms, from a very earthly day-to-day point of view, not a godly one, i.e., not a biblical one. Hence the harsh rebuke. In a way Jesus is telling Peter, in humility, to understand God's plan—as impractical and impossible as it may sound—and do not get caught up in Satan's plan, which sounds very practical (cf. Gen 3:1-4).

Recall, Satan's telling Eve, "No! You will not die!" if you eat the fruit (Gen 3:4). How is that even possible? It is just a fruit of a tree! This is Satan's implication. Humility, however, knows God is in charge. What may sound impractical might just be our limited thinking. God, being in charge, may do what is impractical and impossible in human terms. To understand humility, it is time that we change our desire for earthly practicality or possibility, and in humility *understand* the Wisdom of God even if it sounds impossible or impractical. The Wisdom of God is "not a wisdom of this age" (1 Cor 2:6).

Adding to this, the Wisdom of God is a "mysterious, hidden [Wisdom], which God predetermined before the ages for our glory" (1 Cor 2:7). Yes, it says for *our* glory. As it is written: "Things which the eye has not seen, ear has not heard, nor has it so much entered or dawned on human beings, what God has prepared for those who love Him" (1 Cor 2:9). As Christians, we need to humble ourselves in order to *understand* this particular nuance concerning the Wisdom of God. In fact, through the Holy Spirit, for our glory, God will reveal His Wisdom to us if we are open to it (1 Cor 2:10).

For example, it is not possible for a young *virgin* to be pregnant; Mary knows this, but in humility, she also knows that, for God, all things are possible (cf. Mt 19:26, Mk 10:27 and Lk 18:27); with this she says: "Behold, I am the handmaid of the Lord. May it be done to me according to your word" (Lk 1:34 and 1:38). She shows an essential element of humility, although it is well beyond her comprehension (or even the earthly physical reality of her virginity). It is this part of humility we need to understand. Mary does not limit God with her practicality—she lets *God be God*!

Humility is acknowledging that God is working for us and through us if we allow Him to do so, and to *understand* that this is far beyond our comprehension. With *acceptance* of God's working, in humility, there is a *sigh of relief. Understanding* that God is in charge and not we, is a *sign of relief.* We are not the ones giving the orders. We are not the ones in the driver's seat. It is not about our own strength or abilities. It is about Him. He is in charge. He is the One giving the orders. He is the One in the driver's seat.

All said, avoid the two extremes. A distorted *mea culpa*, in which we say: Look at me, I am unworthy and weak. There is no identity crisis within Christian humility. Or the opposite extreme, by saying: Look at me, how great I am. There is no exalting of oneself, within Christian humility. We work in unison with God, but it is He Who gives us the strength. We are His co-workers, but it is He Who develops us to our full potential. In humility we understand that our identity is in Him; in humility we understand that in our covenant-partnership with Him we will achieve true greatness in Him; and most of all, in humility we understand that it is only "by the grace of God [that] I am what I am" (1 Cor 15:10).

All the while—to summarize—we should realize that the Wisdom of God does not fit into our limited understanding. We should acknowledge that the Wisdom of God is far beyond our comprehension. We should allow God to be God and let Him do great things through us, as impractical and impossible as it may sound. Not for our glory, but for His. Like Mother Mary, let it be *done to me according to His word*, should be our mantra as well. In this, we should be in *awe* of Him and firmly grasp the truth that it is only *by the grace of God that I am what I am*!

This is the example given to us: the Son of God, in humility, recognizes that being judged by a mere earthly ruler, and being put to death by him is part of the Father's plan. We therefore need the Christ Event, for only an incarnation could demonstrate this unfathomable reality, to us. This is the Wisdom of God.

This is why the Second Person of the Trinity became human: to demonstrate and exemplify the true *virtue* of *humility*, so we may truly *understand* it; for left on our own, we would definitely not understand the Wisdom of God as it pertains to the true meaning of Christian humility.

As stated in the Preface: If our beliefs are theologically sound, and we put them into practice, our life will inevitably be sound! If our beliefs are unsound, our life becomes unsound! Through the Revelation of *Yahshua* (יֵשׁוּעַ) the *Mâshîyach* (מָשִׁיחַ), our practical day-to-day living must always be based upon sound theory or theology (i.e., the foundational understanding of God that underlies and therefore enlightens our worldview). If not, we will receive a harsh rebuke just like Saint Peter.

To paraphrase Saint Thomas Aquinas: We must disdain what He disdained on the Cross and desire what He desired.

The Fourth Virtue, Obedience:

> If you seek an example of *obedience*, follow Him who became obedient to the Father even unto death. For just as by the disobedience of one man, namely, Adam, many were made sinners, so by the obedience of one Man, many were made righteous.[275]
>
> | Saint Thomas Aquinas |

When we look at the Cross we see the *greatest* example of *obedience*.[276] The Cross is the true exemplification of this virtue, in which we are called to *live*.

Through the mission of Moses, Israel became obedient to God through the Law. Through the Mission of *Yahshua* (יֵשׁוּעַ), we are presented with a greater reality, Jesus' *direct* obedience to God the Father. The Christ continually states that He is here to do the Father's will (see Jn 8:28 and 7:16). He does not seek His own will but God the Father's will (see Jn 5:30). Even the very *food* of His life is to do the will of the One who sent Him (see Jn 4:34). He demonstrates this in the ultimate act of obedience to the Father, when He goes to the Cross (Phil 2:8). If Jesus had such a desire to do the will of the Father, why should we be any different? We must *desire what He desired.* We are called to *live* out that *same obedience.* We are called to that *same conviction and commitment to obedience* to God the Father.

However, as we studied in Chapter 3, The Absolute Primacy of Jesus, the Wisdom of God places all primacy on *Yahshua* (יֵשׁוּעַ) the Messiah.

I suggest that the transition goes something like this. At the macro level, all of humanity is called to do the will of the Father. Not one human being is *excluded* from His call. So, what is the will of the Father? Simply put, it is to *listen* to His Son (Mt 17:5, Mk 9:7, and Lk 9:35; also cf. Mt 7:21). What we have here is a clear and objective directive from God the Father on His will for us.

There is no guesswork here. Without qualification, it is simply stated—*Listen to Him*!—Listen to My Son. We are the ones creating enmity with God when we go against God's will. Moreover, in this, when we *listen* to His Son, when we *see* His Son, and when we *believe* in His Son, we will have life eternal *with* Him for we will be raised up *in* Him (Jn 6:40). This is the clear and concise *will* of the Father. As we studied, He gives all *primacy* to His Son.

Subsequently, with this directive from the Father, we now logically move to the *will* of the Son. Here, we may scour the Gospels to discover the *objective will* of the Son, i.e., what He wants from us. Additionally, He also gives us a clear and objective directive, which is to *follow Him*; more precisely, take up our cross, and follow Him (Mt 16:24 and Mk 8:34). Even more precisely, He directs us to take up our cross *daily*, and follow Him (Lk 9:23). It does not get any clearer than this. This is the *will* of the Son.

Then, in the Son's will, He imparts to us His Spirit, the Holy Spirit, the Advocate (see Jn 14:16 and 15:26). This is where the subjective element of God's *will* in our life comes into play. This is the micro level of God's *will*. It is in the *take up your cross* part of the Son's directive. For all our crosses differ. They are subjective and personal to us. Your cross is not the same as mine. We even see this in the life of the Messiah, where right after His baptism He was led by the Holy Spirit to begin His particular mission (Mt 4:1, Mk 1:12, and Lk 4:1). Thus the will of the Holy Spirit is to help us and guide us to *take up our personal cross—daily*—and follow the Son. To be precise, "you will receive power when the Holy Spirit comes upon you" (Acts 1:8) to carry out your personal mission, in the Son. This is our very personal and subjective mission within the objective directive of the Messiah.

To state all this in another way, we may connect this to the threefold path of discipleship: "Whoever wishes to come after me must deny himself, take up his cross, and follow me" (Mt 16:24, Mk 8:34, and Lk 9:23). To *deny oneself* is the will of the Father at the macro level—it is where we lose our own interest and listen to His Son. The *follow me* is the will of the Son. Accordingly, the *take up your cross* is the will of the Holy Spirit, the subjective will for you at the micro level. Each will collectively is the total will of God!

Saint Francis gets this point and shares it with his brothers shortly before he passed away to eternal life. He tells them: "I have done *what is mine*, *may* [*the*] *Christ teach* you what is yours!"[277] All the brothers (the Franciscans) are called to *follow* the Christ (this is the objective directive), but they are not all called to follow the Christ exactly as Saint Francis did, that is, they are not all called to be another Saint Francis. Each Franciscan brother has his own personal mission within the overall mission. This also applies to us. The call to follow the Christ is an objective call, but our personal calling is the subjective mission within that objective calling (*Note*[278]).

A vivid example of this is found in the discourse between Jesus and the Rich Young Man, found in both the Gospel of Saint Matthew and the Gospel of Saint Mark (Mt 19:16-22 and Mk 10:17-22). Concerning ourselves with only the point in question, and the subtle movement through which Jesus takes the young man, we start with the young man's question of Jesus, "What must I do to gain eternal life?" (Mt 19:16). Here we get the first tidbit of insight, for Jesus answers "If you wish to enter into life, keep the commandments" (Mt 19:17). If you notice, *the commandments* are a direct reference to the Law, and Jesus does not use the word *eternal*, He plainly states *life*. The Law equals the temporal promise. This is obedience to God through the Law.

To this, the young man replies "All of these I have observed from my youth" (MK 10:20). At first glance, we might question: How's this even possible? How is it possible to keep *all* of the Law? Here is the next tidbit of insight. "Jesus, looking at him, [and] loved him" (Mk 10:21). Love—*agape* (ἀγάπη)—is the Greek word used here. The young man's answer was in simplicity and in good conscience. In his mind he did not lie; he believed what he said. If this were not true, Jesus would have still *loved him* and in that objective *agape* (ἀγάπη) He would have called out his deception (like He has done with others). In addition, the young man had an intense desire—a real commitment to obedience. If we were to stop and think about it, unlike others he does not ask for healings or anything of the sort, but he continues by asking Jesus, "What do I lack?" (Mt 19:20). Continuing this subtle movement, the journey that Jesus is taking the young man through, Jesus' answer gives us another tidbit of insight, for He tells the young man "You are lacking one thing" (Mk 10:21).

Let me interject here; if we were to go to the bank and ask for a loan, and after going through the loan-process the personal banker tells us: Everything looks good, but you are *lacking one thing*. This literally means you are not getting the loan, or at minimum until that one thing is fixed! You can have all ninety-nine things in order, but the *one thing* is the difference between an acceptance and a denial. Well, this is no different.

Even if we believe we are keeping all the Commandments—and for the moment, let us assume we are—we like the young man, are still *lacking one thing*, and that *one thing* denies us entry. Here we not only see the deficiency of the Law, we see the subtle movement from *the commandments* (i.e., Law) to His commandments. For if we *love Him* we will keep *His commandments* (Jn 14:15). Now if *the commandments* and *His commandments* were the same, why would we be still *lack one thing*? As we discussed in previous chapters, it is not about how good of a person we are, how kind we are to one another, or about the love—not *agape* (ἀγάπη)—we show one another. *The Wisdom of God is that eternal life could not be achieved apart from His Son.* This is basically what Jesus is saying to the young man, and by extension to you and me. Yes, keeping the Law is good, but, not good enough—for we will still be *lacking one thing*. That *one thing* is that we need to follow Him, for Jesus tells the young man: "Come, follow Me" (Mk 10:21).

Here is another tidbit. In addition to *lacking one thing*, Jesus' answer also demonstrates the deeper meaning of the Law. He rattled the young man by showing him his misconception of thinking that he had kept the Law. Jesus' answer demonstrates the true cost of loving your neighbour: "Jesus said to him, 'If you wish to be perfect, go, sell what you have and give to the poor'" (Mk 10:21). This is the true cost of loving your neighbour. This also showed the young man that although he sincerely believed he was keeping the Law, he was, in actuality, not.

As mentioned, a journey takes place here, not only for the young man, but also for us. We sometimes mistake, "If you love me, you will keep My commandments" (Jn 14:15) as that of keeping the Law. However, Jesus is not referring to the Law. For even if—through some great miracle—we do keep all the Law, we will still be *lacking one thing*. Besides, Jesus clearly tells us exactly what His commandment is: "I give you a new commandment, love one another, as I have loved you" (Jn 13:34 and 15:12). This is the fulfillment of the Law.

We will explore the second part of this—the continuing dialogue between *Yahshua* (יֵשׁוּעַ) and His disciples—shortly. Until then, another tidbit, concerning the word *perfect*, needs to be stated within this context.

When we hear the word *perfect*, we may think that *Yahshua* (יֵשׁוּעַ) is asking the young man (or us) to achieve a life without fault of any sort. However, this is not entirely the case. The English word *perfect* does not completely capture the underlying Greek word used here (cf. Mt 5:45), which is τέλειος (teleios/*tel'-i-os*); which means to *complete* (in various applications of labour, growth, mental and moral character, etc.), or to bring to completion, or perfection; this word is rooted in the Greek word τέλος (telos/*tel'-os*), meaning the end result of an act or state, to *set out* for a definite point or *goal*, or a fixed end or an end propose, or a natural end.[279]

Therefore, to use the word *perfect* or to achieve perfection, in this context, means to do or achieve or to complete or bring to completion what *you* have been designed to do—your particular ends.

For example, a hammer could be used in various different ways, but, the actual *telos* (τέλος) of a hammer is to pound in nails, this is its end. This is its *telos* (τέλος), what it is actually designed to do. The hammer is at its best and the most happy (if I may jokingly say) when pounding nails.

Likewise, humans are free to do as they wish. We have the free will to go against our own nature, to go against our true identity, and to go against who we really are; but, that does not mean that we do not have an actual *telos* (τέλος), collectively and individually.

Despite the secular world's incantation that humanity is just a random happening of chance, life has purpose, meaning, and direction. We are created for a *purpose*. We have a *true identity*. All of humanity has a *natural order* or *fixed end*. Our life has *meaning*. We all have a precise *direction*. This is what obedience is; it is to *live* out that purpose.

The *Catechism of the Catholic Church* begins with this purpose, meaning, and direction. That is humanity's *telos* (τέλος) at the macro level is that we are all "created by God for God" (*CCC* #27), and, as we just studied, it is to follow the Christ, as an objective calling. This is our collective *telos* (τέλος). Within that calling at the micro level, is the particular subjective mission (our particular direction) that the

Christ wants from us, individually to complete—to *take up our cross.* This is our individual *telos* (τέλος).

Jesus our Messiah defines us. He gives each and every one of us our true identity. In fact, He is our very identity.

Our objective mission is what each one of us is designed to do, and the subjective is what is only ours to do—it is our particular *mission* in life, carried out in *total* obedience to Him. Obedience to Him is paramount (see Gen 2:16-17).

If we were to go back and analyze the last part of the dialogue, it would go something like this: *Jesus said to him, if you wish to be perfect*, that is, if you wish to achieve your *telos* (τέλος), what you have been designed to do, your particular ends, in obedience, *go, sell all what you have and give to the poor*, for this is your particular subjective mission in life at the micro level; it is the "take up your cross" part of your mission (*Note*[280]). Then, *come follow Me*, for this is your overall objective mission; this is God's will in your life; it is what contains your subjective personal mission.

That is why the Second Person of the Trinity had to become human: to exemplify the *virtue* of *obedience*, so we may *live* it. Left on our own, we would definitely not understand the Wisdom of God as it pertains to the true meaning of Christian obedience, nor discover that we are not only created for a general purpose but also for a particular purpose, as an individual within the collective.

To paraphrase Saint Thomas Aquinas: We must disdain what He disdained on the Cross and desire what He desired.

The Fifth Virtue, Despising Earthly Things:

> If you seek an example of *despising earthly things*, follow Him who is the King of kings and the Lord of lords, in whom are hidden all the treasures of Wisdom and knowledge. Upon the Cross He was stripped, mocked, spat upon, struck, crowned with thorns, and given only vinegar and gall to drink. Do not be attached, therefore, to clothing and riches, because they divided My garments among themselves. Nor to honours, for He experienced harsh words and scourging. Nor to greatness of rank, for

weaving a crown of thorns they placed it on My head. Nor to anything delightful, for in My thirst they gave Me vinegar to drink.[281]

| Saint Thomas Aquinas |

When we look at the Cross, we see the *greatest* example of *despising earthly things*. The Cross is the true exemplification of this virtue, of what we are called to *do*.

As a Christian, we are called to *be* unworldly, that is, godly and detached from earthly things. This is counter-cultural. Yet, we are in this world as mere *aliens and sojourners* or *pilgrims and strangers*, so we must "keep away from worldly desires"; for worldliness "wages war against the soul" (1 Pt 2:11). We are called to be *in* this world of humanity, but not *of* this world that is antagonistic to God and His truth (*Note*[282]). Thus, we must be content, settled in, and satisfied with what we have (Heb 13:5 and 1 Tm 6:8).

However, in saying this, we do not denigrate the worth of creation as God's gift to us. Nor does it disparage the goodness of this world or the godly pleasures of this world. God created the world and *the world is good* (Gen 1:1-2:3), for God's goodness is in this world. We should not construct an un-theological dichotomy in which we say the world is somehow evil or bad in its entirety.

The despising of earthly things or worldly desires or sinful pleasures is not our opposing the goodness that God has created in the world. As we read in Appendix A, 8, Holy Scripture uses the word *world* in both a good sense and a bad. The temporal goods, gifts, and pleasures of this world should not be abused, they are to be used in their proper order or *telos* (τέλος), rightly, thankfully, and in that we should rejoice in it (as we will discuss in Chapter 8, "Rejoice . . . Always!").

In other words, in the good sense, being worldly is being caught-up or devoted to the things of our Messiah (see Jn 3:16), in the bad sense, being *worldly* is related to being caught-up or devoted to the ungodly aspects of our society, and being attached to temporal things (see Jms 4:4).

The sinfully worldly *Christian* is one who has faith and trust in Jesus the Christ, but is at the same time caught up with ambition, achievements, sophistication, desire to impress others, to be the envy of others, and so forth. This clinging to, and desiring these things, makes the *worldly Christian* no different from a non-Christian.

The term used by Saint Paul for worldliness in the bad sense is *fleshly people* (1 Cor 3:1). As he speaks to the church in Corinth, he gives us a very simple gauge to determine if a Christian is a *fleshly* person or a *spiritual* person. In his words "you are *still of the flesh* if there is jealousy and rivalry among you; for while there is jealousy and strife among you, are you not of the flesh, and behaving in an ordinary human way? (1 Cor 3:3).

The focus within this virtue is to do away with this *fleshly* person that we might find within us. Because this virtue goes against the grain of the society in which we live (not to mention our own sinful nature), I think this is the virtue that we as Christians struggle with the most (even from a sheer acceptance of it). Yes, I think at some basic level this is not a virtue we desire. In some sense we are scandalized or revolted by this virtue and may very easily rationalize or theologize it away.

Let us therefore present this last virtue in *twelve points*, for I find that because this virtue is extreme, counter-cultural, and intense, we need to recognize the virtue's nuances. It is hoped that, through the grace of God, it will make it easier for us to digest, thus create an appetite for acceptance.

Point Number 1: We should point out that the opposite of this virtue is all seven Deadly Sins[283]: pride, envy, sloth, lust, greed, gluttony and anger. If we do not despise earthly things and worldly allurement, we open the door to *all* Seven Deadly Sins. All that is worldly in the sense of being antagonistic to God (and His design) is rooted in these sins; the lust of sensual craving, the envy and longing of the eyes for forbidden things, the boastful pride of life, a pretentious life, self-determination, self-actualization, a conceited confidence in wealth and resources, or in the stability of earthly possessions, the love or greed for money—these do not come from God, nor are they the Wisdom of God; they are from the world and are rooted in the wisdom of this world (1 Jn 2:16).

Yahshua (יֵשׁוּעַ), Himself, admonishes us to "Watch out and be on our guard against every form of lust or greed" (Lk 12:15). This admonition uses a Jewish writing technique called the Hebrew superlative. This example—*watch out* and *be on your guard*—being a twice-stated emphatic admonition is an imperative, therefore, it should not be taken lightly.

In another example, *Yahshua* (יֵשׁוּעַ) asks us: "How will it profit you if we were to gain the whole world [i.e., wealth, fame, success, and so forth], but, forfeit your souls?" (Mt 16:26, Mk 8:36, and Lk 9:25).

Point Number 2: We began the first of these five *virtues* by arguing that Exodus is a typology. I think this virtue is the strongest reason that can be made for this argument. For example, Israel was promised the geographic area that became known as the Promised Land; it was a productive land "flowing with milk and honey" (Deut 26:8-9 and Jer 32:22). The Promised Land is a territory on physical earth; however, in typology it pointed to a spiritual reality.

That is to say, if Exodus is a type that points towards the spiritual deliverance fulfilled in Jesus the Messiah (*Note*[284]), the Promised Land is also a type that points towards the New Jerusalem (Rev 21:2). The new Promised Land is not in the earthly realm, "for here we have no lasting city, but we seek the one that is to come" (Heb 13:14).

We just need to seek and wait for—"the Name of my God and the name of the city of my God, the New Jerusalem"—the new Promised Land to come down out of Heaven from our God (Rev 3:12). This is the New Mount Zion that cannot be shaken (Heb 12:18-29). This is exactly what we are waiting for.

Jesus' Kingdom does not "belong to this world" (Jn 18:36). This is a core teaching that, sadly, we tend to overlook or water down. Looking for and chasing after earthly power and prosperity in any form is not our goal. If it were or if we think it is, we must re-examine the issue and answer these questions: How do we account for Jesus' virtue of despising earthly things? Furthermore, why did He not seek after earthly power and prosperity while on this earth? Worldly power belongs to Satan. Consider Satan's three temptations to the Christ in the desert (Mt 4:1-11 and Lk 4:1-13). Consider the time that the crowds wanted to "carry Him off to make Him king" (Jn 6:15). He could have easily accepted these earthly honours, but He did not!

Why did Jesus not rebel against Caesar? Why did He not reclaim the Promised Land from the Romans?

Keeping this answer very simple, it is because His Kingdom is in this world but not of this world.

Saint Thomas Aquinas has articulated the example given by Jesus; now we must also be *unworldly* in the proper sense, just like Jesus. This is what we are called to *do*. He completely abandoned Himself to His Father, so we must completely abandon ourselves to Him. He died on a Cross for His Father, so we must be willing to die for Him.

To verify the veracity of this conclusion, we need only consider the Apostles and the Saints. Did the Apostles run after earthly or worldly success? Of course they did not! After Pentecost, they were willing to die for their Messiah. Church tradition tells us that they were all martyred except for John who was banished to a remote island. This doesn't sound like a worldly achievement to me! The Church was built on the blood of these martyrs throughout the centuries.

Even Saints who *had* earthly success of varying degrees had a complete detachment. For example, Saint Bridget of Sweden was of noble decent. Saint Francis of Assisi came from a rich merchant family. Saint Clare came from a wealthy, aristocratic family. Saint Thomas More was a renowned lawyer, who became the equivalent of the Prime Minister of England. Saints Margaret of Scotland and Elizabeth of Portugal were both queens. Saints Elizabeth and Margaret of Hungary were both princesses. Saint Edward the Confessor was a king of England. The list goes on. All of them knew their Kingdom was not of this world and were unworldly just like Jesus. So should we be.

Point Number 3: Dealing with various issues within a first-generation church community formed by Saint Paul in Corinth, Saint Paul gives a description of his ministry as an example and admonishment to the Corinthian church: "To this very hour we go hungry and thirsty, we are poorly clad and roughly treated, we wander about homeless and we toil, working with our own hands" (1 Cor 4:11).

He does not stop there: "When ridiculed, we bless; when persecuted, we endure; when slandered, we respond gently. We have become like the world's rubbish, the scum of all, to this very moment" (1 Cor 4:12-13). Does this sound like he is pursuing earthly prosperity? "Of course not!" He obviously was not a preacher of the Prosperity Gospel, since he was holding up his plight as an example to follow as he goes on to exclaim: "I urge you, be imitators of me" (1 Cor 4:16).

Saint Paul followed the example of *Yahshua* (יֵשׁוּעַ). For comparison, let us paraphrase Saint Thomas Aquinas' description of Jesus: They stripped Him, mocked Him, spat upon Him, struck Him, and crowned Him with thorns. When He was on the Cross, they gave Him only sour wine and gall to drink.

Therefore, do not be attached to earthly things, to clothing and riches, for they divided Jesus' minimal garments among themselves. Do not be attached to honours, for He experienced harsh words and scourging. Do not be attached to high rank, for they twisted a crown of thorns and placed it on His head. Do not be attached to excessive eating and drinking, for in His thirst they gave Him sour wine to drink.

The One who has called us to *follow Him* despised earthly things; in His steps the Apostles and Saints followed His lead and despised earthly things. Therefore, shouldn't we?

As it is written: Jesus "suffered outside the gate, to consecrate the people by His own blood. Let us then go to Him outside the camp, bearing the reproach that He bore. For here we have no lasting city, but we seek the one that is to come" (Heb 13:12-14).

It is elsewhere written: "For to this you have been called, because [the] Christ also suffered for you, leaving you an example that you should follow in His footsteps. He committed no sin, and no deceit was found in His mouth. When He was insulted, He returned no insult; when He suffered, He did not threaten; instead, He handed Himself over to the One who judges justly" (1 Pt 2:21b-23). Let us then go *outside the gates* following the Messiah's *footsteps*, for this is what we are called to *do*.

Point Number 4: We should not make the mistake of thinking that Saint Paul (or for that matter any of the Saints) liked suffering for its own sake. This is a rationalization used by some to water-down this virtue. On the contrary, their example should inspire us, for it is the Saints' conviction and commitment to obedience to God the Father, which allows them to suffer just like the Christ suffered. It is rooted in the realization that doing the will of the Father would inevitability bring about suffering. Why is this so? God's will is in direct opposition to the will of this world; and, here is a key: if we love properly—*agape* (ἀγάπη) our neighbour—we will without doubt suffer (*Note*[285]). This is a *sine qua non* (that is, a direct result of) Christian love. There is absolutely no way around it. However, with this there is also the confidence and assurance that "the sufferings of this present time are as nothing compared with the glory to be revealed for us" (Rom 8:18).

Point Number 5: If we do not despise earthly things, we will find ourselves torn between the will of the Father and the will of this world: for "no one can serve two masters, he will either hate one and love the other, or be devoted to one and despise the other; you cannot serve both God and mammon" (Mt 6:24 and Lk 16:13).

The Greek word that is translated into the English word *mammon*, is μαμμωνᾶς (mammōnas/mam-mo-nas'). It is a word of Chaldean origin, which not only means money, confidence in wealth or possessions, fame, status, greed or avarice, but, it means these traits personified.[286] That is to say, *mammon* is the tangible *personification* of *whatever* is valued to us more than God, which would include social constructs. Mammon goes beyond idolatry. It is not only an idol; it is the deification of that idol where it is eventually opposed to God—an anti-God.

Therefore, we cannot serve any of these things in any manner and think we can serving God at the same time. Another way of putting it is if we do serve any of these things, they, individually or collectively become our god, for the word *mammon* means the act of serving a different entity altogether (or as some academic theologians put it: an idol *par excellence* or *molten god*), which is in exact opposition to God. We may also equate serving mammon with the wide gate and the broad road or path that leads to destruction (Mt 7:13), in opposition to serving God by entering the narrow gate and taking the constricted road or path that leads to *Life* (Mt 7:14).

Keep in mind, belief in a deity is inherent. Every human being has this intrinsic belief—including an atheist (acknowledged or not). We might not worship the God of the Bible, but *we will* end up worshiping something!

Point Number 6: Qoheleth (a.k.a. King David's son, Solomon) audaciously exclaims in his philosophical treatise Ecclesiastes: "Vanity of vanities! All things are vanity" (Eccl 1:2). Again, what we have here is a superlative, a double-fold emphatic admonition: emphasizing that everything is futile; all things are sheer futility; the *utmost* vanity!

This might sound acceptable coming from a poor person but, according to Ecclesiastes this is coming from King Solomon (*Note*[287]) who had had riches humanly unimaginable for its time. To put this into perspective, analysts estimate that his net worth to be somewhere between 2.0 and 2.2 trillion dollars in today's US currency. In fact, some rate King Solomon as the seventh richest person ever to live. With all this wealth, he experienced all earthly pleasures possible at the time. Whatsoever his eyes desired was not kept from him (Eccl 2:10), including seven hundred wives and three hundred concubines (1 Kgs 11:3).

Having all this he concludes that all things are vanity, futile, empty, meaningless, frustrating—it is like chasing the wind (Eccl 1:1:4). Is he trying emotionally to depress us or make us disillusioned? Is, *life meaningless, and an empty void of despair*, as some have concluded?

For the sake of brevity, we will narrow the focus to this context. Qoheleth, even with his incomplete theology (for this was long before the time of Jesus) shares with us something very insightful and profound concerning God's Wisdom.

The answer to the meaningless of life and ensuing emotional depression comes with Jesus the Messiah. Yes, "creation was made subject to futility" as Saint Paul writes in his letter to the Romans (Rom 8:2). Yes, everything is loss, rubbish, and dung . . . but wait for it . . . for here is the exception—*except* for the *supreme good* of knowing *Yahshua* (יֵשׁוּעַ) the Christ (Phil 3:8; also cf. Eccl 5:1-2 and 12:13). This is the answer! *He* is the answer!

All in all, Qoheleth's message to us is that it does not matter how many riches or pleasures we have (or how much power we have, as we will further explore in the next chapter) it is all temporal and fleeting. Now, knowing Jesus the Christ (Saint Paul's message to us) is that *Yahshua* (יֵשׁוּעַ) the *Mâshîyach* (מָשִׁיחַ) is the only answer to having the fullness of life—*in Him and only in Him life is no longer vanity*!

Point Number 7: Let us now return to the dialogue between Jesus and His disciples just after the Rich Young Man went away (Mk 10:23-31 and Mt 19:23-30). Recall, within our discussion on the fourth virtue we ended this dialogue with Jesus telling the young man to sell all he has, give it to the poor, and then to follow Him. "When the young man heard this statement, he went away sad, for he had many possessions" (Mt 19:22).

Continuing the discussion, *Yahshua* (יֵשׁוּעַ) said to His disciples: "How hard it is for those who have wealth to enter the Kingdom of God!" (Mk 10:23). The disciples reacted to this with amazement. Then, Jesus made his surprising statement, "It is easier for a camel to pass through the eye of a needle than for one who is rich to enter the Kingdom of God" (Mk 10:26). When the disciples heard this, in great astonishment, they asked: "Then who can be saved?" (Mk 10:26).

I find this question from the disciples a little puzzling. At first glance, we may want to question the disciples by asking them: Why the astonishment? Why ask who can be saved? Why, do you think *everyone* is rich?

However, Jesus' comment is not as much to do with the wealth or riches in and of themselves (cf. 1 Tm 6:10 and Heb 13:5), but more to do with covetousness. Even the poor love and covets riches—hence *who can be saved*?

The other matter is that within the Jewish context, riches and wealth were considered to be a sign of God's blessing (e.g., Abraham). Thus, the disciples must have also concluded that if those who are wealthy (i.e., blessed by God) have a hard time entering into the Kingdom of God, where does that leave the rest of us who are not considered blessed by God? Hence their, *who can be saved*?

At this point, Peter speaks up. He asks Jesus: "We have given up everything and followed you. What will there be for us?" (Mt 19:27). Listen to Jesus' twofold answer very carefully.

In the first part, He says directly only to the twelve Apostles: "I say to you that you who have followed Me, in the new age, when the Son of Man is seated on His throne of glory, will yourself sit on twelve thrones, judging the twelve tribes of Israel" (Mt 19:28; also cf. Rev 21:14). This is clearly not an earthly or worldly glory; this is a glory within His Kingdom (in which they are currently sitting).

Then *Yahshua* (יֵשׁוּעַ) goes on to say the second part, which is also directed to you and me: "and everyone who has given up house or brothers or sisters or father or mother or children or lands for the sake of My Name will receive a hundred times more, and will inherit eternal life" (Mt 19:29).

This is not a mere earthly reward; this is also a reward in the Kingdom of God. Granted we may argue that He does add the words "now in this present age," as recorded in the Gospel of Saint Mark (Mt 10:30) within this second part, but is this not still spiritual in nature as we are also rewarded here and now? For it would be illogical to think we will be rewarded with one hundred physical mothers or fathers in this life.

Commenting on this passage from the Gospel of Saint Mark, Saint John Chrysostom writes, "This hundredfold reward therefore must be in participation, not in possession, for the Lord fulfilled this to them not carnally, but spiritually."[288]

This is precisely what I am saying. Therefore the Apostles, and all the Saints for that matter, have received one hundredfold in this life and the life to come. This is all about the glory of God, and our preferring the glory of God in the Kingdom of God, to all things of this world. Seek first the Kingdom of God and all things will be given to you (Mt 6:33 and Lk 12:31).

Point Number 8: If you are thinking that giving up house or brothers or sisters or father or mother or children or lands is considerably more extreme than first imagined, you are absolutely correct. It is one thing to give up the house and land part (as we stated when we began discussing this virtue), but brothers, sisters, father, mother or children, as well? With this kind of rhetoric we might ask:

Is this for real? You might be surprised to hear that this is not hyperbole, and it is not only real, but, based on an earthly perspective, we might say it gets even worse.

The extreme language does not stop. Jesus the Messiah does not ease up, for He also says: "Whoever loves father or mother more than Me is not worthy of Me, and whoever loves son or daughter more than Me is not worthy of me" (Mt 10:37).

So then, what is being said here? As a disciple we need to put love in the proper order and perspective. We must not put anything before the Christ, even our family. Everything and everyone takes a back seat. He comes first! This is radical, arduous, and counter-cultural. We may also say that this is to inform us of the cost of being His disciple—the *cost of discipleship*. For that reason, we need to sit down and analyze the cost (Lk 14:27-32). This is a disposition of detachment from all things, in which we place Jesus the Christ first (*Note*[289]), that is, we give Him priority over all relationships, and place Him over and above everything.

"But wait, there's more!" Jesus takes this a step further when He says: "If any one comes to Me without hating his father and mother, wife and children, brothers and sisters, and even his own life, he cannot be My disciple" (Lk 14:26). This is not just loving our relatives a little less or in second place, He adds the word *hate*, and includes spouses and life itself. Now what is happening here?

When Saint Thomas Aquinas tells us that we are to follow the example of despising earthly things, he means *all* earthly things! Again, this is not mere hyperbolic language on the part of our Messiah. The *hate* referred to here goes to our inner disposition. We are called to hate all our carnal desires and pleasures, in our very *life itself* and in family and friends around us. Shunning earthly things includes shunning *sin*. We must *hate* sin.

Clarifying the word *hate* in this passage from the Gospel of Saint Luke, Saint Gregory of Nazianzus writes:

> But it may be asked, how are we bid to hate our parents and our relations in the flesh, who are commanded to love even our enemies? But if we weigh the force of the command we are able to do both, by rightly distinguishing them so as both to

> love those who are united to us by the bond of the flesh, and whom we acknowledge our relations, and by hating and avoiding not to know those whom we find our enemies in the way of God. For he is as it were loved by hatred, who in his carnal wisdom, pouring into our ears his evil sayings, is not heard. Now to show that this hatred towards relations proceeds not from inclination or passion, but from love, our Lord adds, *yes, and his own life also.* It is plain therefore that a man ought to hate his neighbour, by loving as himself him who hated him. For then we rightly hate our own soul when we indulge not its carnal desires, when we subdue its appetites, and wrestle against its pleasures. That which by being despised is brought to a better condition, is as it were loved by hatred.[290]
>
> | Saint Gregory of Nazianzus |

The extreme language used by the *Mâshîyach* (מָשִׁיחַ) is not to tell us to *hate* our parents, but to love our parents by hating all that makes them and us antagonistic of Him. Hating sin in ourselves and those around us is Christian love.

We live in a confused cultural environment that refuses to call sin a sin—or stated differently, regards sin as not being sinful. As previously mentioned, in this we are actually asserting that what was considered sin for the past two thousand years must be discarded, for now, in our new and improved, reformulated and reimagined teachings, it is no longer sin. This is a fallacy.

When we capitulate or promulgate this fallacy we are leading people to the wide gate and road, to a *carnal lukewarm* Christianity which is far from Christian love. Condoning sin is not *agape* (ἀγάπη).

Besides, if we do not know what sin is, how are we supposed to *hate* it? Also as pointed out, if what was sin for the past two thousand years is no longer sin, this inevitably raises doubts, questions, and legitimacy of the new teaching on sin. What is the standard by which we say that this reimagined new and improved teaching is now correct? If we have been wrong for the past two thousand years, who's to say what is being proposed is now somehow right? Would we not be casting doubt upon the so-called new teaching on sin as well? In this continuous change, Christianity itself becomes a mere New Age religion—a potpourri of New Age thought—meaningless, and likewise irrelevant.

Bottom line: *what has been objectively stated in Holy Scripture as wrong cannot all of a sudden be right.* That would absolutely make no sense. Within Christianity, hostility towards Sacred Scripture needs to end. We think we have all this figured in our enlightened, technologically advanced, prosperous era—but have we really? Will our Messiah spew us out of His mouth as Jesus the Christ admonishes and warns the church at Laodicea because of their version of carnality?

> I know your works; I know that you are neither cold nor hot. I wish you were either cold or hot. So, because you are lukewarm, neither hot nor cold, I will spit you out of my mouth. For you say, I am rich and affluent and have no need of anything, and yet do not realize that you are wretched, pitiable, poor, blind, and naked. (Rev 3:15-17)

Moving along, one little side note: from time to time I have heard despising or detachment from earthly things referred to as a sacrifice, not used in a positive sense, but as in the giving up of something desirable for the sake of something else.

This view is problematic on a few levels. For instance, it inevitably classifies giving up earthly things as a sacrifice in the sense of a burden. We want these carnal pleasures, but we are choosing to abstain from it for the sake of the Messiah. With that attitude, it also becomes something we are doing as a *quid pro quo* exchange with the Messiah.

This is the wrong disposition to have. Yes, there is the cost of being His disciple; nevertheless, we are not *doing* this as a mere sacrifice; therefore, the cost becomes no cost if we are truly doing it out of love. For example, we do not worry about the cost, sacrifice, or try to earn credit, when we do things out of love for our spouse, do we? "Of course not!" If we did, it would no longer be love. Why would this be any different? We should want to *be* unworldly, because we love Him. We are doing this in response to the One Who loves us. It is a reciprocation of love, not some sort of distorted sacrifice or *payment* we are making in the hopes of gaining some *reward*.

Besides, in this attitude we are actually missing the greater point here. That is, our true authentic self is only realized when we are totally wrapped up *in Him* (not in worldly things). Again, keep in mind that worldliness does to mean we are opposed to the gifts of creation or the goodness of the world. However, to truly appreciate God's creation, we need to fall in love with the Creator; and as we will see in the next chapter, it is only then that we will know what it really means to be human, and thus live a joy-filled life, here and now!

If we truly do this, and seek first the Kingdom of God, and not give anything or anyone the primacy in our life, "all these things will be given to [us]" (Mt 6:33), one hundredfold and beyond. In applying this virtue, we need to stop being anxious, worried, fearful, and so forth, and put God above all things.

In this eighth point, let us take a moment, refrain from looking at others, look at ourselves, and question: Am I putting *Yahshua* (יֵשׁוּעַ) the *Mâshîyach* (מָשִׁיחַ) before everything and everyone? Am I despising earthly things? Do I hate sin and all its manifestation? What is my inner disposition; despite what I have or do not have? If, through the grace of God, we are able to answer, these question in line with our Messiah's objective teachings, we will be prosperous and successful—but as we will see in the next chapter—not in the way the world defines these words, but how *God* defines them.

Point Number 9: A prerequisite before *we take up our cross and follow Him*; it is that we must first *deny* ourselves. "Whoever wishes to come after me must deny himself" the Messiah directly tell us (Mt 16:24, Mk 8:34, and Lk 9:23). The Greek word used here for *deny* is ἀπαρνέομαι (aparneomai/*ap-ar-neh'-om-ahee*), which expresses the meaning to utterly disown, and abstain; to affirm that one has no acquaintance or connection with someone; to forget one's self, lose sight of one's self and one's interests.[291]

Would this not include the despising of all earthly things? Also would this not include assessing our personal attachment to our current way of life? Denying ourselves consequently refocuses us to Jesus, creating an inner disposition of detachment, a disposition of total abandonment, even to the point of death. Is this natural? "Of course not!"

We might want to argue that this type of abandonment will ruin our lives. On the contrary, the paradox here is that when we lose all, we gain all, when we deny ourselves and lose our life for His sake is when we truly find it: "For whoever wishes to save his life [*in this world*] will [*eventually*] lose it [*through death*], but whoever loses his life [*in this world*] for My sake will find it [*that is, life with Me for all eternity*]" says the Christ (Mt 10:39[292], 16:25, Mk 8:35, Lk 9:24, Lk 17:33, and Jn 12:25). We must believe this and desire this. Yes, with this absolute abandonment, in both big things and small things—comes absolute certitude.

A word of caution, however, this is an all-or-nothing proposition; it is non-negotiable. We should not compartmentalize or decide which parts of our life we will deny or abandon to Him. We are either attached to Him or attached to the world. Therefore, it must be a complete abandonment, to the point of being willing to die for Him! It is better to be an atheist than a lukewarm Christian, because, if we "are lukewarm, neither hot nor cold" He will spit us out (Rev 3:16).

Point Number 10: A key to despising earthly things is to *be* content. Contentment, as alluded, is rooted in Divine Providence. We are content, because we are standing on a strong foundation—we know that God will provide (Mt 6:30 and Lk 12:38)—thus we are not on edge or restless. Here is what Saint Paul has to say about being content:

> I have learned, in whatever situation I find myself, to be content. I know indeed how to live in humble circumstances; I know also how to live with abundance. In every circumstance and in all things I have learned the secret of being well fed and of going hungry, of living in abundance and of being in need. I have the strength for everything through Him who empowers me. (Phil 4:11-13)

In another place, he says:

> [godliness] with contentment is a great gain. For we brought nothing into the world, just as we shall not be able to take anything out of it. If we have food and clothing, we shall be content with that. Those who want to be rich are falling into temptation and into a trap and into many foolish and harmful desires, which plunge them into ruin and destruction. For the love of money is the root of all evils, and some people in their desire for it have strayed from the faith and have pierced themselves with many pains. (1 Tm 6:6-10)

Also, in the letter to the Hebrews, it states:

> Let your life be free from love of money but be content with what you have, for He has said, I will never forsake you or abandon you. Thus we may say with confidence: The Lord is my helper, (and) I will not be afraid. What can anyone do to me? (Heb 13:5-6)

We are not afraid or apprehensive, for we rest in the Providence of our God. Contentment knows that the grace of Jesus the Anointed One is enough (see 1 Cor 12:9). All the Saints understood this principle. So shouldn't we? If we are restless, it is only until we rest in Him (to paraphrase Saint Augustine).

This is a contentment in *all* areas of life. In it, we pray in harmony with the palmist: "O Lord, my heart is not proud nor haughty my eyes. I have not gone after things too great nor marvels beyond me" (Ps 131:1[293]; also cf. Sirach 3:20).

Contentment is the antidote to temptations. Satan's temptations are designed to make us give up our mission (both macro and micro). Think of the temptations of *Yahshua* (יֵשׁוּעַ). Satan will ask you: What? You don't want "all this power and their splendour?" (Lk 4:6). Being content will control all our passions, selfish desires, and worldly allurements. Most of all, personal contentment will help us say: "by the grace of God, I am what I am" (1 Cor 15:10).

Point Number 11: "We have not received the spirit of the world but the [Holy] Spirit that is from God, so that we may understand the things freely given to us by God" (1 Cor 2:12). We speak about these things "not with words taught by human wisdom, but with words taught by the [Holy] Spirit, describing spiritual realities in spiritual terms" (1 Cor 2:13). This is the Wisdom from God the Holy Spirit.

Point Number 12: On the whole, persons accepting worldly wisdom do not accept or have a hard time accepting the Wisdom of God, for they think it is foolishness or plainly incongruent with earthly reality; they cannot understand it because they look at things solely from an earthly perspective, not a godly one (1 Cor 2:14). Although we as Christians acknowledge that all things are lawful or permissible for us (*Note*[294]), we also recognize that not all things are beneficial or advantageous to us, for they do not build our character, nor edify our spiritual life. Therefore, we should be enslaved or controlled by even permissible things (1 Cor 10:23 and 6:12).

As I write about these virtues, I personally debated whether to use a more moderate tone, and thus, give us a way out. To be up front, this debate was not only for your sake, but it was also for mine. As we have discussed, Saint Thomas Aquinas' fifth virtue of despising earthly things is very challenging, to say the least. Thus, I struggle with it. After much debate with myself, I realized that I am not the one to moderate the thrust of these virtues. As stated many times, my opinion does not matter. I am not the moderator of truth. Jesus' vocabulary is crystal clear. He does not moderate His tone, and, His presentation is the Wisdom of God. With this in mind, I believe that the extreme expressions and terminology used by Jesus are designed to shake us, to wake us up!

The shake-up is because He knows that every generation will at some point get complacent. He knows that we, therefore, need to *wake up* and *pay attention*. Being complacently asleep is a problem.

That is why, without theologizing and watering down expressions, the Christ uses the extreme so we may truly grasp what He is telling us!

Just a reminder, a full study of these five virtues is totally beyond this book. This is only a basic study—within a limited demonstration of the Wisdom of God in the irrationality of the Christ Event. We should now take some time to build upon these thoughts. Therefore, I recommend a prayerful discernment and personal refection on all five virtues presented to us by Saint Thomas Aquinas, especially this last one.

As I write this, I am personally wondering what all of this will look like in my own life. What changes must I make going forward? How do I do this? I am guessing that you might be asking some similar questions. I think the starting point (which we will continue to discuss in the next chapter) is to fall in love again and again with the One Who created us: to love Him and Him alone with the totality of our being. With that, we must totally abandon ourselves to Jesus' will in our life, and desire—again with the totality of our being—to carry out His will, no matter what the cost to us. To do this, our heart must not be and cannot be enslaved by anything except Him. He *must* be the absolute centre of our lives. This *must* be our inner disposition—our starting point.

Herewith, may I suggest something. Our objective calling is non-negotiable; however, our subjective calling—what is *ours to do*—is negotiable. Therefore, keeping the preceding in mind, let us sit at His feet and discern and negotiate with Him what He wants us to do. Abraham did it, Moses did it, so why shouldn't we? In the Church's wisdom, use a spiritual director if possible during this discernment. For now,

> have no anxiety at all, but in everything, by prayer and petition, with thanksgiving, make your requests known to God. Then the peace of God that surpasses all understanding will guard your hearts and minds in Jesus [the] Christ. (Phil 4:6-7)

In summation, all these five virtues are the Wisdom of God. On the Cross He exemplifies these virtues, and thus, teaches us what it truly means to be human. As per Saint Thomas Aquinas, the second reason He became human, in His life on earth, was to demonstrate these virtues to us, for as you can see—if we were honestly to look within us—each of us knows that left to our own devices we probably would not and will not do any of these, let alone come to any of these conclusions.

At this moment, the God of the universe, asks us to follow His Son. As previously mentioned, the call to follow the Christ is an objective call, but, what *is ours to do*—the *take up our cross daily* part—is the subjective mission within the objective calling, which we must, through the Wisdom of God, discern and ascertain exactly what God is asking from us as individuals, within the collective. For, these two comprise our direct obedience to God that we as Christians *must* live out.

> So prepare your minds for action, be completely sober [*in spirit—steadfast, self-disciplined, spiritually and morally alert*], fix your hope completely on the grace [*of God*] that is coming to you when Jesus [the] Christ is revealed. [*Live*] as obedient children [*of God*]; do not be conformed to the evil desires *which governed you* in your ignorance [*before you knew the requirements and transforming power of the good news regarding Salvation*]. But like the Holy One who called you, be holy yourselves in all *your* conduct [*be set apart from the world by your godly character*]; because it is written, "YOU SHALL BE HOLY (set apart), FOR I AM HOLY." [Lev 11:44-45 and 19:2]. (1 Pt 1:13-16[295])

To paraphrase Saint Thomas Aquinas: We must disdain what He disdained on the Cross and desire what He desired. For this we need His help, so, before we continue, let us pray:

God our Father,
the contradiction of the Cross
proclaims your infinite wisdom.
Our very existence is a gift from you;
to You we offer all that we have and are.

Grant, we pray,
that, always pondering spiritual things
we may carry out in both word and deed
that which is pleasing to Your Son;
keep before us the wisdom and love
you have revealed in your Son.

Help us to follow Him and praise Him
with our lips, with our hearts, and with our lives.
Help us to see that the glory of your Son
is revealed in the suffering He freely accepted.
Give us faith to claim as our only glory
the Cross of our Lord, *Yahshua* (יֵשׁוּעַ) the *Mâshîyach* (מָשִׁיחַ)
who lives with You and the Holy Spirit,
God, for ever and ever,
Amen.[296]

We are exhorted to *rejoice* always in Jesus the Christ!
Therefore, in order *always* to be joy-filled
we must be centred *in Him*.

Chapter 8 | "Rejoice . . . Always!"

Christians can be some of the gloomiest people in the world. As a whole, we are not really a joyful group, are we? Now I say this with three fingers pointing back at myself. In contrast, as Christians, we need to be joyful and talk about joy more often.

In his letter to the Philippian church, Saint Paul exhorts: "Rejoice in the Lord always," and to make sure that they get his point, he adds, "I say it again: rejoice!" (Phil 4:4; also cf. 1 Thes 5:16).

As mentioned, a superlative such as this is a double-fold emphatic imperative, expressing a supreme degree—thus it should not be taken lightly. This exhortation, this command, is also directed to you and me. This is also *our* command: "Rejoice . . . Always!"

At first, this exhortation is a little confusing. Are we actually *commanded* to rejoice? As academic theologians have commented, how can someone require this of us?

It is easy to rejoice when things are going well—when we have just graduated, when we have just been married, when we have just received a promotion at work, etc. However, to say *always*? To expect it through various trials and tribulations—a parent passes away, a diagnosis of a serious medical illness is received, a job is lost, etc.—isn't it rather cruel or callus to ask this of us?

In any given day, our emotional state may vary from one minute to the next—isn't this our lived reality? Knowing this human condition, is Saint Paul's command even legitimate? "Rejoice . . . [in the Lord, no matter what the circumstance] . . . Always!" Again, if so, how is this possible?

Before we consider the answer to these questions, let us touch on a foundational understanding that we Christians should have to even begin to ascertain what is being commanded here.

To do this, a good place to start is at the beginning of the *Catechism*:

> The desire for God is written in the human heart, because man is created by God and for God; and God never ceases to draw man to Himself. Only in God will he find the truth and happiness he never stops searching for: The dignity of man rests above all on the fact that he is called to communion with God. This invitation to converse with God is addressed to man as soon as he comes into being. For if man exists it is because God has created him through love, and through love continues to hold him in existence. He cannot live fully according to truth unless he freely acknowledges that love and entrusts himself to his Creator. (*CCC* #27)

Saint Augustine summarizes this *Catechism* entry very succinctly when he says: "Thou hast formed us for Thyself, and our hearts are restless until they find rest in Thee."[297] True rest, true peace, true happiness, and true joyfulness, for which we inherently search, is only found in the One Who created us.

Saint Augustine also says: "The peace of all things is the tranquility of order."[298] We are, at our core, ordered or oriented to God our Creator. There is no disturbance within us when we keep our life oriented to Him (i.e., the *tranquility of order*). If we want true peace, it is fundamental that we accept this basic premise.

Similar to what we have studied about love, being joyful or happy is not a fleeting emotion or a feeling of pleasure. Being joyful is a conviction. It is a conviction that comes from faith, through an encounter with Jesus the Messiah. He is the root cause of any joyfulness that permeates our life.

We are never told that life will be easy. Life is a grind. Life may be a daily battle. Nevertheless, the key is to centre our life in the Christ, to grow spiritually. As a result, we will find that inner joyfulness, even in the midst of trials and tribulations that we face in our day-to-day lives. As sufferings and difficulties (or even prosperity and blissfulness) permeate our lives, we will find rest and joyfulness *in Him*—"for rejoicing in the LORD must be your strength!" (Neh 8:10b)—no matter the circumstance. This foundational understanding is the key to finding the real meaning behind Saint Paul's command: "Rejoice . . . Always!"

Before we use this key, just three quick notes: (1) depending on context, *in Him* could mean *we in Him*, or *everything happens in Him*, or both meanings simultaneously; (2) although bits and pieces of the subtitle of this book (*Understanding Who Jesus Is* and *What it Means to be Christ-centred*) appear within the first six chapters of this book, our focus within those chapters have been primarily of the first part of the subtitle, it was in Chapter 7 that we started the transition between the two, now with this command from Saint Paul to rejoice, let us officially change our focus to the second part of the subtitle; and (3) concerning the second part of the subtitle, there are two breakaways—as we studied in previous chapter—our *call to holiness* and our *witness of charity* which should be a continuous study for all Christians.

In biblical Greek, four words are used for *rejoice.*[299] In his command to "Rejoice . . . Always!" Saint Paul uses the particular word χαίρω (chairō/*khah'ee-ro*). This Greek word means to be filled with joy, great joy, or to have joy with intensity; it is also a salutation (*Note*[300])

In the Greek, the word for *joy* is the same word as *happiness*—χαρά (chara/*khar-ah'*). As well, the Greek word for *happy* is the same word as *blessed*—μακάριος (makarios/*mak-ar'-ee-os*).

Therefore, in the Greek, *rejoice* means to be joy-filled; it is an intense joy; *joy* means happiness, or to be happy; and *happy* means to be blessed, to enjoy divine favour, or happy-blessed, as we will shortly see as related to the Beatitudes.

Keeping all these connections and definitions in mind, let us begin with a basic statement concerning happiness: Every human being wants to be happy!

Yes, humans intrinsically desire and seek happiness. In that quest, the first question becomes: How do we *define* happy? Based on our particular definition, the second question is: How is happiness *attained*?

Without getting into the psychology of happiness or the science of happiness, because that topic is well beyond the scope of this book,

I think one of the challenges we have in understanding the command to "Rejoice . . . Always!" comes from the fact that even as Christians some of us tend to define and view the attainment of happiness in a way very similar to that of the secularists. What do I mean by this?

One day I decided to walk around my Cathedral parish and randomly conduct one of my unscientific surveys. I asked fellow parishioners: What is happiness to you? How would you define happiness? How would you attain happiness, or advise your loved ones to attain it? (Now, before you continue, you might want to think of your own answer, or even jot it down).

Just over half of the answers that I received would have been little or no different than if I had received them from a non-Christian.

A non-Christian societal definition of happiness is usually stated in terms of a positive emotional state. It is a feeling or a pleasure-based response (*Note*[301]). Therefore, happiness in this sense could be described in terms of feelings of joy, feeling good, satisfaction with life, social satisfaction, fulfillment of some sort, independence or freedom, and so forth. Notice that this definition is subjective, and is focused on a person's own self-interest (*Note*[302]).

Within this definition, the primary focus of *attaining* this happiness tends to be achievements, physical objects, or building relationships. Corporations, advertisers, and media know this; they constantly bombard us with these concepts. We will be happy if we buy what they are selling. We will be happy if we climb the ladder of success—get into a good college, buy a car, graduate, get a good job or career, get that promotion or make more money, buy a house, get married, have children, do charity work and so on and so forth. This is an illusion. We delude ourselves if we think that the importance, the power, the status, the superiority, the independence, the fame will make us . . . *happy*!

Moreover, this mindset assumes that happiness is essential even though its definition is subjective. Most of us have had a Christian family member or friend express similar sentiments as this: As long as this makes you happy; or whatever makes you happy.

Confronted with these sentiments, one day I started to ask: What does my happiness have to do with it? The usual reaction to this question is bewilderment or shock. Therefore, I follow up with another question: Was Jesus happy going to the Cross? This is not to say that our personal happiness does not matter. I ask the questions to make a point, Christian to Christian.

I find these questions make us Christians stop and think. Individually and societally, we put so much emphasis on the wrong type of happiness, as we have described, that we need to stop to reflect on the scriptural emphasis concerning *happiness*, which is needed in order to "Rejoice . . . Always!"

The Gospel accounts of Jesus' agony in the Garden of Gethsemane make us, at first glance, conclude that (based on our societal definition), He was *not* happy (Mt 26:36-39, Mk 14:32-36, and Lk 22:39-42) for He did not want to be crucified (Mt 26:39, Mk 14:36, and Lk 22:42).

However, the real issue is that the usual societal meaning of happiness (or unhappiness) has nothing to do with the Cross. Therefore, Jesus was not happy about what awaited Him; yet, He was happy, or to give the word some contrast, we may say *joyful*, because He was doing His Father's will. He was accomplishing the mission His Father gave Him to do (Jn 12:27).

Doing His Father's will and completing the mission His Father gave Him (Jn 10:14-18) gave Jesus intense joyfulness—*chairō* (χαίρω). This joyfulness is in sharp contrast to any worldly happiness (*Note*[303]). This joyfulness is something that the world just cannot give (*Note*[304]).

For that reason, Jesus did not subscribe to this societal definition of happiness. Jesus was not independent; He was *interdependent* with His Father. He trusted the Father. Thus, He was joyful in doing the will of His Father. We, consequently, are called to be and do the same. Our true happiness is rooted *in Him*. Like a child, our dependence is on Him. With this understanding, we should *not* conform ourselves to this world, in any way, or be caught up in earthly or worldly happiness—we are to be transformed by the renewal of our minds, so that we may desire and discern God's will in our life, the good, acceptable, perfect will of God (see Rom 12:2). Doing His will brings true happiness and joyfulness. Not understanding this is the *prima facie*—the first and clear—problem in Christians even trying to understand the command: "Rejoice . . . Always!"

What is more, when we look at worldly happiness we instantly realize that it is insatiable. The more we get, the more we desire. As a result, once we get something we eventually desire something else—it is time to move on to the next achievement or gratifying object. This is the continuous cycle of worldly happiness.

That is why this type of happiness is an illusion. This continual cycle of desire is not real happiness, for the element of contentment (as we discussed in the previous chapter) must be present for any type of happiness to be valid.

To understand further, let us now look at this from another point of view. Every human being has an emptiness within that needs to be filled. We deceive ourselves by trying to fill this void with achievements or things. Both are finite; they only please for the moment. The fulfillment is just as temporary and fleeting as that which caused the fulfillment.

Those of us living in affluent countries (and the rich in all countries) tend to take this imprudent path. We move from one purchase to another, from one achievement to another, from one hobby to another, and in some cases even from one spouse to another, all in the hope that the latest thing will bring fulfillment and happiness.

Sensory fulfillments are fleeting; as a result we sooner or later thirst for more. That is, the finite only temporarily fulfills this vacuum—this emptiness or void within us—but does not quench that deep longing inside. It is just a temporary illusion of happiness. The only way our life makes any sense is if it has meaning in our Messiah. If we delude ourselves by trying to give our life meaning through things that perish (finite things, whatever they may be), we will not be truly satisfied. Without a doubt, we will find ourselves craving and desiring more.

Stated in philosophical terms, we humans cannot find the reason for our existence within ourselves (in fact, nothing within creation finds a reason for its own existence). Following the lead of Saint Thomas Aquinas, philosophers say that *the world is contingent.* They observe that everything comes into being and then passes away, including the world itself. In biblical terms, all of creation travails for meaning (Rom 8:22). As rational human beings, we search for a deeper meaning for our lives—the reason for our existence. Our *soul* needs meaning (*Note*[305]).

This search can be intentional or unintentional, conscious or unconscious; nevertheless, it is intrinsically a part of our human condition—for there is a void within every human being that needs to be filled. What sometimes happens is that the searcher attempts to fill this void with a multitude of finite things, which becomes an exercise in futility. To that point, here is a famous quote usually attributed to G. K. Chesterton: *A man knocking on the door of a brothel is unconsciously looking for God* (*Note*[306]).

We all thirst! Now the question becomes: How are we going to satisfy this thirst within us?

The words *insatiable* and *thirst* is not merely a word I choose, it is a theme that runs throughout Scripture, often connected with the image of water. As a Psalmist declares: "As the deer longs for streams of water, so my soul longs [thirsts] for you, O God" (Ps 42:1). There is a thirst within us that only the Infinite can quench (*Note*[307])—this is the only prudent way to quench this thirst.

This thirst is highlighted in the conversation at Jacob's well between Jesus the Messiah and the Samaritan woman (see Jn 4:7-15). In this story, with which most of us are familiar, Jesus asks the woman for a drink of water (Jn 4:7). Jesus moves the conversation from finite physical water to *living water*, the totally thirst-quenching spiritual water that only He offers (Jn 4:10). The Samaritan woman, misunderstanding, continues to focus on finite physical water (Jn 4:11-12). To this *Yahshua* (יֵשׁוּעַ) answers, "Everyone who drinks this [finite] water will be thirsty again, but whoever drinks the [Infinite] water I shall give [which is He Himself, the Infinite] will never thirst" (Jn 4:13-14).

The plight of the Samaritan woman who jumped from one husband to another in her search for happiness—the latest one not even being her husband (Jn 4:17-18)—is also humanity's plight, if we do not realize that our insatiable unquenchable thirst can only be permanently quenched by the Infinite!

We have only one life to live! Live in the moment! Live life to the fullest! These are the mantras of our day. As Christians, we must grasp and declare to the world the fact that nothing finite can fill this inner void, for only the Infinite can. When we seek Him we realize a happy life and when we seek a happy life we seek for Him, as Saint Augustine would say.[308] Seeking Him is the answer to emotional depression, delusion, and despair.

To again paraphrase Saint Augustine, our hearts will continually be restless and agitated in every aspect of their finite quest, until we allow our hearts to rest in the Infinite. Lasting happiness can only be achieved when we find the *true* meaning of life—*in Him*. In this, we can "Rejoice . . . Always!"

Yes, we have one life to live! Yes, live in the moment! Yes, live life to the fullest! Absolutely, yes! However, to live our life to the fullest is only possible in *Yahshua* (יֵשׁוּעַ) the *Mâshîyach* (מָשִׁיחַ)—the Infinite. In Him, we find real happiness! In Him is the truest and fullest life we may live! In Him, we can *rejoice—chairō* (χαίρω)! In Him, we can move from living a mere biological life, a life in *bios* (βίος), to living life as in *zōē* (ζωή), life with the highest good and fullness of life.

Real rest or real happiness is found only in the *Ultimate Good*, the *Highest Good*, the *Supreme Good*, the *Summum Bonum*, so let us make Jesus the Christ the Lord of our *zōē* (ζωή), in this life and also in the next.

When we forgo a twisted notion of worldly happiness and worldly comforts, self-determination and self-reliance, when we stop running after the finite in the hopes of filling a vacuum within, we will find true happiness and joyfulness. Trust in the Messiah, get closer to the Christ, and enjoy true joyfulness *in Him*—a joyfulness that this world cannot understand nor give.

Recall our discussion on Qoheleth's treatise regarding *vanity of vanities*. He concluded that everything is fleeting, that is, everything will pass away. It has been said that wisdom is how quickly we adapt to this fleeting change. That may be in the immediate; however, ultimately, *true wisdom is knowing the One who is not fleeting*, the One in Whom there is no change, the One Who is Infinite, Who will not pass away.

Fundamentally, if all things are *vanity*, if life is just an absurdity, should we not conclude: Why go on living? Many do ask this question. As discussed, Qoheleth's answer is that, *without God*, life is just vanity of vanities. The value of continued life and contentment may ultimately only be fulfilled in *Yahshua* (יֵשׁוּעַ) the Christ, the *Summum Bonum—our hearts will be restless until they rests in Him*.

If we desire riches, we must set our heart on *true* riches. These riches are *not* of this world. "One's life does not consist of possessions" (Lk 12:15).

Worldly ambition (*Note*[309]), pursuit of worldly pleasures, and pursuit of riches will not only keep us from true happiness—inner joyfulness—we will end up worshiping those pleasures and riches (i.e., idolatry). "Take care to guard against all greed" (Lk 12:15), Scripture warns us, for we either worship God or *mammon* (our idols personified).

Do not get me wrong, I am not denigrating achievements, meritocracy, personal responsibility, or social fulfillment, etc. I am not saying that our earthly reality is meaningless—not even Qoheleth is saying that. Our world is objectively real. We need the things of this physical world. However, they are meaningless without God.

Moreover, God created godly pleasures for us to enjoy. Pleasures are God's gift. I have heard preachers declare that God is not a *kill-joy*. He knows that we need weddings to counteract funerals, that is to say, we need joy to offset our afflictions. We need happiness and joy, even in temporal earthly things. So, buy it, use it, and have the benefit of it!

Life is precious. Laugh and have fun. Be joy-filled. All the while, however, recognize that we are only stewards of all of God's gifts, including our talents and possessions. We must use our gifts for His divine purpose.

We are also stewards of our *bios* (βίος), so we must take care of it. Exercise, go to the doctor—feed it, groom it, and dress it! All the while, heed this admonition:

> Do not worry about your life, what you will eat (or drink), or about your body, what you will wear. Is not life more than food and the body more than clothing? Look at the birds in the sky; they do not sow or reap, they gather nothing into barns, yet your Heavenly Father feeds them. Are not you more important than they? Can any of you by worrying add a single moment to your life-span? (Mt 6:25-27)

By the way, do not also mistakenly think that I am speaking of the notion of having some sort of balance or moderation in life. This notion is too simplistic, and may be a copout.

Let me explain again in three summary points.

First: We must keep in mind that our earthly reality is ordered or oriented by God (in fact everything is ordered or oriented by God). Idolatry is rebelling against that truth. All sins are a form of idolatry since they represent rebellion against God.

As Christians, we recognize that contentment is the antidote to worldliness. The secular mantra of eat, drink, and be merry for we will die tomorrow, is *not* Christian. We are not here simply to live a life to the so-called fullest, die, and remain in our graves.

We need to find our purpose in serving God in our real world—*in reality* (*Note*[310])—with a good conscience (*Note*[311]). If not, we may become emotionally depressed. Only living our life for God will make us truly happy-blessed—joy-filled. For God wants us to be happy in that sense. He is about abundance, not scarcity. So again, buy it, use it, and have the benefit of it—but, here is the key, do it all *in Him*.

All Christians are called to live a life of simplicity. Religious Brothers and Sisters take simplicity a step further with an official vow of poverty, that is, to live with nothing of their own (Acts 2:44). Although this is not explicitly required of the laity, we are nevertheless called to live in simplicity of life, with recognition that all we have is *in Him*. That said, we cannot live providing only for our *needs*—God wants us to have and use things, which may aid in enjoyment. In that we may also strive for our *wants*. However, striving for our *wants* should not do away with Him, nor lead us into greed, materialism, or other sorts of sin, if so, it is not *in Him*. Again, both our *needs* and our *wants* must be *in Him*. Therefore, we must constantly check ourselves, and thus, discern *in Him*, what to buy and what to use in aiding with enjoyment.

Here is an understanding that might help in this discernment. First, we must recognize that *needs* are primarily objective, but they may have a subjective elements. *Wants*, however, are 100% subjective to the individual. It is mainly the validity of the subjective aspects of wants that must be constantly discerned. We should ask ourselves: Am I putting it to use for myself, am I putting it to use for others, and more importantly is this aiding me in true happiness. By the way, an annual purging of our possessions is a good habit to form.

Here is a thought from Saint Augustine,[312] there are things to be enjoyed and there are things to be used. The things to be enjoyed bring about happiness; things to be used aid in that happiness. Philosophically speaking, if nothing finite can bring about true happiness, we must conclude that nothing finite can be enjoyed. Thus, all things are only to be used, for the only Object to be enjoyed, that which brings about true happiness, is the Triune God: "Who is our highest good and our true happiness." The finite, those things of use, help us, able us, and aid us to arrive at the fullness of enjoyment and happiness, in the Triune God. Even our very self should be viewed in this light, for we should not love ourselves for our own sake. If so, among other issues, we will occupy our minds on ourselves in a changeable finite condition and not look at ourselves in relation to Him. In this we are also called to "love our neighbour as yourself" (Mt 19:19), so just like we do not love ourselves for our own sake, we do not love our neighbour for their own sake, we love them for the sake of and in relation to the Triune God.

Remember that everything has a *telos* (τέλος), a designed end purpose. We may use the good things in life—congruent with its *telos* (τέλος), while holding on to Him. From that, live as "those buying as not owning, those using the world as not using it fully" (1 Cor 7:70b-31a). In that same attitude, go and build relationships and *achieve in Him* and for Him.

Second: While we are on this earth, and as we seek to improve the present, we must realize that there is something more than this earthly reality, something that transcends it. Life is not relegated to *bios* (βίος); true life is rooted in *zōē* (ζωή), found only in Jesus the Messiah.

Therefore, we must live that something more, here and now, for the Kingdom of God is here. At the same time we watch for His coming Kingdom. This is what academic theologians refer to as the *Already* and *Not Yet*. The *Already* (the Kingdom is here) and the *Not Yet* (the Kingdom is yet to come) is a dual realty we must recognize and live accordingly. In the *tranquility of order* when we seek God's Kingdom first, all be given to us (Lk 12:31 and Mt 6:33).

Third: What Qoheleth and I mean when we saying that everything *without God* is vanity, is that living life without God is *the* absurdity (also Rom 8:20-21).

Why is life without God, an absurdity? It is because we all know that eventually *we will die*. All life comes to an end sometime.

As secular society moves away from God, it refuses to answer the deep-rooted philosophical (and theological) questions that all of humanity inherently ponders—such as: Why are we here? What happens after we die? What is the purpose of our life? Instead, the standard assumption is that we are just a random happenstance—no questions need to be asked!

In dramatic contrast, knowing God gives us a deeper understanding of our earthly reality. We see life as it is. Only a proper understanding of Who God *is* gives life *true* meaning. It instills a divine purpose. We cannot claim to be *enlightened* if we do not know God. We cannot "Rejoice . . . Always!" if we do not know God.

Keeping all this in mind, we must also consider that as human beings, we not only have physical needs (food, shelter, clothing, etc.), but we also have natural and fundamental psychological and emotional needs. We need to belong, we need inherent value, and at its root, our lives need purpose and meaning. Therefore, as our society increasingly moves away from God, His identity, authority and purpose, it becomes increasingly chaotic and confused—which is inevitable.

In addition, a direct correlation exists between *not* knowing God (plus a movement away from God), and our society's *general emotional* depression (to avoid any confusion, I am not speaking of clinical or chemical depression).

For this *general* emotional depression, our society does not need more *Prozac*; it needs an authentic relationship with the One Who created us.

To be clear, I am not suggesting that those who are suffering from *any type* of depression should stop taking their medication. What I am saying, however, is that a personal relationship with God is the ultimate and only enduring solution.

If we were to think about it, the notion that the human race has progressed from some sort of primordial soup, by chance, and therefore humans have no ultimate purpose, consciously and subconsciously affects greatly the mental health of any thinking person. Don't you think? Is it any wonder that society is becoming more and more emotionally depressed (or even clinically depressed)?

We speak of mental health, but we do not want to speak of God. This disconnect is futile in resolving mental health issues. It is great that we now speak openly about mental health issues, but it is sad (and ineffective) that we are doing so without speaking about God. As Christians (and as Church) we have a huge role to play in this conversation.

Bottom line: true happiness is not in isolation from the Infinite, in fact it is only found in the Infinite; therefore, it is pointless to speak about mental health without simultaneously speaking of God—the Infinite. The less we speak about God the less chance we have of mental health issues being resolved. *A world without God is a world without hope and a world without hope is emotionally depressing on one level or another*. In that world, it would be impossible to "Rejoice . . . Always!"

Our Messiah knows all of our needs (physical, emotional, and psychological) and our wants. However, He desires us to seek Him and His Kingdom first; when we do so all our needs and wants will be satisfied. Seek *Him*—family, friends, and possessions, and everything else will be icing on the cake. We must pursue *only* Him, *not* worldly happiness. Paradoxically, in finding Him we find *true* happiness, even in this present age. So, "put to death, then, the parts of you that are earthly" (Col 3:5). "Seek what is above" (Col 3:1), and "think of what is above, not of what is on earth" (Col 3:2).

You will recall that in the preceding chapter we studied the Greek word *telos* (τέλος), meaning the natural order, point or goal, or an end purpose.[313] At that time we also studied the Greek word *teleios* (τέλειος), which is translated into English as *perfect* (most of the time) and its being rooted in the Greek word *telos* (τέλος). To this I will now add another Greek word, τελέω (teleō/*tel-eh'-o*), which is also rooted in *telos* (τέλος), but usually translated into English, as *finished* or *accomplished*.

On the Cross, just before *Yahshua* (יֵשׁוּעַ) our *Mâshîyach* (מָשִׁיחַ) took His last breath, He was

> aware that everything was now finished [*teleō* (τελέω)], in order that the Scripture might be fulfilled, Jesus said, "I thirst." Now, there was a vessel filled with common wine. So they put a sponge soaked in wine on a sprig of hyssop and put it up to His mouth. When Jesus had taken the wine, He said, "It is finished [*teleō* (τελέω)]" And bowing His head, He handed over the Spirit. (Jn 19:28-30)

Some scholars debate *what* was finished. However, the word *teleō* (τελέω), tells us. Jesus *completed*, *executed*, *concluded*, and accomplished[314] His mission, set forth by His Father, and thus, made available salvation for all who believed, because He discharged our debt. He accomplished exactly what the Father asked of Him. This is *perfection*. This was His adventure; this was His happiness; this was His joy. This is the same *perfection* we are also called to complete. It is in this perfection that we may "Rejoice . . . Always!"

Once we are baptized *in Him,* we start a new and beautiful purpose-driven adventure—*in Him*—which the Father has prepared in advance. From our temporal standpoint, we discover the aspects of this adventure by asking: What does the Messiah have in store for me? What does the Anointed One want of me? What does the Christ have in mind for me?

As we pose these questions and embark upon this adventure, we may have joy in everything *with Him* and *in Him*. This is true happiness! Moreover, this joyfulness is our path to holiness, our path to being Saints.

What I am saying is that to find the true purpose of life, we need only look to Jesus the Messiah—then carry out our own particular *telos* (τέλος). This is *perfection* (*Note*[315]). So no moderation, go *all in* on Him—not just achieve some sort of a balance. He is the true key to living a happy-blessed, joyful, meaningful, and purpose-driven life. True happiness is *only in Him*; everything else is secondary.

Saint Paul states the following in a slightly different context, nevertheless, it is apropos here, for "In Him we live and move and have our being" (Acts 17:28). Understanding this, we pray with the Psalmist:

> I take refuge in you. I say to the Lord: "You are my God. My happiness lies in you alone." . . . You will show me the path of life, the fullness of joy in your presence, at your right hand happiness forever. (Ps 16:1-2 and 1:11[316])

In summary, our happiness, our joy *lies in Him alone* and in the purpose-driven life resulting from being in *Yahshua* (יֵשׁוּעַ) our *Mâshîyach* (מָשִׁיחַ). True happiness is not found in the worldly secular understanding of this word. We will *not* find ultimate happiness in family, or friends, or social status, or health, or possessions, or money, or achievement, or even in wisdom or knowledge.

Here is a test we may use. When we as Christians are asked to define happiness and its attainment, do we explicitly say:

- Happiness is not found in the finite, it is ultimately only found in the Infinite?
- Happiness is when we rest in Him, while on this earth and then for all eternity?
- Happiness is to do the will of Him Who created us?

Alternatively, paraphrasing the Beatitudes, which have been called the *Christian ID-card*, do we say the following?:

- Happy-blessed, joyful, and holy are the poor in spirit (Mt 5:3), those who are detached from material things and the addictions of this world, who live in simplicity, and find their security in Jesus the Christ—not those who find security in the wealth and riches of the world.
- Happy-blessed, joyful, and holy are they who mourn (Mt 5:4), those who are detached from feeling-good, who live a life consoled by Jesus the Christ, rather than fleeting pleasures—not those who long, yearn, and run after worldly pleasures.

- Happy-blessed, joyful, and holy are the meek (Mt 5:5), those who are detached from the need for worldly power and domination of others, for they rest in Jesus the Christ—not those who desire any or all powers of this world, and view life as a zero-sum game.
- Happy-blessed, joyful, and holy are those who hunger and thirst for righteousness (Mt 5:6), those who intensely concern themselves with the will of Jesus the Christ—not those who are dominated by their own will.
- Happy-blessed, joyful, and holy are the merciful (Mt 5:7), those who freely give what they themselves freely received from Jesus the Christ—not those who are self-assertive and plot revenge on their own terms.
- Happy-blessed, joyful, and holy are the clean of heart (Mt 5:8), those who have their heart directed towards pleasing Jesus the Christ, with simplicity, purity, and no ambiguity—not those who are filled with guile, deceit, and lies.
- Happy-blessed, joyful, and holy are the peacemakers (Mt 5:9), those who truly make peace, by fundamentally ordering their life to Jesus the Christ—not those who instigate and agitate, or spread gossip, hatred and lies.
- Happy-blessed, joyful, and holy are they who are persecuted for the sake of righteousness (Mt 5:10), those who are detached from worldly honours and admiration, and seek to please Jesus the Christ—not those who are people pleasers.

Well, do you answer in this way? If so, "Rejoice [*chairō* (χαίρω)] and be glad, for your reward will be great in Heaven" (Mt 5:12). If not, at a very minimum, do we answer that true happiness is ultimately only *in Him*, not in isolation from Him, and thus, articulate to some degree this particular understanding, as true happiness, joyfulness, blessedness, and holiness *in Him*?

I acknowledge that living in this way is not easy. It is counter-cultural. It goes against the societal grain. It is even contrary to our natural inclinations.

As the world pushes us towards *its* definition of happiness and attainment of such, the Christian stands up and boldly states a different way of living. In the paradox of the teaching of the Beatitudes, humanity finds the true definition and the true attainment of happiness and joyfulness. As we have paraphrased Saint Thomas Aquinas (in the previous chapter), to be truly happy we must disdain what He disdained on the Cross and desire what He desired. When we do we will be able to "Rejoice . . . Always!"

Another aspect to add to our understanding of what it means to "Rejoice . . . Always! is revealed in the last beatitude stated above. Are we happy, joyful, blessed, and holy when others insult us and persecute us and utter every kind of evil against us because of Him? (Mt 5:11). Well, we are *blessed* to be persecuted in His Name. We are also blessed to suffer in carrying out mission, if that be His will (1 Pt 3:17). So then, do we rejoice—*chairō* (χαίρω)—and are we glad when this happens?

Worldly society knows nothing of mingling happiness with suffering or rejoicing during suffering—for it is contrary to their perspective. However, as Christians, our definition of happiness also fundamentally differs from theirs in this regard.

Remember, happiness, for the Christian, is rooted in Jesus the Messiah. We find our everything *in Him*. Our happiness is rooted in His objective and subjective will for us. We must take up our cross (subjectively) and follow Him (objectively). This is our joy. This is our happiness. This is our mission. This is our adventure *in Him*. Carrying out our *telos* (τέλος) in simplicity and love—*in Him*—will bring us true happiness, for Christian love is joy-filled. There is no greater joy than to respond to His call. In this we are happy-blessed.

This foundational truth is progressively realized: (1) we realize our *very being* is *in Him*, who we *are* is found only *in Him*; (2) we realize that everything that we *are*—our male and femaleness and corresponding abilities, aptitude, talents, etc.—are all from Him, and thus *in Him*; (3) we realize that everything we *do*—the vocation we choose, the tasks we select, the actions we perform, our public life, our private life, etc.—must also be *in Him* (*Note*[317]); (4) we realize that everything we *have*—all our possessions—must also be *in Him*; life is not about getting what is ours to obtain, it is about seeking what is His, for only "In Him we live and move and have our being" (Acts 17:28); and (5) in all this, we ultimately realize that *He* is our *everything*; we *do not* need anything else, therefore, we place all we are and have at His service; in this, we must not seek some kind of balance or moderation, but with intense joy we must go all in, *in Him*.

Great joy is found in answering our mission—our *telos* (τέλος), our natural end for which we have been designed—and happy-blessed is that person.

With these realizations, we also know that we will inevitably suffer, just as the Christ suffered (1 Pt 2:21). Why? The answer requires a book of its own. However, simply put, here are three basic answers.

First: As mentioned, if we love properly—as He loves; i.e., *agape* (ἀγάπη)—we will suffer. This is a fact. For a simple example, just ask any parents, for in their unconditional love for their child will they not suffer?

Second: The Christ's mission is antithetical to worldly perspectives. Jesus said, "If the world hates you, realize that it hated Me first. If you belonged to the world (*Note*[318]), the world would love its own; but because you do not belong to the world, and I have chosen you out of the world, the world hates you" (Jn 15:18-19). This hatred towards the Christian, even from our own family or friends, will manifest itself in one form or another. "Indeed all who desire to live a godly life in [*Yahshua* (יֵשׁוּעַ) the *Mâshîyach*] will be persecuted" (1 Tm 3:12).

Third: Suffering helps us learn obedience—Jesus humbled Himself, being obedient even unto death, death on a Cross (Phil 2:8). In obedience, He patiently endured suffering. It is easy to be obedient when everything is going our way, but not so easy when things are difficult. "Was it not necessary that [the] Christ should suffer these things and enter into His glory?" (Lk 24:26). Why would it be any different for you or me? We should not be unhappy in sufferings. As we suffer, or during our sufferings, we bow down our head to Him in obedience and humility—all the while "knowing that affliction produces endurance, and endurance, proven character, and proven character, hope" (Rom 5:3-4).

> [So] when you come to serve the LORD, prepare yourself for trials. Be sincere of heart and steadfast, undisturbed in time of adversity. Cling to Him,

> forsake Him not; thus will your future be great. Accept whatever befalls you, in crushing misfortune be patient; for in fire gold is tested, and worthy men in the crucible of humiliation. Trust God and He will help you; make straight your ways and hope in Him. You who fear the LORD, wait for His mercy, turn not away lest you fall. You who fear the LORD, trust Him, and your reward will not be lost. You who fear the LORD, hope for good things, for lasting joy and mercy. Study the generations long past and understand; has anyone hoped in the LORD and been disappointed? Has anyone persevered in his fear and been forsaken? Has anyone called upon Him and been rebuffed? Compassionate and merciful is the LORD; He forgives sins, He saves in time of trouble. Woe to craven hearts and drooping hands, to the sinner who treads a double path! Woe to the faint of heart who trust not, who therefore will have no shelter! Woe to you who have lost hope! What will you do at the visitation of the LORD? Those who fear the LORD disobey not His words; those who love Him keep His ways. Those who fear the LORD seek to please Him, those who love Him are filled with His Law. Those who fear the LORD prepare their hearts and humble themselves before Him. Let us fall into the hands of the LORD and not into the hands of men, for equal to His majesty is the mercy that He shows. (Sirach 2:1-18)

When we consign ourselves to His hands and place all we are and have at His service, we will suffer. We will suffer physical and mental pain for Him (just as He did on the Cross), "but rejoice [*chairo* (χαίρω)] to the extent that you share in the sufferings of [the] Christ, so that when His glory is revealed you may also rejoice [*chairō* (χαίρω)] exultantly" (1 Pt 4:13; also cf. Mt 5:12).

There is a positive understanding of suffering in Him. In this positive suffering we now rejoice, so we may rejoice in the future eternally with Him. This is our *joy*. Our true joy is ultimately only in

Jesus the Messiah—everything else is loss (Phil 3:8). He is *the* Way, *the* Truth, and *the* Life (Jn 14:6). We must with intense joy earnestly *desire* Him. Remember:

> Blessed are you when people hate you, and when they exclude and insult you, and denounce your name as evil on account of the Son of Man. Rejoice [*chairō* (χαίρω)] and leap for joy on that day! Behold, your reward will be great in Heaven. (Lk 6:22-23)

Worldly happiness is the easy way out. We are easily tempted to take that path by conformity to this world. Achieving worldly acceptance and popularity are temptations from the world—we tend to gravitate towards these types of happiness. Note that "no one experiencing temptation should say, I am being tempted by God; for God is not subject to temptation to evil, and He Himself tempts no one" (Jms 1:13). Rather, each person is tempted when he or she is lured and enticed by his or her own desire (Jms 1:13-14). These worldly allurements and desires do not bring Christian joy. These types of happiness are temporal and fleeting. Do not grieve our Lord and Messiah by searching for this type of momentary worldly happiness. Instead let us stand firm in *Yahshua* (יֵשׁוּעַ) the Christ, our true joy:

> I appeal to you therefore, brethren, by the mercies of God, to present your bodies as a living sacrifice, holy and acceptable to God, which is your spiritual worship. Do not be conformed to this world but be transformed by the renewal of your mind, that you may prove what is the will of God, what is good and acceptable and perfect. (Rom, 12:1-2)

Some of us Christians are allowing the world to transform us, instead of being the transforming agent—the salt—of the world. We are not flavouring the world and transforming people's lives, for and through Jesus the Christ. Instead, we are allowing the world to make us insipid and diminishing the effectiveness of the Church by aggressive secular and political ideologies.

Christians are called to be the "salt for the earth. But if salt loses its taste, what can make it salty again? It is good for nothing, and can only be thrown out to be trampled under people's feet" (Mt 5:13). We must not lose our saltiness by conforming ourselves to this world, if we do, as a consequence, we will be trampled by a godless society. "We do not want . . . a Church that will move *with* the world, we want a Church that will move the world," G. K. Chesterton writes (*Note*[319]).

God created this world. God loves this world, to the point that He sent His Son to suffer and die for this world. In turn, His Son accepted this suffering, so that He may renew us and transform the darkness of suffering and pain into joy.

Who is our teacher? Is it His Son, or is it the world? Who is our influencer? Is it His Son, or is it the world? Who informs our thinking? Is it His Son, or is it the world? If your answer for all three questions is, *His Son*, then this is what you are called to do: His Son "suffered for you, leaving you an example that you should follow in His footsteps" (1 Pt 2:21).

Rejoice—*chairō* (χαίρω)—in your sufferings (Col 1:24). Suffering is not ultimately gloom and doom. On the contrary, in it, we have Christian hope. The Messiah's sufferings, and ours, are not final (Rev 21:1-8). Therefore, in our sufferings there is a call for rejoicing.

This, incidentally, is contrary to some Eastern thought (or religions) which suggest that we are able to eliminate suffering through detachment. This detachment is virtually impossible. Even so, this is not congruent with Christian thought, for we desire to be attached to our Messiah.

Bear with me as I explain what we have studied thus far with another quick summation.

We are aliens and sojourners in this world. We have no idea what our life will be like tomorrow, for we "are a puff of smoke that appears briefly and then disappears" (Jms 4:14). We have no ultimate control of our life; can any of us "add a single moment to our life-span?" (Mt 6:27). We are all going to die! However, death does not have the final say. We will have life without end *in Him*. Our *zōē* (ζωή) is hidden *in Him*. This is our joy. This is our hope. This is our optimistic outlook.

"I write these things to you so that you may know that you have eternal life, you who believe in the Name of the Son of God" (1 Jn

5:13). Although at present we know partially and "we see indistinctly, as in a mirror" we are confident that we "shall know fully" when we see Him "face to Face" (1 Cor 13:12). This is our confidence. Therefore, rejoice, for we will see Him, our Creator, our Love, *face to Face*.

However, until we die, we live in this world; so, in *bios* (βίος) we will suffer, and in *zōē* (ζωή) we will suffer (*Note*[320]). However, these sufferings may be redemptive. In this, we should rejoice, for we are participating in His sufferings. Therefore, be "content with weaknesses, insults, hardships, persecutions, and constraints" for *His sake* (2 Cor 12:10). "Consider it all joy, my brothers and sisters, when you encounter various trials" for *His sake* (Jms 1:2), "knowing that your fellow believers throughout the world undergo the same sufferings" (1 Pt 5:9b). Likewise, just like Saint Paul, we also must "consider that the sufferings of this present time are as nothing compared with the glory to be revealed for us" (Rom 8:18). Jesus our Messiah,

> suffered outside the gate, to consecrate the people by His own blood. Let us then go [joyfully] to Him outside the camp, bearing the reproach that He bore. For here we have no lasting city, but we seek the one that is to come. Through Him (then) let us continually offer God a sacrifice of praise, that is, the fruit of lips that confess His Name. (Heb 13:12-15)

Do not be ashamed of Him, do not be ashamed of your testimony to Him (1 Tm 1:8), and do not be ashamed to suffer for Him; "but bear your share of hardship for the Gospel with the strength that comes from Him" (2 Tm 1:8). We are told by Him: "Whoever is ashamed of Me and of My words, the Son of Man will be ashamed of when He comes in His glory and in the glory of the Father and of the holy angels" (Lk 9:26 and Mk 8:38).

In our baptism, we have been raised with the *Mâshîyach* (מָשִׁיחַ), therefore, "seek what is above, where the Christ is seated at the right hand of God" (Col 3:1). Yes, we must "think of what is above, not of what is on earth" (Col 3:3). For when *Yahshua* (יֵשׁוּעַ) the Anointed One, our very *zōē* (ζωή) appears, "then you too will appear with Him in glory" (Col 3:4). He did not come to bring us mere *bios* (βίος), to put us in a mere survival-mode; He came to give us *zōē* (ζωή), the fullness of life and life abundantly—here and now and in life eternal.

Rejoice! We will see Him *face to Face*. Furthermore, our rejoicing and hope lie in the fact that He has conquered all suffering and its ultimate manifestation, death (1 Cor 15:55). "Do not let your hearts be troubled" (Jn 14:1), for we are *in Him*. In this world we will have trials and tribulation (this is inevitable), but, we must take courage, for He has overcome the world (Jn 16:33). Therefore, He directly tells us to *have peace in Him* (Jn 16:33). "Let the peace of [the] Christ control your hearts, the peace into which you were also called" (Col 3:15). This peace is not some sort of subjective psychological mindset. It is *His* peace. For that reason, despite what is happening in this world, we can take courage.

Yes, it is time that we move from inner agitation to peace—*in Him*. When we order our lives to Him, we will rest in His peace.

His peace is the next aspect we will consider. Beginning with the fact that we cannot be in His peace—thus "Rejoice . . . Always!"—when we live with an earthly fear or a distorted *fear of God*.

Many of us are motivated by fear, *not* love, which causes agitation, not peace. We see this all around us. I am speaking of that personal inner motivation which tends to be fear-driven rather than love-driven.

For example, most of us try to be good people—that is, go to church, lead an ethical and moral life, treat others fairly, and so on. However, our root motives are sometimes not those of love. To put it bluntly, we tend to do this because of a conscious or subconscious inner fear of going to hell, not out of love (*Note*[321]).

This fear-motivation is detrimental. In this, we respond to the love that *Yahshua* (יֵשׁוּעַ) our Christ extends to us, not reciprocally, but out of fear. Stated differently, we are not responding with a good conscience. I know that I am guilty of this. We do not like goodness for goodness sake, but in fear we respond with the thought that: God will smite me for my transgressions.

This attitude does not bring joyfulness; it brings more fear that eventually may turn into resentment. We lose our peace. This might be the reason why we Christians are gloomy—for we love out of fear.

As stated in the Preface, what we believe has a direct correlation with how we live. When our inner disposition and worldview is wrong, we live out that wrongness, which (in this instance) manifests itself with more fear. When our desire to do God's will is intrinsically wrong (although we might not know that) we inevitably reflect that in our lives. Consider for example the resentment demonstrated by the older son in the story of the Prodigal Son (Lk 15:25-30).

On this note, we may also consider the agitation of peace within the disciples on the road to Emmaus. Without the correct understanding of God's work, in false reasoning (Lk 24:25), they were agitated (visibly angry), emotionally depressed (gloomy, dejected countenance), and downcast (sour and sad)—as the underlying Greek word σκυθρωπός (skuthrōpos/*skoo-thro-pos'*) indicates (Lk 24:17).[322]

Jesus the Messiah needed to give them a lesson in Scripture (Lk 24:27). He needed to correct their partial information with complete information. In this, "they said to each other, were not our hearts burning (within us) while He spoke to us on the way and opened the Scriptures to us?" (Lk 24:32). Proper understanding, complete information, made their heart burn, awakening them from despair and agitation, and gave them peace.

We Christians may worship in vain (Mk 7:8). We may worship with faulty interpretations and understanding (Mk 7:9). We may honour God with our lips, but our hearts may be far from Him (Isa 29:13). Not everyone who calls *Yahshua* (יֵשׁוּעַ) the *Mâshîyach* (מָשִׁיחַ), "Lord, Lord," will enter the Kingdom of Heaven (Mt 7:21; also cf. Lk 13:23-27).

Like the Samaritan woman, we may worship what we do not understand (Jn 4:22); we may cling to our own understanding and human traditions (Mk 7:8 and 7:13). Like the Sadducees we may be easily misled, because we *do not know the Scriptures* (Mt 22:29).

When we worship in ignorance, there is no benefit to us; our worship is deficient; it does not correspond to the Truth, for it is of our own making. In this, how can we have peace?

Like the Samaritan woman, we jump from one thing to another (*Note*[323]). Like the Sadducees, we may have a poor understanding of God's word. So, "see to it that no one captivates you with an empty, seductive philosophy according to human tradition, according to the elemental powers of the world and not according to [the] Christ" (Col 2:8).

With that, what is the correct understanding of these two words, *fear* and *peace*? Beginning with the word *fear*, how do we "Rejoice . . . Always!" if we are living in fear, or have a distorted understanding of the *fear of God*?

Simply stated, there is *good* fear and *bad* fear. We will deal with the latter first.

Bad Fear: God has never called us to live with *bad* fear, i.e., a earthly fear. It may be fear of trials and tribulations, the ups and downs of life, unpleasant events, or even physical or mental harm. Nonetheless, we must face bad fear, and as Saint Francis De Sales states:

> Do not anticipate the unpleasant events of this life by apprehension, rather anticipate them with the perfect hope that, as they happen, God, to whom you belong, will protect you[324]
>
> | Saint Francis De Sales |

Concerning the fear of misfortunes, François-Marie-Jacob Liebermann states:

> Do not ever allow yourself to become upset by your misfortunes. In face of your misery, should you find yourself in this situation by the will of God, remain humble and lowly before God, and be at great peace. Respond to all misfortune, whatever it may be, with gentleness, peace, tenderness and interior moderation before God, abandoning yourself simply into His hands, so that He may make of you and in you what He pleases. Wish calmly and peacefully to live only for Him, through Him and in Him.[325]
>
> | François-Marie-Jacob Liebermann |

The above quotations provide antidotes to *bad* fear. Scripture provides others. As the Psalmist boldly and confidently proclaims: "Even when I walk through a dark valley, I fear no harm" (Ps 23:4; also cf. Ps 91).

We rest in Jesus our Messiah, and we should cast all our worries upon Him because He cares for us (1 Pt 5:7). For He continually reassures us: "be not afraid" (Jn 6:20).

As we are tossed about in turbulent seas (a metaphor for life), we can have confidence that Jesus our Messiah is in charge (see Mk 4:39). We find calmness in Him (cf. Mk 4:39-41 and 1 Kgs 19:12). We must have confidence *in Him* and abandon ourselves to Him. In turbulent seas we do not fear, for we rest in Him.

With this let us move to *good* fear.

Good Fear: The fear of God is *good* fear. The "fear of the LORD" is the beginning of wisdom and the fullness of wisdom, (Ps 111:10; also cf. Prov 1:7, 9:10, 15:33, Isa 11:2, 33:6, Job 28:28, Sirach 1:2, 1:14, 1:16, 1:18, 1:24, 19:17, 21:11).

As you may have recalled, when the word LORD is written in English in all capitals, it refers to the Name of God, *YHWH* (יהוה). The fear of *YHWH* (יהוה) is the true beginning of wisdom.

It is unfortunate that the translated English word *fear* does not give us the full meaning of the underlying Hebrew word יִרְאָה (yir'âh/*yir-aw'*). As a result, we might distort the biblical understanding of this fear.

In Hebrew, *fear* has a twofold meaning, denoting *both* a sense of terror and fear, and a sense of moral reverence, awe and worship (*Note*[326]). To understand properly the *fear of God*, we must recognize the dual disposition we must have in understanding both meanings.

In applying the first meaning, we must be afraid of, in dread of, and frightened of God, including and acknowledging that some things we do offend Him.

Also keep in mind, that the gravity of any offense is not solely based upon the offense itself, but it is also based upon the one you are offending. For example, we may swear at our friend, we may swear at our mother, we may swear at God; now, even though the offense is identical in all three examples, the gravity of the offense increases from our friend, to our mother, to God (*Note*[327]).

Any offense is magnified when we offend God. We should be

fearful of sinning against Him, or fearful of using His name in vain. We should be fearful of the misuse of the Eucharist, and receiving Communion unworthily. We should be fearful of not doing what is right and just. Most of all, we must be fearful of *not* spending all of eternity with Him.

In the second meaning, to fear God is to be in *awe* of Him. We must tremble in joy, in fascination, in reverence of His Majesty and splendor, of Who He *Is*. Again, He is God. In the *awe* of Him, we have peace.

This good fear is a response to the fact that He created us out of love for us! The Psalmist proclaims:

> Let all the earth fear the LORD; let all who dwell in the world show reverence. For He spoke, and it came to be, commanded, and it stood in place. (Ps 33:8-9)

He created us. Our fear is *love motivated* towards Him.

In short, the proper disposition we must have—i.e., the fullness of wisdom—is when we have both a proper sense of fear and a proper sense of awe of *YHWH* (יהוה).

Some scholars favour the latter meaning of the fear of God—and dismiss the former. This is a mistake. We must choose both. I think the reason that they favour the latter is that they fail to recognize the love motivation within the former. Do not make this mistake. We must hold both of these in unison. Our awe of God tempers our dread of God, and our dread of God keeps us in awe of Him.

In both meanings of fear of God, we can be joyful and find peace. Not only do we see His Majesty and splendour and realize that He is the God of the universe, but also we see His love for His creation, in particular His *agape* (ἀγάπη) for us, and this gives us peace.

It is this combination of good fear which we pray to the Holy Spirit in asking the *gift* of fear. For it is He Who gives us joy and peace in connection with God. In this we ask: *veni Sanctus Spiritus* (come Holy Spirit), fill us with your gifts, especially Your *gift* of fear (*Note*[328]). Understanding, that,

> the gift of Fear fills us with a sovereign respect for God, and makes us dread nothing so much as to offend Him by sin. It is a fear that arises, not from the thought of hell, but from sentiments of reverence and filial [i.e., love] submission to our Heavenly Father. It is the fear that is the beginning of wisdom, detaching us from worldly pleasures that could in any way separate us from God. "*They that fear the Lord will prepare their hearts, and in His sight sanctify their souls*."
>
> | Novena Prayer to the Holy Spirit |

Continuing our understanding of *His peace*, we see that His peace however, is not an earthly peace, it is a peace found only in Him; this is a fulfillment of God the Father's love; what is more, it is a peace that is twofold.

First, Relational Peace: When Jesus the Christ speaks of relational peace, He refers to peace on earth relating to other humans. This peace may be seen in three aspects. First, we must cultivate a general peace on this earth (*Note*[329]). Second, we cultivate a peace within ourselves. Third, we cultivate a peace directly with others. For, if possible, we are called to "live at peace with all" (Rom 12:18; also cf. 14:19, Heb 12:14, and Prov 16:7). In the words of the Messiah: "Blessed are the peacemakers" (Mt 5:9).

So then, this should be the *modus operandi* for all Christians (our default mode of operation) that is to say, our inner disposition and natural inclination toward others should be peace at all times (even in the face of hostility).

Keep in mind, that even though this is a relational peace, this nonetheless is not earthly peace (see Mt 10:34)—for peace is found *only in Him* (see Mt 10:35-39). His peace is a peace that has defeated earthly fear. It is a peace that has defeated sin. It is a peace that has defeated death.

Earthly peace is temporal; peace *in Him* is eternal. Chasing after a earthly peace—e.g., some sort of self-serenity, or emotional tranquility, or quietness that is *not in Him*; or Eastern meditative or yogic practices, internal emptying of oneself or balance, political utopia or humanistic ideology, or even some kind of New Age *kumbaya* moment—is futile because it is fleeting and it is not His peace.

Our abiding peace comes only *in Him,* meditating, contemplating, and gazing on Him. Our abiding peace comes from the knowledge that we are standing upon a Rock, and that Rock is the Christ Himself (1 Cor 10:4). We live with an *absolute certitude in Him*. Christians must therefore stop these other exercises in futility.

Remember, "God did not give us a spirit of timidity *or* cowardice *or* fear, but [*He has given us a Spirit*] of power and of love and of sound judgment *and* personal discipline [*abilities that result in a calm and peace, well-balanced mind and self-control*]" (2 Tm 1:7[330]).

Note, however, that the Messiah's peace is sometimes a peace in spite of conflict. Consider the following:

> Do not think that I have come to bring peace upon the earth. I have come to bring not peace but the sword. For I have come to set a man 'against his father, a daughter against her mother, and a daughter-in-law against her mother-in-law; and one's enemies will be those of his household.' Whoever loves father or mother more than me is not worthy of me, and whoever loves son or daughter more than me is not worthy of me; and whoever does not take up his cross and follow after me is not worthy of me. Whoever finds his life will lose it, and whoever loses his life for my sake will find it. (Mt 10:34-39)

As we can see, this is not a earthly peace. Doing the Christ's will bring peace to the doer (*Note*[331]).

In His peace, we find the antidote to loneliness, alienation, isolation, and emotional depression. As many preachers have said: You are known by God; you are not alone; your life is not mere random chance; God knows you by name and loves you; you have a purpose to your life; you have a mission to fulfill; God is watching over you; you are a vessel for Him.

His peace is also understanding our eternal-rest *in Him*—as we have studied, in the fulfillment of the Sabbath rest—even while we are on this earth.

It might be helpful to make a distinction between *worry* (or *anxiety*) and *concern*. Reality may give us concern; however, this concern should not turn into worry or anxiety (cf. Mt 6:25-34). That is, *concern* is okay, but *anxiety* is not:

> have no anxiety at all [do not be anxious], but in everything, by prayer and petition, with thanksgiving, make your requests known to God. Then the peace of God that surpasses all understanding will guard your hearts and minds in [*Yahshua* (יֵשׁוּעַ) the *Mâshîyach* (מָשִׁיחַ)]. (Phil 4:6-7)

Affirming this, Jesus repeatedly tells us throughout the Gospels: "Do not be afraid!" (e.g., Mt 10:28, Mk 6:50, and Lk 8:50). Also, as stated in the Book of Revelation: "Do not be afraid of anything that you are going to suffer . . . Remain faithful until death, and I will give you the crown of life" (Rev 2:10). The letter to the Hebrews states, "Thus we may say with confidence: The Lord is my helper, (and) I will not be afraid. What can anyone do to me?" (Heb 13:6). In Saint John's Gospel, Jesus says, that we will "weep and mourn, while the world rejoices; you will grieve, but your grief will become joy" (Jn 16:20).

Jesus, our Messiah, is *right now* seated at the right hand of God the Father (Heb 10:12), and "now He waits until His enemies are made His footstool" (Heb 10:13). Because of that, even when wars and insurrections trouble the world, do not be alarmed, troubled, or terrified (Mt 24:6, Mk 13:7, and Lk 21:9); for do you not know that in our baptism (*in Him*) "we even now taste the joy of the New Jerusalem" and (*in Him*) we are also *right now* seated at the right hand of God?[332] We are already in possession of this hope. He, the Head, is with His body, consequently, we the body are with the Head. That is, He is not disconnected or dismembered from the body (Acts 9:4, 22:7, and 26:14). Don't be afraid! Don't over-think! Remain in His peace!

Second, Peace with God: When Jesus our Messiah speaks of peace, He also speaks of something deeper than anything this world can give us, or even His relational peace on this earth, as just noted.

This second peace is the more profound of the two. The Christ speaks of peace between us—humanity—and God the Father. It is this peace that gives us tremendous joy—which gives us true *shalom*. In *Yahshua* (יֵשׁוּעַ) the *Mâshîyach* (מָשִׁיחַ), humanity has been reconciled with God the Father; therefore, we have peace with God the Father in our Messiah (cf. Rom 5:1 and Col 1:20). The enmity that once was between humanity and God is no longer. The barrier of hostility is no longer.

> But now in [*Yahshua* (יֵשׁוּעַ) the *Mâshîyach* (מָשִׁיחַ)] you who once were far off have become near by the blood of [the] Christ. For He is our peace, He who made both one and broke down the dividing wall of enmity, through His flesh, abolishing the Law with its commandments and legal claims, that He might create in Himself one new person in place of the two, thus establishing peace, and might reconcile both with God, in one body, through the Cross, putting that enmity to death by it. (Eph 2:13-16)

Yes! We are saved from the wrath of God (Rom 5:9), we are "no longer strangers and sojourners, but [we] are fellow citizens with the holy ones and members of the household of God" (Eph 2:19)—so, rejoice! I say it again: Rejoice!

Note that the peace described above is objective—the removal of enmity between humanity and God—however, this produces a subjective response in us. We rejoice and this rejoicing comes from this ultimate peace He gives us—a peace that is over and above any earthly peace.

This peace and this rejoicing come from the fact that we are now *one body with Him*; we are *a new person in Him*; and we are thus *reconciled to the Father through Him*. In our human condition we live a life not only knowing this fact, but also a life worthy of this designation and destination. For in this peace we can "Rejoice . . . Always!"

As we rejoice—*chairō* (χαίρω)—in His peace. we realize that His twofold peace is intertwined. When we give our lives to Jesus the Messiah, instead of chasing after earthly peace or being troubled by it (again, concern is okay), our lives will have true peace in the midst of *all* of life's trials and tribulations, and we realize that this is only possible because of the ultimate peace He has given us. Everything on this earth is temporal; everything on this earth will pass away; everything on this earth is fleeting (Eccl 3:1-3:8). Therefore, true peace is found only *in Him*.

This is of utmost importance, so we must firmly grasp this: *ultimate peace is found only in Him*. It is through *His* very own blood that we have been reconciled to God the Father (Col 1:20), let us therefore *only* rest in Him.

We may have heard that if we know the Christ we will have that true inner peace. Conversely, if we do not have that true inner peace, it is fair to say we really do not know who the Christ *Is*.

Yes, this might sound harsh. We may even question: Who really has true inner peace? Even so, if you do not have that true inner peace, is it fair to say that means you do not know *Yahshua* (יֵשׁוּעַ) the *Mâshîyach* (מָשִׁיחַ)?

Stated another way, do not say you know Jesus the Christ if you do not have that inner peace. If we do not have His inner peace, we must recover our understanding of Who Jesus the Messiah *Is*, and find that inner peace *in Him*. This is a journey that all those who call themselves Christians must embark upon. We must have a mature understanding of Who He *Is*—so we may live out that understanding as adults in our faith.

What I am saying here is clearly depicted in two Gospel scenes—both of which happen on turbulent seas (as mentioned, a depiction or metaphor of the turbulence in life).

In the first scene, a sudden violent storm arose in the sea and which threatened to swamp the boat in which Jesus and the Apostles were riding (Mt 8:24). This is a picture of the sudden storms of life that each one of us goes through. In such calamities, we might also scream out like the Apostles: "Lord, save us! We are perishing!" (Mt 8:25). To which He will reply: "Why are you terrified? O you of little faith" (Mt 8:26).

In the second scene, the Apostles were again being tossed about by the waves and the winds, but this time Jesus was not in the boat with them (Mt 14:24). We could say that this is a picture of the trials and tribulations of life in which we think that Jesus is not with us. At that point Jesus came to His Apostles, calmly walking on the water (Mt 14:25). He told them and tells us: "Take courage, I AM; do not be afraid" (Mt 14:27).

We, like Saint Peter, stretch out our hand to Him, and He gives us the ability to peacefully walk on the water—that is walk through life's turbulence (Mt 14:28-29). But. we also like Saint Peter, see the turbulence around us, lose our peace, get frightened, start to sink, and thus cry out: "Lord, save me!" (Mt 14:30). In this again, we are questioned: "Why did you doubt? O you of little faith" (Mt 14:31).

So then, are we of little faith? Do we doubt? He is the One Who rebukes the winds and calms the seas (Mt 8:26). He is the One Who immediately catches us even in our doubts (Mt 14:31). He is the One in Whom there is true peace.

When we know who God *Is*, we inevitably know who we are. In the Messiah, we know that we have become children of God. The understanding of this covenantal relationship with God gives us peace. More will be said about this in the next chapter but, for the moment, note that it is precisely this peace that the risen Christ gives us.

Think about the Resurrection appearances, in which the risen Messiah appears in the midst of His Apostles and disciples and says to them: "Peace, be with you" (see Lk 24:36, Jn 20:19, 20:21, and 20:26).

In essence He is saying, I have completed My Mission, which My Father has given Me; in it, I have atoned for you, I have made you righteous, I have justified you, and I have sanctified you. You now have *peace* with God the Father, cancelling the enmity and estrangement that once was between you and God the Father. You have been reconciled in and through Me. So, "Rejoice . . . Always!" For, what you were unable to do, I did. So, "Peace, be with you!"

At these Resurrection appearances, Jesus did not chastise His followers; He did not berate them; He did not humiliate them; He did not admonish them. He did not ask them: Why did you flee? Why were you not there to protect Me? Why did you not help Me? Why did you fail Me? Why were you so useless? He said nothing on those lines, for that would be an earthly peace that He would be questioning.

On the contrary, in tenderness, in *agape* (ἀγάπη), in mercy, without severity, and highly unmerited, He says "Peace, be with you." Do not worry; be not afraid; all is good, for I have done what you are unable to do. In and through Me, you have all been reconciled to God the Father. "Peace I leave with you; My peace I give to you. Not as the world gives do I give it to you. Do not let your hearts be troubled or afraid" (Jn 14:27). So again, *rejoice—chairō* (χαίρω)—and be in *peace*.

Our Messiah has *given* us His peace of reconciliation with God the Father. More than any other peace, it is precisely this peace that we *give* one another—especially in the setting of the Holy Eucharist. When we say, *peace be with you*, to the one standing next to us, we are *giving* His peace and thus essentially saying: My brother, my sister, do not worry, do not be afraid, He has reconciled us to God the Father, and thus (through Him and *in Him*) it is exactly *this* peace (*His peace*) I now give unto you!

In the midst of trials and tribulations, in the midst of life's uncertainties and messiness, in the midst of chaos and moral decay all around us, in the midst of scandal and corruption, "in the midst of a crooked and perverse generation" (Phil 2:15), *Yahshua* (יֵשׁוּעַ) the *Mâshîyach* (מָשִׁיחַ) shows us His redemptive power and calls us to go and persevere; (I deliberately quoted Philippians 2:15 within this context, so that we may recognize that nothing much has changed in two thousand years). Knowing *His peace*, we, one-by-one, give that peace to one another, despite what is happening around us.

We have been given an unmerited gift from God the Father, Who has reconciled us to Himself through His Son. At this moment, our job is to carry out this ministry of reconciliation (2 Cor 5:18). God the Father is making His appeal, through us, to the rest of humanity (2 Cor 5:20). We are the ambassadors of this message: that God the Father has reconciled the world to Himself, in Jesus the Christ, His Son (1 Cor 5:19).

Our Joy-filled Reaction in Saying: Yes!

Speaking of our job, let us now revisit the component of our response within justification and sanctification (*Note*[333]). Saint Peter describes this response as follows:

> According to His promise we await new Heavens and a new earth in which righteousness dwells. Therefore, beloved, since you await these things, be eager to be found without spot or blemish before Him, [and] at peace. (2 Pt 3:13-14)

We also note in another passage that "each of us shall give an account" of ourselves to God (Rom 14:12; also cf. 1 Pt 4:5), as per our response. However, since this is not a book on our *witness of charity* or our personal *call to holiness*, I would like to present our response primarily in the context of Christ-centredness, particularly (and in line with this chapter) our joy-filled reaction in saying: Yes!

Beginning with sanctification, we remind ourselves that sanctification is not perfectionism. It does not mean being sin-free. The call to be perfect—"be perfect, just as your Heavenly Father is perfect" (Mt 5:48)—is better understood as our achieving our end goal, our personal individual *telos* (τέλος), what we have been designed by God to do.

> We [tend to] believe, for example, that to win the spiritual battle we must vanquish all our faults, never succumb to temptation, have no more weaknesses or shortcomings. But on such terrain we are sure to be vanquished![334]
>
> | Fr. Jacques Philippe |

If we believe that we need sinless perfection, we will be defeated before we start.

> A very important, concrete example is the following: when we commit some fault or other, under the assault of a trial that seizes us, we are often tempted to grow slack in our prayer life, to not spend, for example, our usual time, in private meditation. And we managed to find good justification for this: "How can I who have just fallen into sin, who have offended the Lord, how can I present myself before Him in this state?" And we need sometimes several days before we can resume our normal habits of prayer. But this is a grave error; this is nothing but false humility, inspired by the devil. We must above all not change our habits of prayer. Quite the contrary. Where will we find healing for our faults if not close to [*Yahshua* (יֵשׁוּעַ) the *Mâshîyach* (מָשִׁיחַ)]?[335]
>
> | Fr. Jacques Philippe |

Again, do not fall into the misconception that we must be sinless or without fault (*Note*[336]). It is this kind of thinking that pushes non-Christians from Christianity, and our Christ.

We should not create a false image of God, as if He were counting every mistake we make waiting to damn us to hell. We should not make Christian ideals seem unattainable. Even worse, we should not portray ourselves as righteous by our own efforts. It is *in Him* that the high standard is set (cf. Mt 7:13 and Lk 13:24); it is also *in Him* that the high standard is achievable for "before the foundation of the world" He has chosen us *in Him* to be holy and blameless (Eph 1:4). We Christians need to *wake up* from our slumber and understand this.

Stated differently, achieving this perfection is not some sort of path of moral or ethical legalism (*Note*[337]). The *doing* part primarily consists of joyfully and eagerly doing exactly what our Creator designed us to do.

As we have studied, we celebrate the Eucharist, not because we are self-pious or holier-than-thou; we go because *we* acknowledge that we are *not.* Therefore, we should not become discouraged or hide ourselves from Him when we falter and fail in our sinfulness. Even in our sinfulness, even in our failures, we should be vigilant in prayer, we should continue going to the Eucharist, and yes, we can be joyful for we still can achieve our *telos* (τέλος) and be perfect *in Him*. It is this understanding that we should share with non-Christians.

To make my point, let us look at the concept of *sainthood*. The Church, in Her wisdom, canonizes individuals as Saints. In essence, She is declaring that these individuals, are now around the Heavenly Throne of Jesus the Messiah, for while they were on the earth they were *perfect*; which is to say, they achieved their particular *telos* (τέλος) while on this earth. Question: Were they sinless while on this earth? "Of course not!"

A good example in our time is Pope John Paul II. We know that he went to confession once a week. What was he confessing if he was sinless? He was sinful just like you and I. Despite that, he achieved his *telos* (τέλος); therefore, after his death the Church asserted his sainthood—and this goes for all the canonized Saints.

Most of us have continual, habitual sins. Any priest will tell you that 99.9% of us confess the same sins repeatedly. Each one of us has a particular sin with which we struggle. However, this should not take us away from our striving to achieve our natural ends, our *telos* (τέλος), that is, our purpose *in Him*. In Him we will conquer our sins. Our focus should not be *me-focused*; it should be *Christ-focused*. As we have studied, He has sanctified us.

> Blessed be the God and Father of our Lord Jesus [the] Christ, who has blessed us in [the] Christ with every spiritual blessing in the Heavens, as He chose us in Him, before the foundation of the world, to be holy and without blemish before Him. (Eph 1:3-4)

We might ask ourselves, how is it possible to be *holy and without blemish*, when we continually sin in one form or another? The answer is that we are chosen *in Him*. In ourselves, none of us is holy or without blemish, but, *in Him*, we are unblemished (this is the first part of sanctification, where God is the Actor). *In Him*, we are holy. *In Him*, our trespasses and sins are not counted against us. Yes, *in Him*, God the Father *will* impute the Christ's righteousness to us.

This, *in Him* aspect, God the Father, accomplished through His

Son, on our behalf, out of pure love, mercy, and grace. Now, we Christians need to live this reality (our part in sanctification). We need to stop inappropriate introspection and look up at Him.

In some sense, our personal sin also works for our benefit (the key is: only if we are *in Him*). Saint Paul writes that "all things work for good for those who love God" (Rom 8:28), to which Saint Augustine adds: "even sin!" (*etiam peccata*).[338]

Saint Paul goes on to say that we "are called according to His purpose" (Rom 8:28). We need to say to Him: Yes! In this *yes*, we allow Him to carry out His purpose in us, despite our sinfulness. We should allow His grace to shape us, and not let Satan defeat us by making us wallow in our sin and guilt, and thus, inhibit us from achieving our *telos* (τέλος), our perfection *in Him*.

False humility is saying to ourselves that because we are sinful we must hide ourselves from Him. We see this in the beginning with Saint Peter, when he says: "Depart from me, Lord, for I am a sinful man" (Lk 5:8). True humility knows that the Christ still loves us—although we are sinful. Thus, we press forward, carrying out our *telos* (τέλος), *in Him*. We see this change within Saint Peter when he eventually allowed the Messiah to do with him as He willed despite (still) being a *sinful man* (see Jn 21:15-19).

We have not attained perfection, but we press on, *in Him* (Phil 3:12). We need to move forward and focus on what lies ahead of us (Phil 3:13), despite our personal limitations, always continuing our "pursuit toward the goal [our *telos* (τέλος)], the prize of God's upward calling, in [*Yahshua* (יֵשׁוּעַ) the *Mâshîyach* (מָשִׁיחַ)]" (Phil 3:14).

As we study sanctification we realize that there is a paradox between God's act and our response. On the one hand, we will never be without sin (1 Jn 1:8), however, in His sanctification, we are actually without sin. This paradox might even sound contradictory or convoluted; nevertheless its understanding is important. We need to hold both of these statements in harmony without contradiction.

Saint John tells us, that Jesus the Christ came to take away sin, and "in Him there is no sin" (1 Jn 3:5); and, thus, we, being *in Him*, have been bestowed with His sinlessness in the Father's love. It is in this, "that we may be called the children of God" (1 Jn 3:1). "Everyone who has this hope based on Him makes himself pure, as He is pure" (1 Jn 3:3).

Furthermore, Saint John goes on to says, "No one who remains in Him sins; no one who sins has seen Him or known Him" (1 Jn 3:6). How do we understand these statements? To have *known* Him means to have recognized, have had knowledge of Him, or had perceived Him. Thus, we might say: Well I have sinned; does that mean I don't know Him?

Grappling with this question, let us consider justification, for in Him we are righteous. Listen,

> since we have been justified [*that is, acquitted of sin, declared blameless before God*] by faith, [*let us grasp the fact that*] we have peace with God [*and the joy of reconciliation with Him*] through our Lord Jesus the Christ (the Messiah, the Anointed). Through Him we also have access by faith into this [*remarkable state of*] grace in which we [*firmly and safely and securely*] stand. Let us rejoice in our hope *and* the confident assurance of [*experiencing and enjoying*] the glory of [*our great*] God [*the manifestation of His excellence and power*]. (Rom 5:1-2[339])

Understanding this is a cause for rejoicing. Real humility knows that He has done this for us. He has done what we cannot do. Now, in our joy-filled reaction we go and become a *witness of Him*, by allowing Him to do as He wishes with us.

So then, does this mean we do not need to deal with our sinful actions? "Of course not!" Does this mean that we do not take our personal sin seriously? "Of course not!" Does this mean we write off continual sinning as of no consequence? "Of course not!"

That is not what I am saying or what Saint Paul is saying (Rom 6:1-15). Consider this verse, "Do you not know that your body is a temple of the Holy Spirit within you, Whom you have from God, and that you are not your own" (1 Cor 6:19); or consider this verse. "We are not debtors to the flesh, to live according to the flesh" (Rom 8:12).

When our Messiah told the adulterous woman to "Go, and from now on do not sin any more" (Jn 8:11), this command also applies to you and me. When Jesus told the man healed at the pool called

Bethesda, "do not sin anymore, so that nothing worse may happen to you" (Jn 5:14), He was also speaking to us.

At some level we know all this—and this study on our *call to holiness* requires a book all of its own—for we must take our personal sin *very* seriously (and through the grace of God stop sinning by answering this calling). Our bodies *are not our own* to do with them as we wish. However, the focus in this book is Jesus the Christ; therefore, the presentation in the book is Messiah-focused. While we acknowledge our *call to holiness,* we respond to the call by focusing on Him and not on ourselves, for therein lies our intense joy.

That said, let us acknowledge that there are two predominant meanings in Scripture of the English word *sin*: (1) the most common is understood as the transgression of the Law (offence, error, and evil deeds); (2) another literally means *missing the mark* or *not to share* in the prize.[340] In both Hebrew and Greek, when the verb (to sin) is used, it primarily refers to the latter definition, and, when the noun (sin) is used, it primarily refers to the former definition.

Most scholars equate *missing the mark* to the transgression of the Law. However, it has, in turn, more than one aspect. Consider the Scripture "No one who remains in Him sins; no one who sins has seen Him or known Him" (1 Jn 3:6). In the Greek text, the verb *sins* in both places, is ἁμαρτάνω (hamartanō/*ham-ar-tan'-o*), mainly meaning *missing the mark*, not transgressing the Law. Therefore, if we are in Him, we will not miss the mark, for we are focused on Him. Likewise, if we miss the mark we do not *know* Him, for we are not focused on Him, which is sin.

With this, let us also consider the term *repent*. When we hear the word *repent,* as in "Repent, and believe in the Gospel" (Mk 1:15), we think of being contrite or being sorry for our sins (our transgressions of the Law). However, the underlying Greek word is μετανοέω (metanoeō/*met-an-o-eh'-o*), which primarily means to turn around, to change direction, to change one's mind, to return to, or literally to turn around 180 degrees—contrition is secondary, or we might say, would be included in the turning around.[341]

This is akin to the verb *to sin*, *hamartanō* (ἁμαρτάνω). In other words, to change direction, hit the mark, and attain the prize is primary, and contrition due to transgression of the Law is secondary and included.

God has "mercy on all for He loves all things that are; and loathes nothing that He has made; for what He hated, He would not have fashioned" (Wisdom 11:24). Concerning humanity, God "forgets the sins [the transgression of the Law, for it is the noun ἁμάρτημα (hamartēma/*ham-ar'-tay-mah*) used here] of men that they may repent [*metanoeō* (μετανοέω), turn around, come back to Him, and *hit the mark*]" (Wisdom 11:23).

Here is an analogy from archery that might help: If our focus is on Jesus our Messiah, like an archer—focused on the bull's-eye, the goal, the prize—we will not make any errors (transgression of the Law) in the process of attaining our goal. The archer trains and focuses on hitting the bull's-eye, in that achievement few or no mistakes are made. In our 180° turn towards the Messiah, we are literally turning our life away from sin; we are putting sin in the rearview mirror; in fact, we are removing the rearview mirror (cf. Gen 19:26) and discarding it, for we are now only looking forward; our focus is totally on Him.

Here is an analogy from marriage that also might help: In a strong marriage, spouses do not cheat on each other simply because a moral prohibition tells them that it is sinful. No, they do not cheat on each other because they love each other (which is the mark they are trying to hit—they are love focused). No one needs to tell them *not to* commit adultery. For them, no law concerning adultery is needed, for, concentrating on their love, adultery is not even in their minds.

Comparably, our love relationship with Jesus the Messiah must be greater than our love for anyone else, or anything else (particularly sin!). Our goal is not merely to get into Heaven. Our goal is to fall in love with Him. Our goal *is He*. Heaven becomes *Heaven* only because of Him—because He is there. If our focus is completely on Him, sin becomes irrelevant.

"But if anyone does sin, we have an Advocate with the Father, Jesus [the] Christ the righteous One" (1 Jn 2:1; also cf. 1:5-2:2), the One with Whom we are in love. For He is the One Who has justified us and has sanctified us. In Him and for Him, we should "Rejoice . . . Always!" in being a *witness of Him* and in our personal *call to holiness*, because it is something we want and desire to do for Him. We do not need to be told otherwise.

Yahshua (יֵשׁוּעַ) the *Mâshîyach* (מָשִׁיחַ) knows that we fall short, yet He is sympathetic to us. Because He knows our struggles, He bids us to come to Him and be with Him. Through Him, He gives us access to the Father, by justifying us and sanctifying us (*in Him*).

As stated in the earlier chapter, *justification* precedes and secures *sanctification.* Justification is an instant declaration to which we must freely respond and with which to cooperate. This is by becoming a *witness of Him*. On the other hand, sanctification is the ongoing transformation to which we must freely respond and submit, becoming *holy in Him*. We are submitting to an infusion of mercy and grace from Him.

Like Zacchaeus, our encounter with Him makes us want to change our life for Him (see Lk 19:8). Like Zacchaeus, we also freely and willingly lay aside our former way of life "and put on the new self, created in God's way in righteousness and holiness of truth" (Eph 4:24). Note that Jesus did not ask Zacchaeus to do any of this; he did it on his own; therefore, so should we. Recall that this is not only the subjective side of justification and sanctification; it is also the subjective side to our baptism (as we studied in Chapter 5, An Ontological Event). Although we are infused with His grace, it is our responsibility freely and willingly to participate in this grace, and allow it to shape us.

Society, and also, unfortunately, sometimes Christians have de-emphasized personal responsibility. This is a detriment to society and a lack of understanding of the true meaning of justification and sanctification. Recall that justification and sanctification each has a twofold aspect. On the one hand, it is God's doing (remember, He is the Actor). On the other hand, we must give consent (we must respond). This is precisely what Mother Mary's *fiat* is. She had to say *yes* to the outpouring of God's love, mercy, and grace upon her. Unlike us, however, she was already "full of grace" (Lk 1:28). In any case, she (and we) must consent.

Here, is another analogy that might help. Let's call this a *five-step gift analogy.*

First Step, Gift Package Delivery: In the first step, a delivery person delivers a package to you and drops it on your front porch.

Question: Have you *received* the gift? Clearly not. You might not even know that the package was delivered. Compare this situation to that of all humanity. God has gifted us with the Christ Event. This gift has been freely given out of love, from the God Who created us. However, some have not heard of God's Christ Event.

Second Step, Gift Package Delivery Notification: In the second step, you receive a notification that a gift is on your front porch; you open the door and see a beautifully wrapped gift. You pick it up and you take it into your house. Question: Have you received the gift? The answer is: Yes and No. In comparison, this is the segment of humanity that know about the Christ Event gift, but they have not opened the gift for one reason or another; therefore, they have not actually received it.

Third Step, Gift Package Opened: In the third step, you open the gift, to find a stunning, dazzling-white garment. Question: Have you received the gift? The answer is, again: Yes and No. If you have not put on the garment, you represent the segment of humanity who knows more than a little about the Christ Event. This segment of humanity sees, touches, and holds the gift. However, they have not put on the gift; the gift may be ignored, discarded temporarily, or thrown away; therefore, the gift has not been fully received.

Fourth Step, Gift Accepted and Put On: In the fourth step, you see how amazing this garment is, so, without hesitation, you put it on. Question: Have you received the gift? Yes, but, with a caveat. This reception represents the segment of humanity who has accepted the Gift of the Giver and thus has been baptized into Him "from every nation, race, people, and tongue" (Rev 7:9).

Fifth Step, Gift Worn Constantly: In the fifth step, you wear this dazzling white robe all the time. This wearing is the covenantal aspect of accepting the gift (*Note*[342]). These are persons who have received the gift in full. In the words of the Giver: "No one who sets a hand to the plough [accepts and wears the gift; i.e., follows Jesus] and looks to what was left behind [takes off the gift; i.e., stopped following Jesus] is fit for the Kingdom of God" (Lk 9:62).

Wearing the gift constantly is the process of justification and sanctification (*Note*[343]), from the time of our baptism and into eternity.

This is the issue with any form of the idea of *once saved, always saved*, which we briefly mentioned in the prior chapter—we must continually wear the garment; it is not enough to put it on once (cf. 1 Cor 6:9-11 and Gal 5:19-21).

As Christians, putting on the garment for one hour every Sunday is not good enough, e.g., being Sunday-Catholics; nor can we put it on and take it off as we see fit, e.g., being Cafeteria-Catholics. That is not how the Giver of the garment designed it. Here is a little sample of the gift-Giver's criteria:

> Whoever loves father or mother more than Me is not worthy of Me, and whoever loves son or daughter more than Me is not worthy of Me; and whoever does not take up his cross and follow after Me is not worthy of me. Whoever finds his life will lose it, and whoever loses his life for My sake will find it (Mt 10:37-39).

The gift-Giver wants us to be all-in. He wants access to all facets of our life, not neatly compartmentalized parts of it. If we decide to put on the garment it is to be an *all-or-nothing* proposition. It is a total abandonment to Him on our part, without reservation. We cannot divide our life into neat little boxes and say: You can have access to this part and this part, but no, not that part. We need to surrender our lives completely and unconditionally.

Why do we accept this condition from the Giver of the gift? It is because the Giver is God and the gift is so wonderful that words cannot describe it. It "is like a treasure buried in a field, which a person finds and hides again, and out of joy goes and sells all that he has and buys that field" (Mt 13:44)

Or, it "is like a merchant searching for fine pearls; when he finds a pearl of great price, he goes and sells all that he has and buys it" (Mt 13:45-46). It is more precious than anything else on this earth.

We are even willing to lose our very own life joyfully for this gift—for the Giver. We do this out of love for the Giver, and out of gratitude for the gift. Here is the wonderful thing: when we lose our life for Him we actually find our life—we realize what life really is. This is why we accept this condition.

If we are putting on and taking off the garment as we wish, we not only run the risk of losing the garment, there is a good possibility that we essentially will. Putting on the garment is our consent. Like Mother Mary, it is our *fiat* to enter into that covenantal relationship with Jesus the Christ.

From that point, like Saint Paul, we *press forward* in our goal. Like Zacchaeus, our encounter with the Messiah compels us joyfully, freely, and willingly to make every effort to *change* our life. The words *press forward* and *change* mean a continual action on our part. In this continual act of obedience, we work out our salvation with "fear and trembling" (Phil 2:12). Why fear and trembling? Well, "I wish to remind you . . . that (the) Lord who once saved a people from the land of Egypt later destroyed those who did not believe" (Jude 1:5).

> I do not want you to be unaware, brothers, that our ancestors were all under the cloud and all passed through the sea [a typology of baptism], and all of them were baptized into Moses in the cloud and in the sea. All ate the same spiritual food, and all drank the same spiritual drink [a typology of the Eucharist], for they drank from a spiritual rock that followed them, and the rock was [a type of] the Christ. Yet God was not pleased with most of them, for they were struck down in the desert. These things happened as examples for us, so that we might not desire evil things, as they did. And do not become idolaters, as some of them did, as it is written, The people sat down to eat and drink, and rose up to revel [(*Note*[344])]. Let us not indulge in immorality as some of them did, and twenty-three thousand fell within a single day. Let us not test [the] Christ as some of them did, and suffered death by serpents. Do not grumble as some of them did, and suffered death by the destroyer. These things happened to them as an example, and they have been written down as a warning to us, upon whom the end of the ages has come. Therefore, whoever thinks he is standing secure should take care not to fall. (1 Cor 10:1-12)

Here Saint Paul uses Israel as our example and as a warning to us. Just like they, we can lose the gift that has been given to us. In view of that, we Christians should not take this gift for granted—what happened to Israel can happen to us. Vigilance, not complacency is the life of a Christian.

Like Israel, we Christians will also be accountable (as we will discuss soon in the Parable of the Ten Virgins). Judgment day is coming.

> We [*will be called to account and*] must all appear before the judgment seat of [the] Christ, so that each one may be repaid for what has been done in the body, whether good or bad [*that is, each will be held responsible for his actions, purposes, goals, motives—the use or misuse of his time, opportunities and abilities*]. (2 Cor 5:10[345])

Judgment day is coming, and we Christians will face the Messiah as our Judge. Here are our options: we can live in fear of this, we can live in denial or ignorance of this, or we can live a faithful Christian life on this earth without fear, in Him.

Therefore, in reference to our baptismal garment—the *gift* we have been describing—Saint Paul tells us in both an exhortation and in an imperative form to *put on the new self* (Eph 4:24 and Col 3:10). In a continual action, we must look and seek for things that are in Heaven, not things here on earth (Col 3:1). In this, we must kill everything that belongs only to earthly life:

> Put to death, then, the parts of you that are earthly: immorality, impurity, passion, evil desire, and the greed that is idolatry. Because of these the wrath of God is coming (upon the disobedient). By these you too once conducted yourselves, when you lived in that way. But now you must put them all away: anger, fury, malice, slander, and obscene language out of your mouths. Stop lying to one another, since you have taken off the old self with its practices and

have put on the new self, which is being renewed, for knowledge, in the image of its Creator. Here there is not Greek and Jew, circumcision and uncircumcision, barbarian, Scythian, slave, free; but [the] Christ is all and in all [(*Note*[346])]. Put on then, as God's chosen ones, holy and beloved, heartfelt compassion, kindness, humility, gentleness, and patience, bearing with one another and forgiving one another, if one has a grievance against another; as the Lord has forgiven you, so must you also do. And over all these put on love [ἀγάπη (agape/*agápā*)], that is, the bond of perfection. And let the peace of [the] Christ control your hearts, the peace into which you were also called in one body. And be thankful. Let the word of [the] Christ dwell in you richly, as in all wisdom you teach and admonish one another, singing psalms, hymns, and spiritual songs with gratitude in your hearts to God. And whatever you do, in word or in deed, do everything in the Name of the Lord [*Yahshua* (יֵשׁוּעַ) the *Mâshîyach* (מָשִׁיחַ)], giving thanks to God the Father through Him. (Col 3:5-17)

Academic theologians believe that Colossians Chapter 3, is probably an early Christian creed, or at a minimum, some sort of early catechism for baptismal training. Putting on the white baptismal garment symbolizes all the good things that go with it (Col 3:12-13). In contrast, Saint Paul also exhorts us to *put to death the old self*, and the list of sins that go with it (Col 3:5).

In our baptism we have died in the Messiah and we have also been brought back to life *in Him* (Col 3:1). Therefore, our thoughts should be on Him, for we are now hidden *in Him* (Col 3:3).

Saint Paul concludes by telling us that "whatever you do, do from the heart, as for the Lord and not for others" (Col 3:23). That is, in everything we do, whatever that task may be, we must put our whole heart and soul into it, our very best effort, as if we are doing it for Him, for we are in essence working for Him and not for any other.

Why does Saint Paul tell us this? It is because, in the end, he knows that if we do so with an intense, joy-filled reaction to the gift

He has given us, we will receive from Jesus the Messiah the ultimate gift of inheritance (Col 3:24), our prize, our final *citizenship in Heaven* (Phil 3:20).

As Christians, we need to stop occupying our minds with earthly or worldly things (Phil 3:19). We must start living our life in a manner worthy of the Gospel of the Messiah (Phil 1:27). The Messiah is not only our life, we *belong* to the Messiah (Phil 3:20). We have been "purchased at a price" (1 Cor 7:23a), so, do not become a slave of other human beings or earthly things (1 Cor 7:23b). Let money serve you, and do not become a servant or slave of money, wealth, or possessions. In contrast, do not be afraid joyfully to be a *slave* of *Yahshua* (יֵשׁוּעַ) the *Mâshîyach* (מָשִׁיחַ)] (Col 3:24). That is a very good thing!

On the one hand, we work out our salvation with fear and trembling. If, after we have "escaped the defilements of the world through the knowledge of (our) Lord and Saviour Jesus [the] Christ," again become entangled and overcome by those defilements, our last condition will be worse than our first (2 Pt 2:20). As the letter to the Hebrews states:

> For it is impossible in the case of those who have once been enlightened and tasted the Heavenly gift and shared in the Holy Spirit and tasted the good word of God and the powers of the age to come, and then have fallen away, to bring them to repentance again, since they are re-crucifying the Son of God for themselves and holding Him up to contempt. (Heb 6:4-6)

On the other hand, the paradox is that the Christian should have no fear of judgment, for "there is no fear in [*agape* (ἀγάπη)], but perfect love drives out fear because fear has to do with punishment, and so one who fears is not yet perfect in love" (1 Jn 4:14-18).

We need to hold both—the fear of God and the love of God—in unison without contradiction.

On another occasion I again decided to walk around my local Cathedral parish and randomly conduct another one of my unscientific surveys. This time I asked fellow parishioners: What is salvation? Before you continue, like last time, you might want to think of your own answer, or even jot it down.

From this survey, the majority of the answers that I received are what I wrote in the Introduction of this book. For example: salvation is being saved; it is the saving act of God; or the deliverance from sin. Interestingly, for most, even though salvation has elements of an act in the past and present, the answers were mainly relegated to an act in the future (e.g., saved and going to Heaven).

So then, what is salvation? What does it mean to be saved by Jesus the Christ?

To be saved by Jesus, is knowing that despite all my atrocities against Him, my sinfulness and my craziness (as I call it), that—*in Him*—I am a child of God; right here right now as I speak (a reality lived or not); and thus, this is in spite of myself. Therefore, being saved actually means a formation of a relationship; not merely a deliverance from sin or an act of redemption. To be saved by God the Son, is to be reconciled through Him to God the Father—He makes us a child of God the Father, for this relationship is the purpose for which we were created.

As a result, salvation is not relegated to mainly something in the future—salvation is here and now; salvation is being *with* Him and *in* Him, even with my failures and sinfulness, right now while I walk this earth, not sometime just when I die. Why would we want to go to Heaven and spend all eternity with Him, if we don't want to spend our earthly life with Him?

All that said (and the emphasis of this book), *Yahshua* (יֵשׁוּעַ) the *Mâshîyach* (מָשִׁיחַ) is the personification of Salvation, only He provides salvation for all by His death and resurrection. He is the wellspring, the fountain, and the very source of our salvation. He gives Himself as an unmerited gift of love to us. Our personal *yes* is a yes rooted in our reciprocal love for Him, for our goal is to be like Him and to love like Him, explicitly, to be Christ-like—i.e., little christs or images of Him. Thus, like the Saints, we *gaze* upon Him and we *contemplate* Him, so we can be like Him—for this is our calling and thus must be our utmost desire.

Even though, as we continue to study, we can more and more see the *once saved, always saved* idea is much too simplistic, the underlying thought, however, is actually a solid argument; for if we are able to *do* something (bad) or multiple bad somethings that can make us lose our salvation, it is in effect saying that the opposite also holds true, that is, we can *do* something (good) or multiple good somethings that will gain our salvation. Again, this point is a *totally valid* argument. For as we have studied, there is nothing *good* individually or collectively that we can do to merit our salvation, or get into Heaven—we have no righteousness of our own and justification does not come from us (*Note*[347])—consequently, there is also nothing bad we can do to lose our salvation. That said, it is this last part that is a little incomplete and needs clarification.

The clarification is that it depends on what the *something* bad is. We cannot *do* something bad—as in there is no sin (a transgression of the Law)—that will make us lose our Salvation. This is clearly not possible (again, for that would mean the opposite would also hold true). However, here is the caveat: we must remain in Jesus our Messiah and focus on Him, despite our sins. Therefore, the *do something* referred to here is us moving away from the Christ—*missing the mark* (recall the second part in our definition of sin). It is in doing this particular *something* (this particular sin) that *will* make us lose our salvation.

Sometimes Christians (mainly Catholics) tend to be sin-focused (the transgression of the Law). We need to stop worrying about this sin so much; sorry let me rephrase that, we should not be *focused* on this sin and guilt so much, for if we are, we are really not focused on Him and the salvation He gives us. Remember the analogy of removing the rearview mirror. In that we will be focused or be refocused on our Messiah. Like I said before; am I saying: Go out and persist in sin (see Rom 6:1-15)? "Of course not!" For we know that we ourselves are the temple of God (1 Cor 3:16). There is integration within these chapters, so we should hold what has been said in concert with what is being said here. Accordingly, as we have studied, we must *hate* this sin (the transgression of the Law); and this "sin must not reign over [our] mortal bodies" (Rom 6:12).

Here is another image that might help with what I am saying here. When we are focused on our sins we are constantly looking down. In our disposition of navel-gazing we have a greater chance to stumble and fall. Conversely, when we are focused on Him we are always looking up, thus we are able to avoid this sin for we see clearly the path we must walk.

Also, recall the analogy of the archer and that of the married couple. If our focus is on Jesus our Messiah, like the archer's focus on the bull's-eye, the goal, the prize, we will not make many errors (a transgression of the Law) for we are looking and focusing on Him, our Goal. Like the married couple, if our focus is on the love we have for each other, we really do not need a Law to avoid sin. Here is the proper balance from Scripture, in two parts. Part one:

> For by grace you have been saved through faith, and this is not from you; it is the gift of God; it is not from works, so no one may boast. (Eph 2:8-9)

However, we cannot stop there. Part two:

> For we are his handiwork, created in [Jesus the Christ] for the good works that God has prepared in advance, that we should live in them. (Eph 2:10).

Clearly stated, yes, we can lose our salvation, but not due to this sin (a transgression of the Law), for that would not make any sense or be scripturally accurate—keep in mind, that is, *if we are in Him*, we cannot lose our salvation due to any of our sins (transgressions of the Law). It is when we stop God's grace within our lives (the sin of refusing to turn around, the sin of missing the mark); it is when we refuse His mercy, it is when we regard sin as no sin; it is when we are pursuing sin; it is when we sin against the Holy Spirit (cf. Mt 12:31 and Mk 3:22-30), deliberately rejecting the salvation offered by Him (which we may argue is going against our mission, or even not pursuing our *telos* (τέλος) in Him); it is when we take our eyes off the prize and *missing the mark*—it is in *this sin* by which we will inevitably not share *in the prize* (see *CCC* #1864).

In essence, it is when we say *No*! to being a child of God—this is the *do something* on our part by which we can lose our Salvation—for we then hold Jesus the Christ in contempt (cf. Heb 6:4-6).

To "Rejoice . . . Always!" we must fall in love with the One Who loves us. If we want to spend all of eternity with Him, we need to spend all of our earthly existence with Him. If we are focused on Him, everything else as a result—Heaven, salvation, and even sin—becomes secondary. Here is another way of putting it,

> [for] this saying is trustworthy: If we have died with Him [put on the gift] we shall also live with Him; if we persevere [wear the gift continually] we shall also reign with Him. But if we deny Him [take off the garment, take our eyes off the prize, or miss the mark] He will deny us. (2 Tm 2:11-12).

The Greek word used here for *deny* is ἀρνέομαι (arneomai/*ar-neh'-om-ahee*), which means to *contradict*, that is, to *disavow*, to *reject* something offered, *abnegate,* or to *refuse* something offered.[348] Likewise, our Messiah Himself tells us:

> Whoever is ashamed of Me and of My words, the Son of Man will be ashamed of when He comes in His glory and in the glory of the Father and of the holy angels. (Lk 9:26 and Mk 8:38).

If we move our gaze away from our Messiah, if we oppose Him, if we refuse to accept what He is offering, the gift He is giving us in its totality, if we reject Him, He will reject us! Period!

We need to educate ourselves and understand Scripture, for we are culpable if we are ignorant.

As we alluded earlier, this culpability, complacency, and ignorance are at the crux of our understanding of the Parable of the Ten Virgins (Mt 25:1-13). The Early Church Fathers (including Saint Augustine, Saint Jerome, and Saint Gregory of Nazianzus[349]), interpret the ten virgins as two sets of five virgins, all ten as the Church (the bride). The number in each set, five, refer to our five senses, which can either be used foolishly or wisely.

Thus, the Church in Her current condition is a mixture of five wise virgins and five foolish virgins in the parable. The wise are mixed with the foolish. The foolish five are complacent—they use their senses for ill, do not focus on the Bridegroom, and thus, disqualify themselves. When they say: "Lord, Lord, open the door for us!" (Mt 25:11), He replies "Amen, I say to you, I do not know you" (Mt 25:12).

In this context, foolishness of this sort means that we can lose our Salvation. We need to stay vigilant, awake, focused, and be on alert (Mt 25:13), keep our eyes on the prize, and not disqualify ourselves (also compare what was said before this parable in Mt 24:36-51 and after in Mt 25:14-30).

Interestingly, in the Church Father's interpretation they also connect the *oil* with *joy* (with two different understandings). The oil used by the wise virgins is *God's oil of gladness* that does not run out which the wise virgins through God's gift and grace stored by pleasing Him—by being a *witness of charity*, by answering their *call to holiness,* and by achieving their *telos* (τέλος)—while on this earth (*Note*[350]). In contrast, the oil used by the foolish virgins is the joy in the praises of society and the joy found in earthly things, which eventually run out (*Note*[351]). Their eyes were not on the prize, so, they *miss the mark.*

Referring to the *gift*, the *goal*, or *prize*, Saint Paul tells us that he himself, like an athlete, is running a race, in continual focus on the goal, the *telos* (τέλος), the prize of God's upward calling, in *Yahshua* (יֵשׁוּעַ) the *Mâshîyach* (מָשִׁיחַ) (Phil 3:14). Then he states that all of us who have a mature faith should have this same attitude (Phil 3:15), a continual attitude of being alert, pressing forward, and straining toward the goal. This pressing forward is not only to achieve the objective, his *telos* (τέλος), but also, the prize. That is the ultimate goal of God's upward calling, in *Yahshua* (יֵשׁוּעַ) the *Mâshîyach* (מָשִׁיחַ)

Saint Paul had a Christ-centred motivation. His core ambition was to please his Messiah (2 Cor 5:9). Thus, he did not take his gift or the Giver for granted. In reality, to attain the prize, he tells us that he disciplines his body and makes it his slave "for fear that, after having preached to others, [he himself] should be disqualified" (1 Cor 9:27)—like the five-foolish virgins.

Another image Saint Paul uses is that of an athlete in training, which is very apropos for his Greek audience and for us. We all know that athletes do not just show up every four years to the Olympics and win gold medals. No, they train, they exercise, they control their diet and, most of all, they control their thinking. "Every athlete exercises discipline in every way," Saint Paul states (1 Cor 9:25). "They do it to win a perishable crown" (1 Cor 9:25). Accordingly, how much more should we discipline ourselves to win an imperishable crown?

Saint Paul goes on to describe an athlete intending to *win a victor's crown*! He asks us: "Do you not know that the runners in the stadium all run in the race, but only one wins the prize?" (1 Cor 9:24). Therefore, "Run so as to win" (1 Cor 9:24). Run and win the imperishable crown. Saint Paul did not run aimlessly (1 Cor 9:26), nor should we!

Despite Saint Paul's discipline, despite His continual pressing forward toward the goal, he did not claim to say that he had arrived, so neither should we. Branches were pruned off Israel, the olive tree, and we Gentiles were grafted in in their place; thus, we now share in the rich root of the olive tree (Rom 11:17). Saint Paul tells us, however, that if the natural branches were not spared, because they did not bear fruit (cf. Jn 15:2), the grafted-in branches will not be spared, if they do not bear any fruit (Rom 11:20-21; also cf. Jn 15:1-6). Do not take this race for granted. Run to win, before you get pruned! Here is a perfect summary given by Saint Paul:

> I count everything as loss compared to the priceless privilege *and* supreme advantage of knowing [Jesus the Christ] my Lord [*and of growing more deeply and thoroughly acquainted with Him—a joy unequaled*]. For His sake I have lost everything, and I consider it all garbage, so that I may gain Him, and may be found in Him, not having any righteousness of my own derived from [*my obedience to*] the Law *and* its rituals, but [*possessing*] that [*genuine righteousness*] which comes through faith in [the] Christ, the righteousness which comes from God on the basis of faith. *And this, so* that I may know Him and [*in that same way experience*] the power of His resurrection,

> and [*that I may share*] His sufferings, by being *continually* conformed [*inwardly into His likeness even*] to His death [*dying as He did*]; so that I may attain to the resurrection [*that will raise me*] from the dead. Not that I have already obtained it [*this goal of being Christ-like*] or have already been made perfect, but I actively press on so that I may take hold of that [*perfection*] for which [Jesus the Christ] took hold of me *and* made me His own [cf. 1 Cor 9:24 and 1 Tm 6:12]. Brothers and sisters, I do not consider that I have made it my own yet; but one thing *I do know*: forgetting what *lies* behind and reaching forward to what *lies* ahead, I press on toward the goal to win the [*Heavenly*] prize of the upward call of God in [Jesus the Christ]. (Phil 3:8-14[352])

Like Saint Paul, we joyfully continually press forward—in patience, perseverance, and hope—with our eyes on the prize. Not as something already obtained (for, that would be arrogance on our part, not humility), however, without fear, holding on to the fact that we are *in Him*. At the end of our journey, when our death is imminent, we might also say in humility and in concert with Saint Paul:

> I am already being poured out like a libation, and the time of my departure is at hand. I have competed well; I have finished the race; I have kept the faith. From now on the crown of righteousness awaits me, which the Lord, the just judge, will award to me on that day, and not only to me, but to all who have longed for His appearance. (2 Tm 4:6-8)

It is He for Whom we long! Our ultimate goal is He! He is our prize! He is the definitive gift! Not only now, while we are on this earth, but also forever, for all eternity. For it is *only* He, Himself, Who gives our life purpose, meaning, and direction. Therefore, it is only *in Him* that we can unequivocally "Rejoice . . . Always!"

When we read Saint Paul's words above, we see a man who is totally focused on the Christ. Nothing matters to him except *the* ultimate goal, the prize, or gift of being with the Christ for all of eternity. In this, Saint Paul realizes that if the Christ is his ultimate goal for all eternity, then his goal on this earth cannot be any different.

Specifically stated, there is a realization of a congruency of being in the Messiah while on this earth, combined with the gain of the Messiah for all eternity.

Therefore, nothing else and no one else matters in comparison to this. Everything on this earth is loss, is garbage, is rubbish—literally dung—in comparison to gaining the *Mâshîyach* (מָשִׁיחַ). All Christians need to *wake up* and listen: our disposition should not be any different than that of Saint Paul's, or from that of any of the Saints. All things, I mean *all things,* are in Him.

This is the foundational understanding of what it means to live a Christ-centred life. He is our number one goal for all eternity, so we should live our life on this earth with the goal in mind.

Some of you reading this may object to this understanding. For example, a priest I know objected, stating, something on the lines of: Where is myself or my self-realization in all of this? Does it not matter who I am as a person, as an individual?

To this, I answer that it is useless to try to find our real self apart from the Christ; for *who we are* as a person, our true personhood, is wrapped up in Him. It is only when we realize who the Christ *Is*, that we discover who we are as a human beings, as persons, as individuals. In other words, when we discover Him and are in true relationship with Him, we discover our true self—our *true* personhood—what it means to be human, collectively and individually.

The very root of a Christ-centred life is placing the Christ at the very centre of our life. That is, we joyfully and intentionally place the Messiah at the centre of every relationship we have, everything we do, everything we are, everything we have, everything we own, and everything that is life. Therefore, who we are as an individual is illuminated by knowing who the Christ *Is*, and living in the Truth.

In this regard, let us take a moment and listen to a treatise from Saint John Eudes:

I ask you to consider that our Lord Jesus [the] Christ is your true head and that you are a member of His body. He belongs to you as the head belongs to the body. All that is His is yours: breath, heart, body, soul and all His faculties. All of these you must use as if they belonged to you, so that in serving Him you may give Him praise, love and glory. You belong to Him as a member belongs to the head. This is why He earnestly desires you to serve and glorify the Father by using all your faculties as if they were His. He belongs to you, but more than that, He longs to be in you, living and ruling in you, as the head lives and rules in the body. He desires that whatever is in Him may live and rule in you: His breath in your breath, His heart in your heart, all the faculties of His soul in the faculties of your soul, so that these words may be fulfilled in you: *Glorify God and bear Him in your body, that the life of Jesus may be made manifest in you*. You belong to the Son of God, but more than that, you ought to be in Him as the members are in the head. All that is in you must be incorporated into Him. You must receive life from Him and be ruled by Him. There will be no true life for you except in Him, for He is the one source of true life. Apart from Him you will find only death and destruction. Let Him be the only source of your movements, of the actions and the strength of your life. He must be both the source and the purpose of your life, so that you may fulfill these words: *None of us lives as his own master and none of us dies as his own master. While we live, we are responsible to the Lord, and when we die, we die as His servants. Both in life and death we are the Lord's. That is why Christ died and came to life again, that He might be Lord of both the dead and the living*. Finally, you are one with Jesus as the body is one with the head. You must, then, have one breath with Him, one soul, one life, one will, one

> mind, one heart. And He must be your breath, heart, love, life, your all.[353]
>
> | Saint John Eudes |

Practically speaking, what should this look like in our everyday living? How do we "Rejoice . . . Always!" even in unfavourable situations of our day-to-day living? Well, here are nine suggestions.

Suggestion Number 1: Christ-centred Christians joyfully give a deep and an unequivocal Yes! to Jesus the Messiah. We allow Him to *invade* and occupy every facet of our lives. He is our King; therefore, it is His Crown and Kingdom that exercises dominion over our daily life (and not just when it is convenient).

We need to give Jesus the Messiah the controls, the driver's seat in our daily life. Submitting to Him, we must allow Him to live in us and permeate us. Our lives are no longer what we want to do and be, but what He is calling us to do and be. He must be the centre of our private life, our work life, and our public life. He must be the centre of our vocation—our priestly or religious vocation, our marriage vocation, or our vocation to remain single—all vocations are *in Him*.

He must be the centre of our needs and *wants*. He must be the centre of our decisions, including our monetary decisions. He must be the centre of all we own, of all our possessions. He must be the centre of our heart. He must be the centre of our emotions. He must be the centre of our mind, and everything we put into it (via television, books, entertainment, Internet, social media, etc.).

In this disposition we pray unceasingly (1 Thes 5:17) and give thanks to Him unceasingly (1 Thes 2:13); that is we make our very life a prayer, a continual dialog with the One we love. He is our King. Our gaze is fixed upon Him. Every facet of our life belongs to Him. We live solely for Him. For, He is the *Alpha* and the *Omega*, the *first* and the last, the *beginning* and the *end* (Rev 22:13), and *the* Way, *the* Truth, and *the* Life (Jn 14:6) . . . the *love* of our very life.

Suggestion Number 2: To be Christ-centred means that we as Christians need to know Who *Yahshua* (יֵשׁוּעַ) the *Mâshîyach* (מָשִׁיחַ)

really *Is*—hence the reason I am writing this book. We cannot be content with a superficial or personal interpretation of our Messiah. We must let the Holy Scripture confront us and change our lives accordingly. Therefore, the Christ-centred Christian, with full joy, spends time studying, learning, and understanding Who He *Is*.

Now, some of us reading this might question if all this studying, learning, and understanding—i.e., head part—is *really* necessary? Is it not possible to bypass this with infused-grace, or some sort of supernatural vindication? Is it not all about our personal encounter with the love of God?

These are all good questions, but here is the problem. To explain, humour me for a minute: Are you able to lie? Of course the answer is *yes*. Are you able to be lied to? Again, *yes*. Are you able to deceive? Again, *yes*. Are you able to be deceived? Again, *yes*. Lastly, consciously or subconsciously are you able to lie or deceive yourself? Well, if we reflect on it, consciously or subconsciously we are capable of lying and deceiving ourselves. In fact, as the saying goes: our very own eyes may deceive us. So then, how do we know that we are not being deceived by our very own thinking within this *personal encounter*, or *infused-grace*, or *supernatural vindication*?

Here is an important warning we unfortunately tend to miss: Jesus the Christ clearly tells the Samaritan woman that she worships what she *does not* understand, and thus, she is worshiping *in ignorance*, for there is a proper understanding of worship (Jn 4:22). Yes, we could think we are worshiping properly, but all the while be worshiping in lack of knowledge.

He also clearly tells the Sadducees that they are misled, because they *do not know the Scriptures* (Mt 22:29). Yes, we need to know the Holy Scriptures.

These two statements given by the Messiah are extremely profound. We need to have a proper biblical-based understanding. If not, like the Samaritan woman, we run the risk of worshiping our own making and like the Sadducees, we might have an inadequate theology (i.e., understanding of God).

Therefore, the Messiah might also tell us that: "You people worship what you do not understand" (Jn 4:22; also cf. Mk 7:8 and Col 2:8).). Or like He told the Sadducees, He might tell us: "You are misled because you do not know the Scriptures" (Mt 22:29).

If we have a faulty understanding, inevitably it will result in faulty living—which we see in the life of the Samaritan woman (Jn 4:18), and the Sadducees (Mt 22:23).

That said, studying about the Christ, talking about Him—or, for that matter, even writing about Him—is all good and it is needed in our personal and church life, however, alone, it is just *not* good enough. It could be a form of lip service or knowledge for the sake of knowledge. Knowing the Bible from cover to cover is great and vital; however, even Satan knows the Bible.

Knowing about the Christ is good, but again, it is not good enough. To explain (by using this book), note that the first part of this book, *Understanding Who Jesus Is*, must be followed by *What it Means to be Christ-centred.* All that knowledge is empty and meaningless if we only know the Messiah as an academic exercise. If so, we are missing the whole point of this study.

To summarize, if we hold our faith *in Him* simply as a custom, habit, routine, or ritual, we are not being Christ-centred. Conversely, if we simply have knowledge of Him, we are not being Christ-centred. In love with Him, we need to move from a mental assent to a full relational assent. In our practical daily living, being Christ-centred means that we move from having knowledge *in* Him to choosing a relationship *with* Him. Now in this particular case, what matters is not the order as much as having both components. We must choose Him, and thus, be animated by Him. In this, we become what we choose. That is to say, the Christ-centred individual actually becomes *a witness of* Him (which is a great topic for a book on its own).

Suggestion Number 3: Christ-centred Christians acknowledge and rejoice in the fact that between our Messiah's First Coming (when He came in the flesh) and Second Coming, there is an *intermediate coming.* Saint Bernard of Clairvaux teaches us that there are "three comings of the Lord."[354] Between the First and Second Coming is an intermediate coming in which our Christ comes to us individually (for He tells us: "whoever loves Me will keep My word, and My Father will love him, and We will come to him and make our dwelling with him" Jn 14:23), and collectively (for He also tells us: "where two or three are gathered together in My Name, there am I in the midst of them" Mt 18:20). Knowing that our Messiah is with us right here right now as we face our daily life is a cause for rejoicing!

Suggestion Number 4: Our personal, one-on-one encounter with Jesus the Messiah makes us—no, let me rephrase that, *compels us*—to joyfully deny ourselves and take up our cross daily and follow Him. Christ-centred Christians joyfully are willing to lay down their lives for Him (cf. Mt 16:25, Mk 8:25, Lk 17:33, and Jn 12:25). Christ-centred individuals put their *Mâshîyach* (מָשִׁיחַ) before *everything*. The test of being Christ-centred is the attainment our *telos* (τέλος)—the natural end, the authentic purpose, for which we have been designed—and making it a reality *in Him.*

Being Christ-centred means that we are Messiah-focused, not *me-focused*. This can be equated to following the *narrow road*, which we must take (cf. Mt 7:13-14 and Lk 13:24-17). As we have studied, the three parts—(1) deny ourselves; (2) take up our cross; and (3) follow Him—are very difficult because our natural tendency is to be me-focused, and these three go against our natural inclinations.

Nevertheless, Christ-centred Christians strive for all three, and thus, strive for *holiness in Him*: "strive to enter through the narrow gate, for many," our Christ tells us, "will attempt to enter but will not be strong enough" (Lk 13:24). Each morning we need to wake up, and filled with intense joy, pray and ask for strength as we commit ourselves to *all three*!

Suggestion Number 5: Some of you reading this might be familiar with the term *holy indifference*. This begins with the realization that Jesus our Christ knows us and loves us more than we could ever imagine, and even more than we know and love ourselves. Therefore, Christ-centred Christians are indifferent to whatever He wants of them, for they know whatever it is it is the best for them. If He wants us to be sick or healthy, rich or poor, married or single, and so on and so forth, in a way it does not matter as long as all glory goes to Him.

In this we rejoice! We allow our Messiah to do with us as He pleases, for He knows what is best for us. There is no desire for one's own interest. There is no wishing for one's own interest. There is only the desire for perfection and happiness in Him, and for Him. This is a detachment from self, with a corresponding and simultaneous attachment to Him. This indifference is far from being unfeeling or uncaring; it is a detachment from all personal preferences to in turn do all things in Him as He wishes.

Suggestion Number 6: If we are truly living a Christ-centred life, we do not boast about ourselves. If we are Messiah-focused and not *me-focused*, we *cannot* boast about our talents or accomplishments. We realize that it is only "by the grace of God [that] I am what I am" (1 Cor 15:10). Therefore, it would be hypocrisy for us to boast about anything or anyone except Him.

I like the analogy that the prophet Isaiah gives us, when he asks: "Will the axe boast against him who hews with it? Will the saw exalt itself above him who wields it? As if a rod could sway him who lifts it or a staff should lift him who is not wood!" (Isa (10:15).

We know the answers, "Of course not!" Then, how can we—who are in the hands of our Messiah—exalt in ourselves? We cannot. Actually, no human being should or can boast before Him (1 Cor 1:29). On the contrary, whoever boasts, should joyfully boast only *in Him* (2 Cor 10:17). We boast in God the Father, through Jesus the Messiah (Rom 5:11). We also, joyfully, boast in our weaknesses, for we know that He is our strength (2 Cor 12:9). We also "boast in our sufferings, knowing that suffering produces endurance, and endurance produces character, and character produces hope" (Rom 5:3-5).

With this hope, we joyfully boast in the Cross of *Yahshua* (יֵשׁוּעַ) our Messiah (Gal 6:14). The Cross proclaims God the Father's infinite wisdom. Our sufferings are nothing in comparison to the sufferings of His Son—sufferings that He freely accepted on our behalf. They revealed not only His glory but that of the Father's. Therefore, we should not boast in anything but claim as our only glory the Cross of Jesus, our Christ.[355]

Suggestion Number 7:[356] To be Christ-centred (as we discussed in Chapter 3, The Absolute Primacy of Jesus), we need to be like the Magi; that is to say, we need to get out of our comfort zone, take the risk, and search for Him. To do this, we cannot be looking down at ourselves, we need to look up at Him. More importantly, we cannot be caught up in earthly or worldly comforts, for this will immobilize us. We look up and ahead toward the *star* that leads us to the Messiah, positioning ourselves so that we are free of earthly or worldly yokes that hold us back.

The Magi were not only an exemplification, they were a personification of all Christ-centred Christians who desire to leave everything behind, and embark on an extensive journey just to get a momentary glimpse of *Him*. This longing, this yearning, this inner desire helps us battle through all trials and tribulations because our eyes are fixed on Him.

This longing to catch a mere foretaste of Him compels us to take the risk and undertake the journey. With the Magi and in unison with Saint Augustine, we boldly assert: "Thou hast formed us for Thyself, and our hearts are restless till they find rest in Thee."[357]

In this, our own personal desires, wants, and ideologies are shattered. In this, we stop searching for what is best for *me*. For, there are many false stars vying for our attention: the star of stardom, fame, or popularity; the star of fortune, money, or possessions; or even the star of sex, drugs, and rock 'n roll (i.e., pleasures, addictions, and excitement).

We may all choose to follow any one of these stars; however, living a Christ-centred life means that we freely choose the star that leads us to the Messiah. We stop wasting our lives chasing after myriads of illusionary stars. Setting out to find the Messiah is not easy—we all like our comforts and comfortable situations; therefore, many people stay in place—they do not search. The Magi and Christ-centred individuals are not like that. With courage, we joyfully go in search of Him, despite the risk.

Suggestion Number 8: Speaking of courage and taking risks, we cannot claim to be Christ-centred if we are afraid to proclaim Him (again consider Chapter 3). The Christ-centred individual is not afraid to proclaim Him and speak God's Word, in and out of season. Like John the Baptist, we must fearlessly point out: "Behold, the Lamb of God, who takes away the sin of the world" (Jn 1:29). We do not have a private Messiah, a private Cross. Accordingly, we joyfully and courageously proclaim the Christ even if we are put in prison and risk being beheaded like the John the Baptist (Mk 6:27; also cf. Rev 20:4).

In the words of Saint Paul as he admonished Timothy: "I charge you in the presence of God the Father" and of *Yahshua* (יֵשׁוּעַ) the *Mâshîyach* (מָשִׁיחַ) to proclaim the Word, "be persistent whether it is convenient or inconvenient" (2 Tm 4:1a and 4:2a). "Do not be ashamed of your testimony to our [Christ]" (2 Tm 1:8). "For God did not give us a spirit of cowardice [i.e., bad fear] but rather of power and love" (1 Tm 1:7).

We cannot be fearful to enter into dialogue with others, in His confidence. For the One we speak of is the Messiah—Who is God Himself. The greatest act of love we can give others is the gift of Jesus the Messiah. His love—*agape* (ἀγάπη)—is freely given in *love*.

Therefore, in love and joy, let us bravely reenter the synagogues and engage in conversation with our Jewish brothers and sisters, retell them that the *Mâshîyach* (מָשִׁיחַ) that they are waiting for is *in truth Yahshua* (יֵשׁוּעַ). Let us open the Holy Scriptures (Tanakh) and show them this fact just like our *Mâshîyach* (מָשִׁיחַ) did on the way to Emmaus.

Let us lovingly inform Muslims that the only way to God the Father is through His Son, Jesus the Christ, Who is God, the Second Person of the Trinity (as we studied in Chapter 2).

Let us lovingly teach Hindus that there cannot be multiple gods, for we can use scientific principles to deduce that there can only be one Creator God, the Cause of all things (see Appendix B).

Let us lovingly enlighten Buddhists that it is impossible to cease suffering, unless you are detached from love. For, if you love properly, you will suffer as demonstrated by the Messiah Himself. Thus, unless you plan on detaching yourself from *love* in your life, or for that matter even friendships, you will never cease suffering; however, do not fret, for the Messiah has conquered all suffering.

Let us lovingly converse with atheists to demonstrate to them that, through logical deduction, without complication, there has to be an Unmovable Mover or First Cause (see Appendix B).

The Christ-centred individual continually preaches the Word—the Truth—by helping, convincing, and encouraging others through all patience and teaching (2 Tm 4:2b). Accordingly, this is not done with a triumphalism or in an attitude of superiority, or indignation, or self-righteousness; this is done joyfully, in humility and love, through patience, gentleness, and compassion (2 Tm 4:2b and 1 Pt 3:15).

Christ-centred Christians know that their Messiah is patient and gentle with them, so they are patient with others as well. They also know that the greatest gift they can ever give another—the greatest act of love—is the gift of Jesus the Christ. There is no other joy, act of love or gift, greater than this because it is He we offer (cf. Acts 3:6).

Take this next sentence for what it's worth: I'm not a proponent of bringing people to the Messiah by any means necessary just to save their souls or to help them not go to hell in the afterlife; but I'm a huge advocate of bringing others to our Christ so they may *fall in love*—right here, right now—with the One Who created them and truly loves them!

That's my personal goal (and the ultimate goal of this book), to help people fall in love with *Yahshua* (יֵשׁוּעַ) the *Mâshîyach* (מָשִׁיחַ)!

As Christians, we may feed people, we may clothe people, we may help people in every way imaginable. All of that is good, when *only* done in Him. However, none of these can be compared to the gift of the Messiah in their life. Christian social justice endeavours and mission work are important; however, the primary role of any Christian is to bring others to the Messiah (to help them to see their Salvation right in front of them, just as Simeon and Anna saw the Messiah with their own eyes). We *do not* save souls! Only Jesus the Messiah saves souls! Our job is simple to bring them to our Messiah.

Using the analogy from earlier, the Christ-centred individual helps others to open the gift (which has already been given to them), helps them see the dazzling white garment (with their own eyes), and helps them put it on (for all eternity). Just like searching for the Messiah is not easy, preaching the Messiah is not easy. Both are risky endeavours. Therefore, take courage. Being Christ-centred means that the risk is worth it, for we have joyfully entrusted our lives to Him. We trust *in Him*, even if we end up being persecuted and suffer for Him, or even martyred for Him (Jn 15:20)—the Christ-centred individuals know that for His sake all of these are actually very good things!

Suggestion Number 9:[358] To be Christ-centred is also literal. That is, it means for us precisely to be in the centre *with* the Christ. To illustrate this, two different images have been used over the centuries.

The first image is that of the wheel. The wheel turning is life itself; it is the world we live in, constantly turning. As the wheel turns, there will be good times and bad times; but, the wheel continues to turn. Now on a wheel, the greatest turning distance is found at the outer rim. Most of us tend to live on this outer rim. As we move inwards, however, the turning distance is shorter. At the absolute centre of the wheel, there is no movement. This very centre represents the Messiah.

We stay at the centre with Him, as the world revolves around us. Change is inevitable, the wheel keeps on turning, but, when we are Christ-centred—with Him at the centre—there is no movement and there is no agitation. As the world turns we are firmly and securely situated with Him.

This is similar to the motto of the Carthusian monks (founded by Saint Bruno): "*Stat crux dum volvitur orbis*"—which is Latin for, "The Cross stands firm as the world turns." In the Messiah, we stand firm with Him at the centre while the world turns around us. In the centre with Him we can "Rejoice . . . Always!"

In the second image, we have the Christianization of the medieval Wheel of Fortune (*Roda-da-Fortuna*), also referred to as the Wheel of Life. At the top of this wheel is an illustration of a king (depicting prosperity). On the bottom is an illustration of a beggar (depicting poverty). On the right side is an illustration of the king falling to the state of a pauper (depicting the decline). On the left side is an illustration of the beggar climbing (depicting the ascent).

In the Christianization of this Wheel of Fortune, the image of the Christ was placed at the centre. Despite life's ups and downs, emotional highs and emotional lows, prosperity and poverty, the Christ-centred Christian remains stable at the centre with the Messiah.

We Christians should not live on the rim of the wheel of life moving from successes to failures and failures to successes, over and over to the point of exhaustion. No, we live at the centre with Jesus the Messiah—Who "is the same yesterday, today, and forever" (Heb 13:8)—and, from this vantage point we only watch the wheels go round and round (without getting dizzy).

As academic theologians have pointed out, when Saint Paul

commands us to "Rejoice . . . Always!" he cannot be talking about emotions or feelings—he is speaking of an inner objective disposition that is only possible if we are grounded Jesus our Christ. They conclude, that it is as if Saint Paul is commanding us to stop living on the rim of the wheel and with joy-filled intensity live at the centre with *Yahshua* (יֵשׁוּעַ) our *Mâshîyach* (מָשִׁיחַ). This he has the authority to command. When we heed this command, we can "Rejoice . . . [in the Lord, no matter what the circumstance] . . . Always!"

Let us pray:
Yahshua (יֵשׁוּעַ) the *Mâshîyach* (מָשִׁיחַ)
I praise you with my lips,
my heart, my mind, and with my life.
My very existence is a pure gift from You;
to You I offer all that I have and am.

Help me to embrace the world You have given me.
In You:
may I without fear transform the darkness of its pain
into the life and joy of You;
may I use the good things that pass in such a way
as to hold fast even now to those that ever endure;
may I love You in all things and above all things,
and reach the joy you have prepared for me.
Without You nothing has a firm foundation.
Without You nothing has any meaning.

Help me to make You my Ruler and Guide.
Help me to remain in the centre with You.
Help me to "Rejoice . . . Always!" in You.
Amen.[359]

Christians proclaim that they have the Good New! Therefore, should we not know what the Good News is, and then also proclaim what we know?

Chapter 9 | The Good News

On the day that John the Baptist was born, his father Zechariah "filled with the Holy Spirit" prophesied that John would be the one preparing the way of the Lord (Lk 1:68-79).

This prophesy is referred to as the Evangelical Canticle of Zechariah. The Church, in Her wisdom, prays these words of Zechariah every day during Morning Prayer.[360] This is rightfully so. For, as we studied earlier, Zechariah's prophecy is not limited to his son. It is a reminder as we begin our day that this prophecy, in a sense, also applies to you and me—for just like John the Baptist, *you* are also a prophet or prophetess of the Most High, for *you* must go before the Lord to prepare His way, to give His people knowledge of Salvation by the forgiveness of their sins (Lk 1:76-77; also cf. Jer 1:5).

Therefore as prophets and prophetesses, as the forerunners of the Most High, let us go before our Lord and prepare the way for His *Second Coming* by telling those around us: *Now is the time of fulfillment*; *the Kingdom of God is already here*; *so, repent*—turn around, think differently, change your direction from your sinful ways, turn to Him, and hit the mark—*and believe in the Gospel*!

Before we do this, however, it would be good to know what exactly the *Gospel* is. If asked, some of us might say that it is the *Good News*. Well, what then is the Good News?

Suppose we were to stand outside our parish church after a Sunday Mass and ask parishioners as they file out: What is the Gospel message or the Good News that we as Christians proclaim? A majority of church-goers would probably answer with one or a combination of the following:

- *Christmas*! In the incarnation, God, the Second Person of the Trinity, becomes one of us.
- *Easter*! The salvation that God the Father provided through His

Son (*Note*[361]), God the Father so loved the world that He sacrificed His only Son for us, and resurrected Him as our Saviour (Jn 3:16) so that we may go to Heaven.

- The Person of Jesus, the Messiah—God is now with us.
- The declaration from John the Baptist, "Behold, the Lamb of God, who takes away the sin of the world" (Jn 1:29).
- The saving act of God the Father through His Son.
- The reconciliation of the world to God, through His Son.
- The life, death and resurrection of Jesus the Christ.
- We will be resurrected in and through Jesus the Christ.
- Although we deserved God the Father's wrath, we instead received His love, mercy, and grace, through His Son.
- Redemption and forgiveness of sins are available for all who believe in Jesus the Christ (Col 1:14; also cf. Rom 1:16).
- The Christ is "the Way, the Truth, and the Life" (Jn 14:6)
- Our names are written in the Book of Life (Rev 3:5).
- God made us for Himself—we are hand-picked by God.
- We are the righteousness of God, in and through His Son.
- We have a Good Shepherd, who takes care of us, His sheep.
- Jesus the Messiah is the fulfillment of the Sabbath.
- Jesus the Messiah is the fulfillment of the Temple.
- Jesus the Messiah is the fulfillment of the Law and the Prophets.
- Jesus the Messiah is the fulfillment of the Old Testament prophesies and promises.
- The Kingdom of God is now here (Mk 1:15).

I think it would be safe to say that the majority of answers would be something on these lines. Now, some parishioners, a very few for that matter, might answer as follows:

- He is our Groom and we are His bride (Rev 19:7; also cf. Isa 61:10).
- We will see our Lord and our Love *face to Face*.
- *In Him*, the mystery of the Trinity resides in us.
- *In Him*, the Light of God lives in us.
- *In Him*, we are children of God (1 Jn 3:2).
- *In Him*, we right now are sitting at the Father's right hand.
- *In Him*, there is no judgment, and we will not be judged (*Note*[362]).

This second set of answers would be far and few between. However, even fewer parishioners would answer the question as follows:

- God the Father sent His Son to set the earth on fire (Lk 12:49).
- In Jesus the Christ "from now on a household of five will be divided, three against two and two against three" (Lk 12:52).
- In Jesus the Christ "a father will be divided against his son and a son against his father, a mother against her daughter and a daughter against her mother, a mother-in-law against her daughter-in-law and a daughter-in-law against her mother-in-law" (Lk 12:53 and Mt 10:35).
- Because Jesus is the Messiah, our enemies will now be found in our very own household (Mt 10:36).
- Jesus the Christ came not to establish peace on the earth, but rather division (Mt 10:35 and Lk 12:51).

This third set of answers might cause a little bewilderment—for some might ask: How can these statements be Good News? (*Note*[363]). Yet all these answers are correct—all are the Good News. Why is that so?

The *Gospel* or *Good News* is God the Father's *entire* salvific-plan (i.e., His plan for humanity's salvation), a plan which finds its total fulfillment and culmination in His Son (our Salvation)—Whom He sends in the "fullness of time" (Gal 4:4). God the Father is "rich in mercy" (Neh 9:17 and Eph 2:4), and the Face of His mercy is His Son. Therefore, *all* of the Tanakh, or more accurately the Septuagint (i.e., the Old Testament) and the fulfillment (i.e., the New Testament) is the *Gospel* or *Good News*!

Although the Old Testament and New Testament divide history into two periods—and each having its particular significance—the New Testament is a continuation and culmination of the Old. It is this one complete plan of salvation that we hear summarized and proclaimed at every Easter Vigil Mass.

With that, let's take a deeper look at the term *gospel*. The term *gospel* derives from the Greek word, εὐαγγέλιον (euanggelion/*yoo ang-ghel'-ee-on*) or εὐαγγελίζω (euanggelizō/*yoo-ang-ghel-id'-zo*). Included in its meaning is the *act of* declaration, an act of announcing, proclaiming, and preaching of good news.[364] Hence, *euanggelion* (εὐαγγέλιον)—*gospel*—is *both* the message (the good news) and the proclaiming of it.

Within this word is also the act of bringing, showing, and evangelizing.[365] Our English word *evangelize* comes from this same Greek word. The words *preach* or *preaching* are also rooted in this same Greek word. This word was used in the Old Testament (Septuagint), and within the secular Roman Empire to announce *glad tidings* to its citizens; prior to the writing of the New Testament.[366]

At the time of writing the Gospels, the Evangelist Christianized the term to announce the ultimate Good News or the cosmic *Glad Tidings*—in *Yahshua* (יֵשׁוּעַ) the *Mâshîyach* (מָשִׁיחַ).

Mark's Gospel begins as follows: "The beginning of the Gospel [*Euanggelion* (Εὐαγγέλιον)] of Jesus [the] Christ, the Son of God" (Mk 1:1). Therefore, the term we use now as the Good News is for the *Gospel* of Jesus, the *Glad Tidings* of Jesus, the *Good News* of Jesus. It is the *Euanggelion* (Εὐαγγέλιον) of Jesus (*Note*[367])—encompassing God the Father's total and universal plan of Salvation—which is His Son, the wellspring of our salvation. For Jesus the Christ is the "*everlasting Good News*" (Rev 14:6; *emphasis* added).

As mentioned, *Euanggelion* (Εὐαγγέλιον) is also the very act of announcing, proclaiming, teaching or preaching, and evangelizing, His Good News. For that reason, the *Euanggelion* (Εὐαγγέλιον) is supposed to be announced, proclaimed, and preached, for "He commissioned us to preach to the people and testify that He is the One appointed by God as judge of the living and the dead" (Acts 10:42). This commission is an inherent quality within the Greek word itself. The announcement of God the Father's salvific-plan culminating in the *Euanggelion* (Εὐαγγέλιον) of His Son is therefore intended to be a continual proclamation, not mere stagnant information.

This proclamation is a necessity for all Christians. It is an explicit proclamation of the *Euanggelion* (Εὐαγγέλιον) in Jesus the Messiah. We are not called to proclaim a gospel of acceptance, a gospel of open-mindedness, a gospel of tolerance, a gospel of vagueness, a gospel of harmony, a gospel of cooperation, or a gospel of diversity, equity, and inclusion.

None of these supposed gospels is the Good News. None of these gospels will save humanity. These so-called gospels are of persons' own creation and refer to a god of their own creation. As a result, they end up making themselves gods and worshiping themselves. It is equivalent to the grasping of the proverbial apple in the Garden of Eden. As Satan said to Eve, in effect, "Eat the fruit and you will be like gods" (Gen 3:5).

The letter to the Hebrews admonishes: "Do not be carried away by all kinds of strange teachings" (Heb 13:9a). In contrast, the Good News, the Gospel of *Yahshua* (יֵשׁוּעַ) the *Mashiyach* (מָשִׁיחַ) in its fullness is what we proclaim.

As we have studied, we proclaim that *everything converges* on Him. He is the centre, and He is the nucleus of our life. He is *the Way*. He is *the Truth*. He is *the Life*. He *is* the Saviour. He *is* the Sacrifice. He *is* the Redeemer. He *is* Salvation. He *is* Revelation. He *is* Love. He *is* Grace. He *is* Light. He *is* the Actor. He *is* the Rock. He *is* the Unifier. He *is* the Answer. He *is* the Gift. He *is* the Prize. He *is* the Goal. He *is* the Mark. He *is* the *Alpha* and the *Omega*. He *is* the Good News! He is the *Gospel* that we proclaim!

We must not sit on this *Euanggelion* (Εὐαγγέλιον), nor suppress it, nor be fearful of proclaiming it. "While keeping our eyes fixed on Jesus, the leader and perfecter of faith" (Heb 12:2), in courage and joy, we must go forth and tell others.

Here is a good example. Recall the two disciples on their way to Emmaus. The resurrected Messiah corrected their limited understanding of the Old Testament Scriptures. In that correction, their despair turned into joy, and their joy turned into mission. In the middle of the night, they immediately returned to Jerusalem to tell the others about the *Euanggelion* (Εὐαγγέλιον).

As Saint Matthew declared: "This Gospel [*Euanggelion* (Εὐαγγέλιον)] of the Kingdom will be preached throughout the world as a witness to all nations" (Mt 24:14). Well, how is this possible if the onus is not on us to make this happen?

Therefore, in unison with Saint Paul, we collectively say: "If I preach the Gospel [*Euanggelizō* (Εὐαγγελίζω)], this is no reason for me to boast, for an obligation has been imposed on me, and woe to me if I do not preach it!" (1 Cor 9:16; also cf. 2 Cor 5:19).

> For the Scripture says . . . everyone who calls on the Name of the Lord will be saved. But how can they call on Him in Whom they have not believed? And how can they believe in Him of Whom they have not heard? And how can they hear without someone to preach? And how can people preach unless they are sent? As it is written, How beautiful are the feet of those who bring [*Euanggelizō* (Εὐαγγελίζω)] the Good News [*Euanggelizō* (Εὐαγγελίζω)]! (Rom 10:11, 13-15; also cf. Isa 52:7-10).

At the start of His ministry, *Yahshua* (יֵשׁוּעַ) the *Mâshîyach* (מָשִׁיחַ) announced the Good News (Lk 4:17-19). In our baptism, we become priest, prophet, and king, *in Him*. We become His body. We are anointed—*mâshîyach* (מָשִׁיחַ). Therefore, we continue this proclamation just like our Messiah. It is also a part of our mission!

The *Euanggelion* (Εὐαγγέλιον) of Jesus is the *entire* Gospel, the entire Bible message, i.e., God the Father's universal salvific-plan revealed in two periods in history, culminating in His Son—in its entirety, from Genesis "In the beginning" (Gen 1:1) to The Book of Revelation, "The grace of the Lord Jesus be with all" (Rev 22:21).

We need to know the entire Truth. To be Christ-like, as Christians we are obligated to preach the Truth. Evangelization is the telling of the Gospel or the Good News. To the level of our own capacity we *must* evangelize, teach, and preach all parts of God's plan of salvation in history. We are called to do so in and out of season (2 Tm 4:2) until the *Parousia* (*Note*[368]), the Second Coming of our Messiah. Therefore in the words is Saint Paul, I also

> urge you to live in a manner worthy of the call you have received, with all humility and gentleness, with patience, bearing with one another through love [*agape* (ἀγάπη)], striving to preserve the unity of the [Holy] Spirit through the bond of peace: one body and one Spirit, as you were also called to the one hope of your call; one Lord, one faith, one baptism; one God and Father of all, who is over all and through all and in all. But [bear in mind] grace was

> given to each of us according to the measure of [the] Christ's gift . . . And He gave some as Apostles, others as prophets, others as evangelists, others as pastors and teachers, to equip the holy ones for the work of ministry, for building up the body of [the] Christ, until we all attain to the unity of faith and knowledge of the Son of God, to mature manhood, to the extent of the full stature of [the] Christ, so that we may no longer be infants, tossed by waves and swept along by every wind of teaching arising from human trickery, from their cunning in the interests of deceitful scheming. Rather, living the truth in love [*agape* (ἀγάπη)], we should grow in every way into Him who is the head, [the] Christ, from whom the whole body, joined and held together by every supporting ligament, with the proper functioning of each part, brings about the body's growth and builds itself up in love. (Eph 4:1-7 and 11-16)

Speaking of the *Parousia* (the Second Coming), this will happen whether we like it or not. Humanity will be judged, whether we like it or not. "For we shall all stand before the judgment seat of God" (Rom 14:10; also cf. 2 Cor 5:10). At our hearing, we will be asked to give an account of what we did with our gifted personal talents, resources, and time (Rom 14:12), at the level of our given capacity.

Therefore now, picture yourself with the rest of humanity in the heavenly court room of justice. Inside each of us, we know at one level or another that we have sinned against God (Ps 51:4a). All of us know in one form or another, either by thought, word, or deed, that we are guilty of pride, depravity, envy, corruption, sloth, cowardliness, fearfulness, lust, perversion, greed, idolatry, covetousness, gluttony, anger, and so on and so on. We know all this just as much as the person standing next to us (Ps 51:3).

As a result, we all instinctively know that we should be rightfully condemned, that God is solely justified in giving us a verdict of *guilty* (Ps 51:4b).

Nevertheless, here is a part of the *Gospel* message, the *Good News*: if we have *truly* believed in *Yahshua* (יֵשׁוּעַ) the *Mâshîyach* (מָשִׁיחַ)—that is to say, if we have turned around, repented *metanoeō* (μετανοέω), hit the Mark, and carried out our *telos* (τέλος) in Him (the "our response" part, which we have studied in the last two chapters)—we are instantaneously given a verdict of *not guilty*! In Him we are said to be guiltless. Unbelievable! Isn't it? Yes, despite our sinful acts, our sin no longer defines us, for Holy Scripture tells us that "there is now no condemnation [*no guilty verdict, no punishment*] for those who are in Jesus the Christ" (Rom 8:1[369]; also cf. Jn 3:18). Did you hear that? *In Him*, we are blameless in the sight of the Father (Eph 1:4). In view of that, *in Him*, we can, in confidence, give an account for what we did with the talents and the resources given to us, and the time that has been allotted to us.

This is the *Gospel* message! This is the *Good News*! This is what we have been proclaiming! This is what we must continually proclaim!

Now here's the thing. In case you were wondering the opposite also holds true. For, if we are not *in Him* we *must* fear judgment. We need to teach others this truth. Recall, we get to pick between His justice (righteousness) and His justice (judicial). If we are not *in Him* we are picking His justice (judicial), and the judgment that comes with it. So then, let us bring others to *Yahshua* (יֵשׁוּעַ) the *Mâshîyach*!

As we studied, our Salvation comes from Zion (Isa 52:7-10). *Yahshua* (יֵשׁוּעַ) the *Mâshîyach* is the Redeemer. He lifts our sentence of eternal punishment. He is our Resurrection and our Life; even if we die we will live (Jn 11:25). This is the *Euanggelion* (Εὐαγγέλιον) of *Yahshua* (יֵשׁוּעַ) our Christ.

Therefore, we do not live in a cloud of fear—a fear of death or even a fear of going to hell. We live in hope, and thus "conduct ourselves in a way worthy of the Gospel [the *Euanggelion* (Εὐαγγέλιον)] of the Christ" (Phil 1:27).

What is more, we now live in a new hope, awaiting a "new Heaven and a new earth" (Rev 21:1), the breaking through of the New Zion, for the old is passing away, the world as we know it is passing away (1 Cor 7:31). In the risen Messiah everything changes. The *Euanggelion* (Εὐαγγέλιον) conveys this deep message of hope (*Note*[370]). Saint John writes:

> Then I saw a new Heaven and a new earth. The former Heaven and the former earth had passed away, and the sea was no more. I also saw the Holy City, a New Jerusalem, coming down out of Heaven from God, prepared as a bride adorned for her Husband. I heard a loud voice from the throne saying, Behold, God's dwelling is with the human race. He will dwell with them and they will be His people and God Himself will always be with them (as their God). He will wipe every tear from their eyes, and there shall be no more death or mourning, wailing or pain, (for) the old order has passed away. (Rev 21:1-4)

What *Good News* that is. What *amazing news*. What *incredibly amazing news*. We are called to proclaim this eternal reality. This is the joy of the *Euanggelion* (Εὐαγγέλιον)!

On this note, this book is intended to be the *euanggelion* (εὐαγγέλιον), in the sense that it teaches the *Euanggelion* (Εὐαγγέλιον). It is a proclamation of *what is* and (as we will shortly study) *what is to come*. As stated, the *Euanggelion* (Εὐαγγέλιον) is not a stagnant declaration; it is continual. Therefore, the *Euanggelion* (Εὐαγγέλιον) is not of the past—it's here now in Jesus the Messiah. "This is the time of fulfillment. The Kingdom of God is at hand. Repent, and believe in the [*Euanggelion* (Εὐαγγέλιον)]" (Mk 1:15).

We may unequivocally conclude the assertions throughout this book that this proclamation is not subjective—it is not based on our own belief systems. It is not about you or me. As we discussed in Chapter 1, Who Do You Say That I AM?, my opinion or your opinion is not the basis of truth. Truth is totally independent of us.

We are called to proclaim what *is*, what *reality is*. "Ever since the creation of the world" God the Father has made it possible to know Him (see Appendix B), for "His invisible attributes of eternal power and divinity have been able to be understood and perceived in what He has made" (Rom 1:20; also cf. Ps 19:2).

We have no excuse, for not seeing *what is* (Rom 1:20). In this second part of history, the time of ignorance is now over, we must move forward to get to know the culmination of His *Euanggelion* (Εὐαγγέλιον), that is, God the Father's *Euanggelion* (Εὐαγγέλιον) focus on His Son—the mystery of the Christ (Acts 17:30 and Eph 3:4).

However, here is a stumbling block we face. We live in a world that likes to complicate things. I recently learned the term *complexifying*. It means the intentional confusion of matters. So many issues are considered to be grey areas, preventing us from seeing reality, the *what is*. The further we move away from the basics in theology, the more likely it is that we are misled.

Remember the term repent, which we studied in the previous chapter. Adding to our definition of turning around: *metanoeō* (μετανοέω) is a compound word consisting of *meta* (meaning after or beyond) and *noeō* (meaning to perceive or understand or mind).[371] In this *to repent* also means changing of *mindset,* having a new mind, or a transformation of mind. The quote above (from Mark 1:15), directly relates repentance to *meta* (after) change of the *noeō* (mind) with respect to the Gospel—*Euanggelion* (Εὐαγγέλιον).

We need to transform or change our mindset; keep things simple, stop complicating our lives, and focus on our goal. We may call it the turning around from *complexifying* (sin) to simplifying; the turning around from false reality (sin) to reality; the turning around from lies (sin) to the Truth; the turning around from worldly allurements (sin) to God.

Additionally, the previous verse (Mk 1:14) provides the context "after John [the Baptist] had been arrested, Jesus [the Christ] came to Galilee proclaiming the Gospel [*Euanggelion* (Εὐαγγέλιον)] of God" (Mk 1:14), saying: "This is the time of fulfillment. The Kingdom of God is at hand. Repent [*metanoeō* (μετανοέω), change from believing in a false reality], and believe [in reality, the Truth] in the Gospel [*Euanggelion* (Εὐαγγέλιον)]" (Mk 1:15).

The lesson for us is that the Kingdom of God is here, turn around; stop following illusions and false idealisms. It is time to change our attitude, our worldview, our twisted vision, and *repent*—turn from sin and lies, and believe in the Truth, Jesus the Messiah. "It is the hour now for you to awake from sleep; for our Salvation is nearer now than when we first believed" (Rom 13:11).

It is time to come back to the One Who loves us. Our encounter with the risen *Mâshîyach* (מָשִׁיחַ) has to change us. He is our Lord. He is Our God. He is all that matters, and thus, in this disposition, everything that does matter, matters in Him.

Holy Scripture warns us that, "anyone who is so progressive [runs on ahead and does not remain in the doctrine of the Christ, *that is, one who is not content with what He taught*] as not to remain in the teaching of [the] Christ does not have God" (2 Jn 1:9[372]).

"Many deceivers have gone out into the world" (2 Jn 1:7). Do not go after these false messiahs, prophets, and visionaries. Do not run after foolish unloving doctrines made by humans not by Him. Be content in Him. Be alert. Stay vigilant. *Wake up,* pay attention, and "interpret the signs of the times" (Mt 16:3).

Our current, highly secularized society is on a mission to divide people into groups. Screaming their daily mantra of inclusiveness, as they, in fact, reject and exclude.

In *Yahshua* (יֵשׁוּעַ) the *Mâshîyach* (מָשִׁיחַ), there is no polarization, there is no isolation, and there is no alienation: "the same Lord is Lord of all" and calls all to Himself (Rom 10:12, Gal 3:28, and Col 3:11). *In Him* we are all brothers and sisters. "In Him were created all things in Heaven and on earth, the visible and the invisible, whether thrones or dominions or principalities or powers; all things were created through Him and for Him" (Col 1:16).

Therefore, all creation is bound to the mystery of the *Mâshîyach* (מָשִׁיחַ). There is no race or colour, we are all one in Him (Gal 3:28). Even more profoundly, *in Him,* we become "a chosen race, a royal priesthood, a holy nation, a people of His own" (1 Pt 2:9). "Once we were no people but now we are God's people" (1 Pt 2:9). "Once we were alienated from God but now we are His children, who can cry out 'Abba, Father!'" (Gal 4:6).

With all this in mind, we also acknowledge that there are deceivers who want to deceive us, and these deceivers are in fact antichrists (see 2 Jn 1:7). For the past two thousand years, during this *eschatos* (ἔσχατος), these end times, "many antichrists have appeared" (*Note*[373]); and this is sad to say, but many of them that have gone into the world actually "went out from us" the Church (1 Jn 2:18-19; also cf. 2 Jn 1:7). Who are these antichrists? "Who are these liars? Whoever denies that Jesus is the Christ. Whoever denies the Father and the Son, this is the antichrist" (1 Jn 2:22). "Every spirit that does not acknowledge Jesus does not belong to God. This is the spirit of the antichrist that, as you heard, is to come, but in fact is already in the world" (1 Jn 4:3).

Did you notice it is twofold? Yes, there have been and are many antichrists in the world; however, before the *Parousia* takes place, that is,

> before [the] Christ's Second Coming the Church must pass through a final trial that will shake the faith of many believers. The persecution that accompanies Her pilgrimage on earth will unveil the "mystery of iniquity" in the form of a religious deception offering men an apparent solution to their problems at the price of apostasy from the truth. The supreme religious deception is that of the Antichrist, a pseudo-messianism by which man glorifies himself in place of God and of His Messiah come in the flesh. (*CCC* #675)

Again, it is twofold; so, even though there have been many antichrists, there will also be *the final* Antichrist yet to come.

> The English term from the Greek *antichristos* meaning "against [the] Christ" or "adversary of [the] Christ." The term occurs only in 1 John 2:18, 2:22, 4:3, and 2 John 1:7, but similar ideas are found elsewhere in the Old and New Testaments. Basically, the texts speak of a final war of cosmological proportions between the "Antichrist" and God (or the Christ) which will occur prior to the Second Coming of [the] Christ and the final judgment of the world . . . The Gospels speak of "false prophets," etc. (Mt 24:5,

> 23ff. and Mk 13:21ff.). Paul speaks of [the "son of perdition" or] the "man of lawlessness" (2 Thes 2:3-12). A beast from the abyss is mentioned in Revelation 11:7ff., while at 13:1-10 a beast emerges from the sea, followed by yet another beast (13:11-18), etc. These varying images were chosen because they were part of the "language of the day" and because this language represented material especially suitable for what God wanted to communicate about His plans for the end times to the authors of the New Testament and subsequent generations.[374]
>
> | *Catholic Encyclopedia* |

As we currently live in the *eschatos* (ἔσχατος), the end times, and as we pray for the *Parousia*—*Maranatha*: *Come Lord Jesus*!—every Advent, we must in turn prepare for this *final trial*, the final manifestation of the Antichrist who is to come, just in case it happens in our own lifetime on this earth.

Concerning the *Parousia* "and of the end of the age" the Apostles directly ask Jesus what to expect (Mt 24:3). *Yahshua* (יֵשׁוּעַ) begins by telling them the most important thing: "See that no one deceives you" (Mt 24:4). Then He goes on to say:

> For many will come in My Name, saying, "I am the Messiah," and they will deceive many. You will hear of wars and reports of wars; see that you are not alarmed, for these things must happen, but it will not yet be the end. Nation will rise against nation, and kingdom against kingdom; there will be famines and earthquakes from place to place. All these are the beginning of the labour pains . . . Many false prophets will arise and deceive many; and because of the increase of evildoing, the love of many will grow cold. But the one who perseveres to the end will be saved. (Mt 24:5-8 and 11-13)

See, many will be deceived! Please do not be one of them! In addition, "now the Holy Spirit explicitly says that in the last times some will [also] turn away from the faith by paying attention to deceitful spirits and demonic instructions" (1 Tm 4:1) . . . "for the time will come when people will not tolerate sound doctrine [rooted in love] but, following their own desires and insatiable curiosity, will accumulate teachers and will stop listening to the truth and will be diverted to myths" (2 Tm 4:3-4). For even now, many,

> conduct themselves as enemies of the Cross of [the] Christ. Their end is destruction. Their god is their stomach; their glory is in their shame. Their minds are occupied with earthly things. But our citizenship is in Heaven, and from it we also await our Saviour, the Lord Jesus [the] Christ. (Phil 3:18)

Heed all this! "Stand firm in the Lord" (Phil 4:1)! It is time for us to *wake up* from our slumber and understand the *Euanggelion* (Εὐαγγέλιον). "The Church will enter the glory of the Kingdom only through this final Passover" (CCC#677), so be ready and be alert!

All said, we must acknowledge that Holy Scripture is sometimes difficult to understand. "The ignorant and unstable distort [it] to their own destruction" (2 Pt 3:16). However, this difficulty is the incentive to study the whole counsel of God in Scripture, carefully and thoroughly, to understand its truths. As I mention in Appendix A, 12, Christians should be orthodox (that is, have right belief; grounded in sound teaching). To paraphrase Saint Augustine: If we only believe what we like in Sacred Scripture, and reject what we do not like, it is not the Truth we believe, but ourselves. Therefore, "be on your guard not to be led into the error of the unprincipled and to fall from your own stability" (2 Pt 3:17).

> Remember, my dear friends, what the Apostles of our Lord Jesus [the] Christ foretold. "At the final point of time", they told you, "there will be mockers who follow nothing but their own godless desires." It is they who cause division, who live according to nature

> and do not possess the [Holy] Spirit. But you, my dear friends, must build yourselves up on the foundation of your most holy faith, praying in the Holy Spirit; keep yourselves within the love of God and wait for the mercy of our Lord Jesus [the] Christ to give you eternal life. (Jude 1:17-21)

At the start of the time of the fulfillment of the *Euanggelion* (Εὐαγγέλιον)—namely, at the beginning of our Messiah's ministry—when He was in the synagogue, a scroll of the prophet Isaiah was handed to Him. He opened the scroll and found the place where it was written,

> "The Spirit of the Lord is upon me, because He has anointed me to preach Good News [*Euanggelizō* (Εὐαγγελίζω)] to the poor. He has sent me to proclaim release to the captives and recovering of sight to the blind, to set at liberty those who are oppressed, to proclaim the acceptable year of the Lord." (Lk 4:17-19)

After reading this Scripture passage, He rolled up the scroll, gave it back to the attendant, and sat down. Then, He said to those gathered: "Today this Scripture has been fulfilled in your hearing" (Lk 4:21).

Imagine that at the beginning of our ministry, namely our personal continuation of the *Euanggelion* (Εὐαγγέλιον)—that is, in our personal writing of Acts Chapter 29, of and for our Messiah—the scroll of the Gospel according the Saint Matthew (*Εὐαγγέλιον κατά Ματθαῖος*) is handed to us. We open the scroll and find the place where it is written,

> Jesus came up and said to them, "All authority (all power of absolute rule) in Heaven and on earth has been given to Me. Go therefore and make disciples of all the nations [*help the people to learn of Me, believe*

in Me, and obey My words], baptizing them in the Name of the Father and of the Son and of the Holy Spirit, teaching them to observe everything that I have commanded you; and lo, I am with you always [*remaining with you perpetually—regardless of circumstance, and on every occasion*], even to the end of the age." (Mt 28:18-20)

After reading this Scripture passage, we roll up the scroll, give it back to the attendant, and sit down. Then, we also should be able to say to those gathered there: Today this Scripture has been fulfilled in your hearing!

Let us pray:
Ever-living mystery of unity and Trinity,
You gave life to the new Israel and made of it the New Jerusalem
by birth from water and the Spirit,
and made it a chosen race, a royal priesthood,
a people set apart as your eternal possession,
in and through the incarnation.
You are the same yesterday, today, and forever!
For You, time is the unfolding of Truth that already is,
the unveiling of beauty that is yet to be.

God my Abba,
You unveiled Your plan of Salvation
with its culmination in Your Son.
Help me to realize that in Your Son my Lord and my King,
I am already seated at your right hand.

Yahshua (יֵשׁוּעַ) my *Mâshîyach* (מָשִׁיחַ)
You are the Lion of Judah.
You formed Your Church into Your very own Body,
You are the true Peace that came down from Heaven.
Help me fight the good fight!
Help me finish the race!
Help me to realize that knowing about You is good,

but, knowing You is better.
Help me to build a relationship with You in knowledge.

God my Holy Spirit
You are my true Advocate.
You give me my particular mission in life.
Help me to discover my *telos* (τέλος),
and carry it out to its completion,
with you as my Guide.

This I pray to You, Oh Mighty Trinity;
All Holy, All Glorious, All Precious, All Beautiful, All Powerful,
All Knowing, All Good, All Merciful
and All Loving God for ages unending
Amen.[375]

Appendix A | Methodology and Presuppositions

Too many Christian academics, teachers, preachers, and priests believe theology should be relegated only to "theologians" or scholars. They state that theology should not be taught or preached to the average Christian in the pew. That ordinary Christians should only concern themselves with ritual or pious religious practices, and should not trouble themselves with theological issues that are "beyond" them. More than a few Christians, maybe even some reading this, may also agree with the above view. We might say: "I don't have time for theology. I'm not a priest. Besides, I'm also okay with my current understanding of Christianity."

I, however, do not agree with either view. I do not agree with the condescending "there-there" mentality on the one side or with the "indifference to theology works for me" on the other side. On the contrary, I agree with those who believe that *all* Christians should be theologians. Why? The fact that we believe in God and profess our Creed should make us theologians.

Let me explain. The English word *theology* comes from the Greek word θεολογία (theologia/*thē-ə-ˈlō-ja*), which derives from two Greek words Θεός (Theos/*Theós*), meaning God, and λογία (logia/*ˈlo.gi.a*), a Greek word rooted in the word λόγος (logos/*log'-os*), meaning a word, a rational cause, an account, a teaching, or reason. Simply put, then, theology is reasoning or the study about God. As Christians, we must agree that ignorance of God is *not* an option. As a result, we must *study* God—not as an academic exercise or placing Him under a microscope, but leaning about Him—so we may have a mature understanding of who God *Is*. This type of necessary study—by default—automatically makes us theologians.

This book is designed to help us with this study about God, by conveying fundamental theological truths concerning *Jesus the Christ*, with simplicity and clarity, so we may grow in our knowledge of God in this particular area. Moreover, as with any study, it calls us to personal change.

In the words of Saint Teresa of Calcutta, "We must know the faith well, love the faith, and live the faith: know, love, and live."[376] This assertion has three parts:

1. Know: The study of God is not merely an academic exercise or an education in isolation. The study's theological truths are practical; thus, they must become the *foundation* upon which we stand.
2. Love: The study of God must consume us. We must *love* this study, for there is nothing more significant than wholly occupying our minds and our hearts, and entirely focusing our attention on everything that is God (Mk 12:30 and Deut 6:5).
3. Live: The study of God must consequently *change* us, our character and our lifestyle, so that we may live a joy-filled and mature Christian life.

I hope and pray you agree with this.

To borrow from Saint Paul (1 Cor 13:11), when we were babies, we ate baby food. As we grew up, however, were we still content to eat baby food? Or, did we desire something of greater sustenance? Well then, it is time we put aside our childish ways (1 Cor 13:11), and embark upon this necessary study of God, so we may *know* Him, *love* Him, and *live* in Him (see Heb 5:11-14).

As the story goes, Vince Lombardi, the former head coach of the Green Bay Packers (1959–1967), would begin every football season by bringing all the players into the locker room, raising the football, and saying: "Gentlemen, this is a *football*!" Even though some players had multiple Super Bowl rings, and some had lived and breathed football since childhood, he would start every season in the same manner. Some players might be annoyed at the banality or obviousness of this statement; however, this back-to-the-basics mentality garnered him an unsurpassed reputation in the world of football.

I share this story because the approach of this book is the same. Obviousness acknowledged, I am also taking this back-to-the-basics approach in this study. Consequently, I hold up this book and say,

"Ladies and gentlemen, this is *Jesus the Christ*!" With that understanding, here is my *Methodology and Presuppositions*, which I have divided into twelve key areas:

1. God: When I use the word *God*, I am referring to the *Mystery of the Trinity,* the One Who presented Himself to Abraham (Gen 12:1); Who declared Himself to Moses, as subsistent Being (*Ipsum Esse*), the Great "I AM WHO I AM" (Ex 3:14)—in Hebrew אֶהְיֶה אֲשֶׁר אֶהְיֶה (*Ehyeh Aser Ehyeh*), in Greek ἐγώ εἰμί ὁ εἰμί (*Ego Eimi Ho Eimi*) "I AM THAT WHO EXIST"—not a being among beings, but the sheer act of Being Itself, *Ipsum Esse* ("to be"); and, Who, in the fullness of time, revealed Himself in the Christ Jesus (Gal 4:4).

"God alone *IS* . . . God is the fullness of Being and of every perfection, without origin and without end" (*CCC* #213). This God, who is One God, who is Truth itself, who is Love itself, revealed Himself in three Persons: "God the Father," "God the Son," and "God the Holy Spirit" (*CCC* #253–255). As stated in the Athanasian Creed —this is the catholic faith:

> That we worship One God in Trinity and the Trinity in Unity; neither blending their Persons nor dividing their Essence. For the Person of the Father is a distinct Person, the Person of the Son is another, the Person of the Holy Spirit still another. But, the Divinity of the Father, Son, Holy Spirit is One, their Glory equal, their Majesty coeternal.
>
> What quality the Father has, the Son has, the Holy Spirit has. The Father is Uncreated, the Son is Uncreated, the Holy Spirit is Uncreated. The Father is Immeasurable, the Son is Immeasurable, the Holy Spirit is Immeasurable. The Father is Eternal, the Son is Eternal, the Holy Spirit is Eternal. And yet there are not three eternal beings; there is but One Eternal Being. So too there are not three uncreated or immeasurable beings; there is but One Uncreated and Immeasurable Being.
>
> Likewise, the Father is Almighty, the Son is Almighty, the Holy Spirit is Almighty. Yet there are

not three almighty beings; there is but One Almighty Being.

Thus the Father is God, the Son is God, the Holy Spirit is God. Yet there are not three gods; there is but One God. Thus the Father is Lord, the Son is Lord, the Holy Spirit is Lord. Yet there are not three lords; there is but One Lord.

Just as Christian truth compels us to confess each Person individually as both God and Lord; so catholic faith forbids us to say that there are three gods or three lords.

The Father was neither made nor created nor begotten from anyone. The Son was neither made nor created; He was begotten from the Father alone. The Holy Spirit was neither made nor created nor begotten; He proceeds from the Father and the Son. Accordingly, there is one Father, not three fathers; there is one Son, not three sons; there is one Holy Spirit, not three holy spirits.

Nothing in this Trinity is before or after, nothing is greater or smaller; in their totality, the three Persons are coeternal and coequal with each other. Therefore, in everything, as was said earlier, we must worship their Trinity in their Unity, and their Unity in their Trinity.

Anyone then who desires to be saved should think thus about the Trinity. But it is necessary for eternal salvation that one also believe in the incarnation of our Lord Jesus Christ faithfully.

Now this is the true faith:

That we believe and confess that our Lord Jesus Christ, God's Son, is both God and Man, equally. He is God from the Essence of the Father, begotten before time; and He is Man from the Essence of His mother, born in time. Completely God, completely Man, with a rational soul and human flesh. Equal to the Father, as regards to Divinity; less than the Father as regards to His Humanity.

> Although He is God and Man, yet He is not two, but one Christ. He is one, however, not by His Divinity being turned into flesh, but by taking His Humanity into His Divinity. He is one, certainly not by the blending of His Essence, but by the unity of His Person. For just as one human is both rational soul and flesh, so too the one Christ is both God and Man.
> He suffered for our Salvation; He descended to hell; He arose on the third day from the dead; He ascended to Heaven; He is seated at the Father's right hand; from there He will come to judge the living and the dead. At His coming, all of humanity will arise bodily and give an accounting of their own deeds. Those who have done good will enter eternal life, and those who have done evil will enter eternal fire.
> This is the catholic faith: one cannot be saved without believing it firmly and faithfully.[377]
>
> | Athanasian Creed |

2. Jesus-centred: My theological focal point is *always* Christ Jesus. He should always be the *centre* of our lives. For it is God the Father's will and pleasure, that at the Name of Jesus every knee will bend (those in Heaven, all those on this earth, and even all those in hell), and every tongue will confess, to the glory of God the Father, that Jesus the Christ is Lord (Phil 2:10–11).

With this truth, a second point becomes self-evident. Life is not about *you* or *me*. Yes, this is hard to digest in a self-centred, self-determining, *me-me* society. However, in the light of the Christ, this truth becomes blatantly evident (cf. Phil 3:8). We must stop looking at ourselves and turn our gaze to Christ Jesus. Understanding fundamentals is not about getting caught up in theologizing; it is about getting caught up in Christ Jesus—opening ourselves to Him unconditionally, and thus proclaiming with gusto that we belong to Him.

3. Catholic: These books are catholic in the sense of universal, pertaining to the entire Christian church. With this in mind, however, it is grounded in Catholic theology and Catholic teaching, with recognition of *apostolic succession*, an unbroken continuity, congruency, and authority of the Church rooted in and through the Apostles, primarily Saint Peter, until the Second Coming of the Christ (cf. Mt 16:18–19, Eph 2:20, and Ti 1:5).

In other words, I write this for the entire Christian church. However, I write this with total recognition of the authority and succession of all 266 popes and, if God wills, their successors (*Note*[378]). Hence, I assume that you are familiar with Catholic terminology and language. Nevertheless, if you belong to any other Christian group or denomination, these studies are still extremely beneficial. For if you are a true follower of the Christ, a member of the universal church, your calling to live a Jesus-centred life is equally mandatory.

4. Theology: I am categorizing the word *theology* in two different ways: (i) academic theology and (ii) biblical-based theology (*Note*[379]).

The first, academic theology (that is, formal *academic* study or training), is essential for the good of the Church. However, not all Christians are called to engage in this category of theology. Academic theology can be left to individuals called by God to embark on such study for the *good* of the Church.

Therefore, when I use the word *theology* (unless otherwise noted), I am not talking about academic theology. I am more concerned with a foundational, biblical-based theology, upon which *all* Christians are called to embark (*Note*[380]). Learning and living, a biblical-based theology is a fundamental calling for *all* Christians. Our fundamental beliefs—or in other words, what we believe and our foundational thought structure—effect and thus produce the reality we live. It has been said: "When we believe right, we live right!" Alternatively, stated: "Faulty beliefs produce a faulty life."

5. Biblical-based Theology: So, what's a biblical-based theology? A biblical-based theology is based on a *biblical* understanding of God, which has stood the test of time, and that has been repeatedly reiterated and reinforced by the Saints and Church councils alike (*Note*[381]). Simplicity and practicality are in this theology.

By focusing on a foundational, biblical-based theology, we will avoid getting caught up in theological gymnastics, or having an elementary spirituality. Not only do both take us away from the truth, but also they inevitably lead us to pick apart the Gospel message to fit our own personal way of thinking. This is problematic.

On the one hand, we have been blessed with access to multiple theological resources that were not there a mere century ago. The Internet has also given us access to a plethora of theological information, unheard of even a decade ago. On the other hand, we are cursed by being bombarded with so much information that it sometimes becomes difficult for us to decipher the wheat from the chaff. There is so much craziness out there, so many interpretations, and so much misinformation that it can sometimes make our head spin to the point of giving up. With all these interpretations, we have now also divided Jesus into over thirty thousand[382] different denominations within the Christian family.

There will always be misuses of the Bible—it is a given. Remember that even Satan quotes the Bible to his advantage. He "masquerades as an angel of light" (2 Cor 11:14). He takes the sacred and profanes it, using it for evil ends. Therefore, it is vital for us to *know* what the Bible *actually* says, so we may protect ourselves against those who misrepresent and misinterpret it. Yes, we need to study the Bible to defend ourselves from those who will continually abuse it.

So, in one sense, the onus is on us to *really* know our faith. "Do not be carried away by all kinds of strange teaching" (Heb 13:9a). Do not trust every teaching, but test every teaching, and retain what is good (cf. 1 Jn 4:1 and 1 Thes 5:21). We must "beware of false prophets, who come to us in sheep's clothing, but underneath are ravenous wolves" (Mt 7:15). We must "be sober, vigilant, and alert; remember, that our opponent the devil is prowling around like a roaring lion looking for someone to devour" (1 Pt 5:8).[383] We must "resist him, steadfast and solid in our faith" (1 Pt 5:9).

To have a solid faith, we must be grounded in Sacred Scripture—a robust biblical-based theology—so nobody can sway us with falsehoods, with theological gymnastics, with feel-good spirituality, and with subjective personal prophecies or interpretations. "I say this so that no one may deceive you by specious arguments" (Col 2:4). "See to it that no one captivate you with an empty, seductive philosophy according to human tradition, according to the elemental powers of the world and not according to Christ" (Col 2:8).

Therefore, let us read our Bible cover to cover so we may be "steadfast and solid in our faith" (1 Pt 5:9). I cannot emphasize this enough. I am adamant on having a foundational, biblical-based theology, in which the interpretation is congruent with that of the Gospel message that was preached by the Apostles.

"I am astonished on how we are so quick to forsake the One who called us, through the grace of Christ, for a different gospel (not that there is another)" (Gal 1:6–7).[384] We are so easily moved and convinced by "some out there who are disturbing and confusing us, and wish to pervert the Gospel of Christ" (Gal 1:7),[385] with a complicated theology, with a false feel-good spirituality, and subjective personal interpretations.

Even if the greatest orator, Internet sensation, television evangelist, self-proclaimed prophet, preacher, pastor, priest, "or even an angel from Heaven should preach a gospel other than the one that the [Apostles] have preached to us, let that one be accursed! Again, if anyone preaches to you a gospel other than the one that you received, let that one be accursed!" (Gal 1:8–9). We are not called to "currying favour with human beings" or to "seek to please people"—we are called to "be a slave of Christ" (Gal 1:10).

6. The Bible—Our Primary Source: "Ignorance of the Scriptures is ignorance of Christ" Saint Jerome asserts (*CCC* #133). Therefore, there is no way we can say we know Him if we do not know the Sacred Scriptures He has given us.

We need to know the Bible to understand Christ Jesus. How do we build and grow our Christian life if we have laid our foundation on sand? Won't it crumble? Won't it wash away? As the Christ has taught us, we must build our foundation on a rock (Lk 6:48), on a solid foundation that can withstand any force (Lk 6:49).

Keeping with the analogy of a foundation, like a mason who mixes his mortar, we must also use the proper mix to build on a strong foundation. To do this, we must always start from the Bible, for

> all Scripture is inspired by God and is useful for teaching, for refutation, for correction, and for training in righteousness, so that one who belongs to God may be competent, equipped for every good work. (2 Tm 3:16–17)

As a result, the Bible (Sacred Scripture) is *the primary source* of our Christian learning. As mentioned, I encourage all Christians to read the Bible cover to cover. I think by now I have pretty much heard all the excuses on why we do not read our Bible. Excuses notwithstanding, all it takes is a commitment.

For example, if you want to make a one-year commitment, read five chapters a day, five days a week, take the weekends off, and you will have completed the entire Bible (Old and New Testaments), in about one year. If five chapters a day is too much, read four, three, two, or even one. The key is to set an attainable goal for yourself (that will allow for prayerful reflection, absorption, integration, and application) and then go and accomplish it.

If you dislike reading, the Bible is available on audio CD or MP3. If you find listening too distracting, it is also available on DVD, where you can follow along with the words. That is to say, we have absolutely no excuses—all we need is to make that commitment, find a format that works for us, and just read it!

However keep in mind; we must "*Read the Scripture within 'the living Tradition of the whole Church*'" (*CCC* #113) (*Note*[386]). Therefore,

> Scripture must be read and interpreted with its Divine authorship in mind, no less attention must be devoted to the content and unity of the whole of Scripture, taking into account the Tradition of the entire Church and the analogy of faith.[387]
>
> | *Dei Verbum* |

To assist us in this task, we have two *secondary sources* that can help us interpret the primary source (the Bible). The first is the *Catechism of the Catholic Church* (promulgated by Saint John Paul II), which we are blessed to have, for it is a powerful tool that helps us understand the primary source and not misinterpret it. I am also an advocate of reading the *Catechism of the Catholic Church* cover to cover and having it as a reference and resource book in every Christian household. For the principal understanding, which undergirded the promulgation of the *Catechism of the Catholic Church*,

> was to guard and present better the precious deposit of Christian doctrine in order to make it more accessible to the Christian faithful and to all people of good will . . . [And] above all to strive calmly to show the strength and beauty of the doctrine of the faith.[388]
>
> | Saint John Paul II |

The second interpretation key and the final ingredient in the mix is the additional teachings handed down to us from those in authority: the Church councils, popes, and Saints, i.e., Sacred Tradition (*Note*[389]). Again, we are blessed that the Church, in Her wisdom, has preserved the teachings of the Apostles and, in her authority, has handed down these teachings to us during the past two thousand years to keep us from going astray.

In brief, the primary source is the Bible (Sacred Scripture), and the two secondary sources are the *Catechism of the Catholic Church* and Church teachings. Mix this all together, and we have a solid foundation that will make us strong biblical-based theologians.

7. The Bible—Original Languages: The majority of the text, in what we refer to as the Old Testament, was originally written in the Hebrew language, some was written in Aramaic, and some in Greek.

It is also good to know that a few centuries before the Christ, the entire Old Testament Scriptures were translated into Greek. This translation is now referred to as the Septuagint, or the LXX (which means 70), in reference to the tradition that seventy rabbis translated the text (*Note*[390]). Interestingly, the Apostles (e.g., Saint Peter and Saint Paul), used not the Hebrew text, but this Greek text of the Old Testament Scriptures within the early Church as they moved their preaching out of the Temple (and synagogues), and as they moved their evangelization out of Jerusalem. Also, it is good to note that the New Testament writers used the Septuagint text a majority of the time when quoting Old Testament Scriptures within the New Testament.

Now, unlike the Old Testament, the New Testament was entirely written in Greek as the original language (*Note*[391]).

Why's this important to know? First, it is necessary, for when we say "the Word of God," we are referring to the original language; or to be precise, the underlying autograph text, and not any translation. Second, we must always have recourse to the original text among the many translations.

Stating these facts does not necessarily mean we need to learn biblical Hebrew or Greek to study the Word of God—even though that would be extremely beneficial (*Note*[392]). However, acknowledging and recognizing the original languages benefits our study of Scripture by adding nuance (and a deeper understanding) to a word or text, which a translation (English or otherwise) cannot accomplish. Therefore, from time to time I will use the original language to help us grasp this deeper understanding or subtle nuance within the underlying original text.

To give an example of the format I will use, let me use a word found in the Preface: ἀπολογία (apologia/*ap-ol-og-ee'-ah*). First, you will find the word in its original language, in this case, Greek. Then within the parentheses, you will find the phonetic spellings, a slash, followed by the pronunciation. If I use this word again, I reverse the order—e.g., *apologia* (ἀπολογία)—using the phonetically spelt word in *italics* and within parentheses the word in its original language I will, however, not repeat the pronunciation.

8. Words: We should not only be cautious in the words we use (for our words can be taken out of context), but we should also concern ourselves with the original meaning of the written word in its context, for context determines meaning.

Inherently, we recognize that most words have multiple or ambiguous meanings, categorized as either connotative (the secondary meaning or how a word is perceived) or denotative (the dictionary definition), and that words are equivocal (allowing the possibility of several meanings) more than univocal (having only one meaning). We also recognize that over time, some words even change in meaning.

As Christians, understanding that the same word can be used in multiple ways, and also that there is an evolution of words, is vital—for the meaning placed on a word is far more important than the actual *word* being used.

First, let us look at a *word* being used in multiple ways. The main problem we face in Scripture is when a word is used in a good sense or a bad sense. Interestingly, Saint Augustine addresses this issue back in his time.[393] Here are some examples. The word "tradition" is used in a good sense, "hold fast to the traditions, just as I handed them on to you" (1 Cor 11:2; also cf. 2 Thes 2:15), and in a bad sense, "see to it that no one captivate you with an empty, seductive philosophy according to human tradition" (Col 2:8; also cf. Mk 7:13). The word "wisdom" is used in a good sense, "the wisdom from above is first of all pure, then peaceable, gentle, compliant, full of mercy and good fruits, without inconstancy or insincerity" (Jms 3:17; also cf. Eph 1:17), and also in a bad sense, "wisdom of this kind does not come down from above but is earthly, unspiritual, demonic" (Jms 3:16; also cf. 1 Cor 1:12). Another word is "serpent." It is used in a good sense, "be wise as serpents" (Mt 10:16), and in a bad sense, "the serpent deceived Eve by his cunning" (2 Cor 11:3). The word "world" is also used in a good sense, "God so loved the world that He gave His only Son" (Jn 3:16), and in a bad sense, "Adulterers! Do you not know that to be a lover of the world means enmity with God?" (Jms 4:4). Even "bread" and "leaven" are used in a good sense, "I am the living bread that came down from Heaven" (Jn 6:51), and "The kingdom of Heaven is like yeast that a woman took and mixed with three measures of wheat flour until the whole batch was leavened" (Mt 13:33), and in a bad sense, "bread gotten secretly is pleasing" (Prov 9:17), and "Beware of the leaven of the Pharisees and Sadducees" (Mt 16:11). I hope you get the idea.

Second, we shall look at the evolution of words—the changing of the meaning of a word over time. The problem we as Christians face here is that some words have lost their objective meaning, and now have only a meaning determined by the user, (according to societal norms), which unfortunately most Christians have adopted. This issue has become a problem, for we have lost the true Christian meaning of some words. Therefore, I will define words by their original biblical meaning in context. If I may paraphrase Saint Basil the Great:

> We must count terms used in theology and theological details as of primary importance. We must endeavour to trace out the hidden meaning of every word, every phrase, and every little syllable. This is a characteristic lacking in those who are idle in the pursuit of truth. But a distinguishing mark of those who pursue towards the goal, "the prize of God's upward calling, in Christ Jesus" (Phil 3:14). For the prize that is set before us—so far as is possible with human nature—is to be made like unto Him. Now without knowledge there can be no making like; and knowledge is not attained without lessons and study. The beginning of teaching is speech, and syllables and words are parts of speech. It follows then that to investigate syllables and words is not to shoot wide of the mark. Truth is always a quarry hard to hunt, and therefore we must look everywhere for its tracks. The acquisition of truth is just like that of other disciplines, crafts, or trades; it grows bit by bit—apprentices must despise nothing. If we despise the first elements as small and insignificant, we will never reach the perfection of wisdom.[394]
>
> | Saint Basil the Great |

9. Practical Application: Theological study (i.e., a strong biblical-based theology) should be practical in and of itself. If not, we are merely embarking upon an academic exercise. One of the primary goals of this study is not only to help understand *Who Jesus Is*, but also it is about helping us move from mere knowledge or theories into practical application of *Christ-centeredness*. But to do this, we need accurate knowledge. We must make every effort to supplement our faith with knowledge (cf. 2 Pt 1:5). Yes, we strengthen our faith with the theological study, or theory.

Theories are necessary. They contain the foundational theological principles of Christianity that we stand on. Once we have these principles as our bedrock, we, however, cannot remain there—we must allow the movement from one to the other. We must move forward and apply these principles in our day-to-day *practical Christian living*—with the desire to live virtuous lives.

Our goal is *orthopraxy*.[395] That is to practise orthodox[396] theology (grounded in sound teaching). So we have congruency between what we believe and how we live. This is what the Saints precisely have done. They demonstrate a holy *lived theology*.

As said, theological study (done properly) *is* the most practical study that we will ever embark upon, for it penetrates every facet of our lives and teaches us truths that no other study can do.

10. Analogy: When speaking about the Infinite, finite language always falls short. However, analogies, my own or borrowed, convey truths, or at the least help us better understand it. Analogies may also fall apart at one point. So, if they help, excellent. Use them. If they do not help, drop them and move on.

11. Paradox: A paradox, by the definition that Christians most commonly associate with the instances found in the Bible, is a statement or proposition that seems self-contradictory or absurd but in reality, expresses truth. For example, consider the statement, "Blessed are you who are poor" (Lk 6:20). At first glance, this statement seems absurd; but in reality, it conveys a profound truth—most of us are familiar with this example of a paradox, expressed in a single statement. However, less commonly recognized as a paradox are statements in the Bible that do not appear in the text, at the same place, but when placed side-by-side they *seem* contradictory (*Note*[397]).

For example, in the Gospel of Saint Matthew, we are told not to blow our trumpets (Mt 6:2), to give in silence and in secret (Mt 6:4) not letting our "left hand know what our right is doing" (Mt 6:3). However, in the chapter previous, we are told to be a light to the world (Mt 5:14), that we should "shine before others" (Mt 5:16), and not hide "under a bushel basket" (Mt 5:15), so others may *see* our "good deeds" and glorify God (Mt 5:16). At first glance, the commands may sound contradictory. Did Saint Matthew forget what he wrote? How are we to do both without contradiction? However, again on closer examination, in proper contexts, we find that these two seemingly contradictory statements, in reality, also convey different, but equally valid truths.

However, here is the problem with these types of paradoxes. Because these are two completely separate statements, it is somewhat easy for us to be uninformed, to ignore, or reject, or to favour one statement that fits our way of thinking. In so doing, we inevitably move away from the full truth. This favouring is one reason why two people can use the same Bible, and with selective proof-texting, use only one of the statements out of context, to justify their respective position.

Similarly, this also applies to separate statements, one of which is capable of being interpreted as right-leaning and the other statement capable of being interpreted as left-leaning. This paradox also tends to pull us to one side or the other. I think it was Saint Augustine who said, "Holiness lies in the middle" (*Note*[398]). Yes, holiness and truth lie in holding both statements simultaneously and without contradiction or mitigation—recognizing the tension between the two.

On this note—although our personality may pull us toward one side or the other—as Christians, we should *not* be left-leaning or right-leaning, liberal or conservative. A Christian should be orthodox. To paraphrase Saint Augustine: If we only believe what we like in Sacred Scripture, and reject what we do not like, it is not the Truth we believe, but ourselves. In view of that, whenever encountering these examples of paradoxical statements, we must hold both accounts without contradiction. Again, holiness and virtue often lie in the middle. Authentic Christianity is rarely either/or—it is usually both/and. As you might have heard, "Christian commitment is total and not selective."

12. Orthodox: Yes, we must strive for orthodoxy! This study is not a *soft* theology, meaning, this book is not a *feel-good* theology or spirituality. If you are looking for a theological take that is in line with the cultural tendency of exculpation, which says, "You're okay," "I'm okay," "We are all okay," you will be disappointed. If you are also looking for a left-leaning *liberal extremist* position or a right-leaning *conservative fundamentalist* position, you will be disappointed. Having right belief, grounded in sound teaching is our goal.

While we are on the subject, orthodoxy is not about being a moderate; do not confuse this with either *balance* or *moderation*, as proposed within secular thought, or unorthodox Christian thought. It is neither. It is about recognizing both truths (as stated above) and holding both realities simultaneously, without contradiction and without mitigation—an adherence to *Truth* in totality.

Appendix B | Existence of a Creator God

How do we know if a Creator God exists? Namely, how do we know if there is a being sufficient in nature and power to create the universe? Many religions believe in gods that have lesser capabilities but not in an ultimate Creator God. Atheists and theists argue using faith about the existence or non-existence of a God. However, I do not want to engage in the usual *faith* bases of those arguments.

My goal in writing this Appendix B is to give you, the Christian, an entry point of discussion with those around you—e.g., family, friends, co-workers, or even your children—with an argument that is not based on the Bible, religion, or faith.

Intriguingly, the answers to these questions noted above are surprisingly simple. The issue is, however, as soon as one uses the term *God* or even *god*, much less *Creator God*, most persons immediately associate *god* with religion or faith. Any argument used becomes futile because of the assumptions persons on both sides of the argument attach to religion or faith, good or bad.

However, another way of arguing that there is a Creator God is to use observational, scientific and logical approaches. These approaches, although not *proving* a Creator God's existence, establish that something or someone outside of creation *must exist*, an entity that did not have any first cause, that is, self-exists. These approaches are arguments that most people accept as reasonable to maintain or prove a position (*Note*[399]).

The aspect of the discussion that requires revelation or a degree of *faith* is specifically identifying or naming that someone or something outside of physical world. That is where the challenge begins and the disagreements occur.

When we do not separate these two independent inquiries, we inevitably make the argument one and the same, when it is not. We must separate the concept of someone or something outside of creation that created and naming that someone or something, for they are two *separate* issues. I submit that, by using observation, rational thought, scientific principles, and logic, we can establish that there must be a *Creator God* (someone or something that started all of creation as we know it).

As we scientifically know, what we call the *physical universe* has the components of *time*, *space*, and *matter*. We have seen this illustrated as follows[400]:

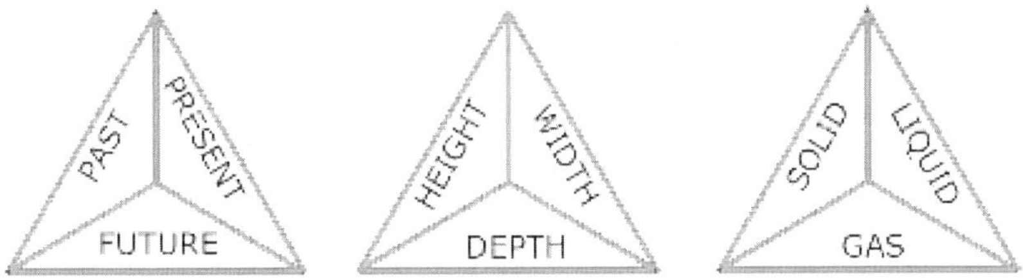

TIME SPACE MATTER

All three components must come into existence simultaneously. These three are what scientists call inherent attributes. Neither time, space, nor matter can exist on its own.

A Creator God logically needs to be outside of what is created (e.g., time, space, and matter). A Creator God cannot be limited or affected by the components of what is created. To state this logic, only *observation* and *reason*—not faith or revelation—is required.

In fact, the *creator* may be described in general, so it does not even matter what name you use. Use whatever you wish: Creator God, Ultimate Being, Ultimate Truth, Supreme Being, Infinite Being, etc. For the sake of simplicity and conversation, I will continue to use the term *Creator God.*

From all the arguments for the existence of a Creator God, I find the following as most compelling (*Note*[401]). What I am about to explain is nothing new. This logic, common to human thinking, has been used throughout the centuries in one form or another. The only way that even staunch atheists can disagree with this is to reject *arbitrarily* the points being made by attributing my arguments to religion or faith (i.e., *retreating* and combining what we have just separated).

I want demonstrate my point by sharing a story about my conversation with a man named Greg. Of all the Tourist Information spots in the world, I happened to walk into his! The two of us started talking; the conversation quickly—and interestingly to me—moved into philosophy and then into religion. Greg was a staunch atheist. Moreover, he was very astute! He was articulate. He was highly educated. He was well read. He knew his philosophers and their underlying philosophy. All of this caught me by surprise.

In our conversation on religion, we soon discussed the question: Is there *a god*? Our friendly but heated conversation (verbal boxing match) lasted about three hours. About God, of all things! In a Tourist Information spot, of all places! Without embarrassment, I can honestly say that I was against the argumentative ropes for the majority of that conversation. He threw me against them and he did not let up!

Every time I used any faith-based arguments, he would quickly retaliate and strike a blow, denying their validity, before I even finished my thoughts. I finally realized that an argument that was not faith-based was a better approach to establish that there must be a Creator God. By using that method, I was able to move off the ropes.

The argument that I presented to Greg, as mentioned, is nothing new. Great thinkers and philosophers have formulated and used this logic in various ways over the years. Scientifically speaking, two principles are at play:

> 1) An object at rest stays at rest, and an object in motion stays in motion with the same speed and in the same direction unless acted upon by an unbalanced force.
>
> | Isaac Newton, First Law of Motion |

> 2) For every action, there is an equal and opposite reaction.
>
> | Isaac Newton, Third Law of Motion |

These two scientific principles can be applied in two analogies—the game of pool and stacked upright dominos falling.

Analogy of the Game of Pool: We know that every reaction begins with an action that causes it. In a game of pool, when a person (let us call that person *The Player*) uses the cue stick to hit the cue ball, the energy expended causes the cue ball to move. The cue ball, if accurately hit, strikes the second ball and transfers energy to cause the second ball to move. Each ball continues to move until the friction of the felt surface of the pool table resists movement, eventually bringing the balls to a stop because insufficient cause exists for each of them to move.

This illustrates Newton's First Law of Motion. The unbalanced force is The Player. The objects at rest are the cue stick and the cue balls. The Player moves the cue stick and the cue stick moves the cue ball. The key principle is that nothing on the pool table has moved by its own initiative, that is, without an external force. That force is separate from and independent of the cue stick and the cue ball.

It is essential to note, in this analogy, that The Player, distinct from the pool table, the cue stick, and the cue balls, does not need to be moved. If The Player were not a self-mover, someone must have moved The Player. In turn, another person must have moved the person who moved The Player. This would need to continue infinitely (i.e., what philosophers call an *infinite regress*), which is logically impossible. Fundamentally, The Player is the first cause in the analogy of playing pool.

Applying the analogy, in the world of pool, to operation of the universe, the first cause (hereafter "First Cause") of the universe's coming into being cannot have been *caused* because that cause cannot exist prior to itself.

Logically, the First Cause, as creator, must be self caused or self-existent, the Unmoveable Mover. This *First Cause* in our universe we can call the *Creator God*.

Analogy of the Dominos: Now let us consider the other analogy. Take a group of dominoes and stand them upright side-by-side against one another. We have all seen this—when someone (let us call him *The Mover*) moves the domino at one end, the remainder fall in succession (i.e., what we call the domino effect!).

Using this analogy, if dominos were lined up in a continuous row, but no one moves the first domino, we have a chain of motionless dominos. Therefore, an Unmoveable Mover, the First Cause must exist to initiate the domino effect. No domino would move without the first move by The Mover.

To extend the analogy, picture the dominoes lined up as described above. Let us assume that each domino represents what we would call the duration of a calendar year of time, defined as meaning that at the end of each year the respective domino falls and hits the subsequent domino, thus starting the duration of that next year.

Arbitrarily, then, starting with Domino 1997, we say that at its end, it falls and hits Domino 1998, causing it to begin its duration. In turn, Domino 1998 does the same to Domino 1999, and so forth. Since we can envision each fall and hit from 2024 back to 1998, we can envision the same pattern occurring for any other year in earth's history.

However, the total number of dominos representing a year in time cannot be infinite. We know that the earth is finite—it has been in existence only so many years. At a point, some cause must have created the first domino year—a "now which has no yesterday."[402] Some scientists refer to the event that caused the first domino year as the *Big Bang*.[403]

As we have noted in the analogy of the pool game, in the case of the dominos, The Mover moving the first domino must obviously be distinct from the dominos, outside the chain of dominoes, unaffected by the dominos, and thus superior to the dominos. That is, The Mover cannot be another domino within the chain. By extension, The Mover in our universe is outside the elements (*time*, *space*, and *matter*) that are needed to make up the Big Bang.

The Mover did not need to be moved. Just like The Player playing pool, The Mover who flicked the first domino is an Unmoveable Mover, the First Cause in the chain of causes. Again, for the same logic as for the pool table, *The Mover* we can call a Creator God.

In conclusion, by using simple observation, rational thought, and scientific principles, we can conclude that an unmoved or Unmovable Mover, or a First Cause, must exist in order for our universe to exist! Assuming the Big Bang Theory, there must be a *Big Banger*, so to speak, a conclusion strangely missing in the descriptions of the Big Bang by secular commentators, even though we instinctively know that matter does not create itself!

Something or someone caused the Big Bang! That something or someone is outside of the Big Bang. That something or someone is that Unmovable Mover, that First Cause. That something or someone is the Ultimate Cause, the First Cause of all causes, which does not have a cause, and thus puts everything in motion—the One who flicked that first domino, the One who put all things in creative motion. If not—without a Creator God—it requires an *infinite regress* or we have something that comes from nothing (*ex nihilo*). Both conclusions go against science and logic.

With that understanding of a First Cause, it is now essential we to move to the second inquiry. That is, don't you think we should discover who that Unmovable Mover *is*? Who is that First Cause? ?

It was the above argument that I presented to Greg. In the end, Greg paused for a long time . . . and eventually said: I will give you that. Although I was the one battered and bruised, Greg finally conceded that there *is* an Unmovable Mover, because there has to be a First Cause—a Creator God, Ultimate Being, Ultimate Truth, Supreme Being, Infinite Being. Greg showed himself to be an honest atheist!

In response, I told him that it is now up to us to search to discover who this Creator God *is*! Then, attending to my psychological wounds, I slowly hobbled out of that Tourist Information spot.

Do you not owe it to yourself to put a name to the Unmovable Mover, the First Cause who set everything in motion, including you?

Endnotes

Preface

1. ***Note*:** "Today, many Christians are no longer even aware of the basic teachings of the Faith, so there is a growing danger of missing the path to eternal life" (Cardinal Gerhard Müller, *Manifesto of Faith*, February 8, 2019).

2. ***Note*:** for further insight, refer to Timothy George, *Theology of the Reformers* (Nashville, Tennessee: Broadman & Holman Publishing Group), 195. According to Saint Augustine, another phenomenon occurs in the *very work of distribution* of God's work. Here is how he put it: "The Lord saith, 'Whosoever hath, to him shall be given' [Mt 25:29]. He will give, then, to those who have; that is to say, if they use freely and cheerfully what they have received, He will add to and perfect His gifts. The loaves in the miracle were only five and seven in number before the disciples began to divide them among the hungry people. But when once they began to distribute them, though the wants of so many thousands were satisfied, they filled baskets with the fragments that were left [Mt 14:20]. Now, just as that bread increased in the very act of breaking it, so those thoughts which the Lord has already vouchsafed to me with a view to undertaking this work will, as soon as I begin to impart them to others, be multiplied by His grace, so that, in this very work of distribution in which I have engaged, so far from incurring loss and poverty, I shall be made to rejoice in a marvellous increase" (Saint Augustine, *On Christian Doctrine*, book 1, chapter 1, number 1).

Introduction

3. ***Pronouns*:** *He* or *Him* or *His* referring to God or Jesus are capitalized to indicate deity.

4. ***Images*:** See cover: "*Simeon and Jesus*" by Andrey Shishkin, 2012; "*Simeon and Anna in the Temple*" by Rembrandt van Rijn (a.k.a. Rembrandt Harmenszoon van Rijn), *c.* 1626-1628.

5. ***Pronouns*:** *She* or *Her* referring to the Church are capitalized to indicate the body or bride of the Christ.

6. *The Liturgy of the Hours* (New York: Catholic Book Publishing Co., 1975).

7. ***Person*:** In reference to the person of Jesus, *Person* is intentionally capitalized, referring to the Divine Person.

8. *Catholic Encyclopedia*, within the definition of "Salvation".

Chapter 1 | Who Do You Say That I AM?

9. ***Synoptic Gospels*:** The first three Gospels, Matthew, Mark, and Luke.

10. ***Note*:** Peter's confession is the defining moment in Saint Mark's Gospel. In the *New Catholic Commentary On Holy Scripture,* commentator Henry Wansbrough states in reference to Peter's confession: "this passage is the great watershed in the Gospel" (968). Philip Van Linden in *The Collegeville Bible Commentary* calls Peter's confession "the first major climax of Mark's Gospel drama (the second climax is the Passion account)" (920). The majority of academic theologians agree that Peter's confession becomes the turning point.

11. ***Academic theologians*:** The term *academic* is an intentional qualification that I will be using in order to differentiate between professionally educated theologians and lay, "biblical-based," theologians, which all Christians are called to be (see Appendix A).

12. ***Ontology*:** "The branch of metaphysics that studies the nature of existence or being." Ontology investigates the nature of being and of the essence of things (*Random House Webster Unabridged Dictionary*).

13. ***Note*:** The Septuagint translates Joshua from Hebrew to the Greek as *Iēsous* (Ἰησοῦς), also spelt as *Iēsou* (Ἰησοῦ).

14. ***Note*:** An example we may use is the name "James," which has variant spellings such as "Jim," "Jimmy," "Jamie," and which is also a variant of the name "Jacob." Likewise, the name "Jesus" is a shorter form and spelling of the variant of "Joshua."

15. ***Mother Mary*:** This is my preferred title for Mary. It is rooted in the understanding that Saint John, at the foot of the Cross, as the beloved disciple is a representation of the Church. Therefore, when Jesus was on the Cross, seeing His mother and the disciple whom He loved, He told His mother that the beloved disciple was her son, and told the beloved disciple, John, that she was now John's mother. Jesus, was telling us (His beloved) to in effect do the same, take Mother Mary into our homes, as per Jesus' declaration (Jn 19:26-27).

16 ***Note*:** "'I AM WHO I AM' is the Name *YHWH* transposed into the first person; it suggests here free choice and unhindered power. God revealed Himself as *YHWH* for the first time to Moses. The etymology of the Name *YHWH* is

disputed. It is surely a form of the verb 'to be' (*hāyā*) and probably the causative form, 'cause to be, create.' Some [academic theologians] suggest that it is a shortened form of a sentence name, '(God who) creates (the Heavenly host)'." (*The New Jerome Biblical Commentary*, edited by Raymond E. Brown, Joseph A. Fitzmyer, and Roland E. Murphy, Englewood Cliff, NJ: Prentice-Hall, 1990, page 47). There is also the shorter form *YH*, יה (*yud-hey*), as used in Psalms 68:4, for example. Also, the Tetragrammaton should not be vocalized, for it is said to be unpronounceable (see: Congregation for Divine Worship, *Letter to the Bishops' Conferences on* "*The Name of God*"; June 29, 2008).

17. ***Note***: Do not take this to the extreme. Some state that only the Hebrew words and pronunciation may be used. In other words, we should not translate these words or names into English or to any other language. This is an unheard of standard that even the Apostles (the evangelists) did not adhere to. Even the seventy rabbis during the translation of the Septuagint did not adhere to this standard. Moreover, in Jesus the Christ there is no primacy of language or race (cf. Col 3:11 and Rom 10:12). Therefore, do not get caught up in this false teaching. The point I am trying to make is that we as Christians should know the name of Jesus in Hebrew, and we should know its meaning.

18. ***Note***: Although the English translations of the New Testament tend to use the word Messiah in various places (e.g. *NAB* uses the word Messiah 59 times, and 2 times in reference to false messiahs), this is not the case in the original Greek New Testament text. It is only in Saint John's Gospel that we find the transliterated title *Messias* (Μεσσίας), which he only used twice (see Jn 1:41: and 4:25) as he himself translates Khristós (Χριστός). Besides these two instances in the entire New Testament, the underlying word/title is Khristós (Χριστός) in all the other 57 times (using the *NAB* example); and, concerning false messiahs, the underlying Greek word is ψευδόχριστος (pseudochristos/*psyoo-dokh'-ris-tos*).

19. ***Note***: The Hebrew word *mâshîyach* (מָשִׁיחַ) is rooted in the Hebrew word משׁח (mâshach/*maw-shakh'*). A primitive root, which means to rub with oil, that is, to *anoint*; by implication to *consecrate* (*Strong's Hebrew Dictionary*). The etymology of the English word Chrism is similar. Although now it primarily refers to the consecrated oil, going back to the Greek, it also refers to the act of anointing.

20. ***Note***: Another example is the Greek word διακονέω (diakoneō/*dee-ak-on-eh'-o*), which is the word for serve—as in, "the Son of Man did not come to be served [*diakoneō* (διακονέω)] but to serve [*diakoneō* (διακονέω)]" (Mt 20:28), which later becomes the title in reference to the office of a deacon—as in, "they should be tested first; then, if there is nothing against them, let them serve as deacons [*diakoneō* (διακονέω)]" (1 Tm 3:10). It is the same word in Greek used

in both places. Although now we use the word deacon primarily as a title, it would be ludicrous to state that Jesus was a deacon.

21. ***Note***: The Greek word *khristós* (χριστός) is rooted in the Greek word χρίω (chriō/*khree'-o*). Which means to *smear* or *rub* with oil, that is, (by implication) to *consecrate* to an office or religious service (*Strong's Greek Dictionary*).

22. ***Eschatology***: "The study and doctrines concerning the 'end times.' The English term is derived from the Greek adjective *eschatos* and refers to the 'teachings about the last things' (or 'end times'). The subject matter of the 'teachings' includes death, [the] Christ's resurrection, the status of the dead prior to [the] Christ's Second Coming (*Parousia*), the general resurrection of the dead, Heaven, hell, judgment, justice, etc." (*Catholic Encyclopedia*).

23. ***Note***: ""Seventy weeks of years" (Dan 9:24) = 490 years. Interestingly, Jesus tells Peter to forgive 70 x 7 (Mt 18:22), which corresponds to Genesis 4:24 and mean the same, a *limitless* quality.

24. ***Note***: Although, scholars' now state that the Book of Daniel was written c167-164 B.C., this is not particularly important for this study. What is important is the understanding (as intended by the writer) within the Jewish community during the first century.

25. *Catholic Encyclopedia*, within the definition of the "Christ".

26. ***Note***: We should note that this is not reincarnation. It is an archetype being fulfilled. For example, in this particular instance, John the Baptist is in the role of Elijah. In addition, the teaching of reincarnation is not taught in Judaism. It is a consensus among Jewish theologians that the idea of reincarnation crept into certain sects of Judaism only around the tenth century. The first-century Jew would never have dreamed of reincarnation—it is theologically incorrect. It is unfortunate that over time, outside influences tend to change sound theology. This is a case in point.

27. ***Note***: There are four tasks of the Messiah: (1) to gather the tribes of Israel; (2) to cleanse the Temple; (3) to deal with the enemies of Israel; and (4) to reign as king.

28. ***Apostle***: The word *Apostle* or *Apostles* is intentionally capitalized when it refers to Jesus' twelve disciples, not when it refers to Christians today who persons are *sent* to proclaim the Gospel or minister in other ways

29. ***Jew***: Used as per the usage within the Old Testament Hebrew Scriptures יְהוּדִי (y^ehûdîy/*yeh-hoo-dee'*), used in the book of 2 Kings, Esther, Jeremiah, etc.; and New Testament Scriptures, in Greek, Ἰουδαῖος (Ioudaios/*ee-oo-dah'-yos*), used 196 times, including references to Jesus (e.g., Jn 4:9), and Saint Paul referring

to himself (Acts 22:3). The meaning is the same in both languages, a *Jehudite* or *Judaean*, that is, a person that belongs to, or is a descendant of *Jehudah*, that is, Judah (*Strong's Greek Dictionary* and *Thayer's Greek Definitions*). I am using this interchangeably with the Hebrew people, or as the descendants of Israel as a nation as the people chosen by God.

30. ***Note*:** "If prosperity charms you into blessing God, but adversity keeps you from blessing Him, then you aren't praising God with your whole heart. You may be praising Him, but you aren't loving Him, because in your praise you're actually seeking some good other than God Himself" (Saint Anselm).

31. ***Cross*:** The word *Cross* is intentionally capitalized when it refers to the Cross on which Jesus died but without a direct reference to Jesus. The symbolic "cross" which each Christian must take up is not capitalized.

32. ***Typology*:** "Christians discern in Old Testament persons and events prefigurements or 'types' of persons and events that occur in the new dispensation. Indeed, the employment of the typological reading of Scripture implies that the 'real' meaning of earlier events is to be found in those consummations in the later events and persons to which they point. This standard way of reading Scripture as a typologically and narrationally unified book, with Jesus [the] Christ at its centre, is clearly reflected in the organization of the lectionary and, indeed, in the very pattern of the liturgy itself" (*Catholic Encyclopedia*).

33. ***Note*:** When reading Scripture we are sometimes quick to assert that we should not take a particular passage literally, only symbolically. Was this the case with Israel? Did they read these particular Scriptural passages about God becoming human, and state, that this is not literal? This is not possible. It has to be only an analogy. Maybe there is a lesson to be learned. These texts were literal. The Creator did become a creature. Even though Scripture clearly stated this is such, this became the stumbling block. Israel could not wrap their heads around God's becoming human. In their mind this idea was utterly blasphemous, not literal. Are we sometimes making the same mistake today?

34. *Catholic Encyclopedia*, within the definition of the "Christ".

35. ***Note*:** Here is Saint Augustine's take on this issue. First, he asks: "Which would we rather live in, in truth or in falsehood?" The obvious answer is, "In truth." Augustine said, "For a happy life is joy in the truth." Now, he goes on to say, that when we speak the truth, it is technically not our opinion, because it is factual information which is independent of us, but also the "common property of all lovers of the truth." We see this in Saint Peter's answers and Jesus' reply (Mt 16:17) (Saint Augustine, *The Confessions of St. Augustine*, Book X, chapter 23, number 33, and Book XII, chapter 25, number 34).

36. ***Note*:** Today, the New Age Movement claim that Jesus is some sort of an enlightened being or messenger. Jehovah's Witnesses state that Jesus is the "archangel Michael." Mormons say that Jesus is the "spirit brother of Lucifer." Even Muslims (Islam) get this answer wrong. They agree with Jesus' Virgin Birth (*The Koran* 21:91); they consider Him a worker of miracles (*The Koran* 1:253); they acknowledge Him as a Prophet or Messenger, but, *only* a man (*The Koran* 4:171), not begotten (*The Koran* 17:11, 18:4, and 112:3). Adherents of Buddhism have a varied response. Some are indifferent; some say that Jesus is another enlightened one (i.e., buddha). Some even claim that Jesus went to India (Tibet) via an ancient trading route, sometime between the ages 12 and 30; and, while in India He studied Buddhism. Personally, I am not sure why Buddhists would make this claim. For argument sake, let us assume that He did go to India and study Buddhism. As we know, His teaching is far from Buddhism. For example, after studying Buddhism, He taught about the Kingdom of God, something totally different. Clearly this is not Buddhism. So, the claim that Jesus studied Buddhism is irrelevant.

37. ***Salvation History*:** "Refers to the whole 'economy' of God's action in bringing about the consummation of His plan for the created natural and human orders, as recorded in the Old and New Testaments, and as continuing throughout history until the end of time [*Parousia*]. The modality and unfolding of God's saving action thus respect the character of the created order which He Himself brought into existence and designed. Human beings, as bodily and time-bound, are historical and social beings. God's plan thus unfolds in stages and through the instrumentality of chosen agents, communities and institutions. A particular people are set aside as the locus of God's saving actions: the people of Israel and the Church. God chooses and sends those who will accomplish His saving work: [the] Christ, the prophets and Apostles" (*Catholic Encyclopedia*).

Chapter 2 | The Second Person of The Trinity

38. *The Liturgy of the Hours* (New York: Catholic Book Publishing Co., 1975).

39. ***Syncretism*:** "The attempted reconciliation or union of different or opposing principles, practices, or parties, as in philosophy or religion" (*Random House Webster Unabridged Dictionary*).

40. ***Relativism*:** "Any theory holding that criteria of judgment are relative, varying with individuals and their environments" (*Random House Webster Unabridged Dictionary*).

41. ***Note*:** Saint John, boldly proclaims, "God is love" (1 Jn 4:16). There are implications to this statement, which as Gentile Christians we might take for granted. Let me explain. We state, "God *is* love." Well, love, to be authentic,

needs both a *subject* and an *object* (a lover and a beloved); if not, it would cease to be love, for it would be self-centred, i.e., self-love. God is the subject of love; therefore, who is the object of love? There are only two options. The first option is creation. However, if the object of love is creation, we must conclude that God would not have been love prior to creation, unless creation was eternal like He is. This option is scientifically, philosophically, and theologically contradictory (for all three disciplines consider the world to be finite). The second option is that the object of love *is* God Himself. If this were correct, it might be construed as self-love; this is why the Old Testament does not make the declaration that God *is* love until the understanding of a triune God was revealed in the New Testament. Within the Trinity, within the unity of One God, *love* is expressed and received by each of the three Persons (God the Father, God the Son, and God the Holy Spirit). *Love*, therefore, *is* the grounds for the claim that God is a trinity of Persons; and vice versa, the claim that God is a trinity of Persons is the basis for Saint John's declaration that "God is love" (1 Jn 4:16). This cannot be said with a Unitarian view of God. In other words, in light of the Trinity, we can legitimately declare that God *is* love. He is the ultimate source of love, and thus He is the cause of all love. Keep in mind, the word *Trinity* is only a word that describes this reality. The word *Trinity* is not found in the Bible, but it was used by the early Church, among other words (e.g., *Hypostaseis*, *Ousia*, *Persona*), to help us apprehend the mystery of the Godhead, the reality of a triune God, the revelation of God that corresponds to the truth found in the Bible (cf. Jn 1:8, 14:9, and 15:26), which was ultimately revealed through Jesus [the] Christ (which we are unable to comprehend totally). Nevertheless, it is only because of this revelation in [the] Christ that Saint John could proclaim, "God is love" (1 Jn 4:16). God can only be love if God is Trinitarian; if not, God would need creation or would be caught up in self-love. We may correctly state that God does love Himself. However, this is not an egocentric selfish idea of love, nor can we acquaint it to the love of self, as understood by humanity, for God is Trinitarian. Again, He Himself is love, and thus He causes all love.

42. ***Note*****:** "By the 360's, *homoousios* was also applied to the Holy Spirit" (*Catholic Encyclopedia*, within the definition of "Homoouios and Homoiousios").

43. ***Note*****:** Stating the three main attributes of God, academic theologians point out the following about Jesus the Christ: (1) Omniscience, Jn 16:30; (2) Omnipresence, Mt 18:20; and (3) Omnipotence, Mt 28:18.

44. ***Note*****:** In the Gospel of Saint John the Greek word structure that Saint John uses in 1:1 is theologically remarkable. In English we translate his word structure as follows: "and the Word was God" (Jn 1:1b). Saint John, however, places the emphasis on the word *God* (for it actually reads: "καί θεός ἦν ὁ λόγος"), so a more accurate rendering would be: "and God was the Word" (Jn 1:1b). In addition, in the Greek, we see another very important theological insight that is

slightly missed in the English. Saint John deliberately does not place a definite article ("the") in front of the word (θεός) God; which in Greek grammar is normally necessary. The lack of a definite article keeps the reader from identifying the Person of the "Word" (God the Son) with the Person of "God" (God the Father); and by avoiding a definite article (*a*) it keeps us from identifying Jesus merely as *a god.* This sentence structure is very deliberate on the part of Saint John, for he needed to put a definite article there, which he intentionally refrains from; thus, he keeps us from theological error (William D. Mounce, *Basics of Biblical Greek Grammar*: *Second Edition*; Grand Rapids, Michigan: Zondervan, 2003; 27). On this note, the next time a Jehovah's Witness comes to the door, patiently point out to them that their sentence structure of this passage within their text—"In the beginning was the Word, and the Word was with God, and the Word was a god" (Jn 1:1, *New World Translation*)—is inaccurate, for it is incongruent with the original Greek, for there is no definite article in front of "God".

45. ***Note*:** In the genealogy within the Gospel of Saint Matthew, "when he comes to listing Jesus' name, the text says, '. . . and Jacob the father of Joseph, the husband of Mary, *of whom* was born Jesus, who is called [the] Christ' (Mt 1:16, NIV). To whom do the italicized words 'of whom' refer? Joseph as father? Mary as mother? Both Joseph and Mary as parents? It is possible for the English words 'of whom' to mean any of these. However, behind the English words 'of whom' stands the Greek relative pronoun ης. The feminine gender of the relative pronoun points specifically to Mary as the one from whom Jesus [the] Christ was born. The genealogy regularly emphasizes the male who fathers a child, but there, 'meticulously [Saint] Matthew' delivers a precise statement of the relationship of Jesus [the] Christ to Joseph and Mary. While the genealogy establishes that Joseph is the legal father of Jesus, [Saint] Matthew emphasizes that Mary is the biological parent 'of whom' Jesus was born. Further, the passive voice of the verb εγεννηθη ('was born')—the only passive among the forty occurrences of γεννάω in the genealogy—indicates [Saint] Matthew's emphasis upon divine action in the conception and birth of Jesus (1:18:25)" (William D. Mounce, *Basics of Biblical Greek Grammar*: *Second Edition*; Grand Rapids, Michigan: Zondervan, 2003; 114).

46. ***Note*:** Some scholars like to point to the Gospel of Saint Luke 2:40 and 2:52, to state that Jesus "grew in wisdom," as if to say, that His divinity was gradually unveiled to Him. If His understanding was gradual, His divinity might also be gradual (e.g., stretching this to concluding that His divinity was infused at His baptism). Besides this conclusion being theologically incorrect for many reasons, it is also a gross misreading of Scripture. For Child Jesus' growing according to normal human biology and His wisdom are written as separate things (see Lk 2:40), in which His wisdom was only limited by His human biology (see Lk 2:52), thus His human biology did not contribute to His

wisdom (cf. Jn 7:15), it only suppressed it (Phil 2:7). So, He did not need to grow in wisdom (cf. Lk 2:47), for "He was filled with wisdom" (Lk 2:40).

47. The Council of Chalcedon, *Definition of the Two Natures of Christ*, no. 148.

48. ***Note*:** A point to ponder: "People like to say that the conflict is between good and evil. The real conflict is between truth and lies" (Don Miguel Ruiz).

49. ***Note*:** Rabbi Kirt A. Schneider asks, "Just how Jewish was Jesus?" to which he replies somewhat of the following: Jesus had a Jewish mother and step-father; He was circumcised on the eighth day; He was dedicated in the Temple; He celebrated Jewish Passover; He studied the Tanakh (Torah); He was recognized as a Jewish Rabbi; He chose twelve Jewish disciples; He was crucified on the feast of Jewish Passover as the "King of the Jews"; He sent His Holy Spirit on the feast of Jewish Pentecost (*Shavu'ot*); and He sits in Heaven as the *Lion of Judah* (Rev 5:5)—"He the lion of the tribe of Judah, the root of David, has triumphed" (*The Lion of Judah*, by Rabbi Kirt A. Schneider, pg. 24-31).

50. ***Note*:** "According to the Christian doctrine of the incarnation, the eternal Son of God assumed a complete human nature and was born of the Virgin Mary by the power of the Holy Spirit. While the incarnation itself is a work of the Blessed Trinity acting together, only the Second Person of the Trinity is united with a human nature. The resulting union is a substantial one, traditionally designated as 'hypostatic,' in which the divine and human natures are joined in the one Person (*hypostasis*) of Jesus [the] Christ. The doctrine of the incarnation received formal expression at the Council of Chalcedon (A.D. 451) after two centuries of controversy. The Chalcedonian definition stated that [the] Christ is 'perfect in divinity and perfect in humanity, the same truly God and truly man composed of rational soul and body, the same one in being (*homoousios*) with the Father as to divinity and one in being with us as to the humanity, like unto us in all things but sin.' The definition sought to exclude views that denied the substantial unity of the divine and human natures in [the] Christ (Nestorianism) and views that denied their distinction in the incarnation (Monophysitism). The Christian understanding of this mystery rules out the notion that the incarnation is a merely transitory theophany: The union of the divine and human natures in [the] Christ is a permanent and abiding one. In addition, a fundamental soteriological conviction is at stake in the doctrine: Whatever is not assumed is not saved. According to the Scriptures, the incarnation has a salvific purpose that embraces both the restoration of the image of God in us through the Cross of [the] Christ and the foretaste of the perfect union with God that is our destiny in [the] Christ" (*Catholic Encyclopedia*, within the definition of "Incarnation, The").

51. C. S. Lewis, *The Complete C. S. Lewis Signature Classics: Mere Christianity* (New York, N.Y.: Harper One, 2007), 50-52.

52. ***Note***: Due to some scholars' questioning the historical accuracy of the Gospels—namely, that Jesus' claim to be God, are not historically true—a fourth option is now proposed (liar, lunatic, Lord, or *legend*). I think that the legend option is a nonstarter. As you read this chapter, you will notice that there is too much Scripture on this topic—not only from the Gospel of Saint John, but also from the Synoptic Gospels, and the rest of the New Testament as a whole. Nevertheless, there are books written that entertain and then debunk the *legend* option (i.e., demonstrate the historical accuracy of the Gospels). Another factor to consider is that, to this very day, Orthodox-Jews understand the trilemma. They do not pick the "Lord" option. Now, if *legend* was an option they would use that option, but they do not, they pick one of the others. May I also suggest that what we said here concerning Jesus also applies to Scripture? It is historically accurate or it is not; there is no other option. To paraphrase Saint Augustine (as stated in Appendix A): when we pick and choose, it is not the Gospel we believe in, but our own ideology.

53. ***Note***: Even Muslims (Islam) consider this reality a total sacrilege; for in reference to Allah, they would state: "He begot none, nor was He begotten"; and thus denying the divinity of Jesus the Christ (*The Koran* 112:1-4).

54. ***Note***: Some scholars are now claiming that there was a "gradation" of divinity. That is, divinity was ascribed to kings, angels, and even to Moses as a second god. This thought is clearly not evident in the text. The blasphemous accusation hurled towards Jesus is in multiple texts, and is strictly attributed to His claim of divinity (God, not a god). If there were gradations of divinity, or if Israel interpreted as such, they would not have been as adamant with their accusation of blasphemy.

55. ***Note***: There are seven attribute of God (I AM): "The LORD, the LORD, a [#1] merciful and [#2] gracious God, [#3] slow to anger and [#4] rich in kindness and fidelity, [#5] continuing His kindness for a thousand generations, and [#6] forgiving wickedness and crime and sin; [#7] yet not declaring the guilty guiltless" (Ex 34:6-7).

56. *Strong's Greek Dictionary* and *Thayer's Greek Definitions*.

57. ***Note***: The Son of Man is a messianic title [based on Daniel 7:13]. It is "A New Testament title for [the] Christ, occurring almost without exception only in the Gospels and only in self-reference to [the] Christ. Perhaps the most significant uses of the title occur in sayings that refer to or predict [the] Christ's future suffering. According to traditional interpretation, 'Son of Man' refers to the emptying or humility of [the] Christ, in particular, whereas 'Son of God' refers to His glory as divine" (*Catholic Encyclopedia*, within the definition of "Son of Man").

58. William D. Mounce, ed., *Mounce's Complete Expository Dictionary of Old & New Testament Words* (Grand Rapids, Michigan: Zondervan, 2006), 69.

59. ***Note***: Some of us might object by questioning: How do we know that Jesus is not simply say I am without implying I AM? First, there are different constructions in the Greek language. Interestingly, even though in some places we read *I am* in our English translations, the underlying Greek is actually constructed differently. For example, when John the Baptist says, "I am not worthy to carry His sandals" (Mt 3:11), or when the centurion says, "I am not worthy to have You enter under my roof" (Mt 8:8); or when Jesus says, "Take My yoke upon you and learn from Me, for I am meek and humble of heart" (Mt 11:29); or we Jesus asks the sons of Zebedee, "Can you drink the cup that I drink or be baptized with the baptism with which I am baptized?" (Mk 10:38), all of these examples do not have the word *am*, it is simply "I" in the Greek. In some case both words the "I" and the "am" are not there in the Greek. For example: "Once more Pilate went out and said to them, Look, I am bringing Him out to you, so that you may know that I find no guilt in Him" (Jn 19:4). Second, we know that it is not a simple "I am" from the immediate reaction from those around, as pointed out.

60. ***Note***: Using Jesus' words—the "Father is greater than I" (Jn 4:28)—some scholars like to point to this phrase as proof that Jesus did not claim to be God. If He were not God, He is blatantly pointing out the obvious. The comparison only makes sense if He was of the same essence as the Father.

61. ***Providence of God***: "Divine Providence is the plan by which God orders all things to their true end. While the plan itself is an act of divine wisdom, it presupposes the willing of an end or goal. Hence, in the first place, divine Providence is itself eternal, identical with the knowledge and will of God. Since God is the universal cause of all causes, nothing escapes His Providence. Moreover, divine Providence embraces the 'hidden plan' that God made 'in [the] Christ as a plan for the fullness of time, to unite all things in Him, things in Heaven and things on earth'" (Eph 1:9–10) (*Catholic Encyclopedia*).

62. ***Note***: Notwithstanding the majority of English translations of Jn 18:31b; the Jewish authorities had the power to put someone to death, but they did not have the power to crucify (or execute) someone. In this instance, *NAB* appropriately translates Jn 18:31b as "execute" not "death". In a way, Scripture needed to be fulfilled, so they could not stone Him (for His bones might be broken), so they needed to crucify Him.

63. ***Note***: Crucifixion was the most barbaric form of execution, which the Romans went on to perfect. Cicero writes this: "the very mention of the cross should be

far removed not only from a Roman citizen's body, but, from his mind, his eyes, his ears" (Marcus Tullius Cicero).

64. ***Note*:** In the ultimate sense, only God can forgive sins. When we sin, even if it is against another, we are actually sinning against God. An example of this understanding is found in King David's sin of adultery (2 Sam 11:4) and murder (2 Sam 11:24). Although the act of adultery was sin against Bathsheba, and the consequent murder of her husband was sin against her and her husband, King David says to God in Psalm 51: "Against You alone have I sinned; I have done such evil in Your sight That You are just in Your sentence, blameless when you condemn" (Ps 51:4).

65. *Strong's Greek Dictionary* and *Thayer's Greek Definitions*.

66. ***Note*:** As we will study in Chapter 8, "Rejoice . . . Always!"; the *fear of God* has two meanings, these two meanings also applies here to the word *tremble*.

67. ***Note*:** If Jesus the Christ is not Lord and God, that means He is not Who He says He is, that means He did not rise from the dead: "And if [the] Christ has not been raised, then empty (too) is our preaching; empty, too, your faith. Then we are also false witnesses to God, because we testified against God that He raised [the] Christ, whom He did not raise . . . and if [the] Christ has not been raised, your faith is vain; you are still in your sins. If for this life only we have hoped in [the] Christ, we are the most pitiable people of all" (1 Cor 15:14-15, 15:17, and 15:19).

68. *The Liturgy of the Hours* (New York: Catholic Book Publishing Co., 1975).

Chapter 3 | The Absolute Primacy of Jesus

69. *The Liturgy of the Hours* (New York: Catholic Book Publishing Co., 1975).

70. ***Note*:** "In His goodness and wisdom God chose to reveal Himself and to make known to us the hidden purpose of His will (see Eph 1:9) by which through [the] Christ, the Word made flesh, man might in the Holy Spirit have access to the Father and come to share in the divine nature (see Eph 2:18 and 2 Pt 1:4). Through this revelation, therefore, the invisible God (see Col 1:15 and 1 Tim 1:17) out of the abundance of His love speaks to men as friends (see Ex 33:11 and John 15:14-15) and lives among them (see Baruch 3:38), so that He may invite and take them into fellowship with Himself" (Vatican II, *Dei Verbum*: *Dogmatic Constitution on Divine Revelation*, number 2).

71. *The Liturgy of the Hours* (New York: Catholic Book Publishing Co., 1975).

72. Ibid.

73. Ibid.

74. Ibid.

75. ***Note*:** "The Catholic Church rejects nothing that is true and holy in [other] religions. She regards with sincere reverence those ways of conduct and of life, those precepts and teachings which, though differing in many aspects from the ones She holds and sets forth, nonetheless often reflect a ray of that Truth which enlightens all men. Yet, She proclaims, and ever must proclaim [the] Christ 'the Way, the Truth, and the Life' (Jn 14:6). In Him, in whom men may find the fullness . . . in whom God has reconciled all things to Himself (2 Cor 5:18-1)" (Vatican II, *Nostra Aetate*: *Declaration On The Relation Of The Church To Non-Christian Religions*, number 2).

76. *Strong's Greek Dictionary* and *Thayer's Greek Definitions*.

77. *Amplified Bible* translation: (The input is not mine).

78. St. Louis de Montfort, *True Devotion to Mary*, part II, section 61. (as found in, *A Year with the Saints . . . The Holy Ones of* God, Day 41, pages 200-202).

79. ***Note*:** Keep in mind that this is not an exhaustive study of any of these areas. Nevertheless, the goal is to give us foundational teaching upon which we may build.

80. ***Note***: "This Sacred Council wishes to turn its attention firstly to the Catholic faithful. Basing itself upon Sacred Scripture and Tradition, it teaches that the Church, now sojourning on earth as an exile, is necessary for salvation. [The] Christ, present to us in His Body, which is the Church, is the one Mediator and the unique way of salvation. In explicit terms He Himself affirmed the necessity of faith and baptism and thereby affirmed also the necessity of the Church, for through baptism as through a door, men enter the Church. Whosoever, therefore, knowing that the Catholic Church was made necessary by [the] Christ, would refuse to enter or to remain in it, could not be saved" (Vatican II, *Lumen Gentiume*: *Dogmatic Constitution on the Church*, number 14). However, "those who, through no fault of their own, do not know the Gospel of [the] Christ or His Church, but who nevertheless seek God with a sincere heart, and, moved by grace, try in their actions to do His will as they know it through the dictates of their conscience—those too may achieve eternal salvation" (*CCC* #847) in ways known to God Himself.

81. ***Note*:** It is better to be hot or cold than being lukewarm (Rev 3:16).

82. ***Note***: In Israel's rejection of their Messiah (Rom 9:4-5), the focus moves from the Jews to the Gentiles (Act 13:48).

83. ***Note***: Political Correctness, in and of itself tends to disassociate our minds from reality.

84. *Strong's Greek Dictionary* and *Thayer's Greek Definitions*.

85. ***Note***: Following is an interesting admonition from Pope Leo XIII: "Everyone should avoid familiarity or friendship with anyone suspected of belonging to masonry or to affiliated groups. Know them by their fruits and avoid them. Every familiarity should be avoided, not only with those impious libertines who openly promote the character of the sect, but also with those who hide under the mask of universal tolerance, respect for all religions, and the craving to reconcile the maxims of the Gospel with those of the revolution. These men seek to reconcile [the] Christ and Belial, the Church of God and the state without God" (Pope Leo XIII, Encyclical Letter, *Custodi Di Quelle Fede*, number 15).

86. ***Pelagianism***: "A heretical theological position regarding grace and free will . . . Specifically, Pelagius held that: (1) Adam was made mortal and would have died whether he had sinned or had not sinned. (2) The sin of Adam injured himself alone, and not the human race. (3) Newborn children are in that state in which Adam was before his Fall. (4) Neither by the death and sin of Adam does the whole race die, nor by the resurrection of [the] Christ does the whole race rise. (5) The law leads to the kingdom of Heaven as well as the Gospel. (6) Even before the coming of the Lord there were men without sin" (*Catholic Encyclopedia*).

87. ***Gnosticism***: "In Christian Tradition after the New Testament period, various sectarian movements (e.g., Valentinians, Manicheans, Mandeans) developed heterodox interpretations of 'revelation,' 'illumination' and 'gnosis.' Differences among these groups notwithstanding, they shared specific assumptions and orientations which collectively are called Gnosticism The characteristic features of Gnostic thought are: (1) Cosmological Dualism: wherein body and matter are diametrically opposed to each other. Spirit is in essence morally good, while matter (i.e., our bodies, creation, etc.) is in essence morally evil (as distinct from being essentially good but under the domination of sin and death). (2) Secret Gnosis: the written words of Jesus in the New Testament are for the commoners and virtually worthless for 'true salvation.' The words and teachings of Jesus were transmitted orally, in secret and only to the Twelve Apostles (Jesus' inner circle of 'true disciples'). This 'secret teaching' was in turn transmitted orally through a line of the spiritually gifted. (3) This 'gnosis' liberates the soul. Salvation occurs by or through enlightenment, and not by means of God's action" (*Catholic Encyclopedia*).

88. ***Note*:** A logical contradiction makes *inclusion* impossible. Inclusion cannot hold contradictory concepts at the same time. For example, a dog cannot also be a cat at the same time.

89. ***Note*:** Some Christians might argue that Mother Mary is not included in the word "all;" this argument, however, is theologically incorrect. She also needed the redemptive work of her Son. The difference was, His grace was poured upon her beforehand. It is only in Him that she was not a sinner, not in her own doing.

90. Pope Benedict XVI, Encyclical Letter, *Spe Salvi* (*Saved In Hope*), number 35.

91. Ibid.

92. ***Note*:** "So it does not matter (comparatively speaking) how often humanity fails to imitate its ideal; for then all its old failures are fruitful. But it does frightfully matter how often humanity changes its ideal; for then all its old failures are fruitfulness" (G. K. Chesterton, *Orthodoxy*, 1908, chapter 7).

93. ***Note*:** "U.S. church membership was 70% or higher from 1937 through 1976, falling modestly to an average of 68% in the 1970's through the 1990's. The past 20 years have seen an acceleration in the drop-off, with a 20-percentage-point decline since 1999 and more than half of that change occurring since the start of the current decade . . . Membership numbers dropped to 50% by 2018, and last year slipped to 47%" (*Gallup*, April 18, 2019).

94. ***Note*:** "This plan of revelation is realized by deeds and words having in inner unity: the deeds wrought by God in the history of salvation manifest and confirm the teaching and realities signified by the words, while the words proclaim the deeds and clarify the mystery contained in them. By this revelation then, the deepest truth about God and the Salvation of man shines out for our sake in [the] Christ, who is both the mediator and the fullness of all revelation" (Vatican II, *Dei Verbum*: *Dogmatic Constitution on Divine Revelation*, numbers 2).

95. ***Note*:** To be clear, on the one hand, "All the Church's children should remember that their exalted status is to be attributed not to their own merits but to the special grace of [the] Christ"; however, on the other hand, "If they fail moreover to respond to that grace in thought, word and deed, not only shall they not be saved but they will be the more severely judged" (Vatican II, *Lumen Gentiume*: *Dogmatic Constitution on the Church*, number 14).

96. *The Liturgy of the Hours* (New York: Catholic Book Publishing Co., 1975), vol II, 416.

97. ***Note*:** Technically speaking, when we ask for help from Mother Mary or any Saint (i.e., intercession) it is a request between us and Jesus, not between us and God the Father. The Saints help us through Jesus to God the Father. It is important to note that we *do not* technically "pray" to the Saints, nor do they intercede between us and God the Father, for there is only one Mediator (1 Tm 2:5). By the way, this is also akin to asking a family member or friend to pray for us.

98. *Strong's Greek Dictionary* and *Thayer's Greek Definitions*.

99. Ibid.

100. Saint Augustine, *The Confessions of St. Augustine*, Book I, chapter 1, number 1.

101. ***Note*:** "In order to be admitted to this meta-religion, the only price the Church would have to pay is giving up Her truth claim. No big deal, it seems, as the relativism dominant in our world anyway rejects the idea that we could actually know the truth, and presents itself as guarantor of peace between all world views and world religions" . . . "God, who is eternal, cannot be changed by the whims of society" . . . "Jesus [the] Christ is not the representation of some supratemporal truth: He is 'the Way, the Truth and the Life' in Person" (Cardinal Gerhard Müller, January 1, 2020). We all have a mind directed *to know*, and the object of knowing *is always* the truth, for none of us wants to live a lie (Fr. John Melnick, SSA—as per Saint Augustine).

102. ***Note*:** Intriguingly, when we say "You have your *informational truth*, and I have mine," it just sounds wrong, for truth is objective, not subjective. For further insight on relativism, I would recommend that you read, Chris Stefanick, *Absolute Relativism* (San Diego: Catholic Answers Press, 2011).

103. *Random House Webster Unabridged Dictionary*.

104. ***Note*:** The Congregation for the Doctrine of the Faith outlines two other tendencies plaguing society (thus affecting the Christian community), which also interestingly resemble aspects of two ancient heresies called Pelagianism and Gnosticism: "A new form of Pelagianism is spreading in our days, one in which the individual, understood to be radically autonomous, presumes to save oneself, without recognizing that, at the deepest level of being, he or she derives from God and from others. According to this way of thinking, salvation depends on the strength of the individual or on purely human structures, which are incapable of welcoming the newness of the Spirit of God. On the other hand, a new form of Gnosticism puts forward a model of salvation that is merely interior, closed off in its own subjectivism. In this model, salvation consists in elevating oneself with the intellect beyond 'the flesh of Jesus

towards the mysteries of the unknown divinity.' It thus presumes to liberate the human person from the body and from the material universe, in which traces of the provident hand of the Creator are no longer found, but only a reality deprived of meaning, foreign to the fundamental identity of the person, and easily manipulated by the interests of man. Clearly, the comparison with the Pelagian and Gnostic heresies intends only to recall general common features, without entering into judgments on the exact nature of the ancient errors. In fact, there is a great difference between modern, secularized society and the social context of early Christianity, in which these two heresies were born. However, insofar as Gnosticism and Pelagianism represent perennial dangers for misunderstanding the biblical faith, it is possible to find similarities between the ancient heresies and the modern tendencies just described . . . Both neo-Pelagian individualism and the neo-Gnostic disregard of the body deface the confession of faith in [the] Christ, the one, universal Saviour. How would [the] Christ be able to mediate the Covenant of the entire human family, if human persons were isolated individuals, who fulfill themselves by their own efforts, as proposed by neo-Pelagianism? Also, how could it be possible for the salvation mediated by the incarnation of Jesus, His life, death and resurrection in His true body, to come to us, if the only thing that mattered were liberating the inner reality of the human person from the limits of the body and the material, as described by the neo-Gnostic vision? In the face of these two trends, the present Letter wants to reaffirm that salvation consists in our union with [the] Christ, who, by His incarnation, death and resurrection has brought about a new order of relationships with the Father and among human persons, and has introduced us into this order, thanks to the gift of His Spirit, so that we are able to unite ourselves to the Father as sons in the Son, and become one body in the 'firstborn among many brothers' (Rom 8:29) . . . In conclusion, to respond both to the individualist reductionism of Pelagian tendency, and to the neo-Gnostic promise of a merely interior salvation, we must remember the way in which Jesus is Saviour. He did not limit Himself to showing us the way to encounter God, a path we can walk on our own by being obedient to His words and by imitating His example. Rather, [the] Christ opens for us the door of freedom, and becomes, Himself, the way: 'I am the Way' (Jn 14:6). Furthermore, this path is not merely an interior journey at the margins of our relationships with others and with the created world. Rather, Jesus gave us a 'new and living way that He inaugurated for us through His flesh' (Heb 10:20). Therefore, [the] Christ is Saviour inasmuch as He assumed the entirety of our humanity and lived a fully human life in communion with His Father and with others. Salvation, then, consists in our incorporation into His life, receiving His Spirit (cf. 1 Jn 4:13). He became, 'in a particular way, the origin of all grace according to His humanity.' He is at the same time Saviour and Salvation" (Congregation for the Doctrine of the Faith, *Letter Placuit Deo*: *To the Bishops of the Catholic Church On Certain Aspects of Christian Salvation*, numbers 3, 4, and 11.).

105. *Random House Webster Unabridged Dictionary.*

106. Congregation for the Doctrine of the Faith, *Letter Placuit Deo*: *To the Bishops of the Catholic Church On Certain Aspects of Christian Salvation*, numbers 11.

107. ***Note***: "Through divine revelation, God chose to show forth and communicate Himself and the eternal decisions of His will regarding the salvation of men. That is to say, He chose to share with them those divine treasures which totally transcend the understanding of the human mind" (Vatican II, *Dei Verbum*: *Dogmatic Constitution on Divine Revelation*, numbers 6).

108. ***Note***: If we lured by relativistic and syncretistic thought patterns, we run the risk of making Jesus the Christ irrelevant.

109. ***Note***: There were two sermons I heard: the first was concerning Eldad and Medad; they were the two that missed the meeting when Moses gathered the seventy elders. Still, they were prophesying in the camp (Num 11:26-29). The second sermon was concerning the healing of the slave of the centurion, who was a non-Jew (Lk 7:1-10). Both stories were used as examples of God's working outside the limits of Israel. This was connected to God's working in non-Christian circles, suggesting that Christians do not have a monopoly on God, and that Jesus is not just for us Christians. This understanding is theologically problematic. If this is a correct rendering, why evangelize? Why baptize the nations? What is more, neither of these examples demonstrates this proposed conclusion. Both Eldad and Medad were Jews who believed in the God of Israel; and the centurion, although a non-Jew also believed in the God of Israel (Lk 7:5). As stated by Saint Peter, "God shows no partiality" (Acts 10:34). The Holy Spirit came upon Cornelius the centurion's household even before they we baptized (Acts 10:44-47). However we should not conclude that this means salvation is possible outside Christianity. On the contrary, Cornelius' household received the Holy Spirit because Saint Peter was speaking the Word of God to them, i.e., evangelizing to them (Acts 34-48). Salvation is open to all, but only through Jesus, the Messiah God the Father sent: "every nation whoever fears Him and acts uprightly is acceptable to Him" (Acts 10:35). The key word here is *Him*; for He is our Salvation.

110. ***Note***: Admonishing one another—Christian to Christian—is rooted in love (Col 1:28, 3:16, Rom 15:14, 1 Cor 4:14, etc.) This is also known as *tough love.* However, important to note, we are not called to admonish the non-Christian.

111. ***Note***: It is important to note, "As a sacred synod has affirmed, God, the beginning and end of all things, can be known with certainty from created reality by the light of human reason (see Rom. 1:20); but teaches that it is through His revelation that those religious truths which are by their nature accessible to human reason can be known by all men with ease, with solid

certitude and with no trace of error, even in this present state of the human race" (Vatican II, *Dei Verbum*: *Dogmatic Constitution on Divine Revelation*, numbers 7).

112. Saint Bernadine of Siena, Sermon 49, art. 1, *Opera Omnia* IV, pp. 495ff

113. Ibid.

114. Ibid.

115. Saint Augustine, *On the Profit of Believing* (*De Utilitate Credendi*), 33.

116. ***Note***: *YaHWeH* (יְהֹוָה) is *the* most scholarly guess we have. Filling in the vowels to create the name Jehovah is not accurate. This is most likely derived from the Latin (Y substituted with J) not Hebrew. That said, we are not supposed to pronounce the sacred Name of God (see: Congregation for Divine Worship, *Letter to the Bishops' Conferences on "The Name of God*"; June 29, 2008).

117. *The Liturgy of the Hours* (New York: Catholic Book Publishing Co., 1975).

118. Ibid.

119. ***B.C. and A.D.***: These abbreviations, respectively, mean "Before Christ" (B.C.), and *Anno Domini* "in the year of the Lord."

120. ***Note***: "Paul's perspective expands to cosmic dimensions, as he describes the climax of history, the end. His viewpoint is still Christological, as in 1 Cor 15:20–23. 1 Cor 15:24, 28 describe [the] Christ's final relations to His enemies and His Father in language that is both royal and military; 1 Cor 15:25–28 inserts a proof from scripture (Ps 110:1; 8:6) into this description. But the viewpoint is also theological, for God is the ultimate agent and end, and likewise Soteriological, for we are the beneficiaries of all the action . . . The last enemy . . . is death: a parenthesis that specifies the final fulfillment of the two Old Testament texts just referred to, Ps 110:1 and Ps 8:7. Death is not just one cosmic power among many, but the ultimate effect of sin in the universe (cf. 1 Cor 15:56; Rom 5:12). [The] Christ defeats death where it prevails, in our bodies. The destruction of the last enemy is concretely the 'coming to life' (1 Cor 15:22) of 'those who belong to [the] Christ' (1 Cor 15:23)" (*NAB* Footnote).

121. ***Note***: "The One who subjected everything to Him: the Father is the ultimate agent in the drama, and the final end of the process, to whom the Son and everything else is ordered (24, 28). That God may be all in all: His reign is a dynamic exercise of creative power, an outpouring of life and energy through

the universe, with no further resistance. This is the supremely positive meaning of 'subjection': that God may fully be God" (*NAB* Footnote).

122. *Catholic Encyclopedia*, within the definition of "Law and Gospel".

123. ***Note*:** In Jesus the Messiah, the Law is fulfilled (Mt 5:17). We know that Jesus did *not* come to abolish the law (Mt 5:17). We also know "it is easier for Heaven and earth to pass away than for the smallest part of a letter of the law to become invalid" (Lk 16:17 and Mt 5:18). On the other hand, in Jesus and "through His flesh," He *does* abolish "the law with its commandments and legal claims" (Eph 2:14–15). In Jesus, the law ends (Rom 10:4).

124. Saint Justin Martyr, *Apology*, 1, 67: pg. 6, 329 and 432 (*CCC* #2174).

125. *Strong's Greek Dictionary* and *Thayer's Greek Definitions*.

126. Ibid.

127. Pope Benedict XVI, Easter Vigil homily (Vatican City), 2012.

128. Ibid.

129. Ibid.

130. Ibid.

131. Saint Ignatius of Antioch, *Ad Magn*. 9, 1: SCh 10,88 (*CCC* #2175).

132. ***Note*:** Interesting to note, Rabbi Kirt A. Schneider states a five-fold purpose of the Law: (1) to reveal God's nature; (2) to set apart God's people; (3) to instruct and guide; (4) to call us to grace; and (5) to make spiritual and practical application (*The Lion of Judah*, by Rabbi Kirt A. Schneider, pg. 128-139).

133. Vatican II, *Lumen Gentium*: *Dogmatic Constitution on the Church*, number 11

134. *Strong's Greek Dictionary* and *Thayer's Greek Definitions*.

135. ***Note*:** In this connection, in the temporal (in time), the Messiah's authority is given to His Church. We need governance, if not, events will turn chaotic. This governance is not democratic, but hierarchical. The Christ is the Head, His authority is invested through His Apostles to their successors, the Bishops; in which, the office of the Bishop of Rome holds the office of Saint Peter.

136. ***Note*:** Pentecost is considered the *birth* of the Church, which occurs 50 days after the Resurrection; it is when the Holy Spirit descended on the disciples—

while they were gathered in the upper room. "Then there appeared to them tongues as of fire, which parted and came to rest on each one of them" (Acts 2:3). Also keep in mind, on the day of the Resurrection, the resurrected Messiah "breathed on them [the Apostles gathered] and said to them, Receive the Holy Spirit" (Jn 20:22).

137. ***Note*:** "One soldier thrust his lance into His side, and immediately blood and water flowed out" (Jn 19:34). What has been described here is the piercing of Jesus' pericardium. Even though visually observed by onlookers, and noted by the Evangelist, it was most likely not biologically known at the time; nevertheless, it was biologically accurately written down. The pericardium is a membranous sac of fluid (i.e., water) around or enclosing the heart (i.e., blood). This also describes the Temple in Jerusalem where the lambs we sacrificed. According to Jewish history: "At the southwestern corner [of the foundation, where the Alter was located] there were two openings like two small nostrils through which the blood which was poured on the western side of the foundation and on the southern side flowed down till the two streams became mingled in the [water] channel, through which they made their way out to the Kidron wadi" (*Mishnah* Middot 3:2).

138. Vatican II, *Lumen Gentium*: *Dogmatic Constitution on the Church*, number 11.

139. ***Note*:** The Temple in Jerusalem was holy because it was the dwelling place of the God of Israel on earth (we can also say the same of the Ark of the Covenant). By no means did the Jews, however, confine God to that limited space. On the other hand, in both, there was a special *Presence* of God over and above everything else. It might help to think of this when we refer to the Eucharist. On the one hand, by no means does the Church say that the *Presence* of the Christ is only in the Eucharist. On the other hand, there is a *special* or Real Presence over and above everything else.

140. ***Note*:** The Hebrew construction of this sentence is fascinating, for it reads something like this: "God He-will-provide Himself the-lamb." Almost as if the lamb is Himself.

141. *Strong's Hebrew Dictionary*.

142. *Strong's Greek Dictionary* and *Thayer's Greek Definitions*.

143. ***Note*:** Interestingly, this is the same word used by Saint John in reference to the incarnation: "And the Word became *flesh* and made his dwelling among us, and we saw his glory, the glory as of the Father's only Son, full of grace and truth" (Jn 1:14; *emphasis* added).

144. ***Note***: In case you were wondering if this—*drinking blood*—violates the prohibition in Leviticus—"you shall not partake of any blood, be it of bird or of animal. Every person who partakes of any blood shall be cut off from His people" (Lev 7:26-27)—it doesn't. For, in Leviticus it also states that "the life of every living body is its blood" (Lev 17:14); therefore, it is the blood that contains life. Jesus makes that very connection: "I am the bread of life" (Jn 6:48); "I say to you, unless you eat the flesh of the Son of Man and drink His blood, you do not have life within you" (Jn 6:53); "For My flesh is true food, and My blood is true drink" (Jn 6:55). Animal sacrifice (or blood) does not bring *life*; but, the blood of the Christ does! So yes, we should not partake in any other blood, but *only* the blood that brings *eternal life* (see Jn 6:54). In this, we may argue that, in essence the prohibition in Leviticus was there in a wait for Jesus the Christ, for we do not and should not want *life* in anyone else. In that regard, the prohibition actually *still* stands (see Acts 15:20), as stated in the First Council of Jerusalem—He being the only exception.

145. ***Note***: Did Jesus have His Passover meal one day earlier? "The Synoptic Gospels give the impression that the Thursday night supper was the Passover meal (Mk 14:12); for John, that meal is still to be eaten Friday night" (*NAB* footnote). The sacrifices for the Passover took place in the Temple at the same time Jesus was crucified.

146. ***Note***: There are many "Eucharist Miracles"—some of them true and some of them not. We should avoid getting caught up in those that are not. That said, we should not be afraid to take a deep look at true Eucharist Miracles, which the Church in Her wisdom has meticulously and scientifically examined and certified.

147. ***Note***: Each of us must discern what it means to receive the Eucharist. This question is not the focus of this book; nevertheless, it requires further study and discernment. On the one hand, we are all sinners, and none of us is "worthy" of the Eucharist; on the other hand, we need to be in line with Church teaching, i.e., the truth that Jesus is presenting to us.

148. ***Note***: In addition, historians tell us that the early Church was accused of incest. The charge of incest was a misunderstanding of Christians' calling each other "brothers" and "sisters" even as married couples.

149. ***Note***: "Jesus tries to remove their difficulties in another way [i.e., Cannibalism as follows, *It is the spirit that gives life, the flesh is of no avail* (*NAB*)—*counts for nothing* (*NIV*)—*is useless* (*NRSV*)—*profits nothing* (*KJV*)—*conveys no benefit* (*AMP*)] that is to say, you ought to understand My words in a spiritual sense: he who understands them carnally is profited nothing. To interpret what Jesus said carnally is to take a proposition in its bare literal meaning, and allow no other. But we should not judge of mysteries in this way; but examine them

with the inward eye. It was carnal to doubt how our Lord could give His flesh to eat. What then? Is it not real flesh? Yes, it truly is. In saying then that *the flesh profits nothing,* He does not speak of His own flesh, but that of the carnal hearer of His word" (Saint John Chrysostom, *Catena Aurea*: *Early Church Father's Commentary on the Gospels*, Jn 6:60-71). "And this food is called among us *Eucharisti'a* [the Eucharist], of which no one is allowed to partake but the man who believes that the things which we teach are true, and who has been washed with the washing that is for the remission of sins, and unto regeneration, and who is so living as [the] Christ has enjoined. For not as common bread and common drink do we receive these; but in like manner as Jesus our Saviour, having been made flesh by the Word of God, had both flesh and blood for our salvation, so likewise have we been taught that the food which is blessed by the prayer of His word, and from which our blood and flesh by transmutation are nourished, is the flesh and blood of that Jesus who was made flesh. For the Apostles, in the memoirs composed by them, which are called Gospels, have thus delivered unto us what was enjoined upon them; that Jesus took bread, and when He had given thanks, said, 'This do ye in remembrance of Me, this is My body;' and that, after the same manner, having taken the cup and given thanks, He said, 'This is My blood;' and gave it to them alone" (Justin Martyr, *The First Apology*: *Of the Eucharist*, Ch LXVI).

150. ***Note*:** "If anyone denies that in the sacrament of the most holy Eucharist there are truly, really, and substantially contained the Body and Blood together with the soul and divinity of our Lord Jesus [the] Christ, and therefore the whole [the] Christ, but shall say that He is in it as by a sign or figure, or force, let him be anathema" (*Council of Trent*, 1551: DS 1651).

151. ***Note*:** Here is another way of looking at it. In the words of Saint Paul: "The cup of blessing that we bless, is it not a participation in the Blood of [the] Christ? The bread that we break, is it not a participation in the Body of the [the] Christ? Because the loaf of bread is one, we, though many, are one body, for we all partake of the one loaf" (1 Cor 10:16-17). Now here is the question: if we, *though many*, become *one body*, because we partake in *one loaf*, how is this possible if the 'loaf' is purely symbolic?" The "many of us" who partake in the one loaf, become *one* according to Saint Paul, therefore, that one loaf cannot be merely symbolic, it *must be* Jesus the Christ Himself, Who makes us *one* in Him. If not, we are saying that it is just a "symbolic" loaf of bread that makes us one. Really? Do you not you think that is problematic? For, if the Eucharist is merely symbolic, our oneness is also symbolic? Therefore, we are not really the body of the Christ, are we?

152. ***Note*:** To make another connection, the Lamb is the Word—the λόγος (logos/*log'-os*); therefore, we are also called to devour and consume the Word, which is also Holy Scripture (cf. Ezek 3:3-4 and Rev 10:9-10).

153. ***Note*****:** "And on the day called Sunday all who live in cites or in the country gather together in one place" (Justin Martyr, *The First Apology*: *Weekly Worship of the Christians*, Ch LXVII). "Therefore, those who were brought up in the ancient order of things have come to the possession of a new hope, no longer observing the Sabbath, but living in the observance of the Lord's Day, on which also our life has sprung up again by Him and by His death" (Saint Ignatius of Antioch, *The Epistle of Ignatius to the Magnesians*: *Let us live with Christ*, Ch IX). "He, in fulfillment of the precept, according to the Gospel, keeps the Lord's day" (Clement of Rome, *Clement of Rome the Stromata*, Book VII).

154. ***Note*****:** The Greeks looked for wisdom (1 Cor 1:22). Some of us go to the Eucharist, looking to be inspired by a powerful homily. We go because we like the priest and his preaching. On the flipside, we do not go because we do not like the priest or his preaching. The Jews demanded sign (1 Cor 1:22). Some of us go to the Eucharist, looking for the spectacular. We want to be mesmerized and inspired. On the flipside, we stop going because we find the Eucharist mundane. Saint Paul could be categorizing this underlying attitude held by Christians in the Corinth community. In today's Christian communities, we may add, the Christian tend to do things out of obligation. Some of us go to the Eucharist out of duty. We go because we feel obligated and duty-bound. On the flipside, we stop going because this obligation turns into resentment. If we belong to any of these categories, Saint Paul would subtly tell us that all of these attitudes are wrong (1 Cor 1:22-24).

155. ***Note*****:** When we pray the *Our Father* (the Lord's Prayer) we say "give us *this day* our *daily* bread": "'Daily' (*epiousios*) occurs nowhere else in the New Testament. Taken in a temporal sense, this word is a pedagogical repetition of 'this day,' to confirm us in trust 'without reservation.' Taken in the qualitative sense, it signifies what is necessary for life, and more broadly every good thing sufficient for subsistence. Taken literally (*epi-ousios*: 'super-essential'), it refers directly to the Bread of Life, the Body of Christ, the 'medicine of immortality,' without which we have no life within us. Finally in this connection, its heavenly meaning is evident: 'this day' is the Day of the Lord, the day of the feast of the Kingdom, anticipated in the Eucharist that is already the foretaste of the Kingdom to come. For this reason it is fitting for the Eucharistic liturgy to be celebrated each day" (*CCC* #2837).

156. ***Note*****:** "If we receive the Eucharist worthily, we become what we receive" (Saint Augustine, *Easter Sermon*, 227).

157. *The Liturgy of the Hours* (New York: Catholic Book Publishing Co., 1975), vol III, 615.

158. *The Liturgy of the Hours* (New York: Catholic Book Publishing Co., 1975).

159. ***Note***: "In order to keep the Gospel forever whole and alive within the Church, the Apostles left bishops as their successors, 'handing over' to them 'the authority to teach in their own place.' This sacred Tradition, therefore, and Sacred Scripture of both the Old and New Testaments are like a mirror in which the pilgrim Church on earth looks at God, from whom She has received everything, until She is brought finally to see Him as He is, face to Face (see 1 John 3:2)" . . . "Hence there exists a close connection and communication between sacred Tradition and Sacred Scripture. For both of them, flowing from the same divine wellspring, in a certain way merge into a unity and tend toward the same end. For Sacred Scripture is the word of God inasmuch as it is consigned to writing under the inspiration of the divine Spirit, while sacred Tradition takes the word of God entrusted by [the] Christ the Lord and the Holy Spirit to the Apostles, and hands it on to their successors in its full purity, so that led by the light of the Spirit of truth, they may in proclaiming it preserve this word of God faithfully, explain it, and make it more widely known" . . . "The task of authentically interpreting the word of God, whether written or handed on, has been entrusted exclusively to the living teaching office of the Church [i.e., the Magisterium], whose authority is exercised in the name of Jesus [the] Christ. This teaching office [i.e., the Magisterium] is not above the word of God, but serves it" . . . "It is clear, therefore, that sacred Tradition, Sacred Scripture and the teaching authority of the Church [i.e., the Magisterium], in accord with God's most wise design, are so linked and joined together that one cannot stand without the others, and that all together and each in its own way under the action of the one Holy Spirit contribute effectively to the salvation of souls" (Vatican II, *Dei Verbum*: *Dogmatic Constitution on Divine Revelation*, numbers 7, 9 and 10).

160. *Catholic Encyclopedia*, within the definition of "Revelation".

161. Saint Augustine, *On Christian Doctrine*, book 1, chapter 39, number 43.

162. Vatican II, *Dei Verbum*: *Dogmatic Constitution on Divine Revelation*, number 2 and 4.

163. ***Note***: We may develop new ways of proclaiming public Revelation (or the Gospel message of our Messiah); however, this is also not private revelation, for we are proclaiming the same Gospel just using new techniques.

164. ***Note***: In the past this term—*development of doctrine*—was used in the same manner as I am using the term *gradual grasping*. For example, Cardinal John Henry Newman used this term—development of doctrine—to describe how public Revelation becomes more and more explicit over the years. This use is

congruent with *gradual grasping*, for it acknowledges that the development is explicitly or implicitly rooted in public Revelation. Unfortunately, today the term *development of doctrine* is not used in the same sense, for now it is used to go beyond public Revelation; hence the reason I qualified it by using the term *so-called.*

165. ***Note*:** "The words of Sacred Scripture contained in the Old and New Testament express truth which transcends the limits imposed by time and place. They are the Word of God expressed in human words and, by means of these words of life, the Holy Spirit introduces the faithful to knowledge of the truth whole and entire and thus the Word of [the] Christ comes to dwell in the faithful in all its richness (cf. Jn 14:26 and 16:12)" (Congregation for Divine Worship, *Letter to the Bishops' Conferences on "The Name of God*"; June 29, 2008).

166. *The Liturgy of the Hours* (New York: Catholic Book Publishing Co., 1975), vol I, 212.

167. Cardinal Gerhard Müller, Vatican City, July 16, 2019.

168. ***Note*:** In the Gospel of Saint John, it is noted that Jesus did His first miracle at the wedding feast in Cana in Galilee, and thus manifested His glory (Jn 2:11). As we know, the miracle He performed was turning water into wine (Jn 2:9). There is a deeper meaning to all of this. Water is a necessity; Moses strikes the rocks so that Israel receives water (Ex 17:6). This expresses the necessity of the Law. Wine shows abundance. It is a necessity for the feast. It brings joy. Jesus takes the water, which was kept for the rites of ritual purification (Jn 2:6), and turns it into *new* wine, better than anyone had tasted (Jn 2:10). This not only points towards the gospel joy, it inaugurates the new covenant, thus it shows the fulfillment of the Law and the Prophets.

169. ***Note*:** Interestingly, this is also the instruction given to us by Mother Mary: "Do whatever He tells you" (Jn 2:5), and it happens to be her last recorded words. Also, just in case you were wondering, listening to Jesus, our Messiah, means listening to the Church hierarchy which He set up. First, this was by giving Saint Peter the "keys to the Kingdom of Heaven," and the powers of binding and loosening (Mt 16:19). Second, this was in the appointment of the greater discipleship, He states: "Whoever listens to you listens to me; whoever rejects you rejects me" (Lk 10:16). This is part and parcel of listening to Him.

170. *Amplified Bible* translation. (The input is not mine)

171. ***Note*:** The Church in Her wisdom does not endorse prophetic utterances (e.g., those by Sister Faustina Kowalska, OLM) while the author is alive. The Church patiently waits until the author passes away. Then She does Her due diligence, before making such approval. In the case of endorsing visions (e.g.,

those by Fatima or at Lourdes), She waits until all visions cease. Then She does Her due diligence, before approving them. One thing that we, the faithful, may do is also patiently wait until She makes such final endorsement.

172. ***Note*:** Satan also uses Scripture, but he discretely twists it. We need to know our Holy Scriptures—Public Revelation—so we may untwist the deception.

173. *Catholic Encyclopedia*, within the definition of "Prophecy".

174. ***Note*:** Keep in mind that the celebration of Christmas is twofold: (1) the First Coming, i.e., the incarnation; and (2) the hope and anticipation of the Second Coming, i.e., the *Parousia*.

175. ***Note*:** Unfortunately, there are those in leadership who consider Church *doctrine* or *teaching* to be bad words. In this, they create a false dichotomy between *doctrine* and *love*. In this dichotomy, pastoral accompaniment is being attached to love and thus pitted against doctrine. In addition, doctrine is also said to be exclusive and pastoral accompaniment is said to be inclusive. This is a twisted, non-scriptural way of looking at pastoral accompaniment. First, we should *not* follow any doctrine which is not from God Himself. Why should we follow human doctrine or precepts? Hence, the Church does not put forward any doctrine or teaching that is not from God. Even Canon Law is rooted in Holy Scripture. Second, if the doctrine we follow is not manmade but from God, it *must* be rooted in love. God's doctrine is rooted in love and thus given with love, for He is love. Therefore, doctrine is not a bad word. To assert this position, that doctrine *is* inclusive and rooted in God's love, all we need to do is look at public Revelation. In the story of the Woman Caught in Adultery (Jn 8:3–11), Jesus the Pastor of all pastors demonstrates the true meaning of these words by accompanying the woman in total inclusivity, and in this accompaniment He tells her with deep and utter love to "Go, and from now on do not sin any more" (Jn 8:11). This is the example we must follow. This is the real meaning of Christian inclusivity and pastoral accompaniment. One cannot be pastoral without love and one cannot love without teaching the truth; therefore, being pastoral means teaching the truth; for it is rooted in the sharing of *God's doctrine of love, with love*.

176. ***Note*:** "Traditional theology has sharply distinguished the reverence accorded to the Saints ('dulia') from the worship and adoration that are due to God alone ('latria')" (*Catholic Encyclopedia*, within the definition of "Veneration of the Saints") (also cf. *CCC* Glossary "Veneration of the Saints").

177. ***Note*:** For a small example, the United Nations Environment Programme (UNEP) stated back in 1989 that "entire nations could be wiped off the face of the Earth by sea-level rise if the global warming trend is not reversed by the year 2000" (James Spielmann, *U.N. Predicts Disaster if Global Warming Not*

Checked). Or, when Al Gore claimed in 2006 that in "10 years, the world will reach a point of no return" (January 26, 2006).

Chapter 5 | An Ontological Event

178. *Catholic Encyclopedia*, within the definition of "Metaphysics".

179. *The Liturgy of the Hours* (New York: Catholic Book Publishing Co., 1975).

180. ***Note*:** The Christ Event has been categorized in various ways. Generally, it refers to the entire accomplishment of Jesus the Christ,: i.e., incarnation, and death and resurrection. Some also include the Ascension and Pentecost. For the simplicity of this study and in reference to the Christ Event, we will look at the entire accomplishment of Jesus the Christ in the main basic categories: i.e., incarnation (celebrated at Christmas), and the death and resurrection (celebrated at Easter).

181. *The Liturgy of the Hours* (New York: Catholic Book Publishing Co., 1975), vol I, 487.

182. Pope Benedict XVI, *Lectio Divina*, Basilica of Saint John Lateran (June 11, 2012).

183. Vatican II, *Lumen Gentiume*: *Dogmatic Constitution on the Church*, number 36. For further reflection on our baptismal roles as priest, prophet, and king also read numbers 34 and 35.

184. ***Note*:** Speaking as a layman; we, the laity within the Church, need to *fully grasp* the dignity bestowed upon us by our Lord in our baptism. In doing so, we do not need to be *ordained*, or *covet* ordained ministries in a disconnected quest for power and authority. This distorted desire for so-called leadership roles within the Church—that some of us continually seek—is very unbecoming of a Christian and undermines our baptismal dignity as the lay faithful. This is not a book on Ecclesiology; nevertheless, we should not confuse the ordained state and the lay state within the Church. The toe does not need to be the arm, and vice versa. Both are crucial and vital. The Ordained and laity have particular roles that need to be faithfully carried out *in Him*. It is not *exclusion* to state that the laity cannot do what the ordained do. "If the foot were to say, 'I am not a hand and so I do not belong to the body,' it does not belong to the body any the less for that. Or if the ear were to say, 'I am not an eye, and so I do not belong to the body,' that would not stop its belonging to the body. If the whole body were just an eye, how would there be any hearing? If the whole body were hearing, how would there be any smelling? As it is, God has put all the separate parts into the body as He chose. If they were all the same part, how could it be a body? As it is, the parts are many but the body is one" (1 Cor

12:15-20). In addition, this is also not a book on our *call to holiness*; therefore I would encourage further study on the triple-office of the Messiah, within our personal call to holiness, which by the way, is our true calling *not* leadership roles.

185. ***Note*:** We can face any issue in Him. As mentioned, rosaries, novena prayers, consecrations, and the like, being done for the right reasons, may be highly beneficial. That said, the advice Sacred Scripture gives us—to live out this dignity bestowed upon us in our baptism—is that we should *put on the armour of God*: "draw your strength from the Lord and from His mighty power. Put on the armour of God so that you may be able to stand firm against the tactics of the devil. For our struggle is not with flesh and blood but with the principalities, with the powers, with the world rulers of this present darkness, with the evil spirits in the heavens. Therefore, put on the armour of God, that you may be able to resist on the evil day and, having done everything, to hold your ground. So stand fast with your loins girded in truth, clothed with righteousness as a breastplate, and your feet shod in readiness for the Gospel of peace. In all circumstances, hold faith as a shield, to quench all (the) flaming arrows of the evil one. And take the helmet of salvation and the sword of the Spirit, which is the word of God. With all prayer and supplication, pray at every opportunity in the Spirit. To that end, be watchful with all perseverance and supplication for all the holy ones" (Eph 6:10-19).

186. ***Note*:** The Christ was raised from the dead, and so will we (cf. 1 Cor 15:13). It is of utmost importance that we demonstrate this in the funerals of our loved ones. In this regard, The Congregation for the Doctrine of the Faith tells us that "all necessary measures must be taken to preserve the practice of reverently burying the faithful departed." Although cremation is not opposed (as long as proper reflection is given to bodily resurrection), the *ideal* is always burial, just as our Lord's was buried. Moreover, if a person is cremated, by absolutely no means should ashes be scattered, divided, or made into keepsakes of any sort. For further study on this, refer to: "Instruction *Ad resurgendum cum Christo* regarding the burial of the deceased and the conservation of the ashes in the case of cremation" (The Congregation for the Doctrine of the Faith).

187. ***Note*:** There are some scholars who mistakenly confuse "resurrection" with "resuscitation." They compare the "raising" of Tabitha or Lazarus to that of the "raising" of the Christ. Although the English word "raising" is used in both cases. In Greek they are not the same.

188. ***Note*:** "'Metempsychosis,' also referred to as 'reincarnation,' is the belief that the soul or character of one who dies is reborn in another appropriate, bodily individual. This belief usually involves a dualistic understanding of the human being, which treats the body and the soul as independently existing things (or non-things, as in Buddhism). The soul is the true self, and the body is the soul's

temporary place of confinement, until the soul is purified of worldly attachments. Thus the soul or true 'self' (or Buddhism's non-self) is not only distinct from the body but is so separable from the body that the soul loses nothing by being separated from the body. According to a dualistic view, when the soul is purified of worldliness, it is freed by death for the state of bliss. However, souls which are not purified are dragged, as it were, by their own 'weight' and attachments, back into an available body which suits their character. This rebirth into a new body is reincarnation or metempsychosis. The character of the previous life's action determines the type of body into which the soul is reincarnated. Doctrines of reincarnation appreciate the truth of the immortality of the soul, but misinterpret its character. In effect, such doctrines despair of the bodily world itself playing any role in the state of beatitude. Reincarnation is regarded in such doctrines as an unfortunate necessity until the soul is perfectly purified from any attachment to this world. Christian Faith holds that perfect purification is from sin, not from the bodily world as such, and the perfect overcoming of sin occurs not in being freed from our bodies in death, but only in our resurrection in the fullness of time, by God's grace, into our own glorified bodies" (*Catholic Encyclopedia*, within the definition of "Metempsychosis").

189. ***Note*:** Who raised the Christ from the dead? As we read in Scripture, there are three different proposals. One states God the Father raised Him from the dead. One states that He Himself raised Himself from the dead. The third states that the Holy Spirit raised the Christ from the dead. It is in fact the full act of the Trinity: for "God raised Him up" (Acts 2:24). It was "God the Father who raised Him from the dead" (Gal 1:1); it was the Holy "Spirit of the One Who raised Jesus from the dead" (Rom 8:11; also cf. Rom 1:4); and Jesus Himself had the "power to lay it down, and power to take it up again" (Jn 10:18; also cf. Jn 2:19). There are scholars who say that this is an evolution of thought that the disciples first stated that God the Father raised His Son from the dead; then they stated that God's Son was the agent; lastly, they stated the Holy Spirit raised the Christ from the dead. This is not an evolution of thought, but Scripture's way of telling us that *each Person of the Trinity was involved* in the resurrection.

190. Regis J. Armstrong O.F.M. Cap., ed., *Francis of Assisi: The Saint*, vol. I, *The Life of Saint Francis by Thomas of Celano* (New York: New City Press, 1999), 255.

Chapter 6 | Why the Incarnation?

191. ***Note*:** In some English translations, for example *KJV*, it says "His only begotten Son" (Jn 3:16). To some the word "begotten" sounds like Jesus was created. This notion would be a poor rendering of the underlying Greek word μονογενής (monogenēs/*mon-og-en-ace*), which means, only or the one and only or sole, or

truly unique, of its own kind, that is the same *Kind* as God Himself (*Strong's Greek Dictionary* and *Thayer's Greek Definitions*). Appropriately, *NAB* translates this as "only Son" avoiding any confusion.

192. *Strong's Greek Dictionary* and *Thayer's Greek Definitions*.

193. Saint, Pope John Paul II, Encyclical Letter, *Dives In Misericordia* (On The Mercy of God), number 8.

194. ***Note*:** For those of you who are interested, here is an abridged version of footnote number 52, from *Dives In Misericordia*: "In describing mercy, the books of the Old Testament use two expressions in particular, each having a different semantic nuance. First, there is the term *hesed*, which indicates a profound attitude of 'goodness.' When this is established between two individuals, they do not just wish each other well; they are also faithful to each other by virtue of an interior commitment, and therefore also by virtue of a faithfulness to themselves. Since *hesed* also means 'grace' or 'love,' this occurs precisely on the basis of this fidelity. The fact that the commitment in question has not only a moral character but also almost a juridical one makes no difference. When in the Old Testament the word *hesed* is used of the Lord, this always occurs in connection with the covenant that God established with Israel. This covenant was, on God's part, a gift, and a grace for Israel. Nevertheless, since, in harmony with the covenant entered into, God had made a commitment to respect it, *hesed* also acquired in a certain sense a legal content. The second word which in the terminology of the Old Testament serves to define mercy is *rahamim*. This has a different nuance from that of *hesed*. While *hesed* highlights the marks of fidelity to self and of 'responsibility for one's own love' (which are in a sense masculine characteristics), *rahamim*, in its very root, denotes the love of a mother (*rehem* = mother's womb). From the deep and original bond—indeed the unity—that links a mother to her child there springs a particular relationship to the child, a particular love. Of this love, one can say that it is completely gratuitous, not merited, and that in this aspect it constitutes an interior necessity an exigency of the heart. It is, as it were, a 'feminine' variation of the masculine fidelity to self expressed by hesed. Against this psychological background, *rahamim* generates a whole range of feelings, including goodness and tenderness, patience and understanding, that is, readiness to forgive" (Saint, Pope John Paul II, Encyclical Letter, *Dives In Misericordia*, On the Mercy of God, number 52).

195. William D. Mounce, ed., *Mounce's Complete Expository Dictionary of Old & New Testament Words* (Grand Rapids, Michigan: Zondervan, 2006), 447.

196. Gordon R. Clark, *The Word Hesed in the Hebrew Bible* (England: Sheffield Academic Press, 1993), 267.

197. William D. Mounce, ed., *Mounce's Complete Expository Dictionary of Old & New Testament Words* (Grand Rapids, Michigan: Zondervan, 2006), 426.

198. Ibid, 1040.

199. *Catholic Encyclopedia*, within the definition of "Mercy".

200. ***Note***: For example, *NAB* uses the word *grace* about seven times, and NRSV about eleven, throughout the entire Old Testament.

201. ***Note***: Just like we use a capital "T" when we speak of *the* Truth (Jesus Himself), or may use a capital "L" when we say God *is* Love, on those bases, we may argue that we can also use a capital "G" when we speak of *the* Grace (or for that matter even *Mercy*), the personification of is Jesus Himself. However, keep in mind this applies only after creation, for prior to creation grace and mercy is not needed. Why would it be?

202. ***Note***: When we understand *grace* as *divine assistance*, and the ultimate divine assistance from God the Father is His Son, Himself—the very indwelling of God's *Grace*—this understanding sheds a different light on the role of Mother Mary. She is the *Mother of God* (*Theotokos*); therefore we may argue that she is the *Mother of Grace* (with a capital "G"). Taking this a step further we may also argue that she is thus the *Mediatrix of Grace*—for through her *fiat*, she becomes the conduit or the one who mediates the indwelling of God's *Grace.* In comparison, with this understanding the title *Mediatirx of all graces* (which now some scholars are arguing in favour of) does not make any sense, not to mention as deduced this title is also theologically problematic.

203. ***Note***: "There are no limits to the mercy of God, but anyone who deliberately refuses to accept His mercy by repenting, rejects the forgiveness of his sins and the Salvation offered by the Holy Spirit. Such hardness of heart can lead to final impenitence and eternal loss" *(CCC* #1864).

204. ***Note***: "Thou didst not create [us] out of any lack but out of the plenitude of thy goodness" (Saint Augustine).

205. ***Hell***: "The place, state, or condition prepared for Satan, his subjects and the unrepentant for all eternity. The term corresponds to the Old Testament Sheol or dwelling of the dead. Theologians generally agree that hell is a place of pain and suffering that is derived from alienation from God. The suffering of those in hell is proportionate to the gravity of their sins, and it is without end. This punishment should not be conceived of as a purely psychological pain, for there is an objective aspect and content to it. Just as Heaven involves an objective relationship to God and an objective pleasure, so also hell involves an objective

condition and an objective punishment and suffering" (*Catholic Encyclopedia*) (cf. *CCC* #1033–1035).

206. *The Liturgy of the Hours* (New York: Catholic Book Publishing Co., 1975).

207. Ibid.

208. Ibid.

209. Pope Benedict XVI, Encyclical Letter, *Deus Caritas Est* (*God Is Love*), number 1.

210. Ibid.

211. ***Note*:** Jesus the Christ is God. How does God die? Well, He had to become human in order to die—for us.

Chapter 7 | Why the Death and Resurrection?

212. *The Liturgy of the Hours* (New York: Catholic Book Publishing Co., 1975).

213. Ibid.

214. Ibid.

215. Ibid, vol IV, 1392.

216. *Amplified Bible* translation: (The input is not mine)

217. Ibid.

218. Ibid.

219. ***Note*:** For further study here are the names of some of the main atonement theories: (1) *Moral Influence Theory*; (2) *Ransom Theory*; (3) *Christus Victor*; (4) *Satisfaction Theory*; and (5) *Penal Substitutionary Theory*. These theories do not need to be held in isolation, they may be held in conjunction. My focus, however, is not so much on the *how*, but on the *Source* of atonement. "New Testament and Christian theology make a distinction between a fact and the interpretation, or meaning, of the fact . . . The fact, itself—that [the] Christ died for man—is like a jewel, a precious jewel, shining in its splendour. Different attempts to explain its meaning are sometimes like different settings in which the jeweler may place a gem; one setting may reveal its beauty more deeply than another; a second setting may make clearer one facet of the jewel in a way that a third setting might fail to do. So it is with the attempts which have been made to explain the meaning of the death of [the] Christ; but here our analogy breaks

down. The jewel can only remain placed in one setting, it cannot be in two or more at the same time. Similarly, if we consider the fact, He died for me, this is the jewel" (H.F. Woodhouse, *Christ Died For Us: What Does That Mean*?, Cincinnati, Ohio: Forward Movement Publications, c. 1957; 3).

220. *Catholic Encyclopedia*, within the definition of "Atonement".

221. Ibid, "Atonement, Day of"

222. ***Note*:** I have used the *Amplified Bible* translation for Hebrews 2:17, for it is one of the few English translations that use the word "atonement."

223. *Strong's Greek Dictionary* and *Thayer's Greek Definitions*.

224. ***Note*:** On the night that the Messiah was arrested, two Apostles in their own way sinned grievously. Judas betrayed Him, and Saint Peter denied Him not once but three times. Interestingly, neither one of them really repented for what they did. As we just studied, in guilt and in self-determination (and a form of self-righteousness), Judas tried to atone for his own sins, so "he departed and went off and hanged himself" (Mt 27:5). In contrast, Saint Peter does not do any of these things, he just broke down and wept bitterly (Mt 26:75, Mk 14:72, and Lk 22:62). In breaking down and weeping, Saint Peter demonstrates his disposition: of a man who just realized that he is not self-determined. Remember, it is in Saint Peter's self-determination—"though all may have their faith in You shaken, mine will never be" he boldly declared (Mt 26:33); and "although I should have to die with you, I will not deny you" he asserted (Mt 26:35)—that Jesus foretells his three-time denial (Mt 26:34). So, here is the bottom line: both Saint Peter and Judas were self-determined; neither of them really repents, however, the difference is, Saint Peter breaks down and surrenders, versus, Judas continued on his path of self-determination. Saint Peter allows the Christ to die for him, while Judas dies for himself. We can learn from this!

225. *Catholic Encyclopedia*, within the definition of "Atonement".

226. Ibid.

227. ***Note*:** This is who Jesus the Christ invites to the Heavenly banquet, the ones who cannot repay Him (see Lk 14:12-14).

228. ***Note*:** As we do future studies into different theories of atonement, we should be cautious if stating that payment is made to Satan, putting him on equal footing as God; or, that it was made to Evil or Death, as if they were entities in themselves; or, that it was even made to God the Father, as an appeasement of some sort of divine wrath. One speculative thought is that payment or ransom

is not made to any entity as such, but it is just the *nature* of sin and justice. We state that *justice demands payment* and *sin have consequences*. In this we are merely stating the *law* of sin and justice. Therefore, payment is made, but not by making sin and justice into entities, but by understanding the nature of the beast itself. For example, if you drop a glass it will shatter, that is just the nature of gravity—nothing more.

229. William D. Mounce, ed., *Mounce's Complete Expository Dictionary of Old & New Testament Words* (Grand Rapids, Michigan: Zondervan, 2006), 592-595. (Note, this entire paragraph is mainly from this source).

230. ***Note*****:** "But what about [Saint] James, who writes that Abraham 'was *considered righteous*' for his deeds (Jms 2:21), and that 'a person *is justified* by what he does and not by faith alone' (Jms 2:24)? Does he not contradict [Saint] Paul? Absolutely not. [Saint] Paul and James each define it differently. For [Saint] James, faith is an intellectual assent to certain teaching, the type of mental activity even demons can perform (Jms 2:19). For [Saint] Paul, however, faith is a personal commitment to Jesus [the] Christ as Saviour and Lord (Rom 10:9), which inevitably leads one to live a life of service to Him and right and holy living (Rom 6)" (William D. Mounce, ed., *Mounce's Complete Expository Dictionary of Old & New Testament Words*, Grand Rapids, Michigan: Zondervan, 2006, 594).

231. ***Note*****:** In fact, this is precisely what we pray for in the *Our Father* (the Lord's Prayer). What is translated as "forgive us our trespasses" is literally "forgive us our debts" in the Greek (Mt 6:9-13).

232. ***Note*****:** In an interesting exchange with the Pharisees, Jesus directly questions them: "Can any of you charge Me with sin?" (Jn 8:46). This question comes just after He tells them that their father is not Abraham (Jn 8:39), and told them that their father is actually the devil (Jn 8:44). If any persons wanted to "charge Him with sin" it was they; however, they were unable to do so, for He was truly without sin.

233. *NAB* footnote (2 Cor 5:21).

234. *Amplified Bible* translation: (The input is not mine).

235. *The Liturgy of the Hours*, New York: Catholic Book Publishing Co., 1975, vol III, 1102.

236. *Amplified Bible* translation: (The input is not mine).

237. *Catholic Encyclopedia*, within the definition of "Mercy".

238. *Amplified Bible* translation: (The input is not mine).

239. ***Note*:** At the time of our trial this is not mercy or grace which is shown to us by our Messiah. Mercy and grace are temporal. This is the realization of our covenantal relationship with Him. In a manner of speaking, we do our part and He will do His.

240. *Catholic Encyclopedia*, within the definition of "Justification".

241. ***Note*:** The assertion or phrase, *sola fide*—faith alone—is not found anywhere in New Testament writings, except once in the negative—"*not* by faith alone" (Jms 2:24; *emphasis* added). Luther, in order to give credence to his assertion, added the word *alone* (*allein* in German) to Romans 3:28. This word—alone or even only—is not in the original Greek text. Here is the German Luther Bible (GLB) translation of Romans 3:28: "So halten wir nun dafür, daß der Mensch gerecht werde ohne des Gesetzes Werke, *allein* durch den Glauben" (*emphasis* added). In addition, he wanted to remove the Epistle of Saint James from the Canon of Scripture. For in-depth exploration on *sola fide*, I would recommend reading *Not By Faith Alone*, by Robert A. Sungenis (Santa Barbara, CA: Queenship Publishing, 1997).

242. ***Note*:** "'Man attains blessedness by a series of acts which are called merit,' writes Saint Thomas Aquinas. But, in saying this, he does not intend to diminish the significance of divine Grace or to transfer the stress in the matter of Salvation from God to man himself. On the contrary, he most emphatically rejects the idea that men might acquire blessedness in his own strength" (Anders Nygren, *Agape and Eros*, New York and Evanston: Harper & Row Publishers, 1969, 621). "If anyone shall say that man can be justified before God by his own works which are done either by his own natural powers, or through the teaching of the Law, and without divine grace through [Jesus the Christ]: let him be anathema [cf. n. 793 ff.]" (Pope Paul II, Council of Trent, *The Creed of the Catholic Faith is Accepted*, number 811, Can. 1).

243. ***Note*:** Righteousness is *imputed* to us; however, we are *infused* with His justifying grace, which leads to *infusion* of sanctification. In his book, *Not By Faith Alone* (Santa Barbara, CA: Queenship Publishing, 1997), Robert A. Sungenis writes: the "Christ does not take on the guilt and punishment of the individual; rather, He appeases the Father so that the latter will not bring His judgment upon His disobedient children" (page 413; also cf. page 115). Nevertheless, Sungenis, himself, goes on to say: "Conversely, Catholic theologian Joseph Fitzmyer argues that even though the Old Testament imagery speaks to appeasement of anger, this was not Paul's intent, rather, Fitzmyer sees *expiation* as the primary effect of [the] Christ's atonement, citing the use of the Greek word ἱλάσκομαι [hilaskomai/*hil-as'-kom-ahee*] in the LXX of God's forgiveness of sins. The problem with expiation, however, is that it can either

be strictly defined (i.e., as payment for sins), or loosely defined (e.g., to make amends, pacify, apologize, etc.). Fitzmyer does not specify which he is using (*The New Jerome Biblical Commentary*, op. cit., page 302). In any case, appeasing God's anger against sin and the subsequent forgiveness for those sins that issue forth from their appeasement are certainly overlapping concepts, neither negates the other" (page 684). This is the stance taken in this study, namely, that it is an *overlapping concept*, thus *neither negates the other*. That said, read carefully what Paul writes to the Romans: "Since all have sinned and are falling short of the honour *and* glory which God bestows *and* receives. [All] are justified *and* made upright *and* in right standing with God, freely and gratuitously by His grace (His unmerited favour and mercy), through the redemption which is [provided] in Jesus the Christ. Whom God put forward [before the eyes of all] as a mercy seat *and* propitiation by His blood [the cleansing and life-giving sacrifice of atonement and reconciliation, to be received] through faith. This was to show God's righteousness, because in His divine forbearance He had passed over *and* ignored former sins without punishment" (Rom 3:23-25) (this is the *Amplified Bible* translation; the input is not mine).

244. ***Note*:** "And where ought [the] Christ to teach, except on the Mount of Olives; on the mount of ointment, on the mount of chrism. For the name [the] Christ is from chrism, chrism being the Greek word for unction. He has anointed us, for wrestling with the devil. They had remarked upon, Him already, as being over lenient. Of Him indeed it had I been prophesied, *Ride on because of the word of truth, of meekness, and of righteousness.* So as a teacher He exhibited truth, as deliverer, meekness, as a judge, righteousness. When He spoke, His truth was acknowledged; when against His enemies He used no violence, His meekness was praised. So they raised the scandal on the score of justice For they said among themselves, If He decide to let her go He will not do justice; for the law cannot command what is unjust: *Now Moses in the law commanded as, that such should be stoned:* but to maintain His meekness, which has made Him already so acceptable to the people, He must decide to let her go. Wherefore they demand His opinion: *And what say You?* hoping to find an occasion to accuse Him, as a transgressor of the law: *And this they said tempting Him, that they might have to accuse Him.* But our Lord in His answer both maintained His justice, and departed not from meekness. *Jesus stooped down, and with His finger wrote on the ground.* As if to signify that such persons were to be written in earth, not in Heaven, where He told His disciples they should rejoice they were written. Or His bowing His head (to write on the ground), is an expression of humility; the writing on the ground signifying that His law was written on the earth which bore fruit, not on the barren stone, as before. He did not say, Stone her not, lest He should seem to speak contrary to the law. But God forbid that He should say, Stone her; for He came not to destroy that which He found, but to seek that which was lost. What then did He answer? *He that is without sin among you, let him first cast a stone at her.* This is the voice of justice. Let the sinner be punished,

but not by sinners; the law carried into effect, but not by transgressors of the law. Having with the weapon of justice smitten them, He deigned not even to look on the fallen, but averted His eyes: *And again He stooped down, and wrote on the ground.* Thus smitten then with the voice of justice, as with a weapon, they examine themselves, find themselves guilty, and one by one retire: *And they, which heard it, went out one by one, beginning at the eldest.* There were left however two, the pitiable, and the pitiful, *and Jesus was left alone, and the woman standing in the midst:* the woman, you may suppose, in great alarm, expecting punishment from one in whom no sin could be found. But He who had repelled her adversaries with their word of justice, lifted on her the eyes of mercy, and asked; *When Jesus had lifted Himself up, and saw none but the woman, He said to her, Woman, where are these your accusers? Has no man condemned you? She said, No man, Lord.* We heard above the voice of justice; let us hear now that of mercy: *Jesus said to her, Neither do I condemn you;* I, who you feared would condemn you, because you found no fault in me. What then Lord? Do You favour sin? No, surely. Listen to what follows, *Go, and sin no more.* So then our Lord condemned sin, but not the sinner. For did He favour sin, He would have said, Go, and live as you will: depend on my deliverance: howsoever great your sins be, it matters not: I will deliver you from hell, and its tormentors. But He did not say this. Let those attend, who love the Lord's mercy, and fear His truth. Truly, *Gracious and Righteous is the Lord*" (Saint Augustine, *Commentary on the Gospel of Saint John*).

245. ***Note*:** To reiterate, upon the Cross, "when Jesus had taken the wine, He said, 'It is finished'" (Jn 19:30). The Greek word used here for "finished" is τελέω (teleō/*tel-eh'-o*), which means to end, to complete, to conclude, but also has an inherent meaning that the debt has been discharged, that the debt has been paid, in full! God in His righteousness—in and through His Son—makes us righteous by paying our debt, completely dealing with the problem of our sins. God does not close His eyes to our sins, no; He clears the debt of our sins, He paid our debt in full—"It is teleō (τελέω)" (Jn 19:30).

246. *Catholic Encyclopedia,* within the definition of "Sanctification".

247. ***Note*:** In the Greek, "Go" is a continuous action (present tense), where the subject does the action on self (middle), and it is making a command (imperative); and, "sin" is also a continuous action (present tense), where the subject dose the action (active), and it is making a command (imperative) (Jn 8:11).

248. *Catholic Encyclopedia,* within the definition of "Sanctification".

249. ***Note*:** "If anyone shall say, that justice received is not preserved and also not increased in the sight of God through good works but that those same works are only the fruits and signs of justification received, but not a cause of its increase:

let him be anathema [cf. n. 803]" (Pope Paul II, Council of Trent, The Creed of the Catholic Faith is Accepted, number 834, Can. 24). "If anyone shall say that the good works of the man justified are in such a way the gifts of God that they are not also the good merits of him who is justified, or that the one justified by the good works, which are done by him through the grace of God and the merit of Jesus [the] Christ (whose living member he is), does not truly merit increase of grace, eternal life, and the attainment of that eternal life (if he should die in grace), and also an increase of glory: let him be anathema [cf. n. 803 and 809]" (Pope Paul II, Council of Trent, The Creed of the Catholic Faith is Accepted, number 842, Can. 32).

250. *Amplified Bible* translation: (The input is not mine).

251. *The New Jerusalem Bible.*

252. ***Note*:** In that regard, it has also been said that the great theologians of the past were also great Saints; unfortunately, rarely are today's academic theologians great Saints.

253. Saint Augustine, *On the Profit of Believing* (*De Utilitate Credendi*), 33.

254. ***Note*:** As mentioned, as we grow in our Christian faith there should be a continuous circular movement from theory (head) to reality (heart) and then back and forth. We cannot be stagnating in our Christian journey—a continuous circular movement from head to heart (or even starting from heart to head), but always a back and forth is necessary.

255. *The Liturgy of the Hours* (New York: Catholic Book Publishing Co., 1975), vol III, 1335.

256. Ibid.

257. Saint Thomas Aquinas, *Summa Theologica*, pt. I–II, question 59, article 4; also cf. Saint Thomas Aquinas, *Summa Theologica*, pt. I–II, question 26, article 4.

258. ***Note*:** To be clear, I am speaking of the particular missions here. I am not saying that the *Law* is not rooted in *love*, *mercy*, and *grace*. However, the Law's fulfillment, or, may we say, true realization comes only in and through Jesus the Christ.

259. *Amplified Bible* translation: (The input is not mine).

260. Ibid.

261. Ibid.

262. Ibid.

263. Ibid.

264. ***Note*:** Read carefully the Amplified translation of the Galatians text, for it expands on the nuances of the original Greek text, thus making it easier to understand: "Brothers and sisters, I speak in terms of human relations: even though a last will and testament is just a human covenant, yet when it has been signed *and* made legally binding, no one sets it aside or adds to it [*modifying it in some way*]. Now the promises [*in the covenants*] were decreed to Abraham and to his seed. God does not say, "and to seeds (descendants, heirs)," as if [*referring*] to many [*persons*], but as to one, "And to your Seed," who is [*none other than the*] Christ. This is what I mean: the Law, which came into existence four hundred and thirty years later [*after the covenant concerning the coming Messiah*], does not *and* cannot invalidate the covenant previously established by God, so as to abolish the promise. For if the inheritance [*of what was promised*] is based on [*observing*] the Law [*as these false teachers claim*], it is no longer based on a promise; however, God granted it to Abraham [*as a gift*] by virtue of His promise. Why, then, the Law [*what was its purpose*]? It was added [*after the promise to Abraham, to reveal to people their guilt*] because of transgressions [*that is, to make people conscious of the sinfulness of sin*], and [*the Law*] was ordained through angels *and* delivered to Israel by the hand of a mediator [*Moses, the mediator between God and Israel, to be in effect*] until the Seed would come to whom the promise had been made. Now the mediator *or* go-between [*in a transaction*] is not [*needed*] for just one *party;* whereas God is *only* one [*and was the only One giving the promise to Abraham, but the Law was a contract between two, God and Israel; its validity depended on both*]. Is the Law then contrary to the promises of God? Certainly not! For if a *system of* law had been given which could impart life, then righteousness (right standing with God) would actually have been based on law. But the Scripture has imprisoned everyone [*everything—the entire world*] under sin, so that which was promised through faith in Jesus [the] Christ might be given to those who believe [*in Him*]. Now before faith came, we were kept in custody under the Law, [*perpetually*] imprisoned [*in preparation*] for the faith that was destined to be revealed, with the result that the Law has become our tutor *and* our disciplinarian *to guide us* to [the] Christ, so that we may be justified [*that is, declared free of the guilt of sin and its penalty*] by faith. But now that faith has come, we are no longer under [*the control and authority of*] a tutor *and* disciplinarian. For you [*who are born-again have been reborn from above--spiritually transformed, renewed, sanctified and*] are all children of God [*set apart for His purpose with full rights and privileges*] through faith in Jesus the Christ. For all of you who were baptized into [the] Christ have clothed yourselves with [the] Christ. There is [*now no distinction in regard to salvation*] neither Jew nor Greek, there is neither slave nor free, there is neither

male and female; for you [*who believe*] are all one in Jesus the Christ. And if you belong to [the] Christ [*if you are in Him*], then you are Abraham's descendants, and [*spiritual*] heirs according to [*God's*] promise" (Gal 3:15-29) (this is the *Amplified Bible* translation; the input is not mine). "Now what I mean [*when I talk about children and their guardians*] is this: as long as the heir is a child, he does not differ at all from a slave even though he is the [*future owner and*] master of all [*the estate*]; but he is under [*the authority of*] guardians and household administrators *or* managers until the date set by his father [*when he is of legal age*]. So also we [*whether Jews or Gentiles*], when we were children (spiritually immature), were kept like slaves under the elementary [*man-made religious or philosophical*] teachings of the world. But when [*in God's plan*] the proper time had fully come, God sent His Son, born of a woman, born under the [*regulations of the*] Law, so that He might redeem *and* liberate those who were under the Law, that we [*who believe*] might be adopted as sons [*as God's children with all rights as fully grown members of a family*]. And because you [*really*] are [*His*] sons, God has sent the Spirit of His Son into our hearts, crying out, 'Abba! Father!' Therefore you are no longer a slave (bond-servant), but a son; and if a son, then also an heir through [*the gracious act of*] God [*through the Christ*]" (Gal 4:1-7) (this is the *Amplified Bible* translation; the input is not mine).

265. ***Note*:** "In the New Testament, the word *basileia* can be translated by "kingship" (abstract noun), "kingdom" (concrete noun) or "reign" (action noun). The Kingdom of God lies ahead of us. It is brought near in the Word incarnate, it is proclaimed throughout the whole Gospel, and it has come in [the] Christ's death and Resurrection. The Kingdom of God has been coming since the Last Supper and, in the Eucharist, it is in our midst. The Kingdom will come in glory when [the] Christ hands it over to His Father: it may even be . . . that the Kingdom of God means [the] Christ Himself, Whom we daily desire to come, and whose coming we wish to be manifested quickly to us. For as He is our resurrection, since in Him we rise, so He can also be understood as the Kingdom of God, for in Him we shall reign" (*CCC* # 2816).

266. ***Note*:** Some of you might have seen the "The Golden Rule" poster, designed and promoted by Scarboro Missions, a Society of Canadian Catholic priests and laity. It depicts the "The Golden Rule" as per various religions and philosophies. For example, the "The Golden Rule" as per the Baha'i Faith: "Lay not on any soul a load that you would not wish to be laid upon you, and desire not for anyone the things you would not desire for yourself." As per Buddhism: "Treat not others in ways that you yourself would find hurtful" (The Buddha, Udana-Varga 5.18). As per Confucianism: "One word which sums up the basis of all good conduct . . . loving-kindness. Do not do to others what you do not want done to yourself" (Confucius, Analects 15.23). As per Hinduism: "This is the sum of duty: do not do to others what would cause pain if done to you" (Mahabharata 5:1517). As per Islam: "Not one of you truly believes until

you wish for others what you wish for yourself" (The Prophet Muhammad, Hadith); and, so forth. Now as per Christianity, the poster uses: "In everything, do to others as you would have them do to you; for this is the Law and the Prophets" (Jesus, Matthew 7:12). Although this is considered to be the so-called "Golden Rule" in Christianity, as we have stated here, Jesus actually takes this a step further. "I give you a new commandment: love one another. As I have loved you" (Jn 13:34). The way Jesus loved us is that He gave His life for us. "No one has greater love than this, to lay down one's life for one's friends" (Jn 15:13). This *new* commandment usurps the Golden Rule. We are not called just to love; we are called to love as Jesus loves. Jesus is the standard of love. May I therefore argue that this is Christianity's real "Golden Rule"—no other religion or philosophy can compare to it.

267. *The Liturgy of the Hours* (New York: Catholic Book Publishing Co., 1975), vol III, 1335.

268. ***Patience***: "A part of the virtue of fortitude, this virtue enables one to endure suffering and evils over a long period of time. While patience may seem to be a less important moral quality, it is in fact quite valuable for the life of charity. The presence of this virtue does a great deal to enhance a person's ability to act in accord with charity, for many of the everyday sins against charity derive from a lack of patience. The theological virtue of patience is an infused virtue which enables one to endure all sorts of ills and sufferings for the sake of love of God and Christian love of neighbour with a sense of composure and self-control" (*Catholic Encyclopedia*).

269. ***Note***: Beginning with the early Church and throughout Church history, we debated whether a Christian should get involved in politics. I have no intention of entering into that debate. My goal here is to simply present *His* example. On the one hand, we must recognize that we "are by nature social," and we have the "right to take an active part in public life, and to make [our] own contribution to the common welfare of [our] fellow citizens" (John XXIII, Encyclical Letter, *Pacem in Terris, Peace on Earth*, number 23 and 26; also cf *CCC* #2238-2242). On the other hand, however, we must discern the clear example that Jesus the Christ gives us as He Himself walked this earth. Therefore, there should be a *tension* within this decrement.

270. ***Note***: "Saint Paul teaches, 'there is no power but from God'. In his commentary on this passage, Saint John Chrysostom writes: 'What are you saying? Is every ruler appointed by God? No, that is not what I mean, he says, for I am not now talking about individual rulers, but about authority as such. My contention is that the existence of a ruling authority—the fact that some should command and others obey, and that all things not come about as the result of blind chance—this is a provision of divine wisdom.' God has created men social by nature, and a society cannot 'hold together unless someone is in

command to give effective direction and unity of purpose. Hence every civilized community must have a ruling authority, and this authority, no less than society itself, has its source in nature, and consequently has God for its author'" . . . "The fact that authority comes from God does not mean that men have no power to choose those who are to rule the State, or to decide upon the type of government they want, and determine the procedure and limitations of rulers in the exercise of their authority. Hence the above teaching is consonant with any genuinely democratic form of government" (John XXIII, Encyclical Letter, *Pacem in Terris*, *Peace on Earth*, number 46 and 52).

271. *The Liturgy of the Hours* (New York: Catholic Book Publishing Co., 1975), vol III, 966.

272. *Amplified Bible* translation: (The input is not mine).

273. *The Liturgy of the Hours* (New York: Catholic Book Publishing Co., 1975), vol III, 1335.

274. ***Humility*****:** "The supernatural virtue by which a Christian gains a proportionate and fitting understanding of his or her relationship to God. This virtue brings recognition that all good is ultimately from God, is the result of His grace and cannot be attributed to human agency. Humility is the basis of authentic love of others, and it draws us into closer conformity with [the] Christ as it harmonizes us with His humility. It recognizes that the humility of [the] Christ enabled Him to bring humanity the gifts of Salvation [i.e., the gift of Himself] by enabling Him to enter our mortal and sinful condition. Even though [the] Christ was utterly sinless, He showed on Calvary how the humility of sinners should be manifested. Although He was not a creature as we are, He submitted to the will of the Father in everything and became the model of humility for us. Humility opens us to the grace of God, and thus the humble one can better resist temptations than can those without this virtue. Humility is at the very foundation of prayer and the spiritual life, for discipleship and the imitation of [the] Christ is not possible without humility. Humility is also the natural virtue which opposes pride, arrogance and vanity, which are the roots of all evil" (*Catholic Encyclopedia*).

275. *The Liturgy of the Hours* (New York: Catholic Book Publishing Co., 1975), vol III, 1335.

276. ***Obedience*****:** "In Sacred Scripture we see a rather different meaning associated with obedience. In the pages of Scripture, we learn of obedience in terms of an individual and whole community response to God's self-disclosure and great plan of revelation. As such, the biblical notion of obedience has to do with responding to and entering into God's life itself (i.e., the goal of Salvation History). The English word is from the Latin *ob-audire*, which expresses the

meaning common to the Hebrew and Greek words in Scripture which mean 'to hear.' That is, in Sacred Scripture to obey is really to "hear" the expressed will of God by responding to it completely and without hesitation (e.g., Gen 22:18, Ex 15:26, Deut 5:31-33, Mt 7:21, Mk 3:35, Jn 12:47, Rom 2:13). Such a definition of 'hearing' opens up new vistas in understanding the great Shema, the "creed" of Judaism: "Hear, O Israel, the Lord our God, the Lord is one" (Deut 6:5). The Lord's requirement of obedience takes precedence over burnt offerings because with obedience there is a relationship with God within all of one's life and not just in the narrower liturgical ritual (1 Sam 15:22). Obedience is the means of fulfilling the human person by principles of logic and reason" (*Catholic Encyclopedia*).

277. Regis J. Armstrong O.F.M. Cap., ed., *Francis of Assisi: The Saint*, vol. 2, *The Remembrance of the Desire of a Soul by Thomas of Celano* (New York: New City Press, 1999), 386.

278. ***Note***: Most of us have heard of the acronym WWJD (What would Jesus do?). I find this acronym interesting. We do know what Jesus did. Even if we project what He would do in our circumstances, how would that help us? I think the better question is to ask: What is Jesus asking me to do? However, I guess that doesn't make a great acronym.

279. *Strong's Greek Dictionary* and *Thayer's Greek Definitions*.

280. ***Note***: Is the part—"If you wish to be perfect, go, sell [all] what you have and give to (the) poor" (Mk 10:21)—subjective; does it apply only to the Rich Young Man, or is it objective; does it apply to all of us? This has been debated. May I suggest that Scripture points to its being *his to do*? It is subjective to him, and to those who are subjectively called to carry out this particular Gospel passage (e.g., Saint Francis). I say this strictly in regard to the totality of what is asked of him—sell all what you have and give to the poor—but not the inner disposition of what is asked of him. For example, we are all called to live that simplicity of life, which was demonstrated in this command; however, we are not all called to sell all that we have. Notice that later, Saint Peter, including all the Apostles, states that they have "given up everything" (Mt 19:27 and Mk 10:28). This is what was *theirs to do*. They did not have to sell everything and give it to the poor. If you recall, "Zacchaeus stood there and said to the Lord, Behold, half of my possessions, Lord, I shall give to the poor, and if I have extorted anything from anyone I shall repay it four times over" (Lk 19:8). This was exactly what was his to do, for Jesus did not correct him and say, "No, not good enough, go, sell all that you have and give to the poor!" May I also add that this has to do with disposition. The Rich Young Man's possessions was his treasure, Jesus recognized this (Mk 10:21), thus the subjective request from him—this was his personal cross!

281. *The Liturgy of the Hours* (New York: Catholic Book Publishing Co., 1975), vol III, 1335.

282. ***Note*:** Thomas A Kempis takes "despising" a step further, for he states: "How blessed are those who know how good it is to love Jesus and to despise themselves for His sake. Jesus wills to be loved alone above all other things and we must forsake all other loves but His" (Thomas A Kempis, *The Imitation of Christ*, A Saint Joseph Giant Type Edition; New York: Catholic Book Publishing Co., 1969;, book 2, chapter 7, number 1.

283. ***The Seven Deadly Sins* (*a.k.a. Capital Sins or Capital Vices*):** "Sins that are sources or causes of other sins. Traditionally, the capital sins were counted as pride, envy, sloth, lust, greed, intemperance and anger. Original sin is the first of all sins as it is the root of our alienation from God. The seven capital or deadly sins are perilous tendencies which threaten the life of charity and the grace of God within us. Saint John terms the root of all sin to be . . . 'the lust of the flesh and the lust of the eyes, and the pride of life' (1 Jn 2:16). The capital sins are disruptions of natural tendencies that are required for our human flourishing and happiness. Pride is a sin by which a person unduly esteems himself or his accomplishments relative to the esteem that should be given to God. Envy is a tendency to begrudge the good of another because it is perceived as a threat to one's own excellence and glory. And the greater the good that is envied, the greater the malice of this sin. Anger is a sin of excessively desiring to suppress what is hostile to us. Anger is morally good when used against true evils and is necessary for true love. However, when anger is imprudent and immoderate, it becomes sinful and destroys harmony and peace. Avarice is an extreme or unruly love of material goods in particular, but it also includes love of worldly honors. Lust is a disorderly craving for sexual pleasure that is indulged in without discipline and without regard for the responsibilities of marriage and family. Intemperance is a lack of restraint in our desire for food, drink, rest or recreation, and its malice lies in the disruption of our dignity that it causes. Intemperance in respect to food often has deep psychological roots. Intemperance in respect to alcohol or drugs is a grave sin because it degrades the person and opens the person to even greater evils. For those who are 'addicted' to either drugs or alcohol, total abstinence is morally imperative. The sin of sloth, involving a lack of enthusiasm for spiritual growth and development, is the antithesis of love of God and leads to undue love of pleasure, discouragement and ultimately despair. Lust of the flesh is a disruptive desire for pleasures. Lust of the eyes is an uncontrolled craving for possessions. And these two combine to create a spiritual laziness and apathy in relation to spiritual growth. The pride of life is a disruptive desire for honors and glory that leads to megalomania, envy and anger" (*Catholic Encyclopedia*).

284. ***Note*:** "Now (even) the first covenant had regulations for worship and an earthly sanctuary. For a tabernacle was constructed, the outer one, in which

were the lampstand, the table, and the bread of offering; this is called the Holy Place. Behind the second veil was the tabernacle called the Holy of Holies, in which were the gold altar of incense and the Ark of the Covenant entirely covered with gold. In it were the gold jar containing the manna, the staff of Aaron that had sprouted, and the tablets [the Ten Commandments] of the covenant" (Heb 9:1-4). Mother Mary is *the* fulfillment of the Ark of the Covenant. For in her womb (i.e., the New Ark of the Covenant), is Jesus, Who is the Real Bread from Heaven (i.e., Manna), the absolute High Priest (i.e., the priestly staff of Aaron), and the fulfillment of the Law (i.e., the tablets).

285. ***Note*:** In Buddhism, the goal is to put an end to suffering. The acknowledgment and understanding of this process is called *Enlightenment*, and the accomplishing of this is called *nirvāṇa*. In simple terms, the final goal of every Buddhist—their "heart's goal"—is *nirvāṇa*, and eventually *parinirvāṇa* (the end to rebirth). The foundational starting point to achieve this goal is the Four Noble Truths. First is the acknowledgment of the disease: i.e., human existence is equated to suffering (*dukkha*). With this acknowledgment, the cause of the disease is explained: i.e., human beings suffer because of desire (*tānha*). Now the remedy for the disease: i.e., in order for human beings to stop suffering, they must stop desiring (*nirodha*). Finally, the treatment to achieve the remedy (*magga*): i.e., the Eightfold Path to help people achieve *nirvāṇa*. When a person attains *nirvāṇa*, Buddhism states that the person is in a state of human perfection. In which, there will be no defilement or sin—no longing, no bad desire, no good desire—within that person and all this happens while they are on this earth. Now, here is the question: Does desire (*tānha*), include the different realities of *love*? For we know, true love *will* cause suffering! It is in human nature to love and to be loved. Moreover, we also know that we readily embrace suffering for the sake of love. All realities and expressions of love will make us suffer. Is this accounted for in Buddhist thought? Does the Buddhist person need to stop desire (*tānha*), which includes love? These are legitimate questions. Again, within Buddhist thought, does the word desire (*tānha*) include the realities of love? Well, we may argue, it must! If not, one would not be able to stop suffering. Therefore, it (love) must be eliminated. Does it not?

286. *Strong's Greek Dictionary* and *Thayer's Greek Definitions*.

287. ***Note*:** Although, scholars' state that King Solomon did not write Ecclesiastes (that it was written about 600-700 years after King Solomon), this is not particularly important for this study. What is important is the personification of King Solomon within Ecclesiastes as intended by the writer.

288. Saint John Chrysostom, *Catena Aurea*, Commentary on the Gospel of Saint Mark chapter 10.

289. ***Note*:** Unlike some Eastern religions, this is not detachment for detachment's sake, and it is not a "complete" detachment. It is a detachment for God, but not from God.

290. Saint Gregory of Nazianzus, *Catena Aurea*, Commentary on the Gospel of Saint Luke chapter 14.

291. *Strong's Greek Dictionary* and *Thayer's Greek Definitions*.

292. *Amplified Bible* translation: (The input is not mine).

293. *The Liturgy of the Hours* (New York: Catholic Book Publishing Co., 1975), vol III, 808.

294. ***Note*:** Contrary to popular secular belief, God does not oppose joy or sensual pleasure. He created things so they may be pleasant to our sight (Gen 2:9).

295. *Amplified Bible* translation: (The input is not mine).

296. *The Liturgy of the Hours* (New York: Catholic Book Publishing Co., 1975), vol III, 956 and 967 (paraphrase of the two closing prayers).

Chapter 8 | "Rejoice . . . Always!"

297. Saint Augustine, *The Confessions of St. Augustine*, Book I, chapter 1, number 1.

298. Saint Augustine, *The City of God*, Book XIX, number 13.

299. *Strong's Greek Dictionary* and *Thayer's Greek Definitions*; and William D. Mounce, ed., *Mounce's Complete Expository Dictionary of Old & New Testament Words* (Grand Rapids, Michigan: Zondervan, 2006), 69-70, 320, 368-370, and 573-574.

300. ***Note*:** Interestingly, and in spite of what we would think, it is the exact salutation used by Judas when he betrayed Jesus with a kiss (Mt 26:49). In this regard, Judas' greeting will actual make sense as we continue our study

301. ***Note*:** Christians are more and more slipping into secular thought. I have heard it said that: "the further into secularism you go, the further away from the Word of God you go" . . . "out there you are swinging in an ocean of your own ego, your own opinions, and your own secular humanistic concepts."

302. ***Note*:** Again, in very general terms, psychologists view happiness, primarily in two different ways: (1) Hedonic/Hedonia: a happiness that is derived primarily from pleasure or enjoyment, thus, doing what "feels good," fulfillment of

desires, and experiencing enjoyment; to give a positive emotional state and general life satisfaction (rooted in the fourth century B.C. philosopher, Aristippus), or even the Epicurean philosophy that pleasure is the greatest good (i.e., "Let us eat and drink, for tomorrow we die"). (2) Eudemonic/Eudaimonia: a happiness that is derived primarily from meaning or purpose, to live a virtuous life; thus, seeking virtue and meaning gives life value and purpose, in which one pursues excellence in work and in relationships (rooted in the fourth century B.C. philosopher, Aristotle).

303. ***Note*:** We also tend to tie happiness with success. In which success is defined in worldly terms (e.g., worldly achievement). However, as with happiness, *success*, from a Christian perspective, is also not worldly. Christians who define success in a worldly sense must change their definition.

304. ***Note*:** We might argue that Jesus did *not want* to be crucified, in the sense it would go against His personal happiness. However, this is not the case; Jesus *did want* to be crucified, in that His joyfulness and His personal happiness were tightly linked. This is the example of happiness that Christians should emulate. Jesus, of course, did not buy into the societal definition of happiness, so, neither should we? Remember, He goes to the Cross of His free will, without coercion (Jn 10:18).

305. ***Note*:** This also applies to love: "(1). All love is acquisitive love. (2). This acquisitive love is the most elementary and fundamental phenomena in human life. God has created man, such that he *must* desire, *must* love and long for something. Since God has reserved to Himself the privilege of 'being sufficient for Himself' and has forbidden man to 'be sufficient for himself,' this is a plain indication to man that he should seek and desire his 'good,' his 'sufficiency,' in something which does not originally belonged to him" (Anders Nygren, *Agape and Eros*, New York and Evanston: Harper & Row Publishers, 1969, 482).

306. ***Note*:** The actual quote is: "The young man who rings the bell at the brothel is unconsciously looking for God" (Bruce Marshall, *The World, The Flesh, and Father Smith*).

307. ***Note*:** "Faith in [the] Christ, rejecting all claims of self-realization, that they can be fulfilled completely only if God Himself makes it possible, by drawing us toward Himself" . . . "No created thing can totally satisfy us because God has destined us for communion with Him" (Congregation for the Doctrine of the Faith, *Letter Placuit Deo*; *To the Bishops of the Catholic Church On Certain Aspects of Christian Salvation*, numbers 6).

308. Saint Augustine, *The Confessions of St. Augustine*, Book X, chapter 20, number 29.

309. ***Note*:** Scripture speaks of a healthy and unhealthy ambition. Here I am speaking only of the unhealthy kind (cf. Mt 20:20-28, Gal 5:15, Phil 2:3-4, 1 Tm 6:10, and Jms 3:16). However, for reference, here are some healthy ambitions (cf. Mt 5:16, 1 Cor 10:23-33, 2 Cor 9:8, and Phil 2:12-18).

310 ***Note*:** What do I mean by purpose in reality? This is a philosophical statement which essentially means that what "is" (i.e., reality) cannot and should not be denied or circumvented. We may look at this in two ways. First, as we have discussed, everything that exists has a *telos* (τέλος), therefore, reality also has a *telos* (τέλος). Using our previous example, a hammer could be used in various different ways, but, the actual *telos* (τέλος) of a hammer is to pound nails, this is its ends. This is its *telos* (τέλος), what it is designed to do. In that reality, we can use it! Keeping in mind, that it must be morally and ethically correct in its usage. We may also argue that purpose in reality is fundamentally based on the sciences—physics, chemistry, and biology—once we deny or circumvent science, we will inevitably be unhappy.

311. ***Note*:** "Have a good conscience and you will always be happy. A good conscience can bear a great deal and still remain serene in the midst of adversity, while a bad conscience is fearful and easily ruffled" (Thomas A Kempis, *The Imitation of Christ*, A Saint Joseph Giant Type Edition; New York: Catholic Book Publishing Co., 1969; book 2, chapter 6, number 1).

312. This entire paragraph comes from his thought: Saint Augustine, *On Christian Doctrine*, book 1, chapter 1, number 1-2; chapter 3, number 3; chapter 5, number 5; chapter 22, number 20-21.

313. *Strong's Greek Dictionary* and *Thayer's Greek Definitions*.

314. Ibid.

315. ***Note*:** Happiness is not the adventure itself. That is to say, do not mistakenly try to fill the vacuum or void with even doing things for God. Christians can be guilty of this. Filling ourselves with mission work, outreach, Christian social justice programs, church committees, and the like, is not what I am describing here. These, in and of themselves, will *not* bring us happiness.

316. *The Liturgy of the Hours* (New York: Catholic Book Publishing Co., 1975), vol II, 1210.

317. ***Note*:** "The poison paralyzing the Church is the opinion that we should adapt to the Zeitgeist, the spirit of the age, and not the spirit of God; that we should relativize God's commandments and reinterpret the doctrine of the revealed faith" . . . "But the one who believes needs no ideology" . . . "We will be happy and free when in the spirit of love we embrace the form of life to which God

has called each one of us personally: in the sacrament of marriage, in celibate priesthood, or in religious life according to the three evangelical counsels of poverty, obedience, and chastity for the sake of the Kingdom of Heaven" (Cardinal Gerhard Müller, January 1, 2020).

318. ***Note***: As mentioned in Appendix A, the word "world" is used in a good sense, "God so loved the world that He gave His only Son" (Jn 3:16), and in a bad sense, "Adulterers! Do you not know that to be a lover of the world means enmity with God?" (Jms 4:4). In this bad sense, therefore, "whoever wants to be a lover of the world makes himself an enemy of God" (Jms 4:4). "Do not love the world or the things of the world. If anyone loves the world, the love of the Father is not in him. For all that is in the world, sensual lust, enticement for the eyes, and a pretentious life, is not from the Father but is from the world. Yet the world and its enticement are passing away. But whoever does the will of God remains forever" (1 Jn 2:15-17). "It is also necessary to affirm that, according to biblical faith, the origin of evil is not found in the material, corporeal world" . . . "On the contrary, this faith proclaims that all the universe is good because it was created by God (cf. Gen 1:31, Wisdom 1:13-14, and 1 Tm 4:4)" (Congregation for the Doctrine of the Faith, *Letter Placuit Deo*; *To the Bishops of the Catholic Church On Certain Aspects of Christian Salvation*, numbers 7).

319. ***Note***: "We do not really want a religion that is right where we are right. What we want is a religion that is right where we are wrong. We do not want, as the newspapers say, a Church that will move with the world. We want a Church that will move the world" (G. K. Chesterton, *Charles Dickens*: *A Critical Study*)

320. ***Note***: This understanding of suffering tends to be what the prosperity gospel preachers miss. Suffering for the Christ is not only good, it is an unavoidable requirement. In this we may also inform the prosperity preacher that being a martyr for the Christ is better than any and all worldly accomplishments.

321. ***Note***: Using everyday life, another example is a story of a landlord who treats his tenants with respect and love; the tenants, unfortunately, do not reciprocate. But they do respond to the harsh treatment of eviction. Some of us may also relate to this phenomenon in an employer-employee situation, where harshness seems to work better than love.

322. *Strong's Greek Dictionary* and *Thayer's Greek Definitions*.

323. ***Note***: In addition, the Samaritan woman's five husbands illustrate an unsuccessful search for happiness and a personal restlessness. Without a proper understanding of Holy Scripture (a biblical based theology), we, like she, are inevitably restless—we move from one thing to another. Moreover, the one that

she is living with was not even her husband (Jn 4:17-18) a further degree of lostness.

324. Fr. Jacques Philippe, *Searching for and Maintaining Peace: A Small Treaties on Peace of Heart* (New York: Society of St. Paul, 2002), 91.

325. Ibid, 101.

326. ***Note*****:** To fear God means to love Him (Mk 12:20), to worship Him (Lk 7:16), to obey Him (Deut 6:24), to serve Him (Deut 6:13), and to live a holy life (2 Cor 7:1).

327. ***Note*****:** It is unfortunate that as a society, in the past few decades, we have moved away from this understanding; and thus, most of us are not even teaching this principle to our children anymore. Our penal system also used to recognize this, however, more and more even our penal system has moved away from it.

328. ***Note*****:** "Come. O Blessed Spirit of Holy Fear, penetrate my inmost heart, that I may set you, my Lord and God, before my face forever, help me to shun all things that can offend You, and make me worthy to appear before the pure eyes of Your Divine Majesty in heave, where You live and reign in the unity of the ever Blessed Trinity, God world without end. Amen" (Novena Prayer to the Holy Spirit).

329. ***Note*****:** I refer you to, Saint John XXIII's Encyclical Letter, *Pacem in Terris* (*Peace on Earth*).

330. *Amplified Bible* translation: (The input is not mine).

331. ***Note*****:** As it has been said: the fruit of silence is prayer; the fruit of prayer is faith; the fruit of faith is love; the fruit of love is service; and the fruit of service is peace.

332. *The Liturgy of the Hours* (New York: Catholic Book Publishing Co., 1975), vol III, Sunday Evening Prayer II, first Psalm Prayer (week I, II, and III), Feast of Saint James Evening Prayer, also cf. Eph 2:13-16.

333. ***Note*****:** "The whole process of the personal supernatural transformation by which we become intimates of the indwelling Trinity. [Justification is] the process by which a sinner is made righteous [and thus, live a life in *witness of charity*]. Sanctification is thus nothing other than the perfection of the life of charity. [It is the movement to living a holy life.] The chief means of sanctification is the infusion of habitual grace which enables us to turn to God in faith, hope and love. The life of grace is continually enhanced in us through our membership in

the Mystical Body of [the] Christ and through our sharing in the sacramental grace that is at the very heart of the Church's life. First through Baptism when we are claimed by [the] Christ, then preeminently through the Eucharist when we receive the food of our sanctification, through the sacrament of Penance as we receive forgiveness for our sins and the strength to respond to our high calling—in all these ways, the work of sanctification is underway throughout our lives. We become holy as God is holy so that we can be fit company for Him for all eternity" (*Catholic encyclopedia* within the definition of "Justification" and "Sanctification").

334. Fr. Jacques Philippe, *Searching for and Maintaining Peace: A Small Treaties on Peace of Heart* (New York: Society of St. Paul, 2002), 11-12.

335. Ibid, 65.

336. ***Note*:** It is important to also keep in mind that, "our struggle is not against flesh and blood [*contending only with physical opponents*], but against the rulers, against the powers, against the world forces of this [*present*] darkness, against the spiritual *forces* of wickedness in the Heavenly (supernatural) *places"* (Eph 6:12) (this is the *Amplified Bible* translation; the input is not mine).

337. ***Note*:** I once heard it said that Christianity or being a Christian it is not about *behaviour modification*, it is about *mind and heart transformation*. When our mind and heart are transformed, our behaviour modifies on its own. The order is important. Do not try as much to change your behaviour, change your mind and heart and your behaviour will follow. Keep in mind, that the acronym T.W.A.R is the process we go through as human beings: it is our *thoughts* that become our *words*, our *words* become our *actions*, and our *actions* become the *reality* we live. Therefore, in order to change the reality we live we must always change our thoughts first. Changing our actions in order to change our reality is futile.

338. Fr. Jacques Philippe, *Searching for and Maintaining Peace. A Small Treaties on Peace of Heart* (New York: Society of St. Paul, 2002), 61.

339. *Amplified Bible* translation: (The input is not mine).

340. *Strong's Greek Dictionary* and *Thayer's Greek Definitions*. And, William D. Mounce, ed., *Mounce's Complete Expository Dictionary of Old & New Testament Words* (Grand Rapids, Michigan: Zondervan, 2006), 654-657.

341. Ibid, 580-581.

342. ***Note*:** When we wear a garment all the time, we are bound to get it dirty (i.e., venial sins). This can be cleaned up, either through the Sacrament of Penance or the Penitential Rite at the beginning of each Eucharistic celebration.

343. ***Note*:** "Justification establishes cooperation between God's grace and man's freedom. On man's part it is expressed by the assent of faith to the Word of God, which invites him to conversion, and in the cooperation of charity with the prompting of the Holy Spirit who precedes and preserves his assent" (*CCC* #1993). To carry out our sanctification, Christians are "sustained by the gifts of the Holy Spirit. These are permanent dispositions which make man docile in following the promptings of the Holy Spirit" (*CCC* #1830). "The seven gifts of the Holy Spirit are wisdom, understanding, counsel, fortitude, knowledge, piety, and fear of the Lord" . . . "They make the faithful docile in readily obeying divine inspirations" (*CCC* #1831).

344. ***Note*:** "Everything is permissible for me, but not all things are beneficial. Everything is permissible for me, but I will not be enslaved by anything [*and brought under its power, allowing it to control me*]" (1 Cor 6:12). "All things are lawful [*that is, morally legitimate, permissible*], but not all things are beneficial *or* advantageous. All things are lawful, but not all things are constructive [*to character*] *and* edifying [*to spiritual life*]" (1 Cor 6:12) (this is the *Amplified Bible* translation; the input is not mine).

345. *Amplified Bible* translation: (The input is not mine).

346. ***Note*:** Society has misconstrued the word *equality*. It is only in Jesus the Christ—i.e., before God—that we are equal. As it has been said, there are no *first-class* or *second-class* citizens in Him. It is *only* in our relation to Jesus the Christ that we find our true equality. For we are not equal, and more importantly we *cannot* say that we are equal in any other way. For example, we are not equal in beauty, but in Him, we are all beautiful. Likewise, we are not equal in our strength, courage, skill, or whatever may be—for we all have been blessed given different talents (Mt 25:15)—but we are all equal before Him.

347. ***Note*:** Based on justification, some scholars argue that "if there is a *hell* there is no one in it." For God the Father in Jesus the Christ atones for all, and thus, forgives all sins. This conclusion is nonsensical. As per our study, we can easily see that these scholars are leading people to the *wide gate* that leads to destruction—not to the *narrow one*!

348. *Strong's Greek Dictionary* and *Thayer's Greek Definitions*.

349. *Catena Aurea*: *Early Church Father's Commentary on the Gospels*, Mt 25:1-13.

350. ***Note*:** Notice that the very next parable is the Parable of the Talents (Mt 25:14-30), immediately followed by the discourse on the Final Judgment, with the reference of separating the sheep from the goats (Mt 25:31:46).

351. ***Note*:** This interpretation by the Early Church Fathers gives us much insight. Not only does it connect the different types of joy represented by the oil (joy in God versus. joy in the world), to what we studied concerning the different types of happiness (a joy-filled-happiness in God versus a worldly happiness), it also answers the question: Why could not the wise virgins help the foolish virgins by giving them some oil (which we may argue is the Christian thing to do)? However, through this interpretation we now see why they could not.

352. *Amplified Bible* translation: (The input is not mine).

353. *The Liturgy of the Hours* (New York: Catholic Book Publishing Co., 1975), vol IV, 1331-1332.

354. Ibid, vol I, 169-170.

355. Ibid, vol IV, 920 (closing prayer).

356. The idea for this fifth thought comes from a homily given by Pope Francis on the Solemnity of the Epiphany of the Lord (Vatican City, January 6, 2018).

357. Saint Augustine, *The Confessions of St. Augustine*, Book I, chapter 1, number 1.

358. The idea for this seventh thought comes from a Bishop Robert Barron sermon on Gaudete Sunday, *Have You Found Joy?*, (December 12, 2021).
Here is the link: https://www.youtube.com/watch?v=L8TxLSDJdtU.

359. *The Liturgy of the Hours* (New York: Catholic Book Publishing Co., 1975), vol II, 344 and 756, vol III, 967, vol V1, 122 (paraphrase of the two alternative closing prayers, and closing prayer with the Collect from Year B, 17th Sunday of Ordinary Time).

Chapter 9 | The Good News

360. *The Liturgy of the Hours* (New York: Catholic Book Publishing Co., 1975).

361. ***Note*:** Christmas and Easter joy and rejoicing is not relegated to the time of Christmas and Easter only. We are a people of *the incarnation*! The incarnation changes all of humanity, it gives life meaning. We are a people of *the Resurrection*! We, in our baptism, participate in His death and resurrection and become one with Him. Yes, this is *the Good News!* We must therefore *live it daily*!

362. ***Note*:** We have heard preachers say that Jesus the Christ did not come to bring judgment on the earth. This is correct for the incarnation—at that time He came to bring salvation. He came to pay our penalty; He came to redeem us, as only He could, for He is God's perfect Lamb. However, because He is the One Who makes payment, because He is the One Who takes our place in the jail cell—which is the Good News—we must now live in and proclaim that Good News. We must now live in that Law of Love and Freedom, which we have been granted. We must now live for our Christ. He does what we cannot do—again, this is the Good News—so we are able to be what He wants us to be, through Him. We must answer our personal *call to holiness*, and in this we must now go out, in His mercy, and show others His mercy and love; i.e., we must be a *witness of charity*—a witness of the love He has shown us. In order to do that, we must first and foremost love Him, and only in that love, can we and do we love others. So again, He did not come to bring judgment upon us, He came to show His mercy and love, and save us from ourselves. All that said, most preachers omit the second part. That is, this is correct *only* concerning His First Coming, for when He comes the second time around (the *Parousia*), He will be coming in judgment!

363. ***Note*:** For further insight on the "Good News" of this last set of answers, I would recommend listening to Bishop Robert Barron's Sunday sermons, *Let Christ Light a Fire in You* (August 13, 2022).
Here is the link: https://www.youtube.com/watch?v=6-7f3izeL0A.

364. William D. Mounce, ed., *Mounce's Complete Expository Dictionary of Old & New Testament Words* (Grand Rapids, Michigan: Zondervan, 2006), 303.

365. *Strong's Greek Dictionary* and *Thayer's Greek Definitions*.

366. William D. Mounce, ed., *Mounce's Complete Expository Dictionary of Old & New Testament Words* (Grand Rapids, Michigan: Zondervan, 2006), 303.

367. ***Note*:** The manuscript titles of all four Gospels are named as such, with the word *Euanggelion* (ΕὐΑγγέλιον): i.e., *Euanggelion* (ΕὐΑγγέλιον) according to Matthew; *Euanggelion* (ΕὐΑγγέλιον) according to Mark; *Euanggelion* (ΕὐΑγγέλιον) according to Luke; and *Euanggelion* (ΕὐΑγγέλιον) according to John. For example, the actual title in Greek for the Gospel according to Matthew is: *ΕὐΑγγέλιον κατά Ματθαῖος*.

368. ***Note*:** On the twofold coming of the Christ: "We do not preach only one coming of [the] Christ, but a second as well, much more glorious than the first. The First Coming was marked by patience; the second will bring the crown of a divine kingdom. In general, whatever relates to our Lord Jesus [the] Christ has two aspects. There is a birth from God before the ages, and a birth from a virgin

at the fullness of time. There is a hidden coming, like that of rain on fleece, and a coming before all eyes, still in the future. At the First Coming He was wrapped in swaddling clothes in a manger. At His Second Coming He will be clothed in light as in a garment. In the First Coming He endured the cross, despising the shame; in the Second Coming He will be in glory, escorted by an army of angels. We look then beyond the First Coming and await the second. At the First Coming we said: Blessed is He who comes in the Name of the Lord. At the second we shall say it again; we shall go out with the angels to meet the Lord and cry out in adoration: Blessed is He who comes in the Name of the Lord. The Saviour will not come to be judged again, but to judge those by whom He was judged . . . His First Coming was to fulfill His plan of love, to teach men by gentle persuasion. This time, whether men like it or not, they will be subjects of His Kingdom by necessity. Malachi the prophet speaks of the two comings. And the Lord whom you seek will come suddenly to His Temple: that is one coming. Again he says of another coming: Look, the Lord almighty will come, and who will endure the day of His entry, or who will stand in His sight? Because He comes like a refiner's fire, a fuller's herb, and He will sit refining and cleansing. These two comings are also referred to by Paul in writing to Titus: The grace of God the Saviour has appeared to all men, instructing us to put aside impiety and worldly desires and live temperately, uprightly, and religiously in this present age, waiting for the joyful hope, the appearance of the glory of our great God and Saviour, Jesus [the] Christ. Notice how he speaks of a First Coming for which he gives thanks, and a second, the one we still await. That is why the faith we profess has been handed on to you in these words: He ascended into Heaven, and is seated at the right hand of the Father, and He will come again in glory to judge the living and the dead, and His Kingdom will have no end. Our Lord Jesus [the] Christ will therefore come from Heaven. He will come at the end of the world, in glory, at the last day. For there will be an end to this world, and the created world will be made new" (Saint Cyril of Jerusalem, *The Liturgy of the* Hours, New York: Catholic Book Publishing Co., 1975, vol I, 142-144).

369. *Amplified Bible* translation: (The input is not mine).

370. ***Note*:** As we think about this Heavenly court room for a moment, we may also conclude that the *Euanggelion* (ΕὐΑγγέλιον) is not about a religion, per se. It is more about a declaration, a declaration of reality. Or to be more precise, it is about the announcing, proclaiming, and preaching of reality. For the *Euanggelion* (ΕὐΑγγέλιον) is reality. The Christ Event is reality. The time of fulfillment is here. It is the time we are living in. It is the love-story of the universe. All of it! The Good News, therefore, is simply about stating *what is*. "But wait, there's more!" the ultimate conclusion of the *Euanggelion* (ΕὐΑγγέλιον) is the nuptial plan, in *Yahshua* (יֵשׁוּעַ) the *Mâshîyach* (מָשִׁיחַ). Yes, not only does He not condemn us, He brings us into the life of the Trinity, as we become God's children (1 Jn 3:2).

371. William D. Mounce, ed., *Mounce's Complete Expository Dictionary of Old & New Testament Words* (Grand Rapids, Michigan: Zondervan, 2006), 580-581.

372. *Amplified Bible* translation: (The input is not mine).

373. ***Note*:** It might come as a surprise to some that the word *antichrist* does not appear in the Book of Revelation! It appears only five times in the entire Bible.

374. *Catholic Encyclopedia*, within the definition of "Antichrist".

375. *The Liturgy of the Hours* (New York: Catholic Book Publishing Co., 1975), vol I, 405, vol II, 864 , vol VI, 662, 663, (paraphrase prayers, with Scripture, and Psalm prayer from The Assumption of the Blessed Virgin Mary, Evening Prayer II).

Appendix A | Methodology and Presuppositions

376. Mother Teresa, *A Call To Mercy: Hearts to Love, Hands to Serve* (New York: Crown Publishing Group, 2016), 147.

377. Athanasian Creed (also known as the Trinitarian Creed or *Quicunque Vult* in Latin). This Creed is attributed to Saint Athanasius (295–373 AD), Bishop of Alexandria, and Doctor of the Church. However, scholars' state that it is Pseudo-Athanasian, written in southern France around the 5th century.

378. ***Note*:** Pope Francis is the 266th pope. He is the pope at the time of writing this book (2015-2020).

379. ***Note*:** Some may argue that speculative theology is its own category. Nevertheless, for our purposes, these two categories are sufficient, because we may place speculative theology as a sub-category within academic theology.

380. ***Note*:** Let me clarify the word "foundational." When I use the word foundational, I am not saying that it is introductory. Here is an analogy that might help. All regions of the world have their staple foods. Here in the West we refer to these as "meat and potatoes"—as our staple diet—our nessasary item of food. This we can call our foundational, staple diet. It has sustenance; however, we do not feed this to our newborn babies. In a sense, staple foods are not introductory, we do not give them to our babies right away, but we gradually introduce them to these foods. So, I use the term foundational in the same way; it is foundational as in, it is our staple diet. However, the new Christian has to be gradually introduced to it.

381. ***Note*:** To be clear, this is not *sola scriptura*. As we know, some things written in Scripture are difficult to understand, and thus can be misinterpreted and/or distorted (cf. 2 Pt 3:16). We therefore cannot read Scripture in a vacuum. Sacred Tradition and Sacred Scripture go hand in hand (*CCC* #80–81 and 2 Thes 2:15).

382. The *World Christian Encyclopedia* counted 33,830 Christian denominations as of 2001.

383. Author's translation.

384. Ibid.

385. Ibid.

386. ***Note*:** The adherence to *Sola Scriptura*—among other issues—faces an inherent contradiction. For nowhere in Scripture does it tell us which books or letters are considered Sacred Scripture. Therefore, we cannot say "Scripture Only" for Scripture does not tell us what Scripture is. It is the Church—through the Holy Spirit—in Her authority that delivers us and tells us what books or letters are to be considered Scripture (a process that started around 365 A.D., with the Council of Damascus and ended on 393 A.D., with the Council of Hippo). If you would like to read more concerning interpretation of Scripture, I would recommend you read, Vatican II, *Dei Verbum*: *Dogmatic Constitution on Divine Revelation*, numbers 11–13, and *CCC*, numbers #109–119. In addition, just as the Word made Flesh, is both Divine and Human, the Word of God (i.e., Sacred Scripture) is also both Divine and human.

387. Vatican II, *Dei Verbum*: *Dogmatic Constitution on Divine Revelation*, number 12.

388. Saint, Pope John Paul II, Apostolic Constitution, *Fidei Depostum*, number 1.

389. ***Note*:** "Sacred theology relies on the written Word of God, taken together with Sacred Tradition, as on a permanent foundation" (Vatican II, *Dei Verbum*: *Dogmatic Constitution on Divine Revelation*, number 24).

390. ***Note*:** Saint Augustine considered the Septuagint to be inspired. In fact, to this day some Orthodox Christians place the Septuagint over the Hebrew text. Although this translation differs in many places from the original Hebrew, it is nevertheless considered inspired. One argument is that the seventy Rabbis (some state seventy-two Rabbis) were inspired while working on the translation. The other argument is that the New Testament writers used the Septuagint over and above the Hebrew text. We see this in many of the quotes within the New Testament, for they were virtually taken word for word from the Septuagint, and not from the Hebrew. This is what Saint Augustine has to

say concerning the Septuagint: "The authority of the Septuagint is pre-eminent as far as the Old Testament is concerned; for it is reported through all the more learned churches that the seventy translators enjoyed so much of the presence and power of the Holy Spirit in their work of translation, that among that number of men there was but one voice. And if, as is reported, and as many not unworthy of confidence assert, they were separated during the work of translation, each man being in a cell by himself, and yet nothing was found in the manuscript of any one of them that was not found in the same words and in the same order of words in all the rest, who dares put anything in comparison with an authority like this, not to speak of preferring anything to it? And even if they conferred together with the result that a unanimous agreement sprang out of the common labour and judgment of them all; even so, it would not be right or becoming for any one man, whatever his experience, to aspire to correct the unanimous opinion of many venerable and learned men. Wherefore, even if anything is found in the original Hebrew in a different form from that in which these men have expressed it, I think we must give way to the dispensation of Providence, which used these men to bring it about" (Saint Augustine, *On Christian Doctrine*, book 2, chapter 15, number 22).

391. ***Note*:** The only admonitory note to this statement is that of the Gospel of Saint Matthew. Some have said that it was originally written in Hebrew (or Aramaic), and then immediately translated into Greek. Most patristic theologians hold this view. Saint Irenaeus (180 A.D.) mentions that Saint Matthew wrote in his own dialect; Origen (244 A.D.) mentions the tradition of Saint Matthew writing in Hebrew; a few others stated such, including Eusebius and Saint Jerome (in the 300's A.D.). Nevertheless, we do not have the Hebrew or Aramaic text; it is therefore generally accepted that the original language of the Gospel of Saint Matthew is Greek.

392. ***Note*:** I would like to outline three options concerning the study of Sacred Scripture. First, and as mentioned, the most beneficial is to study biblical Hebrew and Greek (this might not be practical for most). Second, is to use various Hebrew and Greek study-aids or tools. Third—this being the absolute minimum—is to use multiple translations.

393. See Saint Augustine, *On Christian Doctrine*, book 3, chapter 25, number 35–37.

394. Saint Basil the Great, *On The Holy Spirit*, chapter 1, number 2) (***Note*:** This is a paraphrase of the text).

395. ***Orthopraxy*:** Correctness or orthodoxy of action or practice (*Random* House Webster's Dictionary).

396. ***Orthodox*:** An adherence and conforming to established and correct doctrines and Creeds, in totality (*Random House Webster's Dictionary*); from the Greek, literally meaning "right belief."

397. ***Note*:** These types of paradoxical statements are not the same as those about which some people say, "The Bible is full of contradictions." These types of "alleged" contradictions are not what I am addressing here.

398. ***Note*:** Also stated by Hippolytus of Rome: "Virtue occupies the middle position."

Appendix B | Existence of a Creator God

399. ***Note*:** There are two periods in History, we can call it B.C. and A.D. Saint Paul argues that now the Messiah has come (A.D.): "The wrath of God is indeed being revealed from Heaven against every impiety and wickedness of those who suppress the truth [the truth of the Messiah] by their wickedness. For what can be known about *God* is evident to them, because God made it evident to them. Ever since the creation of the world, His invisible attributes of eternal power and divinity have been able to be understood and perceived in what He has made. As a result, they have no excuse" (Rom 1:18-20). So, there is no excuse in knowing God the Creator, through His creation. Then, once we know this, we move to the time of the Messiah.

400. Dr. Kent Hovind, *Where did God Come From*?: *Hovind vs Reinhold Schlieter Debate*, (accessed January 19, 2023).
Here is the link: https://www.youtube.com/watch?v=w6AHcv19NIc

401. ***Note*:** The other two significant arguments are that of (1) *contingency* which we briefly cited in Chapter 8, "Rejoice . . . Always!"; and (2) the fact we cannot have ethics or morality without a God, as we discussed in Chapter 2, The Second Person of The Trinity

402. Fr. Georges Lemaître.

403. ***The Big Bang Theory*:** "The Big Bang hypothesis states that all of the current and past matter in the universe came into existence at the same time, roughly 13.8 billion years ago. At this time, all matter was compacted into a very small ball with infinite density and intense heat called a Singularity. Suddenly, the Singularity began expanding and the universe as we know it began" (Matt Williams *Universe Today*). Dubbed the *Big Bang* by the astronomer Fred Hoyle, the Big Bang Theory was the idea of Fr. Georges Lemaître. He was a theoretical physicist, a professor of physics at the Catholic University of Louvain, and was also a Catholic priest. The Big Bang Theory does not contradict a Creator God, for not only does the composite of the *small ball* or

Singularity vary, the question—why or how that small ball came into existence?—is not answered. For scientists know that something cannot come from nothing (*ex nihilo*), matter does not create itself. So, there has to be someone or something that created the small ball (the Singularity) whatever that *it* may be—e.g., a *Big Banger*—which did not have any first cause; which was not a part of the small ball; which self-existed prior to the small ball and ensuing Big Bang; and which was (and is) unaffected by time, space, and matter. As we look into space we see, in the words of Fr. Lemaître, a "now which has no yesterday."

Other Books from the Author

Witness of Charity

Understanding the True Meaning of Christian Love

As a Christian, are we a witness *to* something or *of* something? Alternately, are we a witness *to* someone or *of* someone? The way we answer these questions will determine our worldview. Here, we will study these questions from a true Christian perspective.

- What is Christian *charity*?
- What is Christian *love*?
- Are we justified by our *works* or by our *faith*?
- Does the *law* and its commandments apply to us?
- What does it mean to *love our neighbour*?
- What does it mean to *love our enemy*?
- What is Christian *mercy*?
- What is the *Ultimate* source of love?

Once we know and understand the answers, we will ask and answer another: As a Christian, how do we accordingly live a Christ-centred life?

"This little book, *Witness of Charity* ... brings 'fresh eyes' to some of our basic teachings on charity."

Bishop Emeritus F. B. Henry
Diocese of Calgary

"It is my desire that you will use this work to spread the important message of true Christian charity that is so desperately needed in our world."

Bishop William T. McGrattan
Diocese of Calgary

Love Hope Faith

Trinity Project Publishing

Note from the Author

I have been asked why I do not include a biography in my books. Is it an oversight? No, it isn't; for I want my books to stand on their own. Like the majority of the readers of these books I am also a parishioner in the pew. I obtain an Imprimatur and a Nihil Obstat so that the book has received the Church's approval and authority. It does not matter who I am, for in a way I am irrelevant. As I have stated throughout these books, my opinion doesn't matter. Truth is independent of the author's words. As Saint Augustine put it, it is the "common property of all lovers of the truth." What matters then is that these books are written in line with the sound teaching of the Church for the past two thousand years, and reflect the Truth and the truth of God's Gospel message. This is what Saint Paul argues when he says that it is not about Apollos, and it is not about him, it is all about Jesus the Christ (see 1 Cor 3:5). We are merely planters and waterers. It is His vineyard, and He gives the growth, not we (1 Cor 3:6). Our job is that we convey His truth.

As we are baptized into Jesus the Christ we become part of His body. In our singularity we are in unity, *in Him*. In that singularity all the gifts we receive are from Him; and in our unity, we should be putting them into His service. Therefore, my promotion is only the promotion of the Gospel message within these books, and it is not about promoting me.

This is why I do not like signing these books. For all glory must go only to Him Who gives growth!